I've Always Kept a Unicorn

I've Always Kept a Unicorn

THE BIOGRAPHY OF SANDY DENNY

MICK HOUGHTON

FABER & FABER

First published in 2015
by Faber & Faber Limited
Bloomsbury House
74–77 Great Russell Street
London WC1B 3DA

Typeset by Ian Bahrami
Printed in the UK by CPI Group (UK) Ltd, Croydon, CR0 4YY

The right of Mick Houghton to be identified as author of this work
has been asserted in accordance with Section 77 of the Copyright,
Designs and Patents Act 1988

A CIP record for this book
is available from the British Library

ISBN 978–0–571–27890–9

FSC
www.fsc.org
MIX
Paper from
responsible sources
FSC® C101712

To Bert and Loren

Contents

Illustrations

PLATES

Foreword by Richard Thompson

I had the privilege of working with the best. Nothing in the intervening years has changed my mind. As decades pass, and fashions in music come and go, I realise more and more that Sandy Denny was not only the most important singer of my generation, but that no one has come along to touch her since. Who has her dynamic range, from unbelievable power to a whisper, all with the utmost expression? Who has her musical intelligence, her ability to sing the right thing at the right time? Who has her command of the dramatic, and her ability to tell a story by inhabiting the song? Then there is the unique and distinctive songwriting, which few, if any, can match, and the beautiful accompaniment on guitar and piano, and her great charisma as a performer – it leaves the rest of the field forever struggling to catch up.

I think about Sandy a lot, and I suppose through the slightly inaccurate haze of memory I remember mostly the times when she was happy, bubbly and a joy to be with; but what made her a great artist were the inner conflicts and emotional complexities that drove her. I regret deeply the fact that she is not better known these days, and I hope Mick's fine book will go some way towards rectifying the situation. She should be the true yardstick by which all singers and songwriters are measured, and I hope those of her generation who missed her the first time and newer generations will discover her and feel the same.

Preface: Your Fickle Friends
Are Leaving . . .

I was eighteen when I first heard Sandy Denny, early in September 1968. I had been music mad since I was eight or nine years old, spending many long hours in that bedroom world with a radio, a reel-to-reel tape recorder and a record player for company. Sandy's voice raised the hairs on the back of my neck. I was an avid listener to John Peel's *Top Gear* and, that particular night, I was poised to tape the best bits because Fairport Convention were one of the featured groups. I'd seen them play a few times, all at Middle Earth in Covent Garden, but I had no idea they now had a new girl singer. She sang two songs, Joni Mitchell's 'Eastern Rain' and another called 'Fotheringay'; at some point in the course of the show John Peel must have said that her name was Sandy Denny. 'Fotheringay' was like a slap in the face; it stopped me in my tracks.

It was by no means the first time this had happened to me. I can still remember that visceral blast on hearing Johnny Kidd's 'Shakin' All Over', the Kinks' 'You Really Got Me' or the Byrds' 'Eight Miles High'. More often it was voices and moody senti-ments that stuck with me. Having two older sisters exposed me early in life to Rick Nelson's 'Lonesome Town', the Everly Brothers' 'So Sad (To Watch Good Love Go Bad)' and Elvis singing 'I'm left, you're right, she's gone', before discovering such things for myself: Roy Orbison's 'Only the Lonely', Billy Fury's 'Halfway to Paradise', Skeeter Davis's 'End of the World', the Four Seasons' 'Rag Doll', the Beach Boys' 'Don't Worry Baby' and countless other pop songs in which lonesome and sad was the prevailing mood.

Paradoxically, like all the best sad songs, 'Fotheringay' was also uplifting. I whirled back the tape again and again listening to Sandy's featured songs. I had never much cared for girl singers, not until hearing Grace Slick for the first time, again through John Peel. He often played Jefferson Airplane's 'Somebody to Love' and 'White Rabbit' on his *Perfumed Garden* show on Radio London; here was Britain's answer to Jefferson Airplane, with a singer who was Grace Slick's equal. No, Sandy Denny was better. Grace Slick's voice was sexy and just a little sinister but Sandy's could actually reach inside and wring out every ounce of feeling. It still has that effect on me.

By chance, I already had tickets for the Festival of Contemporary Song at the Royal Festival Hall at the end of the month, and Fairport Convention were on a tantalising bill. I'd bought the tickets ostensibly to see Al Stewart; I'd been a fan since hearing him week in, week out at Bunjies folk club and even went to his concert debut at the Festival Hall in 1967. Living in south London, it was a handy venue for me; you could just walk across the bridge and catch the last train home with time to spare. In June 1968 I had seen Pentangle there, and three months earlier, the Incredible String Band, supported by Tim Buckley. But here, lining up for the Festival of Contemporary Song, were the Johnstons, Joni Mitchell, Jackson C. Frank and Fairport Convention, alongside Al Stewart, who unveiled a new, eighteen-minute journey through his adolescent sexual adventures, 'Love Chronicles'. Despite the song's controversial use of the word 'fucking', nobody was noticeably shocked.

Joni Mitchell's debut album had only just been released; within a few years she would become the benchmark by which all female

singer-songwriters would be measured, and none more so than
Sandy Denny. My distant memory of Joni Mitchell was the power
of her voice and a confidence that belied an almost gawky stage
presence. She made a dismissive comment about an Irish group
who had just covered 'Both Sides Now'; unfortunately for them,
that group was the Johnstons, who had already closed their set
with the song, as did she. I'd seen American folk singer Jackson C.
Frank a few times at Cousins and Bunjies. He was a sullen bear of a
man whose songs were appealing but beyond my emotional grasp.
Few in the audience that night – or perhaps even beside her on
stage – would have known that he had once been Sandy Denny's
boyfriend.

Fairport Convention closed the show. Whatever effect listening to the Peel Session tapes had on me, to see Fairport live
– with added Sandy – was something else. It wasn't just about
her, either. They played 'Reno, Nevada', during which guitarist
Richard Thompson let fly with a long, flowing, electrifying solo. If
I remember correctly Sandy sang 'Eastern Rain' and a chilling 'I'll
Keep It with Mine'. Both were on Fairport's *What We Did on Our
Holidays*, released a few months later. What I most vividly remember, however, was how unbelievably exciting Fairport Convention
were that night; the combination of the voices of Sandy Denny
and Ian Matthews was incredible.

They sang Tim Buckley's 'Morning Glory' – this group also
clearly had *the* best taste ever – but the real tour de force was their
version of Leonard Cohen's 'Suzanne'. Fairport were no longer the
frenzied West Coast-sounding group I'd seen bleary-eyed at Middle
Earth. On one side of the stage stood Ian Matthews, motionless,
almost in a dream, and on the other stood Sandy, equally lost in
song; the two swapped the verses back and forth while Richard

Thompson, buried beneath an enviable mound of tousled hair, propelled the song with a rhythmic staccato guitar over which their voices soared. When Sandy Denny came in with the line 'And Jesus was a sailor' it was magical. The next day John Peel repeated the Fairport session, which now included the same brilliant arrangement of 'Suzanne'. Stupidly, I didn't tape it; it was at least ten years before I heard it again on Fairport's *Heyday* collection of vintage Peel Sessions.

A few days later I went off to university to study politics. I hated it, for the most part; my obsession with music helped get me through the next few years. Leicester had little to recommend it but at least was in a broad catchment area that took in Nottingham and Birmingham, where, over the next three years, every great British band or musician – and the odd visiting American – must have played at some point. It's no exaggeration to say that every week there was a great gig happening somewhere within reasonable travelling distance: Family, the Bonzo Dog Band, Love, Liverpool Scene, John Martyn, Blossomtoes, Peter Green's Fleetwood Mac, Free, Caravan, the Move, Derek and the Dominoes, Eclection and so many more. I saw Fairport again twice – once more during Sandy's all-too-brief tenure and then the full-throttle *Full House* band. Even Fotheringay played one of their too few gigs in Leicester, at the stuffy De Montfort Hall in March 1970. For me, they were better than the *Liege & Lief*-era Fairport Convention I'd seen six months before.

More or less a year to the day after the Festival of Contemporary Song, I went along when Fairport premiered the *Liege & Lief* set at the Royal Festival Hall. Nick Drake opened but I would be lying if I said he made any impression whatsoever. We can all be wise after the event. Folk music would never be quite the same again after that night and nor would Fairport Convention, but I wasn't alone in thinking that I preferred the Fairport of old. *What We Did on Our Holidays* and *Unhalfbricking* will always be more moving to me.

My love affair with Sandy Denny continued through *Fotheringay*, *The North Star Grassman and the Ravens* and the *Sandy* albums. By a total fluke I was visiting my mum and dad in Belvedere some time in May 1972 and opened their local paper to see that Sandy was playing a gig at the nearby Well Hall Open Theatre that night, so of course I eagerly went along. The band included Richard Thompson, and even Linda Peters, as she was then, surreptitiously crept on stage at the end. She and Sandy sang the Everlys' 'When Will I Be Loved'. It was a total joy from start to finish. This was the Sandy that friends talk about so affectionately – chattering away, laughing, fumbling and fooling around but singing with impeccable warmth and grace. A tape of the show now reminds me that she sang songs from the *Fotheringay* album, a gripping 'John the Gun' from *The North Star Grassman*, and there were songs from an album she was just recording. I duly snapped up *Sandy* a few months later. It was delightful, but it was the last Sandy Denny album I bought during her lifetime.

I was a typical fickle fan of the day. It now seems as if a lot of us deserted her after 1973. We move on, our taste in music changes, let alone our agendas in life. I never stopped buying records but there was too much good music coming out of America – Little Feat, Steely Dan, the Grateful Dead, Neil Young, Gene Clark, the Flying Burrito Brothers and Jackson Browne spring to mind – and British music was in the grip of glam pop and rock that did absolutely nothing for me. I didn't much care for Fairport Convention any more either; my allegiance had switched to

Richard Thompson's solo records and the albums he was making with Linda.

I find it hard to believe that I didn't hear Sandy's third solo album, *Like an Old Fashioned Waltz*, but if I did I most likely found it too mawkish. I must have heard enough to make such a judgement call, perhaps only the advance single, a cover of the oldie 'Whispering Grass'. I certainly didn't buy the album it trailed. I don't remember checking out Fairport's *Rising for the Moon* either, the album they made after Sandy rejoined the group, but I did see that particular line-up play at Brunel University towards the end of 1975. What I was doing in Uxbridge I couldn't say. It wasn't a great experience. The group was shambolic and, compared to just a few years before, Sandy's voice had less control. She had also lost her *joie de vivre* on stage, replacing it with something more grittily determined. Or am I now guilty of being wise after the event?

I didn't follow Sandy's career too closely after that. Nobody beyond her friends and fellow musicians can have had any idea of how much her life was falling apart. Her final tour in 1977 passed me by, as did her final album, *Rendezvous*. It passed a lot of her lapsed fans by. Then one evening, on 21 April 1978, an old friend rang me, somebody I'd not spoken to in a long while, just to tell me he'd heard – where else but on John Peel's show – that Sandy Denny had died. Feeling sad and not a little ashamed, I dug out my copy of *What We Did on Our Holidays*; side one, track one, 'Fotheringay'. There was that spellbinding voice that once had me in tears, and it did so again that night. It was like hearing about the death of a friend you hadn't bothered to keep in touch with, as Sandy sang, 'but those days will last no more'.

My life changed the following year. I gave up writing about music, which I'd been doing since leaving university to scrape together some sort of living. Quite inadvertently, I ended up becoming an independent music PR and worked with a succession of great bands and musicians over the next twenty years. Being gifted the Sire Records roster in 1979 was the perfect initiation; handling the press for the Ramones, Talking Heads and the newly signed Undertones made it seem easy. I learnt quickly that a PR person is only as good as the acts they choose to take on. Echo & The Bunnymen, the Teardrop Explodes and Julian Cope, the Jesus and Mary Chain, Sonic Youth, Stereolab, XTC, Spiritualized and the KLF were among those I was fortunate to work with at their peak. It was a roster that was light on folk music but these were desperate times for acoustic music in the UK, the 1980s especially. Folk music and folk musicians had all gone to the wall. When in 1995 I was asked by Cooking Vinyl to look after a new album by Bert Jansch, I had to pinch myself. It felt as if I was returning to my roots. Five years later the same label asked if I'd like to work on their latest signing, Richard Thompson. Such are life's twists and turns.

It was around that time that major labels in particular began zealously plundering their archives, systematically reissuing countless classic albums. It seemed as if my entire record collection was being dusted down and upgraded – not always for the better. I was lucky enough to handle the PR or sometimes initiate some of what, for a while, was an endless stream of great records, many originally released by Elektra and Warner/Reprise in America and by Decca, Transatlantic and Island Records in the UK.

Not least among these was the gargantuan nineteen-disc *Sandy Denny* box set in 2010. As a result, I became friends with Elizabeth Hurtt, who administers the Estates of Sandy Denny and Trevor Lucas, Sandy's long-time partner, bandmate, producer and eventual husband. It was Elizabeth who planted the seed for the idea of a new biography, and I can't thank her enough for all her encouragement and help in bringing this book to its conclusion and for allowing me the freedom to tell the story with complete honesty. She also handed over the entire Sandy Denny and Trevor Lucas archive, including documentation and photographs that haven't been seen or accessed before.

This is a book about Sandy Denny, so the weight of responsibility is huge. Writing and researching *I've Always Kept a Unicorn* is easily the most daunting thing I've ever done, but this isn't just about Sandy Denny; it's also about the extraordinary, visionary, talented, complex, feisty and occasionally ornery characters she encountered along the way. It's their story too; the famous, the infamous, the forgotten and the sometimes slighted and snubbed: Jackson C. Frank, Alex Campbell, Bert Jansch, John Renbourn, Martin Carthy, Dave Swarbrick, Al Stewart, Richard and Linda Thompson, Anne Briggs, Dave Cousins, Joe Boyd and plenty more besides, as well as those who passed through Fairport Convention and Fotheringay, and none more so than Trevor Lucas.

Trevor's music has long been overlooked, and unfairly so. From the moment he and Sandy began working together he knew and accepted that she was always going to overshadow him. Their riveting relationship during the 1970s is at the heart of this book; there are loose parallels with Sylvia Plath and Ted Hughes, or George and Martha in *Who's Afraid of Virginia Woolf?*. Theirs was a classic tempestuous relationship – like Bogart and Bacall, perhaps. Sandy liked the old black-and-white movies that used to play on TV in the afternoon, when a film starring Fred Astaire and Ginger Rogers, Bette Davis or Humphrey Bogart always seemed to be on. 'The lady's been stabbed by a bread pudding, do what you can for her,' she scribbled in one of her notebooks, a line out of Bogart's wartime adventure movie *Across the Pacific*. I can imagine her laughing over that.

Sadly, the last few years leading up to Sandy Denny's death had an all too hopeless sense of irrevocability about them. If it was only about the music we could all delight in the unrivalled beauty of her voice and the endlessly rewarding body of work she also produced as a songwriter, but, sometimes, life just gets in the way.

Mick Houghton

2015

1 : *No Fear of Time*
1947–1964

I have lived in the country even though I appear to be a city person. When I was very young we lived in Broadstairs in Kent, and right at the bottom of the garden there was a field, and if you walked through the field there was a deserted beach, and it was absolutely beautiful. I remember it very clearly now although I was very young when we lived there, and I guess that's why a lot of my songs are about the sea. When I'm within walking distance of a shore I go and sit on the beach, especially in the evening. I just love to watch the sea rolling onto the beach and I think a lot when that happens, I get all these romantic ideas.

    SANDY DENNY, *Screen 'n' Heard*, January 1973

Deep down inside me I thought I would do something, but maybe every little girl has that. Everybody has huge fantasies. I thought I was going to be a great ballet dancer, and a sculptor and Edith Cavell.

    SANDY DENNY, *Petticoat*, 20 February 1971

Acoss the distant sky, all the birds are leaving
But how can they know its time for them to go
Before the winter fire, I will still Be dreaming
I have no thought of time.
For, who knows where the time goes

Sad deserted shore — your fickle friends are leaving
Ah, but then you know, its time for them to go
But I will still be here, I have no thought of time
                              of leaving.
I donot count the time.
For who knows where the time goes.

And I am not alone, while my love surrounds me
I know it shall be so until its time to go
So come the storms of winter, and then the birds
        in spring again.
I have no fear of time
For who knows how my love grows
Who knows where the time goes.

| Ballad of Time |

Sandy Denny.

Sandy's original lyrics to 'Who Knows Where the Time Goes?'

Alexandra Elene MacLean Denny was born on 6 January 1947 at the Nelson Hospital, Kingston Road, Wimbledon, in south-west London. 'We chose the name Alexandra because it was the only name we could agree on,' explained her father, Neil. 'My wife Edna used to insist that she be called Alexandra but my own mother called her Sandy, the Scottish diminutive of that name, and within a week of going to school, everyone called her Sandy.' All the family were given the name MacLean, from Neil's mother, Mary Smith MacLean. Sandy's brother, born in 1945, was David MacLean Denny. Elene was Sandy's maternal grandmother's name.

Neil Denny recalled that the year Sandy was born there was snow on the ground until the end of March. The winter of 1946–7 was the coldest of the century and there were serious shortages, strikes and power cuts in what were still very austere times after the Second World War. The following year rationing became even stricter than it had been in wartime and would not come fully to an end until 1954. The middle classes were only slightly less immune from hardship than the majority of the country, and Sandy's early years were bound by the watchword of 'waste not, want not' and by strict family values.

Sandy's great-grandfather, William Denny, had been born in Glasgow around 1842 and became a boilermaker. He was often required to live where his job took him. David Skinner Denny,

Sandy's paternal grandfather, was born in Dundee on 16 October 1873, before the family eventually settled permanently in Glasgow.

Sandy's paternal grandmother, Mary Smith MacLean, was one of the MacLean family of Douart, on the Scottish Isle of Mull, but was believed by her family to have been born in Glasgow, on 14 August 1879. In her youth Mary had been a ballad singer, and so Sandy might be said to have followed in her footsteps. 'My mother spoke Scots Gaelic as well as English,' said Neil Denny, 'and used to sing Scottish dirges like "The Seal-Woman's Croon".'

Sandy's father may have been conventional and conservative, but his father, David Skinner Denny, was a man of tremendous drive and belief. An engineer by trade, he entered local government as a member of Govan Town Council and helped bring about the amalgamation of Govan burgh with Glasgow, later serving on Glasgow Town Council. A leading member of the Independent Labour Party, Denny contested and won the Cowlairs Ward in 1913 and was its representative for ten years. As convener of the Electricity Committee, he was one of the chief supporters of the experimental installation of electricity in working-class tenement houses in the city. He was also a director of the board of the Scottish Legal Life Assurance Company and, on his resignation from the town council in 1923, took up a London-based appointment as superintendent of the board's London, Midland and Wales section. Having been told there were only two places to live in London – Hampstead and Wimbledon – Sandy's grandfather chose the latter, relocating there with his wife Mary and two sons, William and Neil. Sandy's grandparents remained in Wimbledon until David Skinner Denny's death in September 1954, aged eighty. Mary died two years later.

Neil MacLean Denny was born in Govan on 10 August 1912

and was ten years old when the family moved to London. He started part way through the summer term at Queen's Road School in Wimbledon, and later went on to the London School of Economics, where he gained a BSc in Economics and Commerce in 1934. After leaving university he had several short-term jobs before being accepted by the civil service.

Like so many couples in the 1940s, Neil Denny and Edna Jones met during wartime service. 'The civil service was a reserved occupation,' said Neil, 'but I was allowed to go into air crew so I volunteered and became an airman. I flew as an observer or navigator in night fighters, Beaufighters and Mosquitos.' He had enlisted in the air force in 1941, taking the King's shilling in the Long Room at Lord's Cricket Ground, which was being used as a recruitment centre. He was then billeted in luxury flats in Regent's Park before being posted to an Initial Training Wing at Babbacombe, near Torquay in Devon. There he qualified as a radio observer dealing with radar and night fighters.

Edna Marjorie Jones, Sandy's mother, was born in Liverpool on 3 December 1916. 'Edna had a Scots grandfather, an Irish father and a Welsh mother,' said Neil Denny, 'so I think she could justly claim to be British.' She was the daughter of a merchant seaman and granddaughter of a blacksmith who owned property in Llangrannog, a small seaside village in Ceredigion in west Wales. From the age of six, Sandy and her brother David would holiday over Easter with Edna's brother Les and his wife Irene in Liverpool and would visit Llangrannog. Its cliffs and coves became another inspirational place for Sandy.

During the war Edna, like Neil, was in the air corps. 'She decided to post herself to Devon, to Babbacombe,' Neil explained, 'and that's where we met. She was a WAAF who in due course became

a Sergeant WAAF, so she was my superior in rank for a short while.'
Having met in early 1942, the two were married in Newton Abbot
that same year, four days before Christmas. 'We married on the
shortest day, the squadron called it the longest night,' said Neil.
'We had a five-day honeymoon during a truce. The day we got
back, on Boxing Day, they started the bloody war all over again.'

Neil said he never saw any real action. His exploits were confined to the North Sea and Channel patrols, so he was never sent
abroad, and because Edna was in personnel she was able to organise their postings so that they could spend weekends together
whenever possible. When Edna fell pregnant, her Group Captain
was furious: 'he reckoned she planned it deliberately'. David
MacLean Denny was born on 23 January 1945 at Gainsborough
in Lincolnshire, where Neil was posted at the time.

Once he was demobbed, Neil returned to Wimbledon, where
Edna had been living with his parents at 29 Dunmore Road. He
also returned to the civil service, switching jobs in 1948, a year
after Sandy was born, from working in National Savings to the
Ministry of National Insurance. This new role took the family
to Broadstairs for the next four years, where Neil managed the
Ramsgate office, and there Sandy first acquired her love of the sea.

It was only in the last few years of his life that Neil Denny was
asked to talk about Sandy publicly. Most of his comments here are
taken from a series of interviews he did with Colin Davies during
1997–8 for Davies's fanzine *Hokey Pokey*. Listening to Neil speaking is often as heart-rending as hearing some of his daughter's saddest songs. He is every inch the proud father sifting through memories of his daughter and their family life; he is very perceptive and
knowledgeable about Sandy's work, and although he makes light
of it, music was clearly important in his own life.

'Sandy was a one-off really,' said Neil. 'My wife wasn't particularly musical. The family in Scotland used to have these family music gatherings where everybody could do a turn and somebody could play the piano. My brother and I could vamp and we all had our little piece to do but my grandmother was a good singer.

'There was music in the Denny family. I wasn't very good at piano but I've always been interested in music.' Neil sang Gilbert and Sullivan at school but while growing up was more keen on jazz and dance music. The family had a solid collection of classical music, light opera, traditional songs of his Scottish heritage and a 'fair bit of jazz' in the house.*

Sandy once said she used to sing a lot at home and at infant school, but after that 'only inconspicuously in the school choir'. She was barely nine years old when her grandmother died and we'll never know if she ever heard Mary sing the Scottish ballads of her youth. Neil Denny encouraged her to learn some of these, which were collected in Marjory Kennedy-Fraser's books of Highland music. Her three-volume *Songs of the Hebrides* includes 'Fhir a' Bhàta' or 'The Boatman', a late-eighteenth-century lament from the Isle of Lewis which his mother used to sing. Sandy performed 'The Boatman' at floor spots when she was starting out and it was one of two songs she chose for her first radio broadcast in 1966.

The Denny household also had *The Oxford Book of English Verse*; 'Tam Lin' and 'Sir Patrick Spens' appear in it on consecutive pages, from where Sandy once neatly transcribed the lyrics to 'Tam Lin'. 'She'd sing these things to please Daddy, but that

* Much to her father's delight, in 1973 Sandy recorded versions of 'Whispering Grass' and 'Until the Real Thing Comes Along', songs that she knew from his old 78s by the Ink Spots and Fats Waller.

wasn't her real interest,' said Neil. Instead she had discovered pop music – Buddy Holly was her first pop crush. Her cousin Hilary recalled that when her parents met twelve-year-old Sandy at Liverpool docks after an educational cruise in the Mediterranean, she was absolutely distraught. In floods of tears Sandy ran straight into her aunt Irene's arms, declaring, 'He's dead, he's dead . . . Buddy Holly's dead.' She had heard the news on a transistor radio she had smuggled onboard. Hilary describes this as typical Sandy behaviour, saying she was 'a drama queen' and 'so full of life that everything was bigger than life'.

Neil and Edna Denny may not have been musical themselves, but they encouraged an interest in music in both their children and heard something in Sandy's voice to warrant exploring further. 'When she was very young, my wife took her to the Royal College of Music,' said Neil, 'and they said, "She has a very nice little voice and it could develop very well but don't let her join the school choir or take part in amateur dramatics – let her sing naturally and bring her back when her voice breaks." We never did but she had great capability as a singer.'

David and Sandy also studied classical piano – Sandy took lessons from the age of nine – and learnt to play the violin at infant school. David was eventually excused piano lessons so he could study Latin instead. 'I've still got an old record of the famous Beethoven sonatas,' said Neil, 'the Pathétique and the Moonlight and the Appassionata. Sandy used to practise these on the piano; the record is even marked where she used to take it off and put it on.

'I was particularly keen to keep my father's piano, which wasn't very good, but I kept it. Eventually I bought a very good piano – a Challen – especially for Sandy. I thought one of the best things a child could do is to learn an instrument.

'She was a mischievous girl, a great girl, and she used to fool her teachers – she had a wonderful ear . . . She'd ask the teacher to play a piece and then come back next week and she'd play it pretty well, but her teacher must have had some sort of suspicion because one day this teacher made a few mistakes, which Sandy duly repeated. She said, "You're not reading the music, are you?" She was getting away with it, no doubt about it, as she was very sharp.'

Hilary English is Sandy's cousin on her mother's side, the daughter of Irene and Les Jones. Sandy and Hilary were two months apart in age. Speaking to Pamela Winters for her unpublished biography of Sandy, *No Thought of Leaving*, Hilary recalled how David and Sandy would often stay with them in Liverpool over the Easter holidays. She remembers Sandy as a healthy, happy child with a head of wayward golden curls, who even then was free-spirited and impetuous. It was clear to Hilary how close Sandy and her brother David were; they remained so throughout Sandy's life. 'They were great pals,' said Neil sorrowfully.

David and Sandy's first school was Cottenham Park Infant School, on Pepys Road, just on the Wimbledon side of Raynes Park, several bus stops from Worple Road; the Dennys lived in three separate houses on Worple Road when she was growing up. The children then transferred to Old Central Primary School on the edge of Wimbledon Common. In 1956 David – always more methodical and organised than his sister – won a scholarship to King's College School, Wimbledon. The independent King's was, and still is, rated one of the best schools in the UK. There's nothing to suggest that Neil and Edna Denny favoured David over Sandy, but David excelled in all the areas in which Sandy, no less bright, showed little interest or application. When David

left King's in 1963, he had been head of his house, played in the
rugby and hockey teams, and been captain of the cricket eleven
in his final year before going to Imperial College London. There
he obtained a BSc in engineering in 1966, before joining the firm
of Taylor Woodrow, one of the largest house-building and general
construction companies in Britain.

Sandy, meanwhile, 'hated school, every minute of it. I just
resented the way the teachers used their authority. I certainly
wouldn't tell any children of mine that schooldays are the happi-
est of your life. They weren't for me, anyway.' Neil Denny traces
this dislike back to an incident at Cottenham Park, where he says
one of the teachers had it in for her. 'One day, Sandy didn't come
home after half past three. Edna eventually went out to search for
her and she went to the school and this teacher had kept Sandy in
for no reason at all. Sandy was absolutely terrified and desperate
to go home. She never had the same trust in teachers after that.
My wife gave this woman a great dressing-down – she'd done it
as an experiment to see what Sandy's reaction would be. It was a
very odd thing to do and Sandy reacted very strongly against it;
it unhinged her mentally that something like this should be done
for no possible reason. I think that sense of injustice made a big
difference to Sandy's outlook.

'After that she was always rebellious against teachers [and] I
suspect authority in general. Sandy always had a battle at school,
in hot water constantly, inattentive, tremendously loyal; she took
the rap for many things she didn't do. She would never give away
her friends. She wouldn't do her homework in time – she was generally ill-disciplined and didn't do well at school at all. I daren't
show you her school reports.'

Irrespective of her father's concerns about Sandy's attitude, she clouds

Clouds, higher than the trees,
looking down on us from above,
Moving swiftly in the breeze.
More gracefully than a wingèd
                                dove.

In their hundreds they rest on high,
On the sun they seem to lie,
Till twilight comes,
and dark is nigh,

Early poem by Sandy

passed her eleven-plus examination for grammar-school entrance and went on to attend Coombe Girls' School in New Malden in 1958. In one of her notebooks from 1974 she wrote: 'I wasn't like the others, it seemed, and I believe have apparently always lived in a world of my own.' At the foot of the entry she scrawled the name 'Wiggy', one of her school friends. Sandy's other friends included twins Diana and Frankie King. 'We were quite a social group, which was unusual among the girls at Coombe,' they recall. 'Our little group of eight girls always spent lunchtime together and we would have these teenage parties at each other's houses at weekends.' They paint a happier and more carefree picture of Sandy's schooldays than her father does, or Sandy herself.

Coombe Girls' School opened in 1956, so Sandy's year was among the first intakes. The school wasn't full or completely finished; one former pupil observed: 'We watched the building site (and the builders) till the school grew round us.' Some classes took place in prefabs next to the main school building. It was there that Mr Jezierski, an émigré Polish count, taught Russian and art, and Sandy first became interested in drawing and sculpture in his classes.

Frankie King shared a music stand with Sandy in the school orchestra. 'Sandy was the leader,' she says. 'She played violin in the orchestra with us. I remember a concert where the mayor was seated at the front and Sandy was bowing with great vigour and then, whoosh, she let go of the bow and it landed at the feet of the mayor. She just got up, picked up the bow, went back to her place and carried on. That was the sort of thing she used to do.'

'She was very adept at the piano,' says Frankie's sister Diana. 'She would improvise and she could definitely play by ear. At the end of assembly somebody would be asked to play something. I remember her playing the last movement of the Moonlight Sonata and Mummy saying, "If she can play that, then she's a damn good pianist." She was leagues ahead of everybody else in the orchestra.'

As everybody who met Sandy says, she had an infectious laugh. 'She was very smiley,' says Frankie. 'She had short, very curly, perky hair. You would never ever have described her as anything other than bubbly, self-confident, happy and full of life, and this was probably why she fell foul of the teachers sometimes, because she was a little bit of a rebel. She was mischievous, but nothing malicious.'

Coombe was a radical, bilateral school taking grammar and non-grammar streams. Sandy was in one of the grammar streams. 'Sandy wasn't at all academic,' says Frankie, 'but she was very smart and very quick-witted. We were in a different stream to Sandy so we weren't in classes with her. I think we'd have known if she was getting up to anything really awful, although I'm not sure you could have stopped Sandy; even then she was very headstrong.'

Coombe's uniform included grey raincoats down to the ankles, to grow into, long grey socks and brown lace-up shoes. In summer, the girls wore panama hats and gold frocks. 'Sandy would wear her skirt a bit shorter or roll up the sleeves to her blouse, which you weren't supposed to do,' says Diana. 'You had to wear a tie and a panama hat, which she used to squash to make it into a different shape. If you were on the bus without a hat or didn't give up your seat you would be reported. We got into terrible trouble once because we were seen talking to some boys.

'We used to have our lunch together in tables of eight, treacle pudding or spotted dick or something like that, and there was a jug of custard and Sandy poured some of it out and went, "What's this?" and she went up to the serving hatch and asked, "What is this please?" The dinner lady said, "It's custard," and she said, "It can't be, it doesn't have lumps in it." She got in awful trouble for it. That was the level of our insubordination. We were all pretty well behaved, very compliant.'

Another time, Frankie remembers somebody smuggling a copy of *Lady Chatterley's Lover* into the school. 'It was after the famous obscenity court case over the book. The papers said, "Would you let your wife read this book?" There was a copy in a brown paper cover and it did the rounds and everybody read it, sitting on the grass and sniggering over the risqué passages; I don't think we were terribly shocked.'

Although Sandy never sang at school other than at assembly, Diana remembers that she used to sing at their weekend parties. 'We had a terribly jolly time because David, who was two years older, asked his friends along and Sandy asked us and our group of friends and we used to have these wonderful but very innocent parties. We would go to one person's house, and then another. I remember Sandy singing but I have to own up that I never thought, "Isn't she fantastic?"'

'She played the guitar sometimes,' says Frankie, 'or she would just pick something up like a hairbrush that she would pretend was a microphone – and she'd close her eyes and sing and act like she was a pop singer. Probably Buddy Holly or an Everly Brothers hit. If she sang with the guitar she'd sing something folky or country and western by Burl Ives or Joan Baez, that sort of thing. She was very confident. She had no difficulty getting up in front of her friends and singing. Having heard later on that she was very insecure just didn't add up at all to the Sandy we knew at school.'

Frankie and Diana's parents categorically forbade them to have parties at home. 'They were strict,' says Diana, 'but the Dennys allowed this in their house. We didn't go on the rampage and tear the place to pieces. On one occasion one of the boys from King's got very drunk and laid down behind the settee and fell asleep. That was the extent of our wickedness. Teenage rebellion hadn't reached us in Wimbledon. We didn't drink, we didn't smoke. We didn't go to clubs or pubs. We were never that into pop music. Sandy was much more interested in music so we didn't share that. She was much more boisterous than us and independent. If she was going to folk clubs, that's not something we would have done or been allowed to do at that age. Neil and Edna were much easier going than our parents.'

Frankie and Diana say their parents would certainly have frowned upon either of them attending art school. 'That was like dropping out, compared to going to university, which is what we did,' says Diana. 'Neil was a civil servant, he travelled up to London in a bowler hat, carrying an umbrella, and later Edna worked for the Inland Revenue. They were living the cliché. They were very conventional, even for an area like Wimbledon. Sandy becoming a singer must have been completely out of their orbit, but they didn't stand in her way either.'

Neither Frankie nor Diana kept in touch with Sandy; they moved to another school after the fifth year and their group just drifted apart.

It's clear that Sandy was as much a product of her environment as a reaction against it. 'She would say her parents were strict,' says the songwriter and musician Richard Thompson, 'but any-body, parents or teachers, telling her what to do would have met with resistance from Sandy.' The Dennys were defined by Neil's professional occupation but also by values characterised as much by respectability as by income. They epitomised the middle class, which in the early 1960s still embraced moderation in all things and the abiding virtues of good manners, hard work and education.

It has been said that Sandy's parents were unsupportive and that they lacked warmth towards her. Neither suggestion really rings true, although she and her mother were both strong-willed and there would have been flashpoints between them. Edna Denny had a sharp tongue and would always be of the opinion that she knew best, but Sandy would have stood her ground even at a young age.

'I've always had a very straight background,' she said in 1971, 'but my mother always had a fantastic amount of confidence in me, though we never quite worked out what I was going to do.' Edna was definitely a pushy mother. 'She wanted Sandy to get on and do well but also to be seen to do well,' says Linda Thompson, who first met Sandy in 1965. 'Her mother was very ambitious for her kids, but I think that generation really lived through their kids and I can appreciate that since I've had kids of my own.'

Many of Sandy's friends say that Edna was judgemental and reproachful towards her daughter throughout her life. As one friend put it, 'her mother sucked her dry'. While there's no doubt that in later years Sandy's relationship with her parents was more strained, they were unexpectedly supportive when she chose a career in music, whether it was Edna writing to BBC producers on her behalf or Neil picking her up after gigs in the middle of the night or buying her a decent Sony reel-to-reel tape recorder so that she could work on her technique.

Linda Thompson thinks Sandy's relationship with her parents was just typical of the day: 'Her mum was tough. I don't remember her dad saying much, but dads were always more aloof. Her mother reminded me of something Carly Simon said when she won a Grammy; her mother said, "Well, you're not the best singer, that wasn't the best song, but you've won." Sandy's mother was just like that. My mother was the same. You weren't supposed to praise your kids to their face in case they got big-headed. You were very rarely encouraged. Putting somebody down was somehow supposed to incentivise them and make them do better. Our parents were much tougher on us. They didn't give praise lightly or at all.

'Edna was slim. She would have liked Sandy to be thin and

My mum

Sandy's drawing of her mother, Edna

would tell her so. Sandy and I were both born just after the war and in those days we really were pushed: you must work hard, you must study, and we were supposed to be relatively obedient. Sandy had the usual love–hate relationship with her mother like we all do. Edna's favourite singer in the whole world was Shirley Bassey and we used to get sick of her saying, "If only you girls would sing like Shirley Bassey."'

Philippa Clare, another of Sandy's lifelong friends – the two first met in 1966 – saw nothing unusual about her childhood. 'Neil Denny was a normal father of that era. He doted on Sandy and was in denial about everything. He was pretty laid-back; it was her mother who ruled the roost. She was the type who would worry about what the neighbours thought, which was quite normal if you were from that background. We can all tell those stories about how our parents drove us nuts for one reason or another. Sandy had a classic middle-class Wimbledon upbringing.'

Gina Glaser, a traditional singer and one of the life models at Kingston Art School, where Sandy was later to study, remembers a very convivial home environment: 'I would go and spend the night at her house with my kids. She was still living at home when she was at Kingston. I never saw any conflict with her parents. They encouraged her music. Her father didn't say much, would come home from work and read the paper. But her mother would come up, the kids and I would be camped in sleeping bags in Sandy's room – Sandy loved kids – and she and her mother would laugh and chat together with us all. I only saw a side of her mother that was bubbly and loving, and that's where I always thought Sandy got some of her drive.'

'Trevor [Lucas] always thought that Sandy's approach to life came from Edna, who was very demanding, as was Sandy,' says Nigel Osborne, who lived with Marion Appleton, Trevor's sister, during the 1970s. 'Edna could be fearsome. Sandy was a daddy's girl; Neil was rather old-fashioned, from another age, and that appealed to the sentimental side of Sandy's character. Trevor was quite comfortable with Neil as I remember – he kept a lot to himself – but he found Edna much more controlling, just as he found it difficult in the way that Sandy could be controlling and manipulative.' The parallels between Sandy and her mother didn't escape Neil Denny. 'Sandy was a remarkable girl – her mother was the same. Her mother could turn an accusatory conversation into – instead of her being accused, you were.'

Sandy came away with five O-levels at the end of her fifth year at Coombe Girls' School, passing English language, English literature, French, art and music. Initially she stayed on to take art and music A-levels, and passed the former but dropped music because she had a run-in with her teacher. Then in February 1965, after the first term of her final year, Sandy won a scholarship to Kingston Art School. Once she received the letter of acceptance, she immediately abandoned school.

Sandy already knew a number of art students from Kingston through local folk clubs. Although, misleadingly, she said in interviews that she had first got up and sung at the Kingston Folk Barge after she went to art school in September 1965, she had really been doing floor spots in clubs as early as 1963.

Always a music fan, by the time she was sixteen Sandy was already developing her own musical taste. She had made friends with a like-minded girl called Winnie Whittaker, who went to the Roman Catholic Ursuline High School, originally on Worple Road. In Winnie, Sandy had found an equally fun-loving friend who had a greater sense of adventure than her school circle and who was more inquisitive about the social and cultural world opening up for teenagers in the sixties. The self-possessed Winnie certainly shared Sandy's passion for music and had long since discovered Bob Dylan; she was even quite blasé about him because he was becoming too popular.

Both girls had elder brothers with guitars and Sandy soon took advantage of David's lesser enthusiasm. 'David started her on the guitar,' said Neil, 'but he never got very far. Sandy wanted her own guitar because she was immediately better than David.' Sandy found a guitar for sale, advertised as a Gibson, which meant nothing to her father; he dutifully took her along to check it out. 'Sandy was very clever, we got to this house and the chap produced the guitar and Sandy was very non-committal until after we bought it and had left the house and then she said, "Daddy, what a wonderful guitar.'"

Some time in 1963 Sandy and Winnie started going to local folk clubs together. They would take the bus to visit the Kingston Barge, a folk club started in 1961 by local musicians including singer Theo Johnson, and Alan Beach, Roger Evans and Dave Waite, who had formed the Countrymen, inspired by American folk groups such as the Weavers and the Kingston Trio. 'It was a converted coal barge,' says Waite. 'The most you could get in was about eighty people and it was an awful fire trap. People would pack the place out and musicians came from all over. Paul Simon played there, Jackson C. Frank, and Sandy; it's where John Martyn first played when he came down from Scotland.'

The two girls were similar in appearance, both naturally blonde. Sandy's hair was shoulder-length and naturally wavy, framing a round face and a fresh complexion. Winnie was taller than Sandy, who stood a little over five foot, but they often pretended to be each other and would burst into laughter when their true identities were revealed. Folk singer Al Stewart remembers Sandy supporting him at a gig in Portsmouth where she talked Winnie into going on instead of her, before bustling on stage in fits of laughter after the first song.* Stewart says Sandy and Winnie were real 'best friends, always up for a laugh'. 'Sandy would always drag her friend Winnie along to gigs in the early days,' says Richard Thompson; 'she always liked to have a female sidekick. Sometimes it was Linda; she liked to have a pal. It was some kind of buffer, somebody to have a laugh

---

* Sandy and Winnie remained friends, although Winnie, who trained as a quantity surveyor, worked abroad during the 1970s. She was a successful businesswoman and later relocated to Hong Kong, where she died in 2005.

with, or somebody to stick her in a cab and make sure she got home at night.'

If they were such disciplinarian parents, it's surprising that Neil and Edna Denny so readily allowed the sixteen-year-old Sandy to go to folk clubs. But far from barring Sandy from places such as the dingy Barge, the ever-protective Neil would pick her and Winnie up if they missed the last bus home. Eventually they began missing the bus more often because they knew he would come and get them. Perhaps, as Linda Thompson says, 'You couldn't have laid down the law with Sandy, even when she was sixteen. If you said, "Not under my roof you don't," she'd go and find another roof. They probably took the path of least resistance.'

'Sandy's parents were none too happy about her choosing to follow a career in folk music,' says Glasgow-born singer Shelagh McDonald. 'In those days, if you were brought up in a middle-class home, to be a folk singer was like being an artist in Renaissance Italy, you were *ipso facto* a prostitute. Travelling to clubs and stopping over who knows where, you were branded a woman of easy virtue. My parents just hoped I'd give it up, go back home and do something normal. I'm sure Sandy's felt exactly the same.'

Sonja Kristina, best known as the singer with Curved Air in the seventies, started out singing in folk clubs on the outskirts of east London: 'My parents used to drive me to clubs where I was singing and sit outside with a blanket and a Thermos flask and a book and wait for me to come out. When I was sixteen or seventeen I was quite a tearaway anyway so they wouldn't have trusted me to my own devices.' Shirley Collins's mother went a step further: 'My mum came up to London to live with me at one point when I was nineteen or twenty. She didn't like me being up there on my own; coffee houses were dens of iniquity in her eyes. So we shared a bedsit for a while. It was hell. I'm sure Sandy's mother was scared about what she was getting into and, as it turned out, justifiably.'

Geoff Clark was in David Denny's year at Old Central Primary School. His first memory of Sandy was as 'David's little sister, a fairly plump child in a pink pixie hood and very cheery'. Ten years later, by the time he met up with Sandy again, Clark was very much the young idealist who had joined YCND and the Young Socialists: 'I don't think she ever came to any of the serious meetings where we all sat around and discussed how we were going to put the world to rights, but she was often at the parties we had on a Saturday night. I don't think her parents had any issues with it, or her staying out late at parties. I remember a group of us having been to a party in New Malden and pitching up at one thirty in the morning having bummed a lift back to Raynes Park. The driver dropped us all off outside Sandy's house. I can picture her now, taking her shoes off and walking quietly up the garden path and letting herself in.

'I definitely used to see her at the Barge in 1963. Folk music went hand in hand with political idealism; I remember Sandy singing there, though I couldn't tell you what. Nobody who got up from the floor was too adventurous; if it wasn't a Dylan song, it would be something like "Tom Dooley", or by Pete Seeger; among the girls it was usually something they'd heard off a Joan Baez album.'

Dave Waite also remembers seeing Sandy at the Barge. 'It was definitely in 1963 when I first met this dumpy blonde girl who looked like a secretary. She was dressed in a twinset and pearls, pencil skirt and court shoes, and she looked a little out of place on our coal barge, and she asked if she could sing. When she got up and performed we were gobsmacked. We were absolutely stunned.

She had no skills in terms of presentation and she was shy and it was only with a little bit of urging that she did anything at all but she had such a sound – she had one of the most remarkable voices I'd ever heard. That was Sandy Denny and, as far as I know, it was the first time she had got up and done a floor spot.'

Sandy later recalled the incident herself: how she went along to the Barge and came away convinced she could sing better than anyone she saw. The next week, she plucked up courage and returned to the club with her guitar. 'The first time I ever stood up on stage my mouth went all dry,' she said, 'and I could hardly sing but when I came off and everybody applauded, I knew that although it was a great effort, I'd always want to do it.' The nervousness before she went on was understandable but never entirely left her. She had got the bug.

'I don't think any of us woke up one morning and said, "I'm going to be a folk singer,"' says Shelagh McDonald. 'It was the effect of being in a folk club and discovering that world for the first time – it's almost a revelation. You realised that something had been missing from your life; you were tapping into something almost ancestral. So you wanted to be part of it and it gave you strength in a strange way because you could be a part of it. You just had to get up and sing.'

Sandy sang at the Barge regularly from then on: 'First she just sang,' says Waite, 'and then Roger Evans took her aside and started teaching her the guitar – she didn't have too many guitar skills before that. Even then, as untutored as it was, her voice just transported you.' Another local folk fan remembers seeing Sandy at the New Malden Folk Club in the Railway Tavern in 1964: 'I can remember thinking, "What a great voice," and wishing she could tune her guitar.'

Sandy most likely made her first appearance outside London on New Year's Eve 1964; she had been asked if she would entertain at a Young Farmers party at a hotel in Hereford. Unquestioningly, Neil and Edna agreed: 'She was only seventeen, coming up to her eighteenth birthday, but we said alright. We had a word with the pub owners and they were very pleasant, it was a New Year's party and about two in the morning we rang up and said, "How's our daughter getting on?" and the fellow said – "Oh she's still at it." She had a word with us and said she was having a wonderful time. That was one of her first public engagements. The next day she phoned up and said, "I'm staying here – they've got horses" – she stayed a week.'

'I don't think there's any way you could have squashed that drive she had,' says Richard Thompson. 'There is no way you could have sat on that irrepressible creativity. That's the way she was going to go. I don't think her parents stood in her way or could have. She absolutely had the talent and determination to succeed in that world.'

Sandy could not have been better placed to gain further experience. Whether it was folk or jazz or the more electric R & B groups springing up, there were a lot of musical and related activities in and around Wimbledon, New Malden and Kingston. The suburbs and towns along the Thames – starting nearest London with Putney, then Richmond (both on the Surrey side), Twickenham (on the Middlesex side) and Kingston (back on the Surrey side) – were as much at the heart of the folk, jazz and blues scene in the 1960s as Soho. If, as Sandy later described it, Soho had a folk club on every corner, every other pub along the Thames had a regular folk club or folk night, and the same musicians played there.

'I went to the art school at Kingston because I couldn't do

anything else,' says renowned guitarist John Renbourn, 'and it was a bit of a catch-all for drop-outs. Some of the art-school types used to go to a pub in Wimbledon called the Feathers, and we'd sit around playing guitars and that's where I first met Sandy. This was around 1964. We dossed about playing the blues and Sandy used to look in.

'Even then, when she got up to sing she sounded great. She stood out. She became the girlfriend of a singer who I used to play guitar with. He was always standing her up and we became friends. Then the next thing I knew she'd enrolled in the same art school, and I'm sure partly because so many of the musicians who were hanging round at the Feathers were from the art college. It wasn't that she didn't want to do art, she was smitten by the whole music thing and she had aspirations even then, although she was still at school when we first met. The rest of us were just sitting round getting drunk and stoned but Sandy already wanted to become a singer professionally. She was far more motivated than anybody I knew.'

2 : *Learning the Game*
1965–1966

I look back at it with a great deal of affection. There was a folk club on virtually every corner around Soho; there was the Scots Hoose, the John Snow, there was Cousins. God knows how many folk clubs all within throwing distance. You could go up there any night and be sure of finding the little crowd of John and Bert and Jackson Frank and Annie Briggs, and it used to be a really fantastic little community. And Trevor, mustn't forget him; there was his stream as well, the Australian traditional stuff.

SANDY DENNY, interviewed by Patrick Humphries, March 1977

Sandy came with me to the Singers Club to see what it was like but it was not for her. Sandy much preferred the newer folk clubs that were more for her generation where there were no rules about repertoire. She was definitely attracted to modern, contemporary folk music. As much as I encouraged her to learn traditional songs and she sang them so well, she wanted to reach a broader audience and didn't like the staid, collegiate atmosphere of the Singers Club.

GINA GLASER

I was never in the traditional clan – I was in the layabout section with Bert Jansch and John Renbourn and all that lot.

SANDY DENNY, *Melody Maker*, November 1977

KINGSTON SCHOOL OF ART

FULL TIME DAY

PERSON
SURNAME PENNY
CHRISTIAN NAMES ALEXANDRA ELENE MACLEAN
ADDRESS WOMBLE ROAD, WIMBLEDON S.W.20
PARENT'S INITIALS (Mr. or Mrs.) N.M.
AGE 18 yrs DATE OF BIRTH 6.1.47
PREVIOUS SCHOOL COOMBE COUNTY SCHOOL FOR GIRLS
EXAMINATIONS PASSED
PHONE Wim 636
STUDENT'S SIGNATURE Alexandra Penny

COMMENCING DATE 20.9.65
COURSE Pre. Diploma
AIM Dip. A.D.
PROBATION PERIOD
FEE £32.15.0
SIGNATURE OF PRINCIPAL OR HEAD OF DEPT. J.D.B.

REGISTER NOS
9.10

Sandy's registration card for Kingston School of Art

Sandy left Coombe Girls' School in February 1965 to begin work as a temporary nurse at the Royal Brompton Hospital, Kensington. She had heard of the vacancy there through her brother David's German girlfriend and future wife, Irene Eva Gumbel, known as Eva. Sandy committed to working at the hospital for six months before taking up her place at Kingston Art School.

'She went to the Brompton and had quite a tough time,' said Neil Denny. 'They offered her courses but she didn't want them. She said, "I'm only a temporary," so they threw her in at the deep end, just general duties because she didn't have specific skills: attending the deaths, washing the corpses, looking after the grieving relatives. It wasn't fair. She was only just eighteen and because she wasn't going into nursing full-time, she was given the worst jobs.' Neil recalled that Sandy had to deal with a number of dying patients. There was one man in particular whom she liked; she would put bets on for him at the bookmakers. At the end she sat by his bedside and held his hand until he died, and then had to inform his brother he'd gone. 'She had one or two harrowing experiences, no doubt about it, and some of the ward sisters were dragons.'

At one stage, Neil said, Sandy 'just ran away from the hospital, and we didn't know where she was. She finished up in a house in East London where Paul Simon and Jackson Frank lived. I tracked her down and took her back to the hospital.' Sandy later told friends that she really disliked nursing and was deeply shocked by some of the things she saw. 'She didn't take to nursing at all,' says Gina Glaser, 'but she stuck it out and was under no illusions that it would be easy. Today you would say she was a nursing assistant, which meant she was a dogsbody. She told me that many of the nurses were quite nasty to her and made her do the menial jobs that they didn't want to do themselves.'

Nursing was never going to be a vocation for Sandy but it was a shrewd choice, making it easier for her to leave school early without too much objection from Neil and Edna. Nursing and secretarial work were, after all, the two most common profes- sional occupations for girls leaving school in the mid-1960s, and Sandy was never cut out for the dull routine of office work. The unsocial hours at the hospital also enabled her to convince her parents that she needed to live somewhere nearby, so she was able to leave home for the first time and take up a flatshare in South Kensington.

'To understand Sandy,' said Trevor Lucas, 'I think you have to consider she had a very restrictive childhood, until that time when she actually broke away from home. And when she did get out, and saw there was a good time to be had out there, she was determined to have it. When she started working as a nurse, that was really the first time she'd had any freedom at all. And, like most people who have been confined in that way, she was only more eager to live life to the full.'

Living at home can't have been so intolerable, however, given that after Sandy gave up nursing she went back home for the next couple of years. Trevor is certainly right that Sandy grasped the opportunity to live life to the full, but Neil and Edna were by no means blinkered about what their daughter was getting up to and they knew she was being drawn more and more to the folk scene.

The Brompton Hospital had at least one advantage: it was within walking distance of the Troubadour club on Old Brompton Road. The Troubadour was one of the earliest folk venues in London, a basement club that held around a hundred people. It was there that Sandy met Linda Thompson and the two became close and lifelong friends. Born in London, seven months after Sandy, Linda Pettifer – she later changed her name to Peters, before marrying Richard Thompson in 1972 – was brought up in Glasgow but returned to London in 1965, ostensibly to study modern languages.

'When I first moved to London it seemed as if everything was a folk thing,' says Linda. 'Like Starbucks is everywhere now. So

Ad from *Sing* folk magazine, June 1966

many of us started out at the Troubadour. Dylan had played the Troubadour on his first visit. Shirley Collins used to sing there in the fifties. It's where Bert Jansch first played when he came down from Scotland. That's where I first met Sandy some time in 1965. On a typical night at the Troubadour Sandy would be there, or Annie Briggs, Bert, John Renbourn, Martin Carthy. Paul Simon used to come down to the Troubadour on Wednesday nights. You almost took it for granted; it was such an array of talent.

'Sandy used to come down to the Troubadour straight from the hospital with all sorts of drugs stashed in her pockets that she had stolen from the patients, typical nurse thing – uppers, downers, sleeping pills – and then she'd get up on stage and was amazing from the get-go. She was incredible. She smoked like a chimney, took it up with a vengeance when she was nursing and never gave it up; all the nurses and doctors smoked to help get through the long shifts. How Sandy could sing like an angel on all those ciga-rettes I don't know.'

Nursing may have been tough but it had its illicit perks for Sandy and the hours suited her nocturnal activities. 'If she finished at nine o'clock at night,' says Linda, 'she would come straight to the Troubadour or one of the clubs in Soho and she would some-how manage to work her shifts so she didn't have to start too early the next day. It certainly wasn't a calling and I've known her pass out at the sight of blood, so God knows how she coped. Sandy had to do something sensible and proper – like nursing – for her par-ents to go along with her leaving school early. She was definitely quite serious about going to art school but only up to a point; her singing was always going to take precedence.

'When I met her she was eighteen but streets ahead of me as a singer. It was the era of liberation for women, so it was a lot of fun.

The pill made a huge difference. Her behaviour was like a man's – she said and thought what she wanted to, had one-night stands if she wanted to, unusual for a woman in those days – she was wild and wonderful. We shared a couple of boyfriends – we both went out with Joe Boyd, and she went out with Paul McNeill before me. But we never let that get in the way.'

Sandy soon had a regular Tuesday-night slot at the Troubadour, while Linda was still doing floor spots or singing with Paul McNeill.* 'Neither of us had any stage presence – she was always tripping over things and chatting nervously between songs and I always stood there petrified – but when Sandy started to sing it was a completely different matter. I thought she was sublime, the absolute best, and I learnt a lot about vocal techniques, grace notes and that sort of thing from Sandy.'

Shelagh McDonald also remembers seeing Sandy singing at the Troubadour and making an immediate impression: 'I was part of the second wave to arrive in London, not long after John Martyn came down from Scotland in spring 1967. A couple of weeks later, I heard Sandy at the Troubadour and thought, "That's it, I'm giving the whole thing up." She was that good, but because I had had such a battle with my parents to do my folk singing, what was I to do? Either go home with my tail between my legs, admit defeat, or face up to Sandy having this incredible talent and think, "I'm never going to be that good but I'm not giving up."'

---

* Paul McNeill was a traditional singer who recorded a couple of singles with Linda Peters as Paul and Linda. The first, in 1968, was a cover of Dylan's 'You Ain't Going Nowhere'. He recorded two albums for Decca in 1965 and 1966; the second of these, *Traditionally at the Troubadour*, features Trevor Lucas on twelve-string guitar. McNeill was also a guest performer on *Alex Campbell and His Friends* (1967).

33

Philippa Clare, who first met Sandy at this time, was then secretary to actor–producer and king of farce Brian Rix. Richard Thompson describes Clare as 'somebody who always seemed to be somewhere in the mix in that scene. She knew Sandy and Linda, the Strawbs, Swarb [Dave Swarbrick], everybody . . .' 'Back then,' says Clare, 'if you had three chords and long hair you were a folk singer. I wanted so much to be a folk singer but I didn't have the talent. Going on stage, Sandy was very nervous, and that stayed with her. She was very shy too, but usually covered it well by acting the opposite. She didn't find performing easy but by the third or fourth number she had you. You knew even then she was special.'

Sandy finished nursing on 24 August 1965, a month before taking up her place at Kingston Art School. By now she had made the transition from unpaid floor spots in local folk clubs to regular nights at the Troubadour and was breaking into the pivotal network of pubs and clubs running off Shaftesbury Avenue and around Soho. 'One of the things that always struck me about Sandy,' says Geoff Clark, 'was just how single-minded she was. It's incredible when you think about it, but even when she was nursing she was already rubbing shoulders with Paul Simon, Tom Paxton, people like that. She just seemed to take it in her stride.'

The accepted centre of the new contemporary scene was Les Cousins (or just 'Cousins' to the in-crowd there), a basement coffee house at 49 Greek Street, Soho. Les Cousins opened as a contemporary folk club in March 1965, initially only at weekends, but within six weeks it had become so popular that it opened on Mondays and Thursdays as well. A glance at the list of people doing weekly sessions at this time shows Dorris Henderson on Mondays (with John Renbourn playing with her), Bert Jansch on Thursdays (his momentous debut album had hit the shops

Les Cousins membership card

in mid-April), Noel Murphy running the Friday all-nighter and Les Bridger the late-night Saturday show, with the early sessions on Fridays and Saturdays going to visiting Americans and home-grown big names. Almost overnight it had become the place to play for aspiring folk singers, especially on Saturdays. 'To begin with,' says John Renbourn, 'the Cousins was a shady, derelict scene, full of dossers and not the springboard to fame and fortune as it's presented later. It was never that, however much people romanticise about it now. It was just a word-of-mouth joint with no stage at first, but everybody who was anybody and plenty who weren't all played there over the years.'

Les Cousins' broad, open policy saw a roll call of all the folk greats descending its basement steps in its first year. Among those leading the way was a new wave of guitarists: Jansch, Renbourn and Davy Graham were regulars, and occasionally Wizz Jones.

35

The new breed of singer-songwriters followed suit, including Al Stewart, Roy Harper, Ralph McTell and Marc Brierley, as well as Sandy, plus Americans Paul Simon, Jackson C. Frank and Tom Paxton. Other American drop-ins included Sandy Bull, Spider John Koerner and Phil Ochs, alongside jazz and blues musicians like Duffy Power, Alexis Korner, John McLaughlin and Long John Baldry. Old hands such as Alex Campbell, Owen Hand, Les Bridger and Diz Disley also played there, as did the more far-out Incredible String Band, and the soon to be 'in' – Donovan, Marc Bolan and Van Morrison. More traditional music was represented by the likes of the Watersons, Martin Carthy, Anne Briggs and the Young Tradition, who all brought a fresh attitude and approach to traditional repertoires.

'What struck me about that scene in 1965,' said Bert Jansch, 'was that everybody had something to offer. If I wanted to hear a traditional song there was Anne Briggs; or if I wanted to hear a guitarist who was doing something different I'd listen to Davy Graham or Wizz Jones. Clive Palmer would show up and he was a fantastic banjo player. Almost every performer brought something to the melting pot and we all looked to each other and learnt from each other. Cousins was like a magnet and some of the new people didn't do much for me at first but Sandy definitely had something about her, and she sang well, even then. You were definitely drawn to her.'

'I always thought she was more in the Young Tradition mould,' says folk singer-songwriter Marc Brierley, who met Sandy at Les Cousins around October 1965, when he first appeared at the club. 'She had a very English folk voice but more ornate than Anne Briggs or Shirley Collins and, unusually, she played acoustic guitar, softly strummed and with open tuning. She played well enough and mostly sang traditional songs. It was only later her repertoire expanded but I never saw her sing any of her own songs in folk clubs.'

It is remarkable how village-like London was in the mid-sixties. Musicians from all fields became acquainted with one another and crossed over every genre – the mod-soul, R & B, folk, jazz and pop worlds all somehow coalesced in and around the West End's four square miles. It was impossible for musicians not to fall over each other coming out of the Flamingo or the Marquee or the Mandrake. Just about anybody might turn up at Les Cousins. 'I was there when Paul Simon got up,' says future Fairport Convention founding member Ashley Hutchings. 'He was top of the bill with Bert Jansch, Phil Ochs and Danny Kalb, who was in Blues Project. It was quite extraordinary who you could see on one night, one after the other, and Paul Simon got up on stage and said, "Before I start I just want to tell you that I've just had a phone call from America to say that *Sounds of Silence* has just gone number one" – and of course everyone clapped – and he added, "They put Fender guitars on it," with a grimace on his face.' Richard Thompson remembers apprehensively doing a floor spot there in pre-Fairport days: 'It was terrifying and completely embarrassing.'

There were other clubs in the area: the Scots Hoose on Cambridge Circus, the Roundhouse on the corner of Wardour Street and Brewer Street, Bunjies on Litchfield Street, off Charing Cross Road, or the more traditional John Snow off Broadwick Street. Le Duce and the pioneering but short-lived Student Prince were both on D'Arblay Street. Despite the strong camaraderie in the scene, everyone was vying for gigs. John Renbourn remembers bumping into Sandy again after he was kicked out of Kingston Art School. He was washing up in a Soho pub called the Coach and Horses. 'She had followed the migration into that world and she took me to the Pollo restaurant on the corner of Old Compton Street and bought me a really big plate of spaghetti, which, at that time, meant a hell of a lot.

'Sandy used to take me along to a gay joint on D'Arblay Street where she used to sing and she'd smuggle me free drinks. There she was, a full-on red-blooded woman dressed in tight clothes, and all these guys were smooching and dancing together, oblivious to her looks. She couldn't keep a straight face. She'd keep looking at me and bursting into laughter. She was so sweet-natured, had such a sunny disposition and a lovely laugh.'

'She always seemed young to me,' says Marc Brierley, 'and she was terribly nervous about getting up to sing. She would tremble and her voice would shake till she settled into the first or second song. And she would drink a lot to calm those nerves. It was a strange compulsion, that she had to perform but [had] a fear of actually performing. It's not unusual, but at times she was almost paralysed with fear.'

Brierley observes that 'Sandy displayed a definite discomfort with her physicality'; he describes her as 'a dumpy girl, in the nicest possible way'. John Renbourn, Dave Waite, Ralph McTell and Wizz Jones all use much of the same language of the day to describe Sandy's appearance: she was 'chubby', 'plump' or 'round', and 'touchy about her appearance'. Journalists would be equally unsympathetic and insensitive in the future.

'She was self-conscious about her looks,' says Linda Fitzgerald Moore, who was then working in the coffee bar at the Troubadour. 'It's fair to say all women can be insecure about their looks but Sandy actually had a great figure, she was very curvy; she had an hourglass figure that women in previous decades would have killed for. Her face was the first thing to get fat though, it was quite squareish, but her body was much thinner. She was very pretty but she wasn't skinny. She had big tits. Unfortunately, you had to be stick thin in the sixties. And among folk singers you also had to have long, straight hair. That Marianne Faithfull, Mary Travers [of Peter, Paul and Mary], Cathy McGowan look.'

Although Sandy had let her hair grow, it was frizzy rather than falling geometrically and fashionably straight. 'She used to come round to my place and I used to iron her hair between two sheets of brown paper,' says Gordon Graham (aka Doon), who worked at Les Cousins. 'Sandy never felt she looked right and that stayed with her,' says Linda Thompson. 'She was always trying to lose weight; we all took slimming pills then. All her friends were small sizes and I think she found it tough. It was hard to be around all those men, there wasn't the equality and there certainly wasn't today's sense of correctness. She always made herself heard, she always stood up for herself, and I think she found that quite wearing.'

'When I first met Sandy she would get fat and thin, fat and thin, fat and thin,' says Philippa Clare. 'When she was thin her demeanour would change. She would walk into a room in a different way. I remember a certain pair of jeans and when she used to get into that particular pair she would walk taller.'

'The folk scene wasn't exactly dressy,' says Linda Thompson. 'None of us made enough money to spend too much on clothes. Most of the boys only had the clothes they stood up in; they were all pretty scruffy in worn-out trousers, jeans, plain shirts and jumpers. There was still a bohemian hangover from the fifties where black was the colour. Sandy wore what we'd all wear: jeans and everyday tops, ribbed sweaters, pencil skirts and shortish dresses.

The Mary Quant look that was coming in wasn't out of place in folk clubs because it was designed to be functional, so straight tunic dresses and pinafore dresses were in. Nobody wore bright colours in folk clubs. Floral and fabric patterns came later with the hippies.'

'It was a strange existence in folk clubs,' says Brierley. 'We all sat in the dark most of the time. At Cousins it was dark when you went down the stairs, darkly lit inside and still dark when you left. I don't recall seeing Sandy or many of those people in daylight. And after the gig you went to somebody's house or flat and sat in the dark getting stoned. The only light was the glow of cigarettes.'

Sandy would always remember that time in her life with great affection, responding to a question about her fondest memories by recalling 'when everybody used to go down the Cousins when it was open all night and everyone would be on – Martin [Carthy] and Swarb, people like Alexis Korner would do an overnight thing and Bert Jansch and John Renbourn would be there, and the Watersons and Les Bridger. Davy Graham would do the all-nighters as well; those were really good days. John Martyn used to do it too, and Jackson Frank. There were so many visiting American people, Paul Simon, Mike Seeger, Tom Paxton.'

Neil Denny had heard Sandy sing 'Away in a Manger' at Cottenham Park Infant School and play in the orchestra at Coombe Girls' School, but the first time he saw her in a 'professional' show was at Les Cousins in 1965, on a bill with Paul Simon. The supposedly fusty Denny seems to have been unperturbed by his eighteen-year-old daughter playing a seedy Soho dive down among the strip joints. 'I met Paul Simon and Jackson Frank at Les Cousins,' said Neil. 'Jackson used to pick her up or bring her home in his Aston Martin, very polite chap. He was a bit of a wild card, a reasonable musician but nothing special. Paul Simon wrote very literate songs, I thought, but he was an insignificant little chap, wore a cap slightly to one side. He looked a bit scruffy but the last time Sandy saw him, he had his own aeroplane.'

There were few other female singers in Sandy's circle in 1965, says John Renbourn. 'If you went to the Singers Club, there were more female singers in that world. The pedigree folk singers were Isla Cameron, who was very upmarket, Jeannie Robertson and Peggy Seeger, who was in a world of her own, hugely influential but rather under the thumb of Ewan MacColl. The purist clubs were just sheer hell for someone like me or Bert. We didn't do things their way, and nor did Sandy.'

Dave Waite recalls the stringent rules of the Singers Club and the former Ballad and Blues Club: 'It was a bit like going into a church: you couldn't go in while somebody was singing and God help you if you scraped a chair during a song. It was very belligerent and people would split hairs about whether something was a miners' song or a steelworkers' song. Somebody like me in a folk pop group like the Countrymen was regarded as a complete traitor.'

'It was far cooler,' said Trevor Lucas in 1989, 'to say you'd "found" a song from a traditional source, than to actually write anything. History lent virtually anything some kind of credibility. And Sandy, from the time she'd worked the clubs, had always copped a lot of flak for writing her own songs, singing contemporary songs, and not (exclusively) singing traditional things.'

Sandy wasn't entirely alone as a female singer on the more contemporary scene, however. Dorris Henderson was certainly creating a stir.* She was a charismatic black singer who played the

---

* The daughter of a clergyman and the granddaughter of a pure Blackfoot Indian, Dorris Henderson was born in Lakeland, Florida, but raised in Los

autoharp and had arrived in London late in 1964. Like so many, she found her way first to the Troubadour, but she then got a regular spot at the Roundhouse, where she invited John Renbourn to be her accompanist. He describes her as 'a hip, very modern woman who had heard it all before. She thought what we were all doing was so old-fashioned, whereas she was more like Nina Simone in her attitude.'

Streatham-born Jo Ann Kelly was another powerful voice, but she was making a name for herself as an expressive blues singer. Guitarist Wizz Jones, who had been busking his way round Europe and playing Soho clubs since the early 1960s, says she was the only other girl singer who could belt it out like Sandy. 'Jo Ann was an unbelievable blues singer and different from anybody else around. She was inspired by Memphis Minnie but she out-Memphised Memphis Minnie. Jo Ann was a feisty woman, a bit like Sandy, not easy to handle.'

It was Anne Briggs who made the biggest impression on Sandy, as she did on anybody fortunate enough to see her. 'It's obvious that Sandy was influenced by Anne Briggs,' says John Renbourn, 'because Anne was by far the best.'

'Sandy had such incredible soul,' says Linda Thompson, 'she could make you believe in what she was singing, even those endless traditional ballads, and nobody would get bored – she had the audience transfixed. Annie Briggs had the ability to do that

---

Angeles, where seeing the folk-blues singer Odetta perform one night at the Ash Grove changed her life. A jazz singer initially, she was dubbed 'Lady Dorris' by Lord Buckley before she set off for London via Greenwich Village. Henderson recorded two albums with Renbourn accompanying her, *There You Go* (1966) and *Watch the Stars* (1967). Remarkably, she released just one further album, *Here I Go Again* in 2003.

too. We both looked up to her but she was like the wild woman of Borneo to me. She was intense as a singer. I never felt her and Sandy were that close, but nobody was close to Annie. She was a wild thing and could be very intimidating. But people said both those things about Sandy too.'

Anne Briggs's uninhibited behaviour represented the spirit of folk's new age. She had been singing publicly since 1962, aged just seventeen, and made her first appearance on record in 1963.* Briggs was very liberated for the times and Sandy appeared to follow her example. 'People like me and Sandy emerged saying, "Right, we're women, times are changing, we can go out and drink in pubs, we can travel around, we can do anything,"' says Briggs. 'And we did.'

How well they knew each other is hard to say, since Briggs was rarely in one place for very long. By the time Sandy was on the scene in 1965, Briggs was touring in company with the Watersons, or travelling across Ireland, spending time with her boyfriend, the traditional singer Johnny Moynihan, who later formed Sweeney's Men. 'It was hard not to be influenced watching Annie,' said Bert Jansch, whose own guitar playing mirrored her singing for a while, according to John Renbourn. 'Sandy admired her – not just as a singer but her attitude. They knew each other as well as anybody got to know Annie – whenever she turned up in London. The

* Anne Briggs sang 'She Moves through the Fair' on a 1963 Decca anthology from the Edinburgh Folk Festival, released just before her first Topic EP. Briggs recorded only sporadically, mostly for Topic Records, and it was 1971 before her first Topic album was released. In a *Melody Maker* interview in 1970, Sandy named Briggs as one of her 'favourite singers and biggest influences'. She also cited revivalist singer Margaret Barry, whose signature song was 'She Moves through the Fair'.

Cousins was as much a meeting place as a place to play. Everybody seemed to end up there, not just folk musicians. And people would just drop by at the flat John and I shared in Somali Road [in Cricklewood]. Annie might turn up and would usually stay in the flat downstairs with the Young Tradition.

'Annie just came and went as she pleased. Sandy might have liked the romantic idea of being able to do that but Sandy always liked being part of whatever was going on around her too much. She liked to be among friends and she was a bag of nerves sometimes so she needed people she could rely upon. Annie was completely carefree.

'Annie was pretty wild too so we hit it off, I was probably even wilder, and Sandy had that in her. Sandy was completely different though in the kind of songs she would perform. She sang some traditional songs, which she did really well, but she also sang songs by Jackson Frank and Dylan. Very few of the other girls played guitar; Sandy had a good technique but she was a bit too lazy to work at it. There weren't a lot of the other girls who made any impression.'

Briggs was a bridge between the traditional world and the contemporary folk scene epitomised by Les Cousins. Around 1963 she had a loose relationship with Jansch, who was soon the new movement's poster boy. Famously, Briggs taught Jansch 'Blackwaterside', which he then made his own on his classic 1965 debut album, simply titled *Bert Jansch*. Briggs and Jansch also wrote a handful of songs together – 'The Time Has Come', 'Go Your Way My Love' and 'Wishing Well' – although she didn't record any of the songs herself until her albums in 1971 and 1973.*

* Those early songs were kept alive by Jansch: 'The Time Has Come' appeared on *Bert & John* and Pentangle's *Sweet Child*; 'Go Your Way My

More significant was Shirley Collins and Davy Graham's monumental *Folk Roots, New Routes*, released in March 1964, a bold and fascinating, if at first unlikely, collaboration between the more correct Collins and the disorderly Graham. The recordings presented a fusion of folk with Graham's inventive guitar interpretations that was years ahead of its time. 'I used to follow Davy around,' says John Renbourn. 'Along with Bert and Martin Carthy they were the ones everybody looked to. *Folk Roots, New Routes* had a huge impact on all of us. It showed that nothing was sacrosanct.'

Shirley Collins had first arrived in London in the 1950s, when the folk scene was just opening up. She was grounded in folk as a result of her family background and from listening to recordings made in the 1950s through Peter Kennedy in Britain and Alan Lomax in the USA. 'It never left me,' she says, 'and that was always the music I wanted to perform. I was aware of Sandy just as I was aware of Anne Briggs but I hardly knew either of them. People think because we were all singers we were in each other's pockets all the time. I was twelve years older than Sandy and I had family responsibilities so I didn't hang around after gigs. I'd always had my kids to get home to and I never really drank. I don't mean to sound like a goody two-shoes but I just wasn't into it.'

If Briggs was a bridge between the traditional milieu and the Cousins crowd, Jansch's and Renbourn's downstairs neighbours were the London folk underground's equivalent of the revered Hull-based Watersons. The Young Tradition helped introduce the

---

Love' was recorded for *Nicola*; and 'Wishing Well' on *Birthday Blues*. At different times in her solo career, Sandy talked about recording all three of the Jansch/Briggs collaborations for her solo albums; she did record 'Blackwaterside' on *The North Star Grassman and the Ravens*.

traditional repertoire to an audience more used to guitar folk than unaccompanied singing. The flamboyantly dressed trio offered a completely unplugged precursor to Fairport's *Liege & Lief*.

For a time, the Young Tradition's Heather Wood was another kindred spirit to Sandy. She arrived in London towards the end of 1964 and met singers Royston Wood and Peter Bellamy at folk wheeler-dealer Bruce Dunnet's Soho club The Young Tradition – hence the group's chosen name. 'I fell into a folk club and fell madly in love with Bert Jansch,' says Wood. 'Floor singers got in for free, so I learnt a couple of Joan Baez songs. Once I met Royston and Pete, I got hooked on traditional music. Pete and Royston were singing Copper Family songs together and those harmonies left a lot of room for me to play around the edges.

'We were a bunch of heads that happened to be into traditional folk music. We sang what we wanted to sing and we listened to everything, including rock 'n' roll and blues. Royston was into classical music, Peter discovered Bulgarian music, I'd listened to the Everly Brothers. So all of that influenced what we were doing and our attitude to music. And that's how Sandy was, open to everything.

'We weren't on any sort of mission to preserve folk music, nor was Sandy. We were all into free beer and getting laid. We were all stoned out of our gourds. We were singing those old songs because we loved them, not keeping anything alive for future generations. This was fun above all. Sandy was no different. She did what she pleased. She had a gorgeous voice, and knew how to use it.'

The Young Tradition's downstairs flat at Somali Road became a drop-in centre, with the key tied to a string through the letter box, where out-of-towners just drifted through, including visiting Americans like Spider John Koerner, Stefan Grossman and

Jackson C. Frank, who was another to befriend them. 'When Jackson gave us a copy of his album,' says Heather Wood, 'he inscribed it "To the Young Tradition – the in of the out".'

When Sandy was finding herself as a musician and singer, she was most strongly drawn to Frank. 'I think that my first songwriting influences came from somebody called Jackson Frank,' she said in 1972. 'He's an American bloke who made one album over here just called *Jackson C. Frank*. Paul Simon produced it. I really loved the way he wrote, and he has probably had more effect on me than anyone. I can still hear his influences in my songwriting now.'

Jackson C. Frank was born in Buffalo, New York, in 1943. At the age of eleven he was badly injured in a fire at his school in which eighteen children died. Classmates saved his life by using snow to put out the flames on his back, but he suffered more than fifty per cent burns. While he was in hospital a teacher brought him an acoustic guitar as a new interest during his months of recovery.

Frank later became a regular on the Buffalo area's coffeehouse scene, notably at a club called the Limelight, where he became friends with future Steppenwolf lead singer John Kay. Both were heavily into blues music. 'He was bloodied but unbowed, that was Jackson,' says Kay. 'You took one look at him and knew something had happened to him physically, because of the scar tissue on part of his face and his arm. He must have gone through hell with the numerous procedures after the fire but his attitude was, "Dammit, despite all that's visible, I'm going to do something that sets me apart from the also-rans."'

When Frank reached twenty-one he became eligible for $100,000 insurance money as settlement from the fire. 'At the time it was a small fortune,' says Kay. 'We went to Toronto and he went right out and bought a Jaguar XKE convertible

straight from the showroom.' A year later in 1965, he travelled
to England to acquire further cars, specifically an Aston Martin
(he also bought a Bentley and a Land Rover during his year in
London). He had read in *Esquire* magazine that London was the
place to buy cool cars. Frank brought his guitar along, but it was
only on board the *Queen Elizabeth* on the voyage over that he
began writing songs, including his particular calling card, 'Blues
Run the Game'.*

In London Frank was soon drawn into playing folk clubs and
made an immediate impact. Through social worker and folk-scene
mother hen Judith Pieppe he was introduced to Paul Simon† and
Art Garfunkel, who were living at her house on Dellow Street, off
Cable Street in east London. In the room next to Simon was Al
Stewart, an ex-beat-group guitarist newly arrived from the south
coast of England. Frank also became a tenant there.

In a rare interview in 1997, Frank talked about how he first came
across Sandy at Bunjies folk club in London: 'She was a nurse at
the time, and she had been going around singing. When I met her
she was just telling little jokes, and she was singing on stage once

---

* 'Blues Run the Game' became an overnight staple of many a British folk
set list in 1965. Sandy Denny, John Renbourn and Bert Jansch regularly
performed it. Jansch continued to play 'Blues Run the Game' and, much
later, 'My Name Is Carnival', also from Frank's sole album, up until his
death in 2011. 'Blues Run the Game' (along with 'Milk and Honey' and
'Kimbie' from the same album) was one of Nick Drake's early home recordings, and was recorded by Laura Marling in 2012.
† Paul Simon had returned to London for the second time in January
1965, and almost immediately recorded twelve songs for Judith Pieppe's
Five to Ten, a series of morning broadcasts for the BBC's Home Service.
Soon after, he cut most of those songs in London as *The Paul Simon
Songbook* for Columbia Records; it was recorded for £60 in one hour at one
microphone.

Sandy's sketch of Jackson C. Frank

in a while. She had a fantastic voice – I mean, I couldn't believe how lucky I was to run into somebody who was starting that way. She used to make me laugh. God, I would laugh my head off at the things she came up with. I'd never met anybody who had such a voice, such a sparkling personality; she was always a lady.'

The two of them soon got to know each other better, and would both play at the Kingston Barge and at Soho night spots. 'Jackson Frank was an absolute character,' recalls Dave Waite. 'He impressed a lot of people at the Barge. It was a fire risk and when he played there he would have to come up on deck for air after every three or four songs – given what had happened to him in the fire when he was a kid.'

49

Frank's album, released in 1965 and simply titled *Jackson C. Frank*, was paid for and produced by Paul Simon as one of his rare outside projects, and it was through Simon that Frank landed a deal with Columbia. Although he was a compelling, commanding performer in clubs, during the studio sessions the uneasy Frank insisted on being surrounded by screens so those present couldn't see him. Alongside Simon in the CBS studio on New Bond Street were housemate Art Garfunkel, who acted as a runner and tea-boy, and Al Stewart, who played guitar on one of the tracks.*

Although it's usually said that Sandy attended the album sessions and made her recording debut playing the tambourine on one track, Stewart says she was only there when Frank later recorded a single version of 'Blues Run the Game'. 'She was at the session where a different version was cut which has a different guitar part. There is a tambourine on the flip side ['Can't Get Away from My Love'] and I know because I was the one who played it.'

Although it was only 'Blues Run the Game' which caught on, there is no denying the strength of Frank's writing and the raw intensity of what was to be his sole album. His perceptive, open lyricism and a strong sense of melody are clear on its best tracks, 'My Name Is Carnival', 'Dialogue' and the more playful 'Just Like Anything', as well as 'Milk and Honey' and 'You Never Wanted Me', his other most covered songs. Sandy sang the latter two throughout her folk career, always delivering 'You Never Wanted Me' with particular passion.

'Jackson was an amazing person,' says Heather Wood. 'He was

---

* Al Stewart recalls: 'Paul said, "I want you to come along and play some lead guitar on 'Yellow Walls'." I still like the fact that I put a Duane Eddy riff on the bottom string on what's become a classic folk record and Paul said, "Hey, that's good, let's do that again."'

heavily scarred and often in pain. One day he just said to me, "I can't bend down to cut my toenails, so I just let them grow long and then kick walls." And it stuck with me. He and Sandy got together after some gig. He was staying with Judith Pieppe. She assumed they were lovers and put them in the same bed. That's how I heard it. Being around him, something of his approach to writing songs must have rubbed off on her. He was a powerful presence and a great songwriter.'

Frank himself said: 'When I first met Sandy Denny she was a little insecure and somewhat shy. Sandy was working as a nurse and she was just starting out on the folk scene. She was learning the ropes about performing in front of an audience and she was building up her songs. She slowly built up confidence and expanded her material. She became my girlfriend and I got her to quit the nursing profession and stick to music full time.* I remember Sandy trying out her new songs for me, like "Who Knows Where the Time Goes?" and "Fotheringay", and I saw right away that she had tremendous potential.'

Al Stewart remembers first meeting Sandy, who was dressed in her nurse's uniform, in the kitchen at Judith Pieppe's house. 'It was clear to anyone that here was one of the great voices,' says Stewart. 'The first thing I heard her sing was Dylan's "The Ballad of Hollis Brown". I had no idea she could sing and play the guitar and I remember saying, "That sounds pretty damn good, you should be playing in clubs." And she said, "I can't do that because

---

* Sandy was, of course, always going to quit nursing to attend Kingston Art School, but it is more than possible she played Frank early versions of 'Who Knows Where the Time Goes?', which she wrote in 1966, and, if not 'Fotheringay', more likely the song 'Boxful of Treasures', which shared the melody but had completely different lyrics.

Jackson doesn't like me to sing." He was a little stern and didn't want his girlfriend going out and performing in public. Jackson definitely didn't approve. He was pretty possessive. I think he managed to pin Sandy down in many ways and she was always a lot more bubbly when Jackson wasn't around. It was an incredible situation in that house because you had Paul and Art and Jackson and occasionally Sandy all there and playing songs. That's some class of '65.

'At one point Jackson and I were thinking of producing a single for Sandy; we were going to do Paul's "A Most Peculiar Man", with jangly guitars, Byrds-style. "The Sound of Silence" had just taken off. We thought it would be a great idea to do a Sandy Denny record of one of Paul's songs but it never happened.

'[Jackson] would chauffeur Sandy around – she loved the Aston Martin. He'd pick her up from the hospital or drive her back to Wimbledon, he would chauffeur everyone around. Judith had a theory that he was trying to get rid of the insurance money as quickly as possible; he felt it was blood money. He was spending like it was no tomorrow – mostly cars, guitars and good clothes. He ended up broke.'

Stewart remembers there being 'something a little competitive between Bert Jansch and Frank' – including a rivalry over Sandy's affections. 'Jackson is one of the great songwriters,' said Jansch, 'who pointed the way for all would-be singer-songwriters, including me when I was just starting to put words to my guitar tunes. He was a good example to follow because he wrote about how he felt about life and that made it easier for the rest of us to write songs. He made it look simpler than we had thought because we could all now just write from our own personal experience. When his album came out, everyone took note. For a time, he had as much influence on the English folk scene as Bob Dylan, or anyone else, and his album influenced half the folk world at the time.'

'She'd say that Jackson was a bit mean to her,' says Richard Thompson, 'and that he could be moody and I'm not sure it was an entirely happy relationship. He was intense and Sandy was sensitive so it would have been an emotional powder keg, but he was a creative person and it would have been a kind of apprenticeship to be around him as a writer and that circle. And she was absolutely influenced by Bob Dylan and it's not insignificant that when she was involved with Jackson, Dylan was making or had made that transition from writing topical material to deeply personal, more poetic, often quite barbed songs like "Positively Fourth Street", which she liked a lot. Sandy was sensitive but was also very intuitive and she learnt quickly – she had to in those circumstances.'

Philippa Clare describes Frank's relationship with Sandy as slightly bumpy. 'He had the same sort of feeling around him as Van Morrison, a similar aura, large, truculent. The pull for Sandy with Jackson was that he was vulnerable. Bert always looked like he needed looking after, but Jackson was more troubled and they were definitely vying for Sandy's affections, and they both succeeded eventually. Jackson was a very angry man, understandably, because of his disfigurement. And for Sandy, number one, he was burnt so she could feel enough of his pain. He was much older too, and quite a free spirit – that appealed to her.'

Linda Thompson felt much the same about their knife-edge relationship. 'He was another one thundering down the chemical highway. She would stay at the house with him and Paul Simon. A lot of people kept their distance. He was difficult, or could be, and he was another who took a lot of drugs and drank a lot. He had a real presence on stage but he could be quite forbidding off stage. Jackson had a vulnerability that would have appealed to Sandy and they were both self-destructive people. They both took it to the limit and then thought, "Let's go a little bit further." They were just like that. I think it's very brave, others would say foolhardy, but they were up for anything. Sandy was like that even then.'

In the summer of 1966 Frank went home to Buffalo but his album had made no impact whatsoever in America. When he returned to London in 1968, though, he seemed to pick up where he had left off, and a new wave of songwriters were now singing his praises. He played many of the same clubs, including Bunjies and Les Cousins. He appeared at the Festival of Contemporary Song at London's Royal Festival Hall, as did his old girlfriend, now in Fairport Convention, and Al Stewart and Joni Mitchell, after which they all – with the exception of Mitchell – toured Birmingham, Liverpool and Newcastle under the name Folk and Contemporary Songs. 'I have been away from the business now for three years,' Frank wrote in the programme notes, 'and have during that time justified my existence by simply existing.'

It's a chilling description that might just as easily apply to the rest of his life. Frank went back to America again in early 1969,* threatened with deportation from Britain, and from then on tragedy continued to follow him around. In the 1970s he married Elaine Sedgwick, an English ex-model, but after their baby son died of cystic fibrosis and their marriage failed, Frank suffered

---

* Sandy didn't see Jackson again after he left London in 1969, although she looked for him when she was in America during the 1970s. When Al Stewart played with Sandy and Fairport at My Father's Place on Long Island in 1974, he recalls that he and Sandy talked about how neither of them had been able to track him down.

a mental breakdown. During much of the 1980s he was home-less and spent periods in hospital after a diagnosis of paranoid schizophrenia.

'In America he made no impression whatsoever in his lifetime,' says Tom Paxton, who had first met him in England in 1965. 'The last time I saw him, just before his death, he was in terrible condi-tion, drunk and minus an eye.' Jackson Frank died in March 1999, having been unable to revive his career despite another new wave of recognition.

*

1965 was the year that folk went pop in Britain. The Byrds had a number one with 'Mr Tambourine Man' and Dylan, once the young messiah of topical folk, had famously plugged in, scoring five major UK pop hits that year, including 'Subterranean Homesick Blues', 'Like a Rolling Stone' and 'Positively Fourth Street'. Paul Simon had ended 1965 with a US number one hit, 'The Sound of Silence'.* British artists as disparate as Donovan, Marianne Faithfull, the Silkie, even the Searchers – all folk to some degree – graced the charts and the Animals had already taken the traditional 'House of the Rising Sun' to number one on both sides of the Atlantic.

For somebody like Sandy, with her openness towards different types of music – Buddy Holly, the Everly Brothers, jazz standards and classical music – folk was no longer an un-hip, slightly quaint genre that was perceived as a little strait-laced and more often

* 'The Sound of Silence' was never a British chart success but Simon and Garfunkel did have pop hits in the UK in 1966 with 'Homeward Bound', which reached number nine, and 'I Am a Rock', number seventeen.

than not ridiculed. Even the Beatles displayed noticeable folk cre-
dentials, which were particularly evident by the time of *A Hard
Day's Night*.

Stewart thinks it was only after Jackson Frank left Britain in
1966 that Sandy started to come into her own; that, however
much he was an inspirational figure, their relationship did little
for her confidence. Once departed, he no longer cast a shadow
over her. Frank's leaving also coincided with Sandy completing
her first year at Kingston Art School.

Sandy had begun attending Kingston on 25 September 1965
and, at the same time, had given up the South Kensington flatshare, moving back to Worple Road with her parents. If she needed
any encouragement that her singing career was developing, barely
a month later she was able to read her first listing in *Melody Maker*.
Her name appeared on a bill with Jackson C. Frank at Le Duce on
27 October 1965. Moving from uncredited floor spots to having
her name listed was an indication that Sandy was now on her way
and she probably already knew she wouldn't return to Kingston
for a second year.

Sandy had won a further-education award and a reasonable grant of £194 a year to undertake the Pre-Diploma course
at Kingston, which involved a mixture of fine art, painting and
sculpture. 'Sandy wasn't really socially involved in the school,'
says fellow student David Laskey, 'although she occasionally gave
recitals there in the lecture room, playing guitar and singing.'
Other former students remember her occasional performances as
a little more impromptu, jumping up on the table in the canteen
and singing a cappella.

'It was throughout my year at college that [my career] just developed,' Sandy later told the BBC World Service's Clive Jordan. 'I

started doing gigs around the country and then it got to be a little bit too much, going to college and doing gigs and turning up late and having people congratulate me for coming in at two o'clock in the afternoon, so I decided that rather than waste everybody else's time, I'd get out and do it.' After completing the Pre-Diploma course, Sandy told her parents that she wanted to leave Kingston. Neil Denny's account probably reflects her version of events. 'At the end of her first year she was doing quite well in the music business and the school said, "If you want to try making a go of music, do so, and if you don't like it we'll take you back."'

One of the first people Sandy had met at Kingston was Gina Glaser, who became a close friend over the next few years. Glaser was one of the resident artist's models at Kingston Art School, eight years older than Sandy, and an accomplished singer herself who had arrived in London in 1958 with an intriguing history in the American folk revival of the fifties.

'Gina was a great singer, with a naturally good voice,' says John Renbourn, who had also met Glaser when he went to Kingston, 'but she never pushed herself to do anything and never recorded commercially. She was really beautiful and she played a bit of guitar, banjo and dulcimer and had been friendly with Paul Clayton. She knew people like banjo player Derroll Adams and Ramblin' Jack Elliott, and her father was a folk organiser. Dave Van Ronk talks about her in his book *The Mayor of MacDougal Street*. She was part of the early folk movement before Dylan arrived in New York.

'Gina took Sandy under her wing and Sandy absorbed a lot from Gina, who helped Sandy transform herself from being the girl in the pub singing Joan Baez songs to singing beautiful old songs and phrasing more like Gina. Gina was also a stabilising influence on Sandy; she helped her through the various chaotic stages of her domestic life.'

Glaser had come to London having heard there was work in the folk clubs for American singers. 'Jack Elliott told me the clubs didn't pay much but I found if you got three or four bookings a week that wasn't bad,' she says. 'I sang mostly in London, often at the Singers Club, but there were other less rigid folk clubs around Richmond, Putney and Kingston where I ended up living. Aside from maternity leave I was at Kingston Art School throughout the sixties. I met Eric Clapton* at Kingston in 1961, John Renbourn a couple of years later, and met Sandy when I went back there in 1965 after my daughter was born.'

Glaser had no idea Sandy had done floor spots in folk clubs when she invited her to her house for dinner: 'My guitar was there and she just picked it up and started singing, and I was fixated. There were a lot of young women who said they could sing, and I'd go, "Yeah, yeah, yeah." The first song I heard Sandy sing was something by Bob Dylan and I was almost floored. I couldn't believe the power in her voice.'

Glaser says Sandy was definitely interested in finding out more about traditional songs, although places like the Singers Club were not for her. Encouraged by Glaser, she did learn some American folk songs and the two of them would go along to the library at

* In his self-titled autobiography, Eric Clapton says: 'I met, and followed around for a while, an American female folk singer called Gina Glaser. She was the first American musician I had been anywhere near, and I was starstruck. Her speciality was old Civil War songs like "Pretty Peggyo" and "Marble Town". She had a beautiful clear voice and played an immaculate clawhammer style.' As his playing improved, Clapton began playing in a pub in Kingston called the Crown, until he was eventually thrown out of art college at the end of his first year.

16 Croons Hill SE10   22·1·67

Dear Sandy,

   I think this is the song you mean. Country singers
often seem to be in two minds whether the girl's
name is Sylvie or Sophie, and it tends to come out
as Sovay.   I adapted the tune and re-wrote
the words a bit. I recorded it on an album
called First Person (Topic 12T 118) and Martin
Carthy also recorded it on (I think) his first
Fontana album. It's a sweet song, isn't it?
My daughter says Sovay is the kinkiest girl
in folk song.

Letter from A. L. Lloyd

Cecil Sharp House. Sandy had also been introduced to respected
folk scholar and singer A. L. (Bert) Lloyd, who was renowned for
encouraging younger singers; she asked him to recommend songs
to her. She must have mentioned 'The Handsome Cabin Boy'
in particular; he sent her the music and typed words in August
1966, adding, 'I've been thinking about other songs but I need to
hear you a bit more before I know for sure what suits you.' Four
months later he sent her the lyrics to 'Sovay', with a note saying
that Martin Carthy had recorded it on his first album and that
Lloyd's daughter thought Sovay was 'the kinkiest girl in folk song'.

'We talked about phrasing and technique,' says Glaser, 'which
to me is the most important thing about singing. Even if your
voice is shot, it doesn't matter as long as your phrasing is good
– like many old jazz singers. She was listening to Joan Baez a lot

when we first met and Sandy used to screech a little when she sang; I remember explaining how she could counter that.'

Joan Baez had made a remarkable impact in Britain and enjoyed unexpected commercial success with a repertoire of American and British traditional folk songs, including many of the ballads collected by Francis Child. Together with defiant protest anthems, notably her stirring 'We Shall Overcome', these made her a figurehead in Europe and America.*

Sandy never mentioned her specifically in interviews, but Baez was very much the role model for female wannabe folk singers with nothing but three chords and long hair to distinguish them. 'I bought the first Joan Baez album,' says Shelagh McDonald. 'We all did. For that first wave of young folk singers who were drawn to traditional folk it was usually through hearing Joan Baez records. Even Marianne Faithfull discovered folk music through her.' When she was interviewed soon after 'As Tears Go By' reached the Top Ten in August 1964, Faithfull told *Record Mirror*: 'Some critics have called it folksy. Well I'm a folk fanatic. People like Joan Baez impress me – and I could never sing in the same class as her.'†

Gina Glaser says that while she may have helped Sandy eradicate that Joan Baez-style shrill top end to her voice, she doesn't want to exaggerate her part in shaping Sandy's career. 'Sandy used

* Both *Joan Baez 5* and *Farewell Angelina* were UK Top Ten albums in 1965; her 1960 debut album even belatedly made the Top Ten in 1965. Baez's cover of Phil Ochs's 'There but for Fortune' was a Top Ten single in June, and she also had hits that year with 'We Shall Overcome' and Dylan's 'It's All Over Now, Baby Blue'.
† In April 1965 Marianne Faithfull released her dual debut albums, the pop album *Marianne Faithfull* and an album dedicated entirely to folk, *Come My Way*. She said in a recent interview that the fact that the folk album went on to outsell the pop one still pleases her.

to tell people that I influenced her but I think it was more that I encouraged her, especially fostering her interest in traditional songs because that's what I used to sing. And I would encourage her not just to sing traditional songs but to know about them and their origins. She heard me sing "The Water Is Wide" and "Make Me a Pallet on Your Floor", both of which she would sing.

'When Sandy first came to Kingston Art School, most of her experience had been at open mic nights. She was pretty raw but Sandy knew she was better than the others who got up from the floor. She knew she was good, and at home she would record herself and would listen back, and however natural a singer she was, she worked hard to develop her singing. She wanted to improve her phrasing and build up the strength in her voice. She was insecure on many different levels but never about her music, at least not then.'

Glaser thinks the new popularity of folk among people of her own age only strengthened Sandy's desire to pursue music. 'Cousins was the club she loved the most,' she says. 'It was hip and she felt at home there. She was becoming more ambitious – to be famous, to be successful, as well as to be good. She saw that Joan Baez or Judy Collins or Buffy Sainte-Marie were young when they first became successful and she wanted that. She liked the way Buffy Sainte-Marie would attack a song with such power in her voice. "I could be like them," she'd say, "why not me?" Anne Briggs was brilliant and there was nothing stuffy and conventional about Annie. Sandy knew her a little and had seen her sing, so she knew first-hand how hard she had to work at her singing and technique to be as good as Annie.

'I was not surprised when Sandy gave up art and left Kingston. They all gave it up – John Renbourn didn't stay the whole course,

Eric Clapton certainly didn't. There were plenty who stuck around, got their degrees and who would end up teaching, but that's not what Sandy wanted at all. It was a stepping stone to growing up. She enjoyed her time at Kingston. She was good too, her drawings were lovely. Kingston was a very competitive school and she would never have got in without definite skills. She liked sculpture but her thrust was always music; art soon became secondary to her.'

When Sandy left Kingston in the summer of 1966, she wasn't yet the complete package; her voice more than anything was what set her apart from other girl singers, at least to begin with. That's what turned so many heads. 'They had all listened to the Joan Baez songbook,' says Al Stewart, 'and there were a lot of wannabe Julie Felixes* around too. They were pretty interchangeable but Sandy's scan was quite unique, she was deliberately hanging behind the beat all the time, which was very emotive, it was like watching somebody balancing on a cliff edge and I kept thinking she would fall off. Her voice always took you straight there into the heart of the song.' Duffy Power,† one of the best and most

* Julie Felix was a star of the folk world in Britain in the mid-1960s. She recorded four albums between 1964 and 1966 for Decca and though born in Mexico was perceived as a British Joan Baez. To begin with she regularly mixed traditional songs with those of Dylan and Guthrie, and later recorded songs by Bert Jansch, Tom Paxton and Phil Ochs; her *Changes* album also featured Martin Carthy and Dave Swarbrick. Her regular accompanists at different times included Trevor Lucas and John Renbourn. Regular appearances on BBC TV's *The Frost Report* in 1966 made her a household name and two years later she was given her own BBC series, *Once More with Felix*.
† Duffy Power's occasional performances at Les Cousins were said to be electric. Formerly one of promoter Larry Parnes's stable of rockers, by 1963 he had fallen in with blues and R & B kingpins Graham Bond and Alexis

underrated singers of the 1960s, also marvelled at Sandy's capacity to inhabit a song, recalling that whenever he saw her at Les Cousins 'she always sang "Make Me a Pallet on Your Floor" so convincingly that I thought she was homeless'.

If it was Sandy's voice that distinguished her from the pack, Al Stewart knew that she was also discreetly writing songs. 'None of the other girls were doing that, and she had no examples to follow other than men – but she was around Jackson, she was around Paul Simon and Bert Jansch, and she heard the songs they were writing first-hand. That's a special situation to be in and if only by example, it demystified the process. I always felt Sandy was quite shy and very insecure, and that fed into her songs. Even her early songs were very intense, very reflective.'

When Sandy declared she was writing songs it was something that shocked even her close friend Linda Thompson. 'I remember her telling me, and I thought, "How is that going to work, how is that even possible?" She had big goals, not even dreams, she believed she could do these things and worked very hard to get there. The early songs aren't knock-offs of Jackson but they are in that declamatory style that he used and the clawhammer guitar was very Jackson, and then she eclipsed him too.'

Sandy most likely began writing songs in 1965. Her father says she enjoyed poetry and before she wrote songs she would make up rhymes. 'She always read a great deal and had a very good command of the English language. She used to disappear into her room when she was writing,' said Neil. 'She was very secretive.'

Korner. Duffy's Nucleus, whose 1967 recordings were eventually released in 1971 on the Transatlantic album *Innovations*, included the future Pentangle rhythm section Danny Thompson and Terry Cox.

That would never change; Sandy always shut herself away to write and would only play her songs to others when she felt confident they were good enough.

Her cousin Hilary witnessed the more self-absorbed side of Sandy when she came to stay with her aunt at Llangrannog during the summer of 1965, before going off to college. 'Sandy was quieter and more serious,' Hilary told Pamela Winters. 'Her mother warned me, "Go away – Sandy's writing." She said she was writing songs; from my point of view it was very annoying because we were sharing a room.'

'Whenever I sing "The Sea",' reminisced Sandy in 1970, 'I think about a particular beach in Wales where I sat late at night, rather sad, a long time ago when I was about eighteen. It was almost like watching Cinerama as the sun went down.'

Sandy's home demos offer the first insight into her early efforts at songwriting and her influences. There are three reels of demos from 1966 which contain fourteen songs, including the earliest version of her best-known song, 'Who Knows Where the Time Goes?'. She also taped covers of Bert Jansch's 'Soho', Jackson C. Frank's 'Blues Run the Game' and 'Milk and Honey', and a charismatic version of Dylan's 'It Ain't Me Babe', as well as four traditional songs. The remainder are original songs, two of which – 'The Tender Years' and 'Carnival' – are melancholic, a hallmark of her writing to come.

'The Tender Years' drew on an incident at primary school and how she 'never dreamt that we would grow old'. 'There was a boy at Old Central who hurt his knee on the Friday, got blood poisoning and was dead by the Monday,' said Neil Denny. 'She wrote this sad little song for him. So it was a memory that stayed with her. It just indicates what sort of girl she was. It tells the story of this little boy and "the only years he was to know" before he was taken away. It was quite a moving little song.'

The second batch of Sandy's home demos, recorded between January and March 1967, follows the same pattern, with a mixture of traditional songs, including an early 'She Moves through the Fair' and Anne Briggs's 'The Time Has Come' and 'Go Your Way My Love'. The five originals are a second version of 'Who Knows Where the Time Goes?', 'Fotheringay', the confident, bluesy 'Gerrard Street' and the rather more forgettable 'The Setting of the Sun' and 'They Don't Seem to Know You'.

If Sandy wrote any other songs in this period she never left any evidence behind, although Al Stewart recalls her singing a song called 'There's a Red Light in Your Eyes' (written with Wendy Hamilton, another singer). 'I don't think anybody else has ever heard it and it was a great song and I think she only sang it once at Le Duce, which was pretty much empty at the time. "There's a red light in your eyes but in your heart it's a different tale" is how it started, and it stuck in my mind.'

'Boxful of Treasures', another of Sandy's original songs from the 1966 demos, was set to the tune she would later give to 'Fotheringay', abandoning the original lyrical theme of a doomed relationship for the poignant historical setting of the imprisonment of Mary Queen of Scots. Geoff Clark recalls meeting Sandy for the last time during the summer of 1966. 'She'd just got back from a trip to Fotheringay Castle and was full of what a splendid day she'd had, and I think I was the only person there who knew it was where Mary Queen of Scots had been held as a prisoner. We did the Tudors at Old Central, so maybe the seed was sown then. The Elizabeth/Mary complexities and the denouement made a great story.' Sandy would turn them into one of her best early

65

songs; her personal archive includes a guidebook from Fotheringay Castle and a booklet about Mary Queen of Scots, with the now familiar lyrics written inside. '"Fotheringay" came out of my interest in Mary Queen of Scots,' she explained many years later. 'I was fascinated by what it must have been like to spend all those years as a prisoner like Rapunzel or the Lady of Shalott. I've always been fascinated by the history of Scotland. I am naturally drawn to tragic heroines.'

Aside from 'Fotheringay', it was 'Who Knows Where the Time Goes?' which marked Sandy's breakthrough as a songwriter. Whatever or whoever inspired Sandy to write it is still shrouded in mystery; it was originally titled 'The Ballad of Time' in one of her notebooks. Its lyrical themes – the passage of time, the turning of the seasons and 'sad deserted shores' – would recur throughout her work. The 1966 demo, while lyrically the same, is marred by inelegant guitar work that's too indebted to Jackson Frank's style. By the time she taped the second demo, Sandy had streamlined the arrangement, adding the melodic intro. It was now recognisably a Sandy Denny song.

3 : *Alex Campbell and His Friends* 1967

I've never really had any definite plans. Even when I left college to sing professionally I didn't have any future thoughts in my mind. I just wanted to do something from day to day, which is something that I always do.

SANDY DENNY, *NME*, January 1972

We may not be millionaires but we can at least live like them . . . sometimes.

ALEX CAMPBELL

SANDY GLENNON,
PERSONAL MANAGEMENT,
9 BEAUFORT HOUSE,
BEAUFORT STREET,
LONDON, S.W.3
FLAXMAN 9933

Miss Sandy Denny - Commission.

March.				
3rd.	Brighton	9.	9.	0.
6th	"Cellar Full of Folk"	10.	10.	0.
9th	Loughton	10.	10.	0.
13th	Queen Mary College	10.	0.	0.
19th	Troubadour	8.	0.	0.
21st	"Cellar Full of Folk"	10.	10.	0.
22nd	Eros Records	15.	0.	0.
31st	Cousins	15.	0.	0.
April.				
3rd.	Wittering	9.	0.	0.
4th	Leicester	9.	9.	0.
5th	Television	12.	0.	0.
5th	Gt. Yarmouth			
6th	Lowestoft	12.	0.	0.
7th	Norwich	8.	0.	0.
9th	Enterprise	10.	10.	0.
14th	Beaconsfield	10.	10.	0.
16th	Coventry	9.	9.	0.
20th	Airdrie	10.	10.	0.
23rd	Paisley	10.	10.	0.
26th	Eros Records	50.	0.	0.
28th	East Ham	9.	9.	0.
30th	Brentwood	10.	0.	0.

10 %	commission	on	260.	6.	0.

```
            =  26.  0.  0.
            +   2.  0.  0.   Borrowed by you
               28.  0.  0.
            -  19. 17.  2    Received from B.B.C.
                             (20 gns less two insurance stamps).

Total due      £  8.  2. 10.
```

Letter from Sandy's agent detailing her earnings, March 1967

Sandy's first substantial mention in *Melody Maker* was on 17 December 1966 in a round-up of established female folk singers, alongside some of the new crop. The next day she would appear at the concert for peace in Vietnam at St Pancras Town Hall, with Bert Jansch and Julie Felix on a bill that also included Trevor Lucas. The *Melody Maker* piece, headlined 'Fine Feathered Folk', was written by Karl Dallas, Sandy's first and most loyal champion in the press. 'Sandy Denny has the sort of rich, soaring voice that could make her a British Baez,' he wrote, 'though the comparison does her an injustice. There's a great deal of Sandy in what she does, and nothing imitative of anyone.'

The other 'fine feathered folk' were largely 'traditional-style girls' often with strong ties to Ewan MacColl – one of the pivotal figures in the folk revival since the early 1950s – and/or members of the Critics Group, including Frankie Armstrong, Sandra Kerr and Isla Cameron. Sandy was always respectful of traditional music, even if she tended to be less reverential than expected when she introduced songs from the stage.*

In September 1966 Sandy was asked to appear on Peter

* Typical of these was Sandy's giggly introduction to the sombre 'Blackwaterside' at the Lincoln Festival in 1971. 'It's about some poor lady who got led astray by some bloke and found she was in a lot of trouble. But I'm sure she survived. We all do, you know.'

Kennedy's prestigious *Folk Song Cellar*.* She dutifully suggested four traditional songs – 'I Once Loved a Lass' (aka 'The False Bride'), 'Jute Mill Song', 'She Moves through the Fair' and 'Geordie' – but when the programme was recorded on 2 December 1966 she chose to perform two different Scottish ballads, 'Green Grow the Laurels' and 'The Boatman' ('Fhir a' Bhàta'), the latter in the family tradition of her grandmother Mary Smith MacLean.

Sandy's contribution to the programme is one of the few that survives and it's a remarkable performance, heightened by sheer nervous energy. The voice may be thinner but she displays a surprising dynamic range despite a lingering Baez-like tendency to sustain notes for too long. A sense of emotion and her ability to balance vocal technique and stylistic elements are already there for anyone to hear.

Sandy's first work for the BBC had been as a member of the Johnny Silvo Four, whose appearance was taped on 7 November 1966 but broadcast after Kennedy's *Folk Song Cellar*. Sandy performed 'The False Bride', 'Wild Rover' and '3.10 to Yuma', a surprisingly effective version of Frankie Laine's 1957 Western film theme.

Johnny Silvo was also born in Wimbledon, but in very different circumstances from Sandy. His unmarried Irish mother had fled to London to give birth to her son in 1943. She was killed in wartime bombing and young Johnny was raised in a Barnardo's home

---

* *Folk Song Cellar* was an important series of thirty-seven programmes for which Sandy had been recommended by BBC session regulars Dave Cousins and Tony Hooper of the Strawbs. The thirty-minute programme for the BBC World Service was always recorded live in the basement of Cecil Sharp House and set out to reflect what was happening in folk clubs of the day. This key series juxtaposed the mature work of first-generation revivalists (Martin Carthy, Shirley Collins, Cyril Tawney) with that of younger performers such as Sandy Denny and the Young Tradition.

in Kingston. He began singing in the 1950s, drifting from trad jazz into his own brand of breezy post-skiffle folk, which suited his warm voice. Sandy most likely met Silvo while she was doing a residency at the South Ruislip folk club during October 1966, and they worked together up until the summer of 1967, either as a duo or in a quartet. Sandy's initial session was with the quartet, which also included her occasional guitar tutor Roger Evans and David Moses on bass.

'The folk scene in the second half of the sixties,' says Moses, 'tends to be misleadingly divided into two factions: the revivalists or traditionalists and those who favoured blues and American-influenced music. But there was also a third group: entertainers who used music of various kinds as a vehicle for their personalities. Alex Campbell and Johnny Silvo, together with Diz Disley, belonged to the third group. The audiences were quite polarised, as were the clubs. So there were three different circuits, and few artists were able to cross from one to another. Alex Campbell was one of those few.'

While Sandy felt more at home at clubs like Les Cousins, in 1967, her first full calendar year as a professional folk singer, she too was able to move between the circuits that David Moses describes. That year, she found herself rubbing shoulders with Bert Jansch, John Renbourn and friends, and with 'entertainers' such as Silvo, Campbell and Disley, as well as rehearsing and recording with acoustic group the Strawbs. That summer she also met her future producer/manager Joe Boyd, who would be a major player in her career, but for now she was being guided by her first agent and manager, Sandy Glennon, the impresario and folk singer Theo Johnson and the budget-price record company boss Marcel Rodd.

Sandy was taken on by Sandy Glennon not long after she had left Kingston. He also looked after Campbell, Silvo, Disley,

Cliff Aungier and David Moses.* It was Julie Felix who had first introduced her sometime co-manager Glennon to the folk world. 'Sandy would drive me around in his little Mini and he was always so drunk he would hit the kerbs,' recalls Felix. 'I feared for my life every time I got in that car. He was also a film casting agent and a chancer in every sense.'

Martin Carthy burst into laughter at the mention of Glennon's name: 'His influence, his degree of helpfulness would have been patchy. There weren't many agents around working in folk and they weren't very highly thought of. Folk musicians got a lot of the work for themselves. I wasn't on anybody's books – my then wife used to book my gigs. People were suspicious of agents.

'It was a very small world and with all those agents and managers you had the feeling that they had sticky fingers and were great bullshitters, which you probably need to be in that profession, but none of them was a particularly positive force.'

John Renbourn is equally dismissive. 'Guys like Sandy Glennon and Theo Johnson were small fish in a small pond; the folk scene tended to look after itself and was pretty loose, so they could operate quite freely in that world. They were never going to get rich because folk musicians were never much more than self-sufficient in their earnings. They were basically well-intentioned opportunists; Sandy tended to attract such people because she was so trusting.'

Since leaving Kingston Sandy had doubled her fees to £12 or £15 per appearance, and although she still favoured London and its

* John Martyn was also handled by Sandy Glennon, who had advised him to change his name from Iain David McGeachy. 'He was always drunk,' said Martyn, 'which is probably why he thought I could make a go of it as a folk singer; it was only ten quid a night, though, but drinks were usually free.'

outskirts she was now travelling further afield to gigs in Swindon, Norwich, Manchester, Brighton, Coventry and Leicester, even a four-day trip to Airdrie and Paisley. 'My friends all thought I was stupid,' she said later, 'and I know they thought I would never get anywhere. Actually, I enjoyed every minute as a solo folk singer but the loneliness got me down in the end. Travelling from one club to the next wasn't much fun – though everyone was great where I played. I made far more money than I do now. There were no expenses, no equipment to pay for. I could make £75 a week easily, and that's quite a lot, isn't it?' It was indeed: around three times the average weekly wage.

Sandy's earliest professional recordings were made a few months after her first broadcasts for the BBC. Glennon and Theo Johnson brokered a deal for her with Saga Records for two albums, one with Alex Campbell, the other with Johnny Silvo, both released in the summer of 1967. 'Theo Johnson was an entrepreneur, a bit mad and always on the make in the nicest possible way,' said John Martyn about the man who introduced him to Island Records' founder Chris Blackwell. As well as being instrumental in opening and running the Kingston Folk Barge, Johnson had helped establish another of London's earliest folk clubs, in the cellar of Bunjies coffee bar. Originally a skiffle club, Bunjies boasted folk music 'eight nights a week' by 1961 and Johnson had taken over booking all its acts.

'Theo was a big fella, with a booming bass baritone voice,' says Dave Waite. 'He fronted the resident group at the Barge, variously called the Whalers or the Barge Crew.* Sandy sat in with them

---

* Theo Johnson can be heard on the Weavers-style *Hootenanny at the Barge* (1965) and *Bawdy British Ballads*, credited to Big Theo Johnson (1968).

from time to time. He was a marine engineer by trade, a lot of chutzpah, more than his talent justified.'

Johnson's influence even spread to New York, as Tom Paxton recalls: 'One night at the Gaslight in Greenwich Village in 1965 I met a London folk singer named Theo Johnson. Theo was in New York for reasons connected to his day job as a naval engineer and over coffee he assured me he could put together some folk clubs if we ever came over to England.' Paxton had already had the same proposition from Scottish songwriter Matt McGinn, and both were true to their word.*

Between them, Sandy Glennon and Theo Johnson persuaded Saga Records' boss Marcel Rodd† to divert some funds into folk music, although it was never going to be a major investment. Retail laws had lately changed so that records were no longer sold solely in record shops. Now, as Dave Waite recalls, 'you could buy

---

* Paxton's first visit to the UK, in April 1965, coincided with the arrival of import copies of his Elektra debut album, *Ramblin' Boy*. He stayed in London for two months, where 'The Last Thing on My Mind' became a staple in the folk clubs. Sandy recorded the song, as well as 'My Rambling Boy' from the same album.

† Saga had started out releasing soundtracks in the late 1950s as a division of Leonard Cassini's Saga Films, before moving into classical music, providing original and library recordings at a budget price. Saga soon began dabbling in jazz and pop records, one significant offshoot being Joe Meek's Triumph label. In 1964 Saga was sold to Marcel Rodd, and in those days the studio was in the basement of his north London house, while the disc cutting and record pressing was done at a factory in Kensal Road, later the site of the Virgin Group offices. Rodd claimed he was not particularly interested in music, but he made up for it with astute marketing practices. *Best Loved Gems of . . .* was a successful series of portmanteau popular classical music titles culled from tapes in Saga's archive. Saga was undoubtedly a pioneer of affordable records in the UK, long before Decca's Ace of Clubs and Pye's Golden Guinea labels.

them for ten bob at W. H. Smith's, major newsagents, or at railway stations – and all the budget labels came crashing in and cheap was the name of the game. If you couldn't knock out an album in one session they didn't want to know. We all made records for them, and Alex Campbell made more than most. It was money in your pocket. The standard of production was simply switching on the tapes and you played live, but just to be recording was a feather in your cap. It was a step up the ladder and you might get a session fee of £5 per song, or a nominal flat fee of fifty quid. If it was a traditional song, the producer would claim the arrangement credit.' In Sandy's case it was Theo Johnson who claimed the arranger's royalty for the traditional material that was already part of her set.

David Moses was often called in by Rodd for session work: 'I did four folk albums for Saga. I made two with Alex Campbell, *Sandy and Johnny* and a Johnny Silvo Christmas album. Marcel Rodd was a complete cowboy with a tinpot studio just off the Finchley Road. He expected an album to be completed in one three-hour session. Everything straight down to mono, no retakes or editing. I remember one session where he asked the drummer to play louder because they couldn't hear him in the box. After four takes, the drummer playing louder each time, an exasperated Marcel Rodd stomped into the studio to hear how loud the drummer was actually playing, only to discover the drum mic was not switched on.

'My memory of Sandy on those two sessions was that she was a complete pro. I don't remember any tantrums or nerves, just straight down first or second take like the rest of us. The singers were doing material they performed in the clubs every night, so it was just the session players who had to learn the tunes on the day. We did the odd broadcast with Johnny Silvo too. No vivid

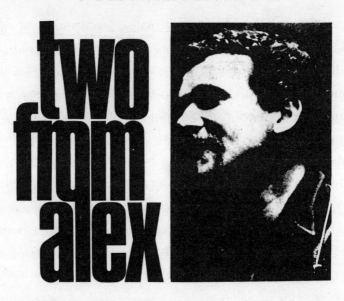

Ad from *Sing* folk magazine, June 1966

memories, I'm afraid, except for Sandy's fabulous voice and sweet, friendly nature.'

'It was a difficult era for guys like Alex [Campbell] and Johnny Silvo,' says John Renbourn, 'because record companies didn't know what folk music was, but realised folk could be recorded cheaply. Even Davy Graham's first album, *The Guitar Player*, came out on Golden Guinea. So folk turned up on the budget arm of major labels like Decca and EMI but they had no idea what slot to put folk into, often pitching it to an easy-listening market. Transatlantic's recordings were done just as much on the cheap, but folk was their niche, so being on Transatlantic had kudos. And Transatlantic had its budget arm, XTRA. The albums Sandy did for Saga went unnoticed and certainly didn't do her justice.'

Yet it was a step up for Sandy to have recorded at all, at a time when she was mainly dependent on playing folk clubs. 'It was a very big deal to have a record out,' says Martin Carthy. 'When I got my Fontana deal it just opened the door wider for me, and being on Fontana would have made more of a difference than being on Saga but it was still a calling card. It's like having something on your CV.'

The two albums Sandy made for Eros, one of Saga's offshoots, were *Alex Campbell and His Friends*, recorded on 22 March 1967, and *Sandy and Johnny*, recorded on 26 April 1967. *Alex Campbell and His Friends* is a hootenanny-style get-together involving Sandy, Silvo, Cliff Aungier and Paul McNeill, to which she contributes three showcased songs: a rushed, high-spirited 'This Train', 'The False Bride' and, by far the best, a heartfelt cover of Jackson C. Frank's 'You Never Wanted Me'. Poet and songwriter Sydney Carter's review in *Gramophone*, September 1967, singles Sandy out for praise: 'Alex's friends include Sandy Denny, a young girl singer of whom I think we shall hear more. Her voice, though pure, seems surrounded by a kind of breathy haze. She struck me most, if only because girl folk singers are so rare.'

Sandy gets co-billing on *Sandy and Johnny* but is only occasionally given the opportunity to assert herself other than as part of Silvo's exuberant but lightweight group. Again, her finest performances are saved for another Jackson C. Frank song, this time 'Milk and Honey', and Alex Campbell's calling card, 'Been on the

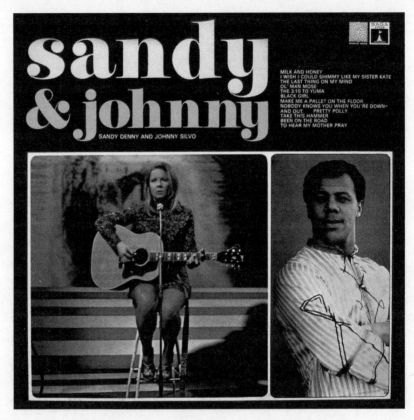

Front cover image for Saga's *Sandy & Johnny* LP

Road So Long'. Less impressive, 'The Last Thing on My Mind' was in every other folk singer's set list, and she reprises '3.10 to Yuma', but her indifferent versions of 'Pretty Polly' and 'Make Me a Pallet on the Floor' don't rise above the stiffness of the session.

Sydney Carter also reviewed *Sandy and Johnny*, again focusing on Sandy as 'the only British girl folk singer I can think of who might become a challenger to Julie Felix in the charts. She has the youthful image and can hang on to a note as long as Joan Baez if necessary. She can sing well, but in a way which will win success in the field of pop rather than in the stricter folk conventicles.'

Carter's point about Baez holds true, but already Sandy's strong sense of phrasing is apparent and there are clear indications of her broad dynamic range.

'She was a natural singer,' says Richard Thompson, 'but she also worked very hard on her singing. If you listen to her Saga recordings and the early radio recordings, she had a much lighter voice and she really worked at the power of her singing. Singing in folk clubs, often without a mic, really helps in developing a vocal strength to fill a room, but on those early recordings she doesn't have the technique to convey that.'

Joe Boyd met Sandy the summer those albums were released and says the experience she gained shouldn't be underestimated. 'She was ambitious. She wanted to make those records. It was a logical process of evolution for her, even though they were low-budget recordings, and it wasn't Topic and it wasn't Transatlantic. Saga didn't signify quality but I was conscious of those albums. They were around; I would go into flats and see them. Alex Campbell's reputation was very much "what you see is what you get", but at the same time he was an inspiration to the next generation of folk musicians that Sandy also hung out with. The Incredible String Band certainly knew Alex's pedigree. It wasn't always easy for Sandy but Alex would have showed her that it was possible to escape the single-mindedness of the purists, who had always thought of her as a bit of a "corrupter" because she sang with a guitar and wrote her own songs.'

Alex Campbell provided the blueprint for the 1960s folk singer in Britain. He had learnt his craft in the late fifties busking in the streets of Paris alongside Derroll Adams and Ramblin' Jack Elliott, and such was his notoriety on the west bank of the Seine that he was mentioned in some Paris guide books as *Le Cowboy d'Ecosse*.

Born in Glasgow in 1925 and orphaned when young, Campbell had fought his way up through the education system against the odds. After the Second World War he went to London, where he became the youngest executive officer in the Inland Revenue. Following a confrontation with a senior colleague over a woman, Campbell resigned and made his way to Paris with the intention of studying at the Sorbonne. En route he ran out of money and began busking to subsist rather than return home. The civil service's loss was folk music's gain.

Just about everybody who came through the folk mill in the late fifties and sixties felt they owed Campbell a debt. He embodied the romantic beat lifestyle embraced by the folk revivalists and he passed on that sense of wanderlust to a succession of young bucks, from Davy Graham, Clive Palmer (of the Incredible String Band) and Wizz Jones through to Bert Jansch, Billy Connolly, Roy Harper, Meic Stevens, Ralph McTell, Dick Gaughan and, of course, Sandy.

Campbell spread the word to people who knew nothing about folk music, while Ewan MacColl was the champion for those who agonised over its significance. Despite their differences, however, Campbell helped out MacColl and his American girlfriend Peggy Seeger by marrying Seeger in January 1959 to prevent her being shipped unceremoniously back to the States. 'However much they were at daggers drawn,' says Martin Carthy, 'never in print did Ewan ever bad-mouth Alex, because Alex married Peggy so she could get a British passport. She was hugely pregnant by Ewan and they were in Paris, where her passport was about to be revoked – because she's a dirty commie, of course – and Alex said, "OK, I'll marry you," and he did. Peggy and Ewan's son was born six weeks later. What a gent.'

Nevertheless, Campbell couldn't resist reminding Ewan MacColl of the favour he had done: 'The story goes,' says John Renbourn, 'that Alex got pissed one night, stormed into one of Ewan and Peggy's clubs where they were playing and shouted out, "Christ, it's God and the Virgin Mary."'

Like Jackson C. Frank, Alex Campbell is unsung today, yet for a time he was the undoubted king of the folk scene and among the highest-paid performers on the circuit. 'He was it,' says Renbourn. 'He was a Glasgow cowboy who looked like Desperate Dan and thought he was Ramblin' Jack Elliott. Once he heard from Wizz [Jones] and Davy [Graham] about the scene over here, he would come back and do the folk clubs – earn some money – then head off again. He was always pissed, told plenty of jokes and played a big flowery Gibson guitar. He really entertained people. He was a top guy – the top dog.'

Wizz Jones first met Campbell in Paris in 1959: 'Alex was a superb entertainer and had terrific charisma. That was never captured because he was a victim of that situation whereby someone would say, "Would you like to make a record, here's some money," and he'd say yes – mostly in Europe, but Marcel Rodd at Saga offered those sort of cash-in-hand deals.'

By his own calculation, Alex Campbell made more records than anybody in folk. It's been claimed he made over a hundred titles: an exaggeration, but not by much.*

---

* Beginning with *Chansons populaires des Etats-Unis* ('Popular Songs of the United States') in 1958 for a small French label, Alex Campbell racked up a further ten albums on the continent before he began recording for British labels including Fidelity, Saga and Transatlantic's XTRA imprint in 1963. The recordings all followed the same approach; he would only do a retake if there was a technical problem.

Campbell never made that one album that would have immortalised him – if anything, the Saga release featuring Sandy Denny is his best known. And though he wrote other songs such as the autobiographical 'My Old Gibson Guitar', he is remembered mainly for the world-weary anti-nuclear lament 'Been on the Road So Long'. Campbell recorded it countless times, including a version with Sandy for *Alex Campbell and His Friends*. 'Sandy was very fond of Alex. She often used to play "Been on the Road So Long",' says Richard Thompson. 'She did it in 5/4 and had her own version which was really good.'

As Sandy would have appreciated, Alex Campbell believed in living the high life whenever he could afford it. Unusually, he had a passion for going to the opera and he loved Wagner. He also liked staying in the best hotels and drinking fine wine and whisky. It's not difficult to see why it's been said by his contemporaries that he was the best-loved folk singer of the 1960s. 'He would have been a positive influence on Sandy,' says Wizz Jones, 'and on anybody starting out, because he was living proof that the folk lifestyle and all that went with it was within your reach. He never saw it as a career but he showed you could make a living just by playing the clubs and always giving your best – and you need to discover that to sustain you and keep you honest.'

Ralph McTell adds: 'Whatever else she learnt from Alex and Johnny Silvo, she would have learnt about playing to an audience. Alex was a master of presentation, could handle an audience like nobody I ever saw. Sandy picked up on that; she always had a great rapport with audiences, very down-to-earth. On the downside, she couldn't have had two worse teachers than Alex Campbell and Johnny Silvo, who both drank like fish till they fell down.'

'Sandy took Alex Campbell home one night,' says John Renbourn, 'to show her parents that there was such a thing as a professional folk singer. That was considered a great joke among everybody.'

'I'm not sure he was a role model to take home and introduce to your parents,' says Julie Felix, 'though he would have been charming and they probably had a lot of values in common. He would tell me I should wear make-up, and I said, "I don't want to," but he thought women should wear make-up. He was old-fashioned in that way.'

'Sandy adored Alex,' says Philippa Clare. 'He was a father figure and he protected her and she felt safe with him. Alex would never take advantage of anybody; he was a very upright, stand-up guy and a generous soul. And his music was like that. Alex was generous to a fault and never felt threatened by the new blood coming in, certainly not Sandy. And unlike some, he didn't want to fuck her; he wanted to work with her.'

'Early on, Sandy was drawn to people who had strong personalities,' says Joe Boyd, 'and she fell for Jackson Frank, and Danny [Thompson], and she got to know Alex Campbell. In those days, particularly if you were a girl, you tended to defer or look for leadership from older males. I mean, she was a girl and she was looking for action; she liked to drink, she liked to flirt, she liked to smoke, she liked having a good time. Alex would have offered a safe environment for her early on.'

Campbell had started up the popular Richmond Folk Club in the 1960s, run for him by Anthea Joseph, who also helped manage and arrange bookings at the Troubadour.* Many of the old guard

---

* Campbell remained a draw in the clubs and worked with equal fervour through the 1970s, but in John Renbourn's words, 'By then he'd peaked;

of entertainers lived in and around southwest London and played the folk clubs in Richmond, Surbiton, Hounslow, Twickenham and Kingston, and Sandy would remain in the area until she moved to the country in the mid-seventies. 'Cliff Aungier, Royd Rivers and Gerry Lochran shared a residency at the Half Moon in Putney,'* says David Moses. 'It was one of London's leading clubs at the time. Alex Campbell, Johnny Silvo, Sandy Denny, Diz Disley, Steve Benbow and Derek Brimstone were all regular visitors.' Theo Johnson and his brother Evan had a flat in nearby Twickenham, while Silvo shared a flat in Richmond with Diz Disley. 'After gigs, all the folkies met up at Davina's on the King's Road, Chelsea,' Philippa Clare remembers. 'The outskirts of London were overrun with folk clubs.'

Dave Waite remembers Diz Disley as another stunning performer in the folk clubs: 'All those guys understood that entertainment wasn't a dirty word. If people went home happy having had a good time, they'd done their job. Aside from anything else it meant they would book you again. Diz was always in work, whether it was playing banjo with Chris Barber or Ken Collier, playing Django in a night club or knocking around in a folk

---

folk music was getting airs but he was still churning out records that never sold and he suddenly didn't slot in any more.' With folk clubs in Britain on the wane, Campbell began spending more time in Europe, notably in Germany and Scandinavia. He relocated to Denmark in the 1980s, where he continued to live the life of the hard-drinking folk singer, still on the road until he died on 3 January 1987.
* The Half Moon on the Richmond Road began as a music venue in 1963 with its Folksville sessions and has endured to this day. When Sandy and Trevor Lucas lived not too far away, in Parsons Green, from 1969 to 1975, the Half Moon provided a link to Sandy's past and to old friends from the folk world who played there regularly.

club.'* Philippa Clare says that 'Sandy felt safe' with Disley: 'Diz was another ladies' man but he didn't want to fuck her either. He used to drive a painted Rolls-Royce; many a time Sandy and I would help him push it up the hill. One of his catchphrases was that "I only drink to steady myself . . . sometimes I get so steady, I can't move."'

'Sandy was at home in that world, which provided a degree of stability in her otherwise disordered life,' says Richard Thompson. 'Linda knew them too and she would say how close-knit it was as a community and, certain rivalries aside, they looked after their own. Alex Campbell was a great guy. He was very encouraging and helpful when we began playing folk clubs together in 1972. His free-spirited approach influenced Sandy. Bert Lloyd was helpful to her; he was always approachable and far more flexible in his ideas than Ewan MacColl. She knew all these great characters like Cyril Tawney or Luke Kelly from the Dubliners, and most of them were a lot older and would have been protective of her because she was a young singer.'

For some on the scene, the face Sandy presented to the world was one of somebody trying too hard to get on, loud and self-confident. Julie Felix's description of her during that year is harsh but not entirely wide of the mark: 'I remember Sandy as being almost like a camp follower and she would follow us around, those of us who were more successful, mostly the blokes. She was a regular around a number of different scenes, whether it was with Alex

---

* In 1967 Diz Disley was a guest alongside Martin Carthy on Dave Swarbrick's first instrumental album, *Rags, Reels and Airs*, produced by Joe Boyd. It's a near-forgotten gem of an album, full of the sort of instrumental pieces that Swarbrick later returned to with Fairport Convention during the 1970s – only electrified.

Campbell, Danny Thompson, Bert and John. We'd always end up in a bar somewhere; she liked a drink, so did everybody, that was the culture. It was pre-women's lib but not in the folk scene. You had to have the strength of a man to get by.'

'She was definitely one of the boys,' says Marc Brierley, 'and she had a strong presence and a real attention-grabbing personality. When she entered a room you knew she belonged there, no question about that, but she literally barged into rooms sometimes. Sandy loved playing and hanging out at Cousins but she also bustled in and out of various different in-crowds that some of the Cousins regulars weren't so comfortable with.'

John Renbourn feels she was misunderstood by one or two diehards. 'Sandy really was, on some level, a bit of a go-getter and wanting to get famous, without a doubt. Not at any cost, nothing like that, but she could be brash and impetuous. She would sometimes hobnob with some pretty smarmy, unsavoury characters around Denmark Street, wheeling and dealing in all-day drinking clubs in Tin Pan Alley and the West End.* Some of the Cousins lot could be a bit snobby and thought that because they were doing something that wasn't commercial it was somehow more worthy. Some of the old-timers like Owen Hand saw Sandy as pushing a little too hard. I never saw her that way, not calculated; but she would get sucked into all those different worlds.'

'What you have to remember,' says Martin Carthy, 'is that,

---

* The Colony Room on Dean Street, run by the infamous Muriel Belcher, was a favourite drinking club of Sandy's for a few years. Linda Thompson says: 'We hung out at Muriel's club with Jeffrey Bernard, Peter O'Toole, Francis Bacon. Sandy could drink the boys under the table. Muriel was a fearsome châtelaine: if she didn't take to you, you were not allowed in. It was a louche and interesting time.'

above all, it was a very, very exciting time. You were part of this huge community. We had our own community, particularly in the sixties, and it carried into the seventies because we had all forged these relationships, and it was a real cross-section of people, different ages and from all over the country, but what we all had in common was the love of this music in all its ramifications.

'I heard things when Sandy was doing solo stuff and I remember thinking – and I didn't think in these terms in those days – that she needed direction. She knew she wanted to sing and she was a decent guitar player and, with hindsight, we now know she wanted to write songs, and that was unusual. I just don't think she really knew where she was going.'

'I really don't think Sandy used people,' says Philippa Clare. 'I think she literally went where the journey took her. There wasn't anything about her that was planned, she was chaos. Everybody wanted Sandy because she was absolutely the best, and Dave Cousins recognised that and Alex Campbell recognised that. It made them all the better for having Sandy involved. She was very open, so somebody comes up and says, "Why don't you come and do this?" – like join the Strawbs – and she'd say, "Oh alright."'

4 : Two Weeks Last Summer
1967–1968

I wasn't really looking to join a group. But they asked me, and I thought 'Oh, well, it's something to do.' Anyway, it didn't last all that long, because I wasn't doing what I wanted to do. Not that I didn't like them all – I really had some good times.

SANDY DENNY, *NME*, 15 January 1972

All Our Own Work was, in my opinion, the first British folk-rock album, and it predated Fairport's first album with Judy Dyble by a year. I always had my eye on the charts and we could have had a couple of hits under our belt by then had Sandy stuck with it. She could have left folk music behind and followed a totally different direction. Sandy hated being thought of as a folk singer and she knew that held her back.

DAVE COUSINS

EFDSS

THE ENGLISH FOLK DANCE & SONG SOCIETY

CECIL SHARP HOUSE
2 REGENT'S PARK RD.
LONDON   N.W.1.
Tel. GULliver   2206

PK/PG

18/10/66

~~30th September, 1966~~

Dear Sandy and the Strawbs *

CELLAR RECORDINGS FOR BBC

Many thanks for sending details of your programme and availabilities.

We would very much like you to come to Cecil Sharp House on FRI....
....DEC..2.

10 a.m. ~~12 p.m.~~	Rehearsal
4.30 p.m.	Balance
7.30 p.m.	Recording with Robin and Jimmie and Audience

For this session we can offer you a payment of 25 gns. incl....
for the Society to have the right to offer the recordings to the BBC
Transcription Service. These will be made up into radio programmes which
are offered to "overseas broadcasting organisations for the sole purpose
of their broadcasting the records from transmitters situated outside the
U.K." (Great Britain, Northern Ireland, the Isle of Man and the Channel
Islands.)

In the event of the programme being broadcast in the BBC's Service
for the U.K. or External Services you will receive £2 10s. per minute for
the first reproduction and £1 5s. per minute for each subsequent reproduction. For
mechanical reproduction in the External Services only: for the first five – 10/- per
minute and 5/- per minute for each subsequent reproduction.

Will you please confirm as soon as possible on the enclosed form
that you are still free on the above date and the suggested terms are
satisfactory.

* Check that they
can come on that
day to accompany
please

Yours ever,

Peter Kennedy

Recorded programme
there lived solo artists
fee of £10 . 10s

President: Her Royal Highness the Princess Margaret   Vice-Presidents: Douglas and Helen Kennedy
Chairman: Dr. L. C. Luckwill   General Secretary: Kenneth F. Goode

Letter from Peter Kennedy confirming a Folk Song Cellar
recording with the Strawbs

Sandy's tenure with the Strawbs is one of the most misunder-stood passages of her career. She sang and rehearsed with the group for the best part of a year, yet they played only one UK gig together, at Nottingham University, plus a brief floor spot at the Greyhound pub in Fulham and a week of shows at the Tivoli Gardens in Copenhagen in July 1967. It was a project kept almost under wraps which should have been launched by *All Our Own Work*, the album that Sandy and the Strawbs recorded in Copenhagen. As it turned out, the album remained unreleased for six years and Sandy rarely mentioned it. It is, however, easily the best of her early work and, significantly, it contains the first professionally recorded version of 'Who Knows Where the Time Goes?'.

When Sandy hooked up with them, the Strawbs were a trio led by banjo player, guitarist and chief songwriter Dave Cousins, with guitarist Tony Hooper and double bass player Ron Chesterman. Cousins can't put an exact date on when he first approached Sandy to join, but her association with the group had begun by October 1966. We know that Peter Kennedy wrote to Sandy and the Strawbs on 18 October at her parents' Worple Road address to arrange a date for them to record *Folk Song Cellar*.*

* Sandy and the Strawbs didn't record together for Peter Kennedy but did record a session in February 1967 for the World Service – long ago lost: 'The Strawberry Hill Boys Sing and Play Folk Songs'. Sandy sang 'Blues

Dave Cousins has often told the story of how he first saw Sandy at the Troubadour sitting on a stool playing an old Gibson guitar and 'wearing a white dress, a straw hat, with long blonde hair, and singing like an angel'. 'When I walked down the steps, there she was, playing guitar and singing. I was absolutely stunned. She was singing "Fhir a' Bhàta" and I went up to her afterwards and said, "I want to introduce myself, I'm Dave Cousins – would you like to join a group?" She asked, "Who are you?" I said, "The Strawbs," and she said, "Alright." I then had to get on the phone to Tony Hooper and say we'd got a girl singer. He thought I'd gone mad. So we went round to her place in Wimbledon a few days later and we were there all night. My wife went crazy when I got home and asked where I'd been, and I said, "Singing." We literally sang all night.'

Cousins had been surprised that Sandy agreed to join more or less there and then. 'We were reasonably well known but not a successful act by any means. We had just begun calling ourselves the Strawbs. She knew us as the Strawberry Hill Boys.' Named after Strawberry Hill in Twickenham, where they used to rehearse, they were another west London group making their way on the folk circuit in 1964. Cousins even co-ran a popular folk club at the White Boar in Hounslow, which had opened in 1965. They were originally a bluegrass group, one of the first in Britain, and later shifted towards the lighter, close-harmony folk style of American groups such as the Limeliters and the Chad Mitchell Trio. The Strawbs were also known for BBC sessions, *Melody Maker* reporting that by Christmas 1966 they had appeared on thirty BBC radio shows, everything from *Friday Night Is Music Night* to *Saturday*

Run the Game' and 'Pretty Polly', as well as three Dave Cousins songs, later recorded in Copenhagen.

Club. Dave Cousins proudly boasts that he and Tony Hooper first appeared on *Saturday Club* in 1964 at the foot of a typically mixed bill that included the Beatles, Chris Barber's Jazz Band, Eden Kane and Brian Poole.

'I think Sandy knew us more from the radio,' says Cousins. 'I always did lots of sessions. I played banjo on Leonard Cohen's only BBC session, but I could never get anybody interested in recording the Strawbs.' The first time their name appeared on a record was in 1966, with *Songs of Ireland*, credited to Steve Benbow and the Strawberry Hill Boys. Benbow was one of the better known folk musicians of the day thanks to regular appearances on radio and television, starting with the radio programme *Guitar Club* in 1957, and regular slots on *Saturday Club* and *Easy Beat*.

'Sandy and I were seriously good friends,' Cousins says, 'and remained so up until she died. I always got on famously with her parents and we would rehearse at her house in Wimbledon, or she would come to my place in Hounslow. We used to record demos on a two-track tape recorder, with heavy curtains up against the windows and a mic hanging down from the light fitting.'

It was effectively a marriage of convenience between Sandy and the Strawbs, both she and the group maintaining separate careers around the folk clubs but regularly rehearsing together. Cousins knew about the albums she had recorded with Alex Campbell and Johnny Silvo, 'which made no impact, none whatsoever. She wasn't ashamed of them but she never told anybody she had made those records. It was all just experience for her, as it was rehearsing and recording with us, but she definitely liked the songs we were doing. It was something new to her. There was never any question of doing traditional songs with us, or the contemporary covers she sang in clubs. We talked about wanting to make an album, and we were always going to call it *All Our Own Work* and it would be all original material.'

The Strawbs were never a folk outfit within the strictest parameters of the scene. 'We played acoustic songs with a folk flavour,' explains Cousins, 'rather than being a folk group as such; some people called it folk pop, but because the Strawbs was predominantly an acoustic group we played folk clubs.' Other, far more middle-of-the-road 'light entertainment' groups – often fronted by a girl singer and with a stand-up bass player – were more pop than folk and usually played the cabaret circuit. The model for most of these was either the Springfields (who had split up at the end of 1963 when Dusty Springfield went solo) or the Seekers, who had become hugely successful in 1965 after coming to the UK from Australia.

'There was a no-man's-land that was neither folk nor pop,' says Dave Waite of the Countrymen, 'and our group was in that territory, so were the Settlers, and the Strawbs were only just outside of it stylistically, except that they wrote their own material.* That was the big difference. We were all plundering Weavers records, the Kingston Trio, Burl Ives, that kind of light country and western and popular folk. I take my hat off to Dave Cousins; he was trying something very different. They were serious folk musicians but

---

* Groups such as the Settlers and the Countrymen relied on a repertoire including American folk hits like 'Tom Dooley', 'Where Have All the Flowers Gone', 'Greenback Dollar', 'Kisses Sweeter than Wine', and more gentle contemporary folk songs like Tom Paxton's 'The Last Thing on My Mind', Hedy West's 'Five Hundred Miles' or Gordon Lightfoot's 'Early Morning Rain'. If they ever graced the pop charts it was usually by covering a Beatles album track – the Overlanders had their sole hit with 'Michelle' and the Silkie with 'You've Got to Hide Your Love Away', while the Settlers breezed meaninglessly through 'Nowhere Man'.

their approach was very pop-orientated – only more tuned-in than the rest of us. Groups like the Countrymen only ever set out to please the audience by playing stuff they knew; Dave's aim was to do his own thing and he very much called the shots in the Strawbs.'

It was seeing Donovan on *Thank Your Lucky Stars* that motivated Dave Cousins to start writing songs. '"Inspired" is the wrong word; I thought, "If he can do it, I can do it,"' says Cousins. 'The most obvious influence for me at first was the Beatles. Then I saw Bob Dylan on a late-evening BBC concert recording broadcast over two nights in 1965, and that was an eye-opener. We all know Sandy loved Dylan but she was a huge fan of the Beatles too. She had very broad taste, and pop music was at its most creative and inventive then. It was when the pirate radio stations were popular, so you just couldn't escape all this wonderful music and, unlike the BBC, the pirates played all this great stuff that was in the American charts.

'I was listening to the Byrds and the Lovin' Spoonful, but our direction was more the Mamas and the Papas, or Simon and Garfunkel, and Sandy knew Paul Simon, don't forget. I got into writing in that vein, very taken by the harmonies that all the American groups used. They had all come out of folk music and, like us, a lot started out playing bluegrass. The Strawbs were much more influenced by traditional American folk music than by British folk music. Our initial influences were derived from the Harry Smith folk anthology.* I got my guitar tunings from banjo tunings, and that's what made us sound individual. The Strawbs were not at all influenced by English folk music – the Beatles and Searchers were more important.'

Songs like 'And You Need Me' and 'Stay Awhile with Me' on *All Our Own Work* have a strong, barely disguised Beatles influence.

* Harry Smith's *Anthology of American Folk Music*, released in 1952.

'They were the songs we started to rehearse with Sandy. She was singing her socks off the minute we started; her harmonies just fell into place.'

Having made crude demos in Cousins's living room in Hounslow around March 1967, Sandy and the Strawbs made more professional demos at the hallowed Cecil Sharp House. These featured Cousins's friend Trevor Lucas beating out percussion on a guitar case. (Although Cousins says he introduced the two of them, it's almost certain Sandy and Trevor had already crossed paths on the folk circuit.) It was through these tapes that Cousins finally found somebody who wanted to record his group.

Tom Browne, a friend and colleague of Cousins, was a DJ and producer for the BBC World Service who had, by coincidence, known Sandy when they were both fifteen; he used to take her to the cinema in Kingston. He was doing folk programmes and a pop news show with Cousins for Danmarks Radio, and he took the Cecil Sharp House tapes over to Copenhagen to try and secure a couple of weeks' work for the Strawbs at the Tivoli Gardens. He also played the tapes to jazz specialist Karl Knudsen, whose Storyville label was now allied to Sonet Records in Sweden. Knudsen decided straight away that he wanted to record the Strawbs. 'Since no one in England was interested, we agreed,' says Cousins. 'I knew Alex Campbell had gone over to Denmark and done an album there for £100 and I thought, "Why not?"'

The Strawbs opened their season at the Vise Vers Hus in Tivoli Gardens on 24 July 1967 and began recording two days later, doing the sessions by day and appearing at the club at night.* The studio

* Sandy is listed as playing the Troubadour on 16 July 1967 and she recorded a home tape with Alex Campbell in Glasgow in 5 August 1967. This

was actually on the stage of the Vanløse Bio cinema and had to be packed away from mid-afternoon until 10 p.m. while the cinema was open, so the band began recording in the early mornings or after their shows at the Tivoli.

The cinema was located in the suburbs of Copenhagen and the equipment was owned by the session engineer, Ivar Rosenberg. As with the Saga sessions, everything was recorded live, straight onto tape, although this time onto two-track stereo. A Danish drummer, Ken Gudmand, was called in for the sessions. On the strength of the demos, Knudsen's vision for the Strawbs was definitely pop. He brought in producer Gustav Winckler, a popular Danish crooner in the Bing Crosby mould who had sung his country's third-place Eurovision entry in 1957. Knudsen usually employed Winckler to record Danish pop acts on his label. The mawkish strings that were added to a handful of songs, including 'Who Knows Where the Time Goes?', give a clear indication that the album was being pitched to the pop market.*

Tasked with securing a deal on their return from Copenhagen, Cousins managed to drum up interest from the German-owned Polydor and the independent Major Minor, but Sandy wouldn't

---

dates the Copenhagen sessions to the intervening time. Until Cousins's Witchwood Media label reissue of *All Our Own Work* in 2012, which reprints extracts from his diary, there was considerable confusion as to when the Copenhagen sessions took place and for a long time the date usually suggested was May 1967. The original 1973 Hallmark album release is even further off the mark: the rear jacket dates the sessions to August 1968, by which time Sandy had been a member of Fairport Convention for three months.
* The strings were arranged by trumpeter Svend Lundvig, a local jazz musician who played with the likes of Stan Getz, Ben Webster and Stan Kenton in Denmark. The strings were not included in the mix used for the LP release but were used on the CD which Joe Boyd's Hannibal label released in 1991 as *Sandy Denny and the Strawbs*.

SANDY DENNY,
244,Worple Rd.
Wimbledon S.W.2o.   AGREEMENT   Copenhagen: 1st Aug.1967
London.-

Hereby the undersigned author transfers to MUSIKPRODUKTION
WINCKLER,Dortheavej 39,Copenhagen NV. Denmark - for ever
and for all countries the full,unrestricted and transferable
rights,herein also included the right to reproduction of
any kind of mechanical music instruments,sound-film,TV etc.
for the following by me composed/written work:

WHO KNOWS WHERE THE TIME GOES

Words & music:Sandy Denny

with exclusive rights for the publisher to printing,publication
and all commercial distribution and exploitation of this work,
separate or in connection with the written text/music.

As compensation for the tranference,the author receives from the
publisher a royalty of:

       lo % of the marked retail selling price for each sheet copy.

All other editions are free of royalties.

Furthermore the author receives from the net income of the publisher:

       5o % of mechanical,sound-film and TV rights etc.

       5o % by sale of publishing rights to other countries.

The performing rights in the composition including broadcasting
rights shall be administered by the performing right society
(Koda) or societies affiliated with this society.

Special clauses:

The publisher agrees to render accounts up to June 3oth and
December 31st each year and send such account with corresponding
remittance to the author as soon as possible after the respective
dates,but not later than 6o days from each date.

THE AUTHOR: MUSIKPRODUKTION WINCKLER:

Sandy's first publishing agreement for 'Who Knows Where the Time Goes?'

consider either offer. 'Polydor heard the tapes but they wanted
us to re-record it,' says Cousins, 'and Sandy said, "Oh no." We
even had Tito Burns wanting to take us on,* but in the mean-

* Showbiz impresario Burns was the sometime manager of Cliff Richard,

98

time Sandy got tired of waiting and left. It was a very frustrating time.' 'Over my dead body' was Sandy's response to the offer from Major Minor, an Irish label run by Radio Caroline co-director Phil Solomon which had already achieved a couple of unlikely pop hits by the Dubliners that year.

Like Sandy's other 1967 recordings, the album eventually came out on a budget label. Owned by the American label Pickwick, Hallmark was known for releasing a highly successful *Top of the Pops* series of soundalike cover versions. *All Our Own Work* was housed in a cheerful, garish sleeve while the group's intended front cover artwork was relegated to the rear: a caricature of those in the group, drawn by Sandy. 'She was a good artist,' says Cousins. 'She caught everybody perfectly in that drawing, which was done with coloured chalks like a pavement artist. The front cover of Fairport Convention's *What We Did on Our Holidays* nicked the idea of a chalk drawing, although done on a blackboard, which I'm sure Sandy must have suggested.'

All Our Own Work is completely elevated by Sandy's voice and presence whenever her singing is to the fore. Her only song on the album is 'Who Knows Where the Time Goes?'. The rest are written by either Dave Cousins or Tony Hooper. Cousins knew a good song when he heard it: 'Months before we went to Copenhagen, we were demoing songs on my home tape recorder, and I asked, "Have you written any songs?" It must have come up before but on this occasion she said, "Yes," and proceeded to sing "Who Knows Where the Time Goes?". I was absolutely stunned. It was the only song she ever played us. She had obviously written others but that was the only song she felt was good enough to share with anybody

the Searchers and the Zombies.

else. We demoed it in my living room. I said, "There's nothing we can add to it that you're not doing already." In fact, she was playing in this guitar tuning that I didn't think I could play.'

'Dave was an ambitious musician,' says Philippa Clare, who knew the group well, 'nothing wrong with that, but his ego was on top of the roof. Dave was happy to involve Sandy as a singer because he knew what she brought to his songs. He always saw himself as the chief songwriter in the Strawbs, but he wasn't stupid, he knew how good Sandy's song was and he wasn't going to turn down the chance to have the publishing for "Who Knows Where the Time Goes?" or to record it for the album. And he was smart enough that the Strawbs had their own publishing company, Strawberry Music. And for an unknown group to have formed its own publishing company back then, that was very forward-thinking.'

It was probably more forward-looking than even Cousins can have dreamt. 'Originally, we owned "Who Knows Where the Time Goes?",' he says, 'but we lost the song to Irving Music in the US, who part-owned A&M.' Strawberry Music was named as publisher when the album was finally released by Hallmark in 1973 and Cousins has proudly retained the documentation showing Strawberry Music held the publishing when Judy Collins first recorded the song.

There's much to admire about *All Our Own Work*. Sandy and the Strawbs brilliantly and confidently pull off the Mamas and the Papas-style close harmonies Cousins was aiming for on 'Nothing Else Will Do', 'On My Way' and the Byrds-like 'All I Need Is You'. The strident folk harmonies on 'Sail Away to Sea' wouldn't be out of place on a Peter, Paul and Mary album. In fact, it's the more Paul McCartney-style pop of 'And You Need Me' and 'Stay Awhile with

Me', the songs they first sang together in rehearsal, that fares less well and where Sandy's voice is more hesitant and stretched. She is superb on the drone-folk 'Tell Me What You See in Me', embellished by sitar and tabla. This was the only song from *All Our Own Work* that the Strawbs returned to on their 1969 A&M Records debut, re-recorded with Cousins voicing Sandy's part.

On the original twelve-track album, Sandy takes the lead on seven songs. Outtakes released later include a version of 'Nothing Else Will Do' sung by Sandy rather than by Dave Cousins, as well as her first attempt at one of Cousins's finest early songs, 'Two Weeks Last Summer', which she later recorded with Fotheringay. Had these songs been substituted for some of the existing tracks it would have made the album much stronger. It's likely that Cousins didn't want to demote himself entirely as a singer and also wanted to accommodate co-founder Tony Hooper, who contributes two bubbly songs where he also sings the lead, 'Sweetling' and 'Always on My Mind'. The album also acknowledges the Strawbs' origins with the bluegrass-style workout 'Wild Strawberries'.

Dave Cousins still believes the album could have broken the band commercially, if Sandy's resistance hadn't cost them a deal and a potential release in 1967. 'Had the Sandy and the Strawbs album come out on a label geared to the mainstream market there is every chance we might have had a hit single and Sandy might have become a major star in the way that Dusty Springfield did after leaving the Springfields. I think Sandy suddenly got cold feet about what the pop world might entail and preferred the safety blanket of the folk world.' *All Our Own Work* does present Sandy in a considerably better light than her two Saga albums, even if Cousins's dream of it yielding a pop hit seems optimistic.

'She liked the Strawbs,' says Gina Glaser, 'and I know she

enjoyed singing with them. What excited her was that she had never sung in a group before and she liked singing those pop harmonies. Sandy was always very open-minded but I never felt she was going to be entirely happy with what the Strawbs were doing musically, however much she liked them as people.'

'I'm not sure she was ever integrated into the group or felt it was right for her,' says Richard Thompson. 'They were an acoustic group and still part of the folk scene when Sandy sang with them and I think she was itching to get out of that world. The difference with Fairport was that we were not coming out of folk; we were a rock 'n' roll band, so it was a very different experience for Sandy.'

'It always seemed as if Sandy was passing through the Strawbs,' says Philippa Clare. 'She was wary about where it might lead and she never put her stamp on the group, whereas she was committed to Fairport. And although Dave was in awe of Sandy, he would also have been wary of her because when Sandy got up to sing the limelight was off Dave.'

Joe Boyd makes the interesting point that Sandy was happy to record the album with the Strawbs and to contribute the first – or best – song she had written to it, but then refused to stick with the group. 'You have to be a strong character to do that,' says Boyd. 'She turned Dave Cousins down and broke his heart when there was nothing else on the table for her at that point. It wasn't that she had Fairport knocking on the door – that was at least six months away.' Dave Cousins's bitterness remains to this day. He is still somewhat irrationally convinced that it was Joe Boyd who advised Sandy against signing any of the deals on the table, telling her, 'You don't want to be a pop singer,' because he wanted her to join Fairport Convention.

'If you ever have any doubt about whether Sandy had a strong will or clarity of vision, that's a pretty good foundation,' says Boyd. 'It could have been a stepping stone for her but it wasn't enough, it wasn't the right move for her. She said, "Count me out," when there were offers on the table from Major Minor and Polydor, both of which were happening labels in some way. This wasn't another Saga but she was saying, "I'm going to wait for something better." Her experience of being in the studio with them had been fascinating; she really loved it and she'd seen the possibilities but also the limitations of what she could do with them.'

Soon after she became a member of Fairport Convention in 1968 Sandy told *Melody Maker* that when she had joined the Strawbs she 'wasn't really ready for it'. She remained close friends with Dave Cousins, who often visited her in the country, but there's no definitive evidence of how she felt about the album they made together, although some time in 1971 *Sounds* writer Jerry Gilbert commented that she had 'shivered with horror' when she heard that *All Our Own Work* might be released.

After Sandy left, the Strawbs continued with the same melodic pop approach and brought in Sonja Kristina, who again Cousins first saw at the Troubadour, working up a set list based on the songs from *All Our Own Work* before reverting back to being a trio again. 'I think it was more that Dave fancied me at first,' says Kristina, 'but he did like my singing and I did sing with the Strawbs a few times, although we played only one show that I can remember [in Brentwood, December 1967], but then Dave decided not to pursue that direction. The Strawbs were in transition towards Dave's more personal songs, which he mostly sang himself. So they decided not to have a girl vocalist. I don't think his heart was in it because he associated that pop-folk approach too much with Sandy and he was pretty devastated by her leaving.'

Dave Cousins admits he felt hurt and let down by Sandy at the time and he returned to very few of the songs they had recorded together. 'It was very difficult to re-record those songs which Sandy had sung,' he says, 'because her singing was so wonderfully free. I just didn't have the flexibility in my voice. Sandy was mesmerising. If I had to pinpoint anything I'd say it's her phrasing, which could go from a whisper to a roar in a sentence or word. And even then, emotionally Sandy had a depth to her singing that nobody else had – there was nobody else to touch her at that time. She wasn't the melancholy person you hear on her solo albums; she was a fun-time girl who enjoyed a laugh, liked a drink and could sing with a power that was amazing.'

It took almost two years before the Strawbs clinched the deal Dave Cousins so desperately wanted, signing to A&M Records in 1969. Indirectly at least, Sandy did play a part in this. Karl Knudsen distributed A&M Records in Denmark and he had sent Jerry Moss (the 'M' in A&M) a tape of *All Our Own Work*. 'Jerry Moss went apeshit when he heard it,' says Cousins, 'and wanted to sign us immediately till he found out Sandy had left. Then he said, "Well, we didn't want to sign the group, we wanted to sign her."'* A&M did, however, ask the remaining Strawbs to record a provisional single, 'Oh How She Changed', which eventually resulted in the group becoming the label's first UK act.

Strawbs, their debut, was released in June 1969.† 'When the

---

* A&M would eventually get Sandy on their books in 1969, since the label had options on selected Island releases, including Fairport Convention.
† A second Strawbs album was recorded in 1968, in between *All Our Own Work* and their eponymous 1969 debut, but it was immediately rejected by A&M. It was finally released in 2012 after Cousins recreated it from the

first A&M album came out,' says Cousins, 'we were much darker and we found ourselves part of the underground scene. It probably worked to our advantage because we were no longer seen as a folk group.' In fact, Dave Cousins very effectively demonstrated how to make folk albums which had an appeal outside the genre. He would go on to reinvent the Strawbs' style in the more progressive pastoral direction that reached maturation with *From the Witchwood* and *Grave New World* in 1972. Cousins still relishes the commercial success of the Strawbs, both in Britain and particularly in North America, compared to those who were considered his folk-rock rivals: Fairport Convention, Pentangle and Steeleye Span.

It was business as usual for Sandy on her return from Copenhagen. She went straight up to Scotland, where she had dates lined up in Glasgow, Perth and Aberdeen; she and Johnny Silvo also appeared on Alex Campbell's *My Kind of Folk* for Grampian TV. It was the first TV outing for 'Who Knows Where the Time Goes?', long ago wiped, but Danish folk fan Carsten Linde at least captured a good-natured song session at Campbell's house at 19 Rupert Street in Glasgow on Saturday 5 August. Despite the indifferent sound quality of the tape, it's a charming, intimate snapshot of Sandy relaxed and among friends – Campbell, his partner Patsy and their kids – everybody getting tipsier and jollier as the night wears on. Sandy is surprisingly intense performing 'The Leaves of Life' (aka 'Seven Virgins'), 'She Moves through the Fair' and a beautiful sixteenth-century lullaby, 'Balulalow', before the entertainment

---

original tapes as a fascinating period piece which he entitled *Of a Time*. It included three of the songs that had originally been sung by Sandy Denny, all re-recorded and revoiced by Cousins.

gets looser and bawdier. Sandy duets with Campbell on a couple of slapdash skiffle standards and has a stab at John Martyn's as yet unrecorded 'Fairytale Lullaby'. 'Can I sing one of my own?' she asks, before singing a ragged 'Who Knows Where the Time Goes?', her guitar horribly out of tune. These tapes were never meant to be heard publicly (though they were eventually released by Dave Cousins's Witchwood Media in 2011), and they give you a sense of the Sandy her friends knew: her warmth, an irresistible sense of fun, and the laugh everybody remembers so affectionately.

At the end of her week of engagements with Silvo and Campbell, Sandy went to Edinburgh to meet up with her boyfriend, Danny Thompson; they had been in a relationship since the beginning of the year. Sandy had been doing occasional guest spots on Sundays at the Horseshoe hotel on Tottenham Court Road, an informal open residency for Bert Jansch and John Renbourn with singer Jacqui McShee.* It was here that Pentangle became a reality after Danny Thompson and drummer Terry Cox committed to the project. Sandy asked Danny if he'd help her with her piano playing. He explained he was no teacher, but he told Jim Irvin in 1998 how he 'fell for her immediately. She had an amazing chuckle. She was larger than life, a great bird to be with.'

Danny also lived in Wimbledon, and would pick Sandy up from Worple Road in his Bentley. Edna Denny, now working at the local tax office, was none too impressed with the imposing, bluff

---

* Jacqui McShee became hooked on folk in 1961 after meeting musicians including Ralph McTell, Cliff Aungier, Gerry Lochran and Chris Aycliff on CND marches with her sister Pam. McShee later came across Bert Jansch and John Renbourn at the folk club she and her friends started up at the Red Lion in Sutton. She began singing with Renbourn and made her debut recording on his second album, *Another Monday*, in 1966.

jazz musician. Danny recalls: 'Sandy met me one night and said, "My mum's checked up on you and found out you're married with a son."' Sandy already knew this, and if Edna had hoped to put her off Thompson, her ploy didn't work. The relationship would last for well over a year.

'Sandy would come along to gigs and there'd be huge rows between her and Danny,' recalls Jacqui McShee. 'It was a pretty volatile relationship. I remember one time she got out of the van with her guitar in the middle of nowhere, and I said, "You can't," and Danny said, "Leave her there, she's too argumentative."'

'She was always up for a laugh,' Danny remembers. 'She'd let stuff happen and wouldn't stand for any pomposity. She did all the things a singer wasn't supposed to. I used to nag her about the smoking, but I wouldn't have stopped her drinking – we were all big drinkers. I did try and keep her off the brandy. She got aggressive on brandy.'

'I was never that close to Sandy,' says McShee; 'we used to natter about clothes and men and we'd have a moan and laugh. I was very fond of her. It wasn't on a very deep level. She was always crying on my shoulder, usually about Danny, and I knew Danny would never leave his wife.'

When they met, Danny Thompson was already an in-demand session player and was appearing regularly at Ronnie Scott's, working with Tubby Hayes, Stan Tracey and Scott's quintet. 'I had my Bentley and loads of money, we'd clear off to Scotland and all that. I suppose she was quite impressed, though she'd never say.'

'Danny was young and they had a lot of good times together,' says Linda Thompson. 'He liked partying a lot and she liked partying a lot. There was more to it than that but it was a relationship that was never going anywhere.'

Andy Roberts was appearing at the Edinburgh Festival with the Scaffold at the Traverse Theatre that summer. In the afternoons, the tiny theatre held poetry readings and a lot of folk musicians would come along. At one of these afternoon gatherings, he recalls that 'Sandy arrived on Danny's arm, and on the basis of what I saw I thought she was a blues singer, a hard-drinking Bessie Smith character; she was Janis Joplin before we knew who Janis was. She really went for it. She was young and a real rough diamond but she played strong guitar, had an absolutely sensational voice and Danny backed her to the hilt. It certainly wasn't a typical folk set. She was very unrefined but had a very, very powerful voice, a raw talent but loads of charisma. When I eventually heard her again it was with Fairport and it was hard to believe it was the same singer.'

Come September, having left the Strawbs and clearly wanting to express her independence and show she had other plans, Sandy spoke to Karl Dallas of *Melody Maker*. Under the headline 'I Don't Want to Be Labelled', she announced: 'I'm collecting material together for my first solo album. I really want it to represent what I'm trying to do. Of course, what I really want to do is sing jazz.' One wonders if this was in part to please Dallas – who said that Sandy had a sense of timing that many would-be jazz singers would envy – or Thompson and his friends at the Capricorn Club on Goodge Street. Run by Acker Bilk and his brother, it was a regular hangout for off-duty jazz musicians. The Mandrake, on Meard Street, was another jazz bar Sandy liked to frequent; but however much she enjoyed the company of jazz musicians, if she had really wanted to make a jazz record she would only have been switching from one marginal genre to another. Sandy wanted broader success than either jazz or folk could offer her. That summer she met somebody who might just be able to make that happen.

Joe Boyd was unlike anybody else Sandy had known on the fringe of the folk scene. 'I was working in a different area, more underground and not exclusively folk, and that intrigued her,' says Boyd. 'Sandy was very independent but I never felt I was being used, that was never Sandy's way, although she always quickly got the measure of people.'

Boyd paints a vivid picture of Sandy, just twenty years old and, however vulnerable at times, no pushover: 'She had a very quick mind, jumping from one subject to another, dropping in comments obliquely, interrupting herself with footnotes, a kind of chaotic intelligence just pouring out. Witty, barbed, very quick with the vicious put-down; she didn't suffer fools gladly. At the same time, she also had a good heart.'

At twenty-five Joe Boyd had already chalked up a near lifetime of experience. He was born in Boston and graduated from Harvard in 1964, where he once roomed with folk singer Tom Rush, and was a close friend of the Doors' producer Paul Rothchild, who became his mentor as a record producer. Rothchild recommended Boyd to Elektra's Jac Holzman, who was setting up a London office in November 1965 and needed someone to run it. Arriving in London just ahead of the pivotal year of cultural change in 1966, Boyd helped open UFO, London's first underground ballroom, with John 'Hoppy' Hopkins, while holding down his Elektra position. Most of Boyd's early production work for Elektra was folk-based: an EP by Sydney Carter, the compilation *A Cold Wind Blows*, featuring Cyril Tawney, Matt McGinn and Johnny Handle, and an eccentric album by Oxford philosophy scholar Alasdair Clayre. He also signed Edinburgh-based trio the Incredible String

Band, Elektra's only British act of any real substance in its sixties heyday.

Sandy didn't know the Incredible String Band well, since Boyd had strategically repositioned the band away from the folk scene: 'From the moment Joe signed us,' recalled Mike Heron, 'he didn't think of us as a folk band but as an "underground" band. It was to our advantage that we'd play alongside Pink Floyd or the Move at underground clubs like UFO.' Produced by Boyd, the Incredible String Band released their self-titled debut in 1966, but it was their second album that shook the folk world. After co-founder Clive Palmer drifted away, the remaining duo of Mike Heron and Robin Williamson abandoned the group's folky, jug-band style for something more bizarre and exotic that epitomised the changing times. *The 5000 Spirits or the Layers of the Onion* proved to be a defining moment in 1967; housed in one of the great mystical, psychedelic covers of the era, it was effectively the *Sergeant Pepper* of the folk world. Their 1968 album *The Hangman's Beautiful Daughter* actually reached number five in the UK charts, unheard of for what was in effect a folk album. The success of the Incredible String Band was crucial in realigning folk within the burgeoning underground, and it wouldn't have gone unnoticed by the determined Sandy that Boyd had been pivotal in making this happen. More than anyone she had met before, Joe Boyd opened Sandy's eyes to the wider possibilities that were in front of her in 1967.

Boyd was unconvinced by Sandy's talents to begin with. 'I'd seen her a few times at places like Cousins and we'd met but we had never really talked, and I was resistant because she touched a certain button for me, which was the big voice, the Judy Henske or even Baez, that room-dominating voice that was a hallmark, quite logically, of people singing in cafes or pub back rooms. I'd seen too much of it in America and what appealed to me was more intrinsically English folk music; I loved the Ian Campbell Folk Group because of Swarbrick's playing but I also loved Ian's singing, and I loved the Watersons, Anne Briggs, Jeannie Robertson, Cyril Tawney and Louis Killen – that was the revelation for me in going into an English folk club. So when I heard singer-songwriters strumming guitars I just thought, "Oh God, this American disease is spreading." And I kind of ran for the hills.'

Then, one particular night after meeting at Les Cousins, Sandy and Boyd ended up having a few drinks and bringing in the dawn at her home in Wimbledon. 'She persuaded me to give her a ride home in exchange for listening to *Sergeant Pepper*, which she'd taped off the radio, and that was how we became friends. And I got the feeling in the stunned aftermath of listening to *Sergeant Pepper* that she was really eager to sing with a band rather than just to her own guitar accompaniment.'

When Boyd eventually heard Sandy and the Strawbs' version of 'Who Knows Where the Time Goes?' it confirmed that he'd underestimated her abilities: 'For a first song to have written, or the first she felt confident about, it was remarkable. When I heard the sound of her recorded voice I could remove myself from that belting voice I'd heard in a small room. She was also very appealing and obviously a lot smarter than my first impression. Once I grasped that my whole perception of her changed.

'We talked vaguely about making a record and, looking back now, it seems incomprehensible that I wouldn't have said, "I'll get you a deal as a solo artist and I'll produce it." But I hadn't heard any other songs she'd written. We continued to talk about it but I was desperately dealing with huge problems at UFO and still feeling the great blow of having Pink Floyd taken in-house by EMI after having produced their first single, "Arnold Layne". And so it was "Let me think about that." Then, very shortly after, I saw Fairport Convention and I began managing and producing them.'

Boyd did find time to produce Shirley Collins's *The Power of the True Love Knot*. He was 'the first proper producer' Collins ever worked with, although she felt he didn't understand English traditional songs or singing at all. 'Joe was a real go-getter and I think I was a real disappointment to him. I remember there was one song – "Lovely Joan" – and I have such a clear memory of it because he said, "Why don't you put some action into it?" He thought I was too straightforward a singer, that I needed to dramatise the stuff more; I couldn't and didn't and Joe quickly lost interest in me. I'm sure he could see that I was never going to be a popular figure in the way that somebody like Sandy was going to be. She was far more marketable than me and I was never going to change.'

'Joe definitely had ambitions for Sandy and could see her potential,' says Philippa Clare, 'but the idea of Sandy making a solo album in 1967 wasn't practical. She hadn't written a lot of songs and she liked the idea of making a solo album but hadn't thought it through at all. Joe did all the right things for Sandy, he was supportive and encouraging, but he had too many things on his plate to be able to help her find the right direction. Sandy wasn't ready and Joe didn't have the time.'

Having had the courage of her convictions to pull away from the Strawbs, Sandy found herself treading water while most of her male singer-songwriter friends and Cousins contemporaries seemed to be moving on apace. Al Stewart, Roy Harper, even John Martyn, who had only arrived from Scotland that spring, were already signed to significant labels and had well-received albums out by the end of 1967; her friends in the Young Tradition had by now released two albums for Transatlantic, and Bert Jansch and John Renbourn had moved to another level of recognition and critical acceptance. Jansch had four albums under his belt, Renbourn two, plus the 'must have' *Bert and John* album they made together in 1966. Jansch and Renbourn were, like the Incredible String Band, dragging the folk boom into the Swinging Sixties, giving folk an air of cool it had never had before.

Sandy must have felt she was going nowhere. She was the best of the British girl folk singers on the circuit but she'd been ill served by the workmanlike albums she had made with Alex Campbell and Johnny Silvo. As traditional singer Tim Hart observed: 'There was nowhere to go once you got £25 at clubs and could headline at occasional festivals. You either became a folk intellectual or you became an alcoholic.'

Maddy Prior, who had teamed up with Hart in 1967, can now take the long view. 'Joan Baez was the one who made English folk music alright,' she says, 'so I got to know Donovan and guitarist Mac Macleod in St Albans and we started going to folk clubs and, next thing, Mac and I started playing some gigs together. I remember I made ten quid working in a Wimpy bar and eight quid doing a gig on my own with a banjo, and I thought, "I'll do this for a bit." There was no question of career. You just muddled along until you did something else really. That's what Sandy was doing. I think she knew she wanted to do something different, but what? The folk scene was very limiting if you weren't content to stay at the same level. And eventually she fell into Fairport, far more by chance than when Tim and I joined Ashley Hutchings to form Steeleye Span, because by then Fairport had paved the way.'

Despite the conviction with which she had launched herself in 1966, two years later Sandy's career was in need of some impetus. This was just at the point when Pentangle – which not only included her boyfriend Danny Thompson but also old friends Jansch and Renbourn – were about to be transformed from 'a ramshackle, happy-go-lucky' bunch, as Colin Harper later described the group, into 'a streamlined machine of efficiency and purpose'. Pentangle had more or less drifted together, a loose combo which by the summer of 1967 had acquired a degree of permanency as well as a name. Progress was fitful, however, and the occasional tours and few gigs Pentangle did other than at the Horseshoe hotel were usually disastrous. The turning point was when Jo Lustig became their manager in February 1968. A Brooklyn-born New York press agent, Lustig had come to Europe in 1960 with Nat King Cole but decided to stay on. His first success was in promoting Julie Felix, but it was Pentangle that would establish his reputation in folk-rock circles.

Lustig immediately repositioned Pentangle just as Joe Boyd had done with the Incredible String Band. He terminated the Horseshoe residency and withdrew Jansch and Renbourn from the folk clubs, before unveiling Pentangle at the Royal Festival Hall on 29 June 1968 off the back of an album produced by Shel Talmy, whose pop credits included the Kinks and the early Who. Lustig presented Pentangle as something fresh and exciting, exploiting the group's unclassifiable musical hybrid to move them onto the concert circuit in the UK, Europe and America, taking in major folk festivals, jazz festivals and the new rock festivals that were springing up. For the next five years, the group were constantly touring or recording, their solo careers virtually put on hold.

Soon after taking them on, Lustig decided that singer Jacqui McShee wasn't marketable enough for his vision of the band. 'After about a year,' says McShee, 'he tried to get me out and bring

Sandy in; I didn't know anything about this at the time and I don't think Sandy was ever even asked. John only told me later but he just said no outright. I think he even threatened to leave. Bert was always so laid-back and I'm not even sure he was aware of what was going on behind the scenes.'

'Jo Lustig was a PR man of the old school,' says Renbourn. 'His forte was drumming up publicity and no shot was too cheap. There was never any question of any singer other than Jacqui. The group wasn't put together as a commercial package with "names", it was a musical entity and Jacqui was integral to that, not just a voice. As a rule Jo never interfered with the music, but he did float the idea of Sandy replacing Jacqui; he even suggested Julie Driscoll at one point.'

Jansch had, indeed, no idea what was going on: 'I don't remember any attempt by Jo to get Sandy into Pentangle. I don't think Sandy really knew what she wanted to do anyway. She could have done anything if she only knew what – and she proved that when she joined Fairport Convention, which came right out of the blue.

'We had no idea how long Pentangle would carry on. Much of that time we were in a daze, which is probably why it lasted as long as it did. When it ended it just seemed the right thing to do. I'm not sure Sandy would have stuck with anything for that long or been able to deal with the amount of touring we did. That's what drained the rest of us, it was relentless.'

'Right from our early days in folk clubs, when Sandy stood up to sing, everyone was spellbound,' says McShee. 'There was nobody else like her and she was very recognisable – you knew it was Sandy. But I always felt she was quite shy behind the front she put up. That's what John said, that she had too big a personality. Pentangle was about the balance between three very strong personalities in Bert and John and Danny. There was no room for another one. I kept everyone's feet on the ground. I was a calming influence, which wasn't Sandy's strong suit.'

Al Stewart recalls an incident around this time that illustrates Sandy's volatility. 'I once "saved her life" following a love affair that had gone wrong. She was hysterical and she was standing in the middle of the traffic on Cambridge Circus. I saw this girl running in front of taxis, crazy stuff, out of control, and I realised it was Sandy. I ran out into the street and just grabbed her and got her into a cab. She was living in Wimbledon, and I remember to this day it was thirty-eight shillings and sixpence on the meter by the time we got to her house. By then she'd calmed down and she said, "What do you think you are doing? Look at the meter; I can't afford to pay that." And I thought, "Didn't I just rescue you?" Neither of us had enough money so she had to go indoors and her dad came out and paid off the taxi. She'd calmed down completely so it was my fault because I'd run up this huge bill. It was interesting how quickly she went from being manic and near-suicidal to being totally in control.'

In those early months of 1968 Sandy's date sheet on the folk circuit was sketchy and remained at much the same level she'd reached a year before. She was, if nothing else, at home in that world. Her audience knew her and she had a lot of friends in folk. Here she could just play music in a scene which was largely free of the glitz she openly disdained. Sandy may have had broad musical tastes but one reason she had been reluctant to take up the Strawbs' offer was that she was never attracted to the pop world. 'It always seems so phoney,' she said in 1971. 'I could never see myself standing up and singing a really phoney pop song which didn't mean anything to me.'

Sandy also knew she did not fit the pop industry's image of the girl singer, another reason she felt safe in folk music. 'Somehow I don't look like a dolly-bird singer. I never have looked like the sort of glamorous chick who has made it in the past. I'd like to, but I don't.'

'I think it was very difficult for Sandy, growing up in that era and not looking a certain way,' says Gina Glaser. 'Sandy was attractive but the record industry almost demands you look a certain way, and that wasn't how she looked. It may not have mattered so much for a folk singer but it still mattered to Sandy as a woman.'

Richard Thompson thinks Sandy was desperate to move on in 1968, and to do that she had to leave the comfort of the folk scene behind. Fairport Convention offered an easy transition on many different levels. 'Image was never exactly our strong point in Fairport,' says Thompson, 'nor did it matter to our audience. As with folk music, you could just be who you were and dress how you wanted. We were a real bunch of scruffs.

'Folk musicians can be quite unforgiving towards anybody being seen to try anything commercial, but Sandy wasn't even a star in the folk world, so she could do as she pleased and she never conformed to strict rules anyway. And nobody in the folk scene had heard of Fairport Convention, so nobody thought she was selling out by joining a rock 'n' roll band.'

5 : I Must Have Grown Some Wings
1968–1969

The difference between the first and second album, once Sandy joined, is massive. People often make the mistake of saying that it was only after Sandy came into the group that we became a folk-rock group, well, we knew all about folk music years before and loved it. It was that suddenly the light went on after Sandy joined.

ASHLEY HUTCHINGS

You must philosophise
Why must you bore me to tears
You're red around the eyes
You tell me things yours else bears
You spend all your time crying
Crying the hours into years

Come lend your time to me
And you will know that you're still free
And when you look at me
Don't think your owning what you see
For remember that your free
And that's what you want to be
So just lend your time to me.

Sandy's lyrics to 'Autopsy', December 1968

Fairport Convention were one of very few groups to emerge in 1967 that were in no way tarnished by their past. Like Pink Floyd or Soft Machine, both of which had formed the year before and had helped define the possibilities of the new underground era, Fairport Convention had no background of slogging it out around the country playing R & B retreads on the club circuit. Their pre-history was in a handful of schoolboy and kickabout groups whose common denominator was usually Ashley Hutchings. They took a variety of names, such as Dr K's Blues band, Tim Turner's Narration (Turner narrated the *Look at Life* documentary series shown in British cinemas) and the Ethnic Shuffle Orchestra, whose name identifies their acoustic jug band/Lovin' Spoonful orientation. It was this group which evolved organically into the fully electric Fairport Convention that played its first gig on 27 May 1967 at St Michael's Church Hall, Golders Green, featuring versions of 'Hey Joe' and Love's 'Seven and Seven Is' in its set. Muswell Hill is usually seen as the focal point because the group rehearsed there in Simon Nicol's family home – called 'Fairport' – but the group's individual backgrounds took in a wider north London catchment of Bounds Green, Hampstead, Highgate, Totteridge and Harrow, all broadly middle-class areas.

Bass player and de facto leader Ashley Hutchings was the eldest, born in 1945, but the rest of the group – Simon Nicol and Richard Thompson, guitars, Martin Lamble, drums, and singer

Judy Dyble – were all eighteen or younger in that summer of 1967. They were all coming at it fresh.

'I would say there was a special atmosphere in Fairport that has never been recreated,' says Ashley Hutchings. 'If you ask Simon or Richard, I bet they would say the same. It's all to do with youth, but also with the things that come out of youth. It's the fact that you have this enthusiasm and bravery which you are never able to hang on to as you get older.'

All five members of Fairport Convention shared an eclectic taste in music and each of them brought songs to the table, although few were ever recorded either officially or for BBC radio sessions. Two of the best songs on their debut, *Fairport Convention*, were barely known covers: 'One Sure Thing' from Jim and Jean's *Changes*, and Merry Go Round's 'Time Will Show the Wiser', written by Emitt Rhodes. 'We dug around and we sought obscure unknown songs by obscure groups and songwriters,' says Hutchings, 'and that formed the basis of what we did. We were always a song-based band, and that was pretty unusual. What struck a big chord was the American singer-songwriters like Phil Ochs or Richard Fariña. There weren't too many English singer-songwriters. We all contributed original songs, often inter-group collaborations, but there was nothing outstanding until our second album, *What We Did on Our Holidays*.'

Judy Dyble had first come to Ashley Hutchings's attention because she was carrying an autoharp, and they struck up a conversation. 'I had done songs like "The Water Is Wide" and "Come All Ye Fair and Tender Ladies" at one or two folk clubs,' says Dyble, 'but there was no music that I didn't enjoy, and that went for all of them. We were all music nuts. I remember transposing Bert Jansch's "Strollin' Down the Highway" so that I could play it on the harp. Incorporating folk music didn't start when Sandy joined, although it tended to be American contemporary folk songs. We made every song our own – they were not just covers but very different arrangements – and that was always the hallmark of Fairport. Richard was the standout musician but he couldn't have done it without the others.'

'We all went to a lot of folk clubs,' says Hutchings; 'we all explored classical music, including modern classical people like John Cage, and jazz as well. I went to Ronnie Scott's a number of times, and I was always going to blues clubs. It was the same for the others and you can hear that when you listen to the first Fairport album. It's a clumsy hotchpotch of influences.'

Fairport started out as a bunch of friends who all had jobs and didn't view being in a rock group as a prospective career, though Dyble believes Hutchings was always ambitious. 'We only really started to take it seriously once people started asking us back and we started getting paid,' she says. 'And once Joe Boyd became involved it went to another level.' Boyd had first seen the group at Happening 44 (a club operating out of a strip joint in Soho's Gerrard Street), but it was after he booked them at UFO on 28 July 1967, where they supported Pink Floyd, that Boyd became involved as manager, signing them to his newly formed Witchseason production company. The *Hornsey Journal* reported on 11 August that Muswell Hill pop group 'The Fairport Convention' were recording and that Boyd was managing them. By then the group were regulars on London's underground circuit, playing venues like Middle Earth, the Electric Garden, UFO and in-crowd hangouts like the Speakeasy, where they even jammed with Hendrix.

Kingsley Abbott went to University College School in Highgate with Martin Lamble and drove the band to many of their early out-of-town gigs. He considered Boyd was behind the first in Fairport's long history of personnel changes: 'Joe was really smart and he had a very clear idea of what was possible for Fairport, and it definitely centred on Richard. He would very quickly have seen Jude as a weak link. Vocals were not Fairport's strength. None of the boys wanted to sing at all. They all took turns but it was usually a competition to see who could stand furthest at the back.'

Joe Boyd may have thought Judy Dyble was a weak link in the band but for the time being he was content to wait and see what developed. 'It seems strange now,' says Boyd, 'that I wasn't driving Sandy into Fairport even then, but it did cross my mind. My God, there was this great singer over here and this great group with a weak singer over there, but Judy was Richard's girlfriend, and although I definitely had a lot to learn in terms of tact, I was at least tactful enough to realise that the first thing you did when you signed a band was not to fire the star's girlfriend.' Boyd's response was not to replace Dyble with Sandy – or anybody – but to add Ian MacDonald to the vocal mix.*

Dyble says she doesn't think she was ever consulted about the decision to add a male singer. 'That was how a lot of things were happening in the band once Joe was managing us. I know I found being in the studio a little overwhelming and uninvolving, more of a boy's thing. I more or less did what I was asked to play and sing and then sat quietly in a corner of the control booth.'

MacDonald, born in 1946 in Lincolnshire, was from a completely different background to the rest of Fairport and had previously been in a group called the Pyramid, which had released one single for the

---

* Born Ian Matthew MacDonald, between the release of Fairport's first and second albums he changed his surname to Matthews to avoid confusion with King Crimson's multi-instrumentalist Ian MacDonald. Later, he would also add a second 'i' to his first name.

The Fairport Convention

Management:	Agency:	Recording:
John Penhallow, Witchseason Productions Ltd., 83 Charlotte Street, London, W.1.	The Bryan Morrison Agency Ltd., 142 Charing Cross Road, London, W.C.2.	Joe Boyd,
01 636 9436	TEM 0171/0606	01 636 9436

The group's very first publicity shot, taken in the garden at Fairport

Deram label. 'I'd never heard of Fairport when they approached me,' he says. 'A reliable source told me they were new on the scene and very good. He was right on both counts. They were really look-ing for a keyboard-playing singer and settled for me.'

MacDonald first met them at Sound Techniques studio,* which

---

* Sound Techniques began as a recording studio at 46A Old Church Street, Chelsea, London SW3, in December 1964. It was set up by Geoff Frost and John Wood and was one of the earliest independent sound recording studios in the UK. It was managed by Wood up until 1976. 'We did a lot of work for Elektra through Jac Holzman, including Judy Collins's *In My Life*, and Joe was by then running the Elektra office in London. That's how Joe and I met.' Boyd and Wood became the team behind almost all recordings by artists on Witchseason's books until 1971, and more besides, usually operating out of Sound Techniques.

would become a second home to Fairport and its many spin-offs, arriving with a suitcase and a bundle of LPs under his arm. 'The first person I met was Ashley, and he wanted to know which albums I had. It was a mishmash – from Tim Hardin to the Kinks. I probably got the job because of my taste in music. I'm not sure that I ever really "slotted in".' There was no conventional audition; MacDonald joined the group while they were recording their debut album during August and September 1967, with Joe Boyd producing and John Wood engineering.

'The first album has no particular direction,' says Hutchings. 'It's full of eccentric ideas – "Oh let's throw that in," or "Let's try this."' Simon Nicol agrees that no one in the band was entirely happy with the first album. 'It tried so hard to show everything that we could do that it didn't really represent what we did at all.'

The album, completed by October 1967, was delayed for several months until Boyd clinched a deal with the trendsetting Track Records, a Polydor imprint run by Kit Lambert and Chris Stamp that had already released recordings by the Who, as well as underground artists like Arthur Brown, John's Children with Marc Bolan, and Jimi Hendrix. Fairport's debut single, 'If I Had a Ribbon Bow', was eventually released on 25 February 1968, although the group were far from convinced that this jazzy 1930s song represented what they were about at all.

Two months after the single release, Ashley Hutchings sat Judy Dyble down at the local bus stop and told her she was no longer in the group. 'Being asked to leave came completely out of the blue,' says Dyble. 'It was like being told, "You're not our friend any more." I was told I sang out of tune or off-key. I always felt mine and Ian's voices didn't really blend. We got on well enough but Ian was always an outsider; we had shared the vocals a lot originally, there'd be different leads on certain songs but Ian was beginning to do more. I felt I was relinquishing the role of being in the forefront.'

Melody Maker's 'Raver' column reported that Judy Dyble left Fairport on 4 May 1968, although her final gig was in Rome the next day, at the International Pop Festival at the Palazzo dello Sport. Just two weeks earlier, she had had no inkling anything was wrong when Fairport played shows in Paris and Monteaux. This was when the sole footage of early Fairport Convention was filmed, for the French TV programme *Baton Rouge*. It's an astonishing performance and it's hard to believe Dyble was sacked just days later, although MacDonald does take the lead on all three songs. Dyble plays recorder on Tim Buckley's 'Morning Glory' and sings with MacDonald on 'Time Will Show the Wiser', as well as on 'Reno, Nevada', a showcase for Thompson's exhilarating guitar skills, during which she sits on the drum riser at the back of the stage for much of its eight minutes.* There would be no footage of Sandy during her first stint with Fairport at all.

'The singing was less important in the early days,' says Hutchings, 'it was more a choice of songs and how we arranged them, but after a while we realised that we needed stronger vocals. People loved Judy, and quite rightly, but we were getting louder. Judy was an integral part of the band. We were called the English Jefferson Airplane – we were billed as "England's Top West Coast Group" – and that was purely because Judy was in the group, so we stood out. There were very few rock bands with a female singer up front.'

At first the group had no intention of bringing in a replacement

* Al Stewart recalls that he once saw Dyble knitting during one of Thompson's long incendiary solos: 'not something I imagine Sandy ever did'.

for Dyble. 'Then we found the reaction at the handful of gigs where we played without her knocked us back,' says Simon Nicol. 'It was "Where's the chick singer?" People expected us to have that boy/girl-fronted line-up.'

'I think everyone missed that female vocal presence,' says co-singer MacDonald, who was by now calling himself Ian Matthews. 'That was one of the strong elements in making the band special. Joe very subtly called the shots. It was quite subliminal, but I think all involved would admit to it now. He planted the seeds for thoughts like my coming in, and leaving. Also Judy leaving, and definitely Sandy joining. I'd never heard of her. I wasn't really plugged into the folk scene.'

The auditions for Judy Dyble's replacement took place at the Eight Feathers Boys' Club in Fulham in the week of 13 May; nobody involved is certain of the exact date. Having realised they needed another girl singer, the group and Witchseason already had a shortlist. 'I suspect none of us knew who Sandy was,' says Hutchings. 'I'm certain none of us had seen her. I always had my ears open and was pretty knowledgeable. We didn't know about the albums she made with Alex Campbell and Johnny Silvo – nor do I remember Sandy ever speaking about them.'

'I knew Sandy's name,' says Simon Nicol. 'I knew she was one of the Cousins crowd. We just asked around, and between us and Witchseason we put the word out. If it was Joe Boyd's idea to put Sandy in the frame, we weren't aware of that, but she would have cropped up through other avenues anyway. We auditioned about twelve girls and it was torturous. It was all done in a day and a half and, honestly, nobody else left any impression.' The entire band now claim to be unable to remember – most likely out of politeness – who the other candidates were. Nicol would later make an oft-repeated remark about Sandy 'standing out like a clean glass in a sink full of dirty dishes', which, says Hutchings, 'is a bit offensive to the others who came along, but there was absolutely no contest when we heard Sandy. That was it.'

Sandy said it was Heather Wood of the Young Tradition who told her about the auditions. 'When Judy Dyble left,' says Wood, 'Steve Sparkes, who was part of the Witchseason set-up, asked if I would be interested in joining. It wasn't even put as strongly as that. I was with the Young Tradition and I had no desire to leave, so I said, "Why don't you ask Sandy?" The rest is history. I don't think I was the only one who suggested her, though. Also, I met the Witchseason crew through Anthea Joseph, who used to run the Troubadour. Anth and I were friends; Anth may have had a hand in Sandy going along.' Karl Dallas says he also put her name in the frame.

In the meantime, Joe Boyd was in America with the Incredible String Band and was famously concerned 'she'd eat them for breakfast' when he heard about Sandy joining Fairport. 'I went "Wow." I was thrilled but I was also slightly alarmed. I think at least some of them knew about Sandy because I know I had talked to them about her. They used to come over to my flat and the test pressing of Sandy's record with the Strawbs was lying around, and I used to play it a lot to people and say, "Listen to this song." It's quite possible I played it to them but I picked out a lot of stuff I would want them to hear because they were so open to it. So it's one of those things that are in the mists of history. I only have the headlines. Sandy certainly knew about them from me but the fact of the matter is that I was out of town and had nothing directly to do with it. I had misgivings beforehand but once it happened it was clear that it was just great.'

Sandy had been no shrinking violet at the auditions. 'When she met Fairport,' says Linda Thompson, 'it was like, "You first. I want to hear something." And for a girl in those days it was absolutely unheard of. They asked her to join that day. I don't think she would have auditioned for them unless she knew something about them.'

Sandy sang 'You Never Wanted Me', which became part of Fairport's repertoire for a few months. 'We all just knew,' says Hutchings. 'I don't think we even discussed it. One song and she was in if she wanted to join.' Richard Thompson adds: 'She said, "I want to hear something you do," which was fair enough, and we did Tim Buckley's "Morning Glory". I don't remember her saying, "Can I let you know in a couple of days?" or anything like that.' Iain Matthews has a slightly different take on proceedings: 'I'm not so sure she auditioned! It was more a rehearsal. There were lots of nods of approval and positive murmurings. Our voices went together OK and in she came.'

Even today, it's obvious that Judy Dyble still feels hurt at the way she was dismissed from Fairport Convention. 'I'm sure that because Sandy had no history with them,' says Dyble, 'she was accepted on a more equal footing. And she had a more forceful personality than me. I did meet Sandy at her flat once. I felt I had to somehow, and it was very strange – I gave her a recipe for mead.

'I just wish they had had a really terrible singer between me and her. I'll always be compared to her. For a brief while Sandy sang several of the songs that I sang with Fairport. I had thought of them as "my" songs, but I was more jealous because she sang them so well.'

Sandy's first gig with Fairport Convention was on Saturday 20 May at Middle Earth – remarkably, less than a week after the auditions. She also travelled with the band to Portsmouth Guildhall in the week and may have got up onstage with them. Kingsley Abbott remembers that even at the first Middle Earth gig she was already well integrated into the group and not just providing back-up to Ian's leads but singing her featured songs. Her audition song, 'You Never Wanted Me', was included in her first Peel Session as a member of Fairport, which was recorded on 28 May and broadcast on 2 June. Fairport's debut album, *Fairport Convention*, was released on 1 June, but the session featured only one of its tracks, 'I Don't Know Where I Stand'. For the first time, but certainly not the last, a Fairport Convention album was released which featured a line-up that had already changed.

Sandy's first mention in the press as a member of Fairport also came on 1 June, in *Melody Maker*'s 'Raver' column, which noted that 'Sandy Denny is the new singer' and that Fairport had just recorded 'Some Sweet Day' for intended release in July. An unusually straight cover of a song most associated with the Everly Brothers, sung by Matthews, it was in fact never released.

A cassette recording exists of Sandy's second Fairport appearance, at the Whittlesey Barn Barbecue Concert and Dance on Whitsun weekend, Sunday 2 June, headlined by Donovan. Perhaps it's the recording quality but Sandy's vocal cuts abrasively through everything else, even when she is singing with Matthews. Her bellowing voice is a sign that she is not accustomed to having an electric band behind her. She takes the same leads as on the Peel Session, but not only is Sandy's voice too shrill at times, she is also playing a Fender Telecaster, an electric guitar known for its cutting tone, which is conspicuously too loud during some of the set.

At the end of the month, *Melody Maker* interviewed Sandy, who

Sandy's second appearance with Fairport Convention

considered that Fairport 'does a mixture of country and western, folk adaptations, blues – but not like John Mayall of course'; musically they are 'flexible but not self-satisfied'. 'We've all got our own ideas,' she says. 'There's not much conflict inside the group. They're all easy going; I'm the one who tends to get uptight. They let me blow up then cool down.' With a band there is 'no more standing alone with your thoughts on draughty railway stations. In the group there's always someone to talk to or at – even if they are asleep.'

The following month Tony Wilson spoke to Sandy, also for *Melody Maker*. Explaining her move to Fairport she says: 'I wanted to do something more with my voice. Although I can play guitar adequately I was feeling limited by it, it was a kind of stagnation. I was developing but the guitar was restricting. Once you know what can be done with six people and like the result, the simplicity and naivety of one voice and guitar is rather insipid.'

John Renbourn remembers just how excited Sandy was and how much she blossomed in Fairport. 'Her phrasing totally loosened up. There was a big change from the kind of level she was playing with Alex Campbell and Johnny Silvo to having the chance to play with Richard Thompson and those guys and sound so wonderful. The quality of her voice and the absolute volume she could project was out of this world. It stuns other great singers.'

'When she joined Fairport she was flying,' agrees Gina Glaser, 'because this was what she wanted to do – her folk music in a contemporary band. She loved it. I think she knew immediately it was what she really wanted to do but without realising it till it happened. Whether it was her songs, Richard's songs, the contemporary covers they did or traditional material, Fairport never lost the respect for the music that was at the core of what they were doing. It's what made them the best of those English folk-rock groups.'

Fairport Convention played some memorable gigs that summer after Sandy joined, including Hyde Park on 24 August, the Isle of Wight Festival on 31 August and the Hampstead Heath Free Festival at Parliament Hill on 6 September with the group they were so often compared to, Jefferson Airplane. 'Sandy was late,' remembers Iain Matthews. 'I always sang with my eyes shut and as we cruised into the solo of a particularly inspired vocalisation of "Reno, Nevada" there was a tremendous burst of applause and I remember thinking, "Yeah, I was pretty good there, wasn't I?" only to open my eyes and glance left to see Sandy, guitar in hand, waving a cheeky "Am I forgiven?" and "Hello" to her adoring fans. That's who she was, and you loved her for it.'

By the time Fairport closed the Festival of Contemporary Song

on 28 September at the Royal Festival Hall, they had all but finished recording their second album, which they began at Sound
Techniques on 3 July and wrapped up on 11 October with the
recording of 'She Moves through the Fair'. The album, *What
We Did on Our Holidays*, was planned for release in November
1968 but was delayed because of the sleeve and worries about the
Christmas market. Interviewed for the November issue of *Beat
Instrumental*, Thompson gives an insightful view as to how the
group was already changing since Sandy had joined. 'We think of
ourselves as a folk-based band. This is even more pronounced now
that Sandy Denny is with us – she was singing pure folk for a long
time on her own, before she joined the Strawbs, and then us. She
really knows what the folk tradition is all about, and the group as
a whole are drawing from the English roots. The fact that we are
electric doesn't make any difference.'

Sandy had fitted into Fairport with remarkable ease, although
Matthews may have been less enthusiastic than the others. 'Sandy
joining was more a sense of relief for me than excitement,' he says.
'I was nowhere near ready to be the sole vocal presence. Sandy gave
off a mixed vibe. She could be quite brassy and loud and yet insecure
and hesitant. She had that songwriter insistence about her material
and Richard seemed to be the one she turned to for approval.'

'Sandy sang with us like she'd been singing with bands all her
life,' says Hutchings. 'We didn't find out till later that she'd sung
with the Strawbs, and that would have helped, but basically she
took to it like a duck to water. What certainly made the transition into Fairport easier was that she already performed songs
by American singer-songwriters, so there was a certain common
ground as well as the awareness we had about British folk music,
even if we hadn't really tapped into that yet.'

Iain Matthews again offers a more sceptical analysis: 'We didn't work closely on vocal arrangements. You have to understand – and don't confuse this with sour grapes – there was an unspoken pecking order within the band and I was down there at the bottom. I wasn't an assertive character. I looked, I listened and I learnt as much as I could. Before Sandy joined, most songs were learnt in a suitable key for soloing on. After she became part of it, keys on her songs were determined by her.

'Sandy arriving was a leap of faith on their part and a whole new direction for the players to chew on. Of course they wrapped themselves around her music. It was new and exciting. She had a different vocal sound to Judy, she projected more. So her role as a lead singer became more assertive. The band took to her approach and her songs like fish to water and it was all a new and confusing experience for me.'

The non-singing musicians in the band felt less threatened. 'She changed the dynamic in the group,' says Simon Nicol. 'She really shook things up and everybody's tastes and palettes changed a little, whereas Ian had just fitted into the group dynamic and relieved the rest of us from having to sing up front. There was an instant melding of the two core repertoires. We had to create middle ground but our repertoire was changing weekly anyway. We were all familiar with the language of folk music idiomatically, which is what she was bringing to the table. At the same time she was taking that same step towards what we were doing. She particularly loved standing in front of a rhythm section and having that force behind her, but above all she worshipped Richard. She really felt at home with Fairport from the get-go.'

Despite Joe Boyd's initial fears, Sandy also fitted in socially with the band. 'We were a pretty easy-going group,' says Hutchings, 'considerate, well-brought-up boys. We invited her in and were pretty sympathetic and she hardly corrupted us at all.

'I made her welcome as the oldest member of the group and, to a certain extent, leader in those situations, and took her under my wing and spent a lot of time chatting with her. She always used to sit next to me in the van, and would very often fall asleep with her head on my shoulder. Her relationship to me was different to the others because I was older and a father figure.'

For her part, Sandy never thought of herself as the star or even projected a role as the lead singer out front. She often stood to one side of the stage; she merged into the group, happy to be an equal part of Fairport Convention. 'She was quite loud and blustery on a personal level,' says Abbott, 'but the one impression I always had of Sandy was that there was always a little girl struggling to get out. She wasn't like the north London girls we knew as friends. She had been around but there wasn't too much hanky-panky going on within the Fairport ranks at the time. I think it was significant that she wasn't in a relationship with any of them and as a result she shared the chumminess that she wouldn't have got elsewhere.

'Socially, Ian never fitted in as well with their London middle-class ethic. When Sandy came in she did; she liked to have a laugh and humour was always a very strong element of Fairport, always lots of wordplay, good jokes. Sandy responded to that whereas Ian tended to take himself off away from it a bit.'

Joe Boyd felt Sandy's inclusion fostered a new-found confidence in them all. 'There was never any time I can remember where I thought they weren't holding their own with Sandy. In fact, I'd say it was almost the opposite. She was the one who was in awe because they gave her something that she never had before – a ready-made group of male chums she wasn't sleeping with – and I think she liked that.'

'We worked well together but we all had independent lives,' says Nicol. 'She had a much more active social life outside of the group with her old gang of friends and folkies. We were buttoned-up middle-class grammar-school boys. She had a much wider and more interesting circle of friends. It was never a question of her ringing any of us up and saying, "Why don't we go out for a meal?"'

Before joining Fairport, Sandy had moved out of the family home in Wimbledon and she and Winnie Whittaker had found a furnished top-floor flat in Stanhope Mews, with private gardens, off Gloucester Road. Their flatmate there was Kate Partridge, whom Sandy had met at Les Cousins, and they were renting the flat from Kate's father, the Canadian artist and sculptor David Partridge.

'We didn't know and were too polite to ask about her life as a single woman living the other side of town from us,' says Hutchings. 'Southwest London might as well have been Leeds to us north London boys. Trevor Lucas wasn't around at the beginning. Trevor sings back-up on *Unhalfbricking* and one or two things we did on the radio, but we weren't aware of him being part of Sandy's life until 1969.

'She never lost that need to have a protective music group around her, and maybe we started her out on that trail when she joined Fairport because we did look after her. And they were happy times. I feel privileged to have been there at the start of that realisation of her creativity. Importantly, we gave her Richard, not only as a guitarist but also as a benchmark to write against. It pushed her on further and Richard responded in the same way.'

'She didn't want to put a foot wrong,' says Boyd, 'particularly with Richard, she had such high regard for him she wasn't going to rock the boat. She was still herself but her social persona, the thing that had worried me before, was that she was very aggressive, very dismissive of people, very sardonic and generally loud, and they were the opposite, mild-mannered, well-behaved boys from Muswell Hill. She quietened down and behaved in a more serious way about her music and, for a while, she was more secure in herself.'

That friendship and camaraderie would remain important to Sandy. Throughout her solo career during the 1970s she wrestled with the dilemma of whether she should be a solo artist or part of a group but, either way, she invariably surrounded herself with the same pool of musicians whom she felt comfortable with and whom she could trust.

By the time Fairport came to record with Sandy in the group Boyd had forged a deal with Island Records for his Witchseason production company. Island already had a strong reputation, often for left-field signings who later grew in importance: Traffic, Free, Spooky Tooth, John Martyn and Jethro Tull were already on the roster when *What We Did on Our Holidays* was released in January 1969. 'The step up we made from the first album is transparent,' says Hutchings. 'Even though it's still very diverse in its influences, it has uniformity. Unlike our debut, it hangs together as an album.' Island had nothing musically to compare to Fairport.

'Witchseason artists were part of the underground in the same way as Traffic or Spooky Tooth,' says Chris Blackwell. 'I had always seen Fairport as a folk-rock band right from when I first heard them, although their musical identity became clear when *Liege & Lief* came out. Since then Witchseason has become synonymous with British folk rock, but that was a very fertile period in

British music. People were experimenting with all kinds of music. Traditional boundaries or categories didn't count for anything.'

Chris Blackwell had immediately seen something in Joe Boyd's judgement. 'I was lucky enough to work with a number of people with great taste,' says Blackwell. 'Joe Boyd was certainly one of them and Witchseason was absolutely Joe's label, it reflected his taste, his everything. All I did was put the records out and support them in every way possible. Witchseason didn't reflect my taste necessarily. I'm more of a groove man.'

Blackwell was, however, very taken with Sandy Denny and says, like everybody, it was her voice that drew you in. 'We none of us found out till later that she was such a great songwriter,' says Blackwell, 'but when she performed you couldn't take your eyes off her. She was fun, and though she had the voice of an angel she could be as raunchy as the best of them. I liked her a lot. She was shy but a very funny person and she had a wicked sense of humour.'

On paper, as with Fairport's first album, the songwriting is shared throughout *What We Did on Our Holidays*; only drummer Martin Lamble fails to get a credit. Sandy and Richard Thompson contribute a song apiece that each would continue to be irrevocably associated with: Thompson's 'Meet on the Ledge', which has since become Fairport's anthem, and Sandy's 'Fotheringay', which opens the album. The two-year-old song is framed perfectly. It's a simple statement in itself, unlike anything from Fairport's first album, and the transformation in Sandy is remarkable. Barely a year since recording with the Strawbs, her voice is no longer high-pitched, there is no trace of vibrato, her confidence is brimming and her breathing is effortless. The album was also an exploratory step towards the British folk rock Fairport later became synonymous with but it's still American singer-songwriters whose music takes precedence, including Sandy's empathetic reading of Dylan's 'I'll Keep It with Mine' and Joni Mitchell's 'Eastern Rain', which was learnt from a demo that came via Joe Boyd. It was a song Mitchell never released.

'There were very few songs Sandy wrote during her time with Fairport,' says Ashley Hutchings. Sandy once said that the way Hutchings encouraged everybody to write was almost like setting homework after school. 'She wasn't good at coming forward with anything she had written. I've found in life that insecurity and massive belief in one's abilities very often go hand in hand – it's very strange but she had that in spades. She knew she was good but she was also incredibly insecure. "Fotheringay" sets up the album so well; it's such an indication of how far we had come as a group and what a great singer she had become. Just compare her singing to any earlier recordings.'

The album's two traditional arrangements also bear Sandy's hallmark as much as 'Fotheringay'. 'She Moves through the Fair' was based on the melody of a traditional Irish air, its lyric written by the Irish poet Padraic Colum. It was a particular favourite of the Irish traditional singer Margaret Barry and of Anne Briggs and had long been in Sandy's solo set. Richard Thompson describes the process of assimilating the folk songs Sandy brought to the band as 'wrapping themselves around her arrangements' from her folk club days.

The other traditional song on the album was already familiar to Hutchings: 'I already knew "Nottamun Town". Shirley Collins recorded it with Davy Graham on *Folk Roots, New Routes*, and I knew Jean Ritchie's version [on her Elektra debut album from 1953]. They were exciting, exciting times, so much good music, and we took it all in.'

If *Liege & Lief* gets all the plaudits, *What We Did on Our Holidays* was more than a mere stepping stone. 'Before Sandy joined Fairport Convention, how many other bands or the kids who bought pop records were the slightest bit interested in folk music?' asks Shelagh McDonald, who had been snapped up by Sandy's former agent Sandy Glennon after Sandy joined Fairport. 'Folk still had that tag to it that it was so uncool. *Liege & Lief* is held up as the album that changed that, but Sandy singing "She Moves through the Fair" or "Nottamun Town" was the start of making it cool to like folk, or at the very least check it out. I noticed folk clubs drawing in new people because they heard what Fairport was doing even then.'

Sandy didn't just encourage Fairport to meet her halfway on traditional material; she was the catalyst for the group raising their game on every level. 'What we were able to do when Sandy joined,' says Hutchings, 'because of the dramatic quality, the expressiveness of Sandy's voice, was to be able to carry off really dramatic songs like Leonard Cohen's "Suzanne", which was remarkable in our particular arrangement.'

Richard Thompson recalls a particular ploy by engineer John Wood to capture that broad range in her voice. 'She could have a huge dynamic range as a singer, a very good quiet tone and a very good loud tone, not all singers have that, and to the frustration of John Wood in the studio it was quite hard to mic her. She didn't have the technique of leaning in or moving back from the microphone, so he used two mics on her, a close mic and a mic further away, and would switch between the two.'

'Although we never recorded it other than for a radio session,' says Nicol, '"Suzanne" is the song a lot of people remember from that time after Sandy joined and many regard it as the pinnacle of her and Ian Matthews singing together. It still sounds so impassioned – having the two voices sing the song and that swelling rhythmic arrangement, Richard with a tremolo pedal which produced that surging, stuttering effect. It's lovely. The voices of Ian and Sandy trading off each other was never fully explored on record. Nor should Martin's contribution be overlooked either.' It's one of the standout tracks on the *Heyday* album.* 'Ian was good,' agrees Hutchings, 'that should never be forgotten, and Ian and Sandy singing together was incredibly dynamic.'

Yet Ian Matthews would effectively leave Fairport within three months of the release of *What We Did on Our Holidays* and would be featured on just one song on the group's next album, *Unhalfbricking*. 'It wasn't that we felt we'd explored all those possibilities with Ian and Sandy,' says Hutchings, 'but we were starting to get more folky. We'd done "Nottamun Town" and "She Moves through the Fair" and were starting to see new possibilities. It was quite obvious to us that Judy had to leave for us to go further; it was quite obvious to me – if it wasn't to the others (though I suspect it was) – that in order to move in the direction that we were favouring, certainly once you get to "A Sailor's Life", that Ian would have to leave.

'Ian was pushed, and he remembers that I told him in brutal terms that he was out of the group, which I don't remember; I

---

* Fairport had recorded their first BBC radio session for John Peel's *Top Gear* on 24 November 1967. *Top Gear* was co-presented by Peel and Tommy Vance, the person who first branded Fairport Convention 'the English Jefferson Airplane'. Peel would become a major champion for Fairport and Sandy. Fairport were the first group to release an album drawn entirely from their radio sessions for Peel. Initially only available on cassette, it was called *Heyday* and covered their sessions of 1968–9, including many songs that were never recorded for their official albums.

must have expunged that from my memory. And he may have felt himself that it was time to move on. It was nothing to do with his quality. Ian has always been a good singer.'

Matthews has given mixed messages as to whether he jumped or was pushed out of Fairport. 'Leaving had never entered my mind at that point,' he told me in 2012. 'I was trying to come up with a way to be more involved in the process. Being asked to leave came completely out of the blue.' Yet in interviews nearer to the time – in 1976, for example – he said that 'I wanted to leave but not as much as they wanted me to leave.'

Either way, Matthews was finding that Sandy had brought something into the band that he was wholly unfamiliar with, and he was a little intimidated by her. The crunch song for him was 'A Sailor's Life'. 'The first time we did "A Sailor's Life" on stage, I remember they worked it up in the dressing room,' he told Patrick Humphries in 1996, 'and I had never worked up a song in the dressing room in my life, it had always been done at rehearsal and it didn't appeal to me at all. I think it became increasingly clear that there was really no place for me in a band playing that type of music.'

Sandy would always sing traditional songs in the van and during downtime at gigs, and that's how 'A Sailor's Life' came to the band's attention. Speaking about the track in 1977, she explained: 'I'd been singing "A Sailor's Life" in the clubs for years. It was one of the first real folk songs I learned. I think I probably got it from Bert Lloyd's *Penguin Book of English Folk Songs*. Carthy had recorded it and there are a lot of variants.'

Having rehearsed it that afternoon in the dressing room where Matthews felt so ill at ease, they first played 'A Sailor's Life' at Southampton's Adam and Eve Club on 26 February 1969. When it was recorded a few weeks later, with virtuoso folk violinist Dave Swarbrick augmenting the group for the session, Ian Matthews was absent. Once again it was *Melody Maker*'s 'Raver' column that broke the news, on 29 March: Ian Matthews had left Fairport and Sandy would carry on as the main singer.*

For many Fairport fans, the line-up with Sandy and Ian Matthews was when the group came of age, became more than just a thrilling West Coast-sounding covers band, and many regret that the potential of their two voices together was never fully explored. 'I don't think that was the question really,' says Matthews. 'It was more about direction, and I was offering little of that. Fairport was always a band evolving daily. I don't think you can point to any specific recording. We were all so young, searching for direction. Anything and everything was considered . . . and daily. *Heyday* gives an indication of the process, but by no means does it define anything.'

When the group assembled at Sound Techniques on 11 January 1969 – just as *What We Did on Our Holidays* was being released – it was to record a Dylan song dating back to 1963 which had yet to appear on any of his albums. 'Percy's Song' turned out to be Ian

* Even after he had left the group Matthews continued to share a flat in Brent with Richard Thompson and Simon Nicol. Along with Ashley Hutchings, they all played on his *Matthews' Southern Comfort* album, which was recorded later that year but not released until January 1970. Matthews decided at the last minute not to release his immediate first post-Fairport record as a solo album, adopting the name Matthews Southern Comfort. The group would have a surprise number one hit with 'Woodstock' in September 1970. 'Apart from having her sing and play on my record [*If You See thru My Eyes* (1971)], I hardly saw Sandy after the split,' says Matthews. 'I wasn't much of a communicator in those days. I was the quiet, shy, northern lad.'

Matthews's final recording with the group. His and Sandy's voices combine grippingly and distinctively, the performance galvanised by their layered harmonies; the live version on *Heyday*, recorded soon after Matthews left, is far less powerful. Yet the way the album took shape it's hard to see where Matthews could have made any meaningful contribution. He certainly wasn't writing songs at this time. When sessions for *Unhalfbricking* continued during March and into April, Thompson, Nicol and Hutchings had to step up to the plate again to cover backing vocals; each of them even tackles a verse, along with guest Marc Ellington, on the boisterous *Basement Tapes* singalong 'Million Dollar Bash'.

'I was a huge Fairport fan,' says Al Stewart, 'and they just got better after Sandy joined. "Percy's Song" was one where Ian and Sandy's voices went so well together that it was absolutely compelling when they performed it live. Sandy always had the ability to transform even the most depressing songs and hold your attention. The way she and Ian combined to sing "Percy's Song" was fascinating. It was a cappella to begin with and then the band would come in and build it to a real crescendo. Fairport made something absorbing out of what was a lengthy, obscure Dylan song, just as later on they were able to engage audiences in multiversed traditional folk songs.'

Intriguingly, given the reasons for his departure, Matthews's parting shot with the group found them adopting a template that was similar to the way in which Fairport would approach a number of the epic traditional ballads on *Liege & Lief*. To complete the irony, his and Sandy's harmonies most closely resemble those of radical traditional folk groups such as the Watersons or the Young Tradition rather than their usual more American folk/country rock approach. 'I have regrets about leaving,' said Matthews a few years after departing, 'but at the same time I'm glad I did, because the next two albums were just amazing albums that I could never have taken part in. I could have taken part in some of *Unhalfbricking*, but *Liege & Lief* was just way beyond what I was into.'

'Sandy and Ian got along fine,' says Joe Boyd, 'but Ian was always to a certain degree the odd man out. He was from a working-class background and I think that was a barrier, whereas her middle-class upbringing helped Sandy bond with the group. *Unhalfbricking* really benefited from Sandy now being fully integrated, and her stimulating a different kind of record. She was very much part of the process in creating the ideas behind that record. "A Sailor's Life" of course originated with her and it was her idea to do Dylan's "If You Gotta Go, Go Now" in French as "Si tu dois partir". Someone suggested doing the song in a Cajun style and she capped it by saying, "Let's do it in French."

'The two tracks on *Unhalfbricking* that I saw as pointing to the future were "A Sailor's Life" and "Autopsy", a no less staggering piece of work, the culmination of Sandy's song and Richard's 5/8 rhythm feel. I was very excited about what this said about the development of the group as songwriters and the music generally.'

'Autopsy' is one of Sandy's more unusual songs, which Neil Denny said was written 'about a girl that's always telling her troubles'. It was also autobiographical; the often tearful Sandy was known to 'spend all [her] time crying'. The change of tempo from her original demo into a predominantly 5/8 time signature, which Thompson had suggested, reflected a more collaborative process than the group's usual 'fleshing out' of Sandy's songs.

'She didn't have songs we were turning down,' says Thompson. 'She wasn't writing that much during Fairport, I wasn't writing that much, and at first it was mostly co-writes within the group because we wanted to make that transition away from covers. Ashley encouraged us all to write songs. I tended to reject more songs than I actually completed or submitted to the group and Sandy presented even less, but you have two of Sandy's best early songs, "Who Knows Where the Time Goes?" and "Autopsy".'

Unhalfbricking was completed on 9 April, when 'Who Knows Where the Time Goes?' was attempted for the second day running and was eventually nailed in one take. Hutchings remembers this because he says he fluffed the bass line at one point but the rest of the performance was so perfect he had to let it go. It was also Martin Lamble's last recording with Fairport Convention.

Sandy's first recorded performance of 'Who Knows Where the Time Goes?' with Fairport was at a BBC session on 4 February 1969. By then Judy Collins had made it the title track of her latest album, released in November 1968. It was also the B-side of Collins's first Billboard Top Ten hit, 'Both Sides Now' (from *Wildflowers*). 'Who Knows Where the Time Goes?' spent nine weeks in the American Top Forty, peaking at number eight.* Kingsley Abbott remembers Sandy's delight when she calculated she would make around £10,000 in royalties. 'I don't have any way to say why it's such a great song,' says Judy Collins. 'That's a secret that can never be revealed by me or anybody else. It's a mystical question. Sandy's lyrics had overtones of that Celtic folk tradition, the clarity and the beauty of the story. She transcended folk in the way she sang and in the songs that she wrote.'

Richard Thompson says Sandy only played him 'Who Knows

* In the UK, where 'Both Sides Now' was also a hit for Judy Collins at the beginning of 1969, the B-side was switched to Leonard Cohen's 'Hey That's No Way to Say Goodbye'.

Where the Time Goes?' because he asked her about it, having heard that Judy Collins had recorded one of her songs. It was Thompson who suggested Sandy change the opening line from 'Across the purple sky', which is how it appears on the Strawbs' version, to 'Across the evening sky'. He once said that he thought it would avoid any association with Jimi Hendrix's hit 'Purple Haze'. Interestingly, in her recording, Judy Collins sings 'morning sky', while in Sandy's first draft in one of her notebooks, where the song is titled 'The Ballad of Time', the first line is 'Across the distant sky'.

'You had to prise her songs out of her,' says Simon Nicol. 'Sandy was always reticent about us hearing them, but I don't know why she held that one back – perhaps because she'd already recorded it with the Strawbs? It was certainly one of many highlights on *Unhalfbricking*. That was a strong album, and another step up for the group. It has Sandy's greatest song, or best loved song, and "Autopsy" is another fascinating song. It also has Richard's "Genesis Hall". Both those songs show what they were capable of.'

John Wood considers *Unhalfbricking* to be his favourite record of Sandy's because, for him, it's the best she ever sang. '*What We Did on Our Holidays* wasn't cohesive,' he said; 'it always struck me that each person had their own compartment, there wasn't the unity that there was on *Unhalfbricking*.' Wood also singles out 'A Sailor's Life' as truly remarkable: 'Richard and Sandy came in and said, "We really think we can only do this once." They'd already got Dave Swarbrick in to play on it. It was done in the old Olympic 1, a big room. We put Sandy in a vocal booth (she had an awful cold that day too) and everybody else in a big semicircle. When you want to cut that sort of track, it's not easy for people to work if it's all sectioned off, so it was very open and that was it, one take, done. No overdubs.'

'I wasn't involved in the rock arrangement at all,' said Sandy. 'It was a bit like – here I am with my old ballad and there's the band I joined and what they have done with it. At least, on stage. On record, of course, it's "new, improved, with added Swarbrick".'

Sandy had met Dave Swarbrick during her folk days – Swarbrick once said they were introduced by John Martyn – and they knew each other socially. By 1967 Swarbrick's reputation was already second to none. He had joined the Ian Campbell Folk Group in 1961 and embarked on a prolific career with them between 1963 and 1966, recording seven albums with the group. He also played on recordings by A. L. Lloyd, Ewan MacColl and Peggy Seeger, and in 1965 had begun a famous and fruitful association with Martin Carthy, playing on Carthy's first two albums. The two of them mostly toured as a duo, until Swarbrick was recruited by Fairport in 1969, and in between Swarbrick and Carthy recorded two of the most influential and celebrated albums in folk music, *Byker Hill* in 1967 and *Prince Heathen* in 1969.*

'It was Joe [Boyd] who called me,' says Swarbrick. 'We already knew each other from my days in the Ian Campbell Folk Group. Joe was road-managing the Reverend Gary Davis when we met. The first time I met the others was at the *Unhalfbricking* session.' Boyd had also produced Swarbrick's *Rags, Reels and Airs* with Carthy and Diz Disley. 'I see Joe as an enabler,' says Swarbrick.

---

* Recorded immediately before Dave Swarbrick joined Fairport and released by Fontana in 1970, *Prince Heathen* is arguably Swarbrick and Martin Carthy's finest work together. It was described by Simon Nicol as an acoustic version of *Liege & Lief*, 'like listening to the same thing but without the bass and drums'. 'Sometimes I think Martin invented folk music,' says Swarbrick; 'he for sure invented a method of accompanying song, as well as a guitar tuning to enable him to do it. Long life to the man, he is the best.'

'He has a very laid-back way of getting what he wants; he is cool, doesn't waste time in a studio and does a good job. All the times I spent with Joe in a studio he worked in a kind of partnership with John Wood. It was a great partnership too. He also had a special relationship with Fairport, it seems to me, and was trusted.'

When they recorded 'A Sailor's Life', Swarbrick once quipped, he was just told to 'come in when the singing stops'. He found Sandy's singing a revelation; she had moved up several gears from when he had heard her in folk clubs. Swarbrick was also mightily impressed by the group. 'Sandy had a great band to soar over,' he says, 'and a great bunch of musicians who were sympathetic. Richard and Sandy worked closely together. Richard was awesome, of course; that should be his middle name. But the band was cohesive and so special, the chemistry worked and the line-up was sensational. Richard always knew how to set her off; they had a lovely sharing relationship musically. She must have been very excited; in fact, being excited and happy back then seemed to be her default setting.'

Martin Carthy agrees with his long-term partner. 'Sandy didn't do anything with her voice till she met up with people who put her through her paces. You play with someone like Richard and, excuse the expression, it's shit or bust.

'There was a hooligan busting to get out in Sandy, and Fairport released that. I think they were sometimes fairly surprised at the size of the hooligan,' he continues, laughing wildly. 'And there was this musical hooligan trying to get out of Fairport too, and she helped that along. They were terribly English and reticent and had an attitude that "This is serious music but we don't want to upset anybody." Once Sandy joined they were able to stomp on the stage and it was "This is ours, take it or leave it." You add

Swarb to that mix and if they had any reticence left about what they were doing and upsetting the traditionalists, he would have made them believe in it. Swarb's very much a take-it-or-leave-it person. He has a supreme confidence in whatever he does.'

Martin Carthy chuckles when he recalls Swarbrick first being asked to do the session with Fairport. 'He went off grumbling,' says Carthy, 'and the next day, very apologetically, he said, "Don't take this the wrong way but I just met the guitarist I want to play with from now on." He had been blown away by Richard's playing but also by the attitude of the rest of the band, including Sandy, who neither of us had ever worked with. It was like they had no fear, which was what he found so appealing. Not everybody in the folk world took to it but I thought it was remarkable, mind-boggling.'

That one day's session made just as much of an impression on Fairport and on Joe Boyd, but whether they immediately discussed the idea of asking Dave Swarbrick to join the group, nobody can say. They had an album to add finishing touches to and dates lined up, including a return to Mothers Club in Birmingham for the second time that year. Everything changed for Sandy and Fairport Convention that night and any question of Dave Swarbrick joining them was deferred for several months.

6 : The Wild Colonial Boy
1943–1969

When Trevor first came over he connected with Bert Lloyd, who was very excited to meet a singer like Trevor. He was an Aussie who could sing the pants off those bush ranger songs and he had a wonderful presence. He was a good musician, a great singer. The *Overlander* album has some good stuff on it. Very few people know Trevor made that record.

MARTIN CARTHY

Trevor Lucas is big, brash and Australian. He joined pop to see the world. Son of a gold miner and building contractor, he toured everywhere bringing hastily mugged up Australian folk music to the people. The artificiality and triviality of folk accelerated his reconciliation with pop. The 'new freedom' of Eclection takes the form of a series of simple, life-enhancing songs which have been thrown together to make a commercial record.

TONY PALMER, *Observer*, August 1968

Melbourne's Jazz and Folk Centre

FRANK TRAYNORS

287 Exhibition Street, Melbourne

Telephone 32-2374

Every night (Mondays excepted) at 8.15 p.m.

Folk Singing and Coffee with

BRIAN MOONEY	MARTIN WYNDHAM-READ
GLEN TOMASETTI	MARGARET SMITH
DAVID LUMSDEN	DENNIS GIBBONS
LENORE SOMERSET	TREVOR LUCAS
GARY KINANE	SUSAN LEE ARCHER
GAY HARTLEY	GRAHAM SQUANCE

Rent Party Jazz every Saturday midnight to 2.00 a.m.

Tuition in jazz and folk music is available. Instruments are for sale. Upstairs we have our own specialist jazz and folk record shop. Bands, musicians and folk singers are available for all occasions.

TELEPHONE: 32 2374

Melbourne's leading jazz and folk club, which opened in late 1963

Trevor George Lucas was born on Christmas Day 1943 in Melbourne, although he would usually tell people he was born in Wagga Wagga because it sounded better than Richmond, then a poor inner suburb of Melbourne. Trevor liked to kid people his father, Frank, was a gold miner but he actually started out as a builder. By the time Trevor and his elder sister Marion were in their teens, Frank Lucas had prospered and he ran an upmarket painting and decorating business. Trevor's mother, Ada, was a skilled tailor and before she had children had dressed models for couture houses; she provided the cultural push in Trevor and Marion's life.

'Frank was a real character,' says Nigel Osborne, Marion's partner in London during the 1970s, 'that's where Trevor's hail-fellow-well-met attitude came from. Frank was a very bluff character and a true self-made man. He worked hard, made a lot of money, so they were pretty comfortable by the sixties and moved to Camberwell, a better part of town. Frank was always the guy down at the bowling club, smartly turned out, as Trevor always was; he played tennis and could tell a good story. He would drink neat gin, pull a face, and say that "it gets you there more quickly" – like Trevor, who could drink and drink but never fall over.' It was a background about as far from posh leafy Wimbledon as you could get.

'Trevor was pretty much the classic sporty Australian in some respects,' says Elizabeth Hurtt, who first met Trevor and Sandy in 1972 in Chipstead Street, when she was going out with Dave Swarbrick. Elizabeth and Trevor would marry in 1979. 'He was a good tennis player who was offered state coaching, but the family couldn't afford it at the time. He was the Victorian under-fifteen breaststroke champion, and reached state level at water polo as a goalie. He was an all-round lad but at school he was considered stupid because he was dyslexic, something that wasn't recognised, of course. Some time in his primary school days they trialled a new IQ test and he aced the whole school. Like a lot of dyslexic people he was actually very clever, very smart, but putting words and letters down wasn't his forte and that immediately marked him down as dumb.

'He didn't like to be alone,' continues Hurtt; 'he didn't like to sleep alone, which stems back to him having peritonitis as a three-year-old. He was in hospital for three months, during which time his parents were only allowed to visit once every two weeks, for one hour, and see him from behind a glass screen. So he learnt to charm the nurses and extended that in later life to charming girls into bed. That illness as a child had a big impact on his life, especially if you combine that with his dyslexia – dyslexics learn to think on their feet, and to listen well. They can be very articulate despite not being able to read.'

Hurtt describes Trevor as an incredibly engaging person: 'He was Mr Charm. Our son Clancy comes out of the same mould; his fifth-grade school report read, "Clancy needs to learn that a charming smile will not get him out of trouble every time." And you could probably have written that about Trevor.'

When he was twelve, Trevor learnt to play the guitar because of his dyslexia; the family doctor suggested that his mother should get him 'something to do with his hands'. After leaving school he did an apprenticeship as a carpenter in Melbourne but was soon more enthusiastically pursuing his new passion for folk music. Once he discovered he could earn more in one night at Tom Lazar's Little Reata coffee bar than he could in a week as a carpenter, that was the end of his career in carpentry.

'Trevor had started playing American folk and blues as a teenager,' says Martyn Wyndham-Read, the Sussex-born singer and guitarist who is now a renowned exponent of and authority on Aussie 'bush folk'.* 'Trevor was one of the first people to introduce the music of people like Bob Dylan and Leadbelly to Melbourne.' Trevor often played and toured with Wyndham-Read and with Brian Mooney, Garry Kinnane, Glen Tomasetti and others who were the core names of the Melbourne folk boom and on the coffee bar circuit stretching to Sydney. In Melbourne, they would play at the Emerald Hill Theatre and its leading folk and jazz club, Traynor's, where Trevor had a residency.

'Trevor saw the light and abandoned his trade to become a musician, and into the folk world he went,' says Wyndham-Read. 'Trevor was one of the first people to use a twelve-string guitar in Australia; he impressed everyone with his playing of Leadbelly and Big Bill Broonzy songs. Folk music was very popular in those days, with loads of venues around Melbourne, Sydney, Adelaide and places in between and all around the country.'

* Martyn Wyndham-Read went from his grandfather's small farm in Sussex to work as a hand on a sheep station at Emu Springs in South Australia in 1960. 'There was no idea of it being a folk revival or anything like that, they weren't really known as "folk songs", just songs that people sang. First time I heard them being sung by the other station hands my jaw dropped, I thought they were wonderful.' He recorded regularly in Australia before returning to the UK in 1967; his UK debut for Bill Leader's Trailer label in 1970 was *Ned Kelly and That Gang*.

Trevor had already had a taste of the hard-drinking, sexually liberated bohemian lifestyle when, as a fifteen-year-old, he tagged along with his elder sister Marion to some of the Sydney Push gatherings around 1958. The Push adopted a rebellious, anti-intellectual/anti-elitist stance, even though most of its members were writers, filmmakers, artists and musicians. By the late fifties it had shifted from its Sydney University origins to gather in cafes and pubs in downtown Sydney. Germaine Greer once disdainfully commented that the Push embraced 'folk singing' but not music. Greer was one of the renowned London-bound members of the Sydney Push who made a significant impact in sixties Britain, along with Clive James, Barry Humphries and art critic Robert Hughes. Poet Richard Appleton was another of its driving forces and, after Marion became pregnant at seventeen, they were briefly married.*

Visually, Trevor stood out too with his flaming red hair and beard and his tall, wiry frame towering over most other perform-ers. 'He had a deep, rich, pleasant voice,' says Garry Kinnane, 'which he adapted well to blues, work songs, shanties and bush ballads, shifting his accent around from "black" American to "Outback Oz" without ever sounding like anybody but himself.

---

* Sydney-born Appleton met Marion when he was at college in Mel-bourne; he became editor-in-chief of the *Australian Encyclopedia* in 1977, and also compiled the *Cambridge Dictionary of Australian Places*. Nigel Osborne says: 'Marion had a lot of mutual friends in that London Australian fraternity. Every so often around twenty people, mostly expats and including Trevor and Sandy sometimes, would go off to restaurants like Khan's in Bayswater, where everyone would get completely smashed. Marion was well connected; she knew people like *Newsweek* foreign editor Tony Clifton, who was also from Melbourne, John Pilger, Don McCullin, Germaine Greer, Clive James and Barry Humphries. Sandy and Germaine were usually at each other by the end of the night.'

His guitar playing was better than just about every other singer's in Melbourne – a knowledgeable left hand for blues, and some good right-hand picking which he eventually did using metal finger-picks – probably the first in Melbourne to do so. He also had a fierce, driving, flat-picking style when playing twelve-string guitar, which he used on songs like "Walk Right In", "Black Girl" and "Corinna" after the manner of Leadbelly.'

Trevor's recording career started in 1963, when he appeared on the EP *The Folk Attic Presents** for the local Folksong label; he featured on two tracks, 'Old Time Religion' and 'Dem Bones Gwine to Rise Again'. Trevor can be heard on *Australian Folk Festival*, a compilation of performers associated with the Four Capitals Folk Song Tour, and his first solo album soon followed in 1964 on the East label. *See That My Grave Is Kept Clean* includes folk blues standards 'Casey Jones' and 'John Henry', Dylan's 'Talking World War III Blues' and Garry Kinnane's topical 'The Voyager', written after HMAS *Voyager* sank off the New South Wales coast in 1944, killing almost a hundred men. Trevor's concession to bush folk was represented by 'The Flash Stockman' and 'Bluey Brink'.

Like many, Trevor was struck by Dylan, but his greater passion at the time was for American folk blues. 'That was what Trevor was focusing on, but there was also a very strong Australian folk song movement,' says Wyndham-Read, and in some venues musicians were required to play native folk to get work. 'In Melbourne you had the Victorian Folk Music Club and they did urge us professionals to sing Australian songs. Trevor went along with that up to a point but he preferred Leadbelly and Broonzy. Then before

* Trevor would revive the Folk Attic name in the 1980s as the label for various Fairport and Sandy Denny-related rarities, *The Attic Track Tapes*.

he left for England Trevor came to me and asked if I'd teach him a few more Australian folk songs.'

'Trevor was smart,' says Hurtt, 'and he took a chance that if he presented Australian folk song in a more serious way when he arrived in England, then he could find a niche for himself. I don't know how much he knew about this before he arrived but he went prepared, although he also spent time at Cecil Sharp House to gen up even more.' It meant he could play at the Singers Club, or anywhere that adhered to Ewan MacColl's policy of only sing-ing songs in your own language and from your particular culture, because he was an Australian singing Australian folk songs.

The Australian music charts in the 1960s were dominated by American and British music, and however much the gov-ernment tried to encourage the native music industry by lim-iting radio airplay of music from elsewhere, local acts were still strongly influenced by overseas trends. Few Australian musicians enjoyed international success, but the Seekers became massively popular in Britain during 1965, becoming the first Australian group to sell over a million records, including the chart-topping hits 'I'll Never Find Another You' and 'The Carnival Is Over'. Trevor knew the Seekers very well; they had formed out of the Escorts in Melbourne in 1963 and they had all played the same clubs. Trevor shared a flat with Bruce Woodley at one point.* He

---

* Bruce Woodley met Paul Simon when both were living in London in 1965 and the two wrote a few songs together, including the million-selling 'Red Rubber Ball' for the Cyrkle in the US. They also wrote 'I Wish You Could Be Here' and 'Cloudy'. The Seekers later recorded all three songs, and 'Cloudy' became an album track on Simon and Garfunkel's 1966 album *Parsley, Sage, Rosemary and Thyme*. It's another indirect connection between Sandy and Trevor Lucas in the mid-sixties.

made contact with them again when he came to London.

'The Seekers were daggy,' says Hurtt, 'so he didn't want to be too associated with them. And Trevor was moving into real folk – rather than pop folk – and dressing the part. He was sporting his Van Dyke beard and polo-neck Arran sweaters.' Trevor was described in the programme notes for a Royal Albert Hall folk package as having 'a face like El Greco, with Biblical looks and a neat beard and untrimmed hair'. 'Biblical' wasn't a word many would use to describe the man, whose characteristic, exaggerated, colourful Australian language shocked his bandmates in Eclection. Once he is recorded as saying, 'I'm so hungry I could eat Jesus Christ off the Cross and lick the nails.'

The term 'cultural cringe' was coined after the Second World War by a Melbourne critic to describe the ingrained feelings of inferiority within Australian literature, theatre, music and the arts in general at the time. 'In the sixties,' says Hurtt, 'the general trend of what young Australians aspired to do before going to college or after completing an apprenticeship was to go to Europe. You did the overseas trip. You went OS.'

The intrepid young Australians usually travelled by boat. Trevor had married Cheryle Marjorie Hickey on 19 December 1964, just before his twenty-first birthday, and the newlyweds left for Europe, with Marion and Garry Kinnane and his wife, on the Greek ship RHMS *Ellinis* on New Year's Day 1965. 'He wanted to go to Europe, and England in particular,' says Hurtt. 'As much as he knew something about the folk scene in London, it was more "Hey, let's do this" rather than a calculated career move. Trevor's attitude was always, "That's a great idea, let's go do it." He could also lie around in bed till midday but generally he was always working on a scheme, an idea.'

The trip was meant to last six weeks, but Trevor and Cheryle disembarked in Piraeus in Greece, where the Kinnanes stayed on while Marion went ahead to London. Trevor and Cheryle hiked, hitched and drove through Yugoslavia before arriving in England early in the spring. Initially they moved into a bedsit in the building where Marion was living, on Talgarth Road in West Kensington. Over the next year Trevor and Cheryle drifted apart and they split up in 1966; she later returned to Australia and they divorced in January 1973.

Starting out at the Hammersmith Folk Centre at the Prince of Wales pub on Dalling Road, and other local folk clubs, Trevor was a good hustler. His first mention in *Melody Maker* is a listing for Saturday 1 May 1965, a Hootenanny at Ballads and Blues on Berwick Street in Soho, as support to popular children's TV host and former skiffler Wally Whyton. A comparison of their engagements at the end of 1966 suggests that Trevor's career was a lot more solid than Sandy's. Their work diaries reveal that he had more regular work, and far more outside of London.

Unlike most folk performers, Trevor was able to switch between the rival factions in London's folk clubs. When Ewan MacColl's Singers Club moved to the John Snow pub in April 1966, Trevor was among the first guests, Karl Dallas commenting that he 'must be one of the few singers who have been able to bridge the biggest gap in the London scene for he was recently booked at Les Cousins'. A few months later, *Melody Maker* reviewed Trevor's set at Les Cousins, where 'his Australian repertoire took a back seat at an all-night session, including outstanding renditions of Leadbelly songs with some good twelve-string work and a duet with Heather Wood of The Young Tradition'. By November 1965, Trevor had been taken on by Roy Guest's leading Folk Directions agency,* and he had appeared on a number of high-profile multi-artist folk concerts and tours.

Soon after his arrival Trevor landed a tour with Odetta, the Alabama-born folk singer and civil rights activist, and leading Canadian folk duo Ian and Sylvia, taking in major UK cities. In 1966 he played an Anglo-American folk concert at the Royal Albert Hall with Ian and Sylvia, Gordon Lightfoot, the Settlers and the Ian Campbell Folk Group, as well as Folk Sound at the Royal Festival Hall, alongside Dominic Behan, Mike Seeger, the Young Tradition and Isla Cameron. He performed what he called his 'professional Australian' repertoire, backed by Dave Swarbrick and the much respected concertina accompanist Alf Edwards, known for his work with A. L. Lloyd and Ewan MacColl.

Trevor's determination to be at the centre of things meant that he even managed to infiltrate Dylan's hotel room in 1966: 'In the film *Don't Look Back*,' says Garry Kinnane, 'documenting Dylan's visit to England in 1966, there is a scene in a crowded room of people attending to the master's fame, who I think is amused at learning of an imitator of his called Donovan. As the camera roams around the room, you will see for a brief moment the face

---

* A one-time folk singer, Turkish-born Roy Guest came to prominence in the 1960s as a promoter with both Harold Davison and Brian Epstein's NEMS enterprises, but is best remembered for his association with folk music, representing or promoting leading folk musicians including Paul Simon, Tom Paxton and Judy Collins. He also managed Al Stewart. Guest promoted a number of major folk tours and concerts and ran the Folk Directions agency from the mid-sixties (originally based in Cecil Sharp House). He had also run the pivotal Howff folk club in Edinburgh in the early sixties, where the likes of Bert Jansch and the Incredible String Band played early on, and would open a London-based Howff on Primrose Hill in the early 1970s.

of a bearded Trevor Lucas, sitting against the wall looking stoned to the nines.'

If Trevor was getting himself in the right places at the right time and marketing himself as a serious folkie when it suited him, a review from a folk festival at Louth Town Hall in north Lincolnshire in 1966, supporting the Spinners and Dominic Behan, gives a sense of the other side of Trevor's stage persona, a forte for dubious outback jokes and showmanship: 'the lanky ginger-whiskered Australian playing a Pete Seeger instrumental while whistling a different tune at the same time'.

'We did the odd club and were often on the same bill,' says Dave Swarbrick. 'I met him very shortly after he came here. He was mostly known then for a native Australian repertoire – "The Drover's Dream", "Rocking the Cradle", things like that – but he made an impression on the scene, he was a striking figure with charisma. He was well received, didn't go short of work and was ambitious to succeed.' The two became firm friends, both with a mischievous, laddish streak.*

Known to enjoy the odd prank at friends' expense, Trevor once turned up unannounced when Swarbrick and Martin Carthy were doing an iconoclastic cabaret-type show at the Prince Hamlet Theatre in Copenhagen. Most uncharacteristically, the two future folk legends appeared wearing skin-tight trousers, each leg a different colour. Carthy was in orange and green, Swarbrick in blue and yellow plus fetching knee-length pixie boots. Trevor had flown over specially to surprise his mates. 'He turned up for

---

* Trevor joined Fairport between 1973 and 1976; Swarbrick describes him as 'a solid rhythm player, a strummer, major, minor and sevenths kind of a player. Dependable as hell, once he was in a groove you could count on him not to waver, the kind of guitarist you would want on a bear shoot!'

the premiere,' says Swarbrick. 'We had to appear at the back of the theatre and play while walking down the aisle to the stage. Poor Martin supported me all the way to the stage; I had been to a family dinner and was the worse for wear. Trevor's loud and inimitable guffaw coming from the front seat nearly sobered me up. We were wearing silly and embarrassing costumes, which delighted him no end.

'We had a lot of fun together,' says Swarbrick. 'One time he bought a hearse for about £30. The undertaker threw in a coffin for another ten bob. We just used to drive it round London. One of our most successful missions was when we drove it up to Cecil Sharp House. We took the coffin out and took it upstairs to the shop, where we put it on the counter and told the poor girl at the desk it was a two-man dulcimer that they had ordered.'

Trevor had plenty of male friends as well as a reputation 'as a bit of a ladies' man', as John Renbourn rather quaintly describes him. 'I used to see him sitting outside the Troubadour,' says Renbourn, 'and he had a lovely Guild twelve-string guitar. He used to play a couple of Eric von Schmidt songs – "Joshua Gone Barbados", "Panama Limited" – and he was really good, a very accomplished twelve-string player. I liked him an awful lot and I used to go round to his house in Hampstead; he was a very decent fellow and we had plenty of adventures together.'

In 1966 Trevor recorded his second album, *Overlander*, with backing by the Alf Edwards Group. A new Watford-based indie folk label, Reality Records started life with a batch of simultaneous releases, including albums by Nadia Cattouse, Steve Benbow and Cy Grant, plus Trevor's 'songs of the Australian bush and its tough wild men – sung by an Australian singer with a difference – red-bearded Trevor Lucas can accompany himself on the guitar with the consistency of a gale-force wind, or the soothing sweetness of a gentle zephyr'.

Overlander is a fine example of Aussie folk, much of which might raise a smile today, but it includes some stirring performances, notably an adapted version of the nineteenth-century ballad 'Banks of the Nile' (later recorded so memorably by Fotheringay). Lucas is at his very best on this; it suits his dark, booming voice. 'Banks of the Nile' had spread to the US and Australia, and in Queensland it became 'Banks of the Condamine', where the hero was no longer a soldier but a horse breaker or a shearer. A. L. Lloyd had first recorded it in the 1950s on a 78 rpm record, coupled with 'Bold Jack Donahue'. Trevor also sings 'Bold Jack Donahue' on *Overlander*, another song later recorded by Fotheringay. *Overlander* included a version of Australia's best-known bush ballad, 'Waltzing Matilda', with a rare alternative tune that Trevor had sourced. Reality even released this as a single.

Trevor's growing standing in the folk community was confirmed when, in 1967, he guested on A. L. Lloyd's album of whaling songs, *Leviathan*, released by Topic. He also appeared (alongside Dave Swarbrick and Isla Cameron) on the soundtrack of the film *Far from the Madding Crowd* that year. Although he was an excellent twelve-string guitarist, arguably all that distinguished Trevor from others on the folk scene was a reputation for singing Aussie folk songs, which was now wearing thin, especially in Swinging Sixties London. He was never going to settle for being a 'professional Australian' and was always going to break out of folk as soon as the opportunity presented itself. That happened in the summer of 1967, when he met up with a disparate group of musicians from all over the world who would, almost by chance, form a group he described as 'a very underground, flower power group, based on a cross between the Jefferson Airplane and the Mamas and the Papas'.

The group was called Eclection, comprising one Brit, two Australians, a Canadian and a Norwegian, who came together in an Australian-run restaurant called Bangers on the corner of Queensway and Moscow Road in Bayswater. Georg Hultgreen, who wrote nine of the twelve songs on the group's sole album, has a colourful background. He was born in Norway, the son of a Russian father of royal blood and a Finnish mother, respected sculptor Johanna Kajanus.* The family moved to Paris just before Hultgreen hit his teens, and then emigrated to Canada, where he learnt English. By 1967 he had made his way circuitously round the world to arrive in London.

'I was playing my twelve-string guitar from table to table in Bangers,' says Kajanus, 'and singing Gordon Lightfoot's "Early Morning Rain" when I was approached by an impossibly tall Canadian guy called Michael Rosen, who was curious as to where I was from, why I was singing Canadian songs. That was the start of Eclection.' It was through Rosen that Trevor became involved; they had recently met when both appeared at the third Cambridge Folk Festival. Trevor then brought Australian singer Kerrilee Male into the group. She was only on stopover from a holiday in Canada when Bruce Woodley introduced them. Kerrilee had been a regular on an Australian music-based TV show called *Dave's Place* (presided over by the Kingston Trio's Dave Guard). She had already released a couple of EPs in Australia and sang with a Sydney trad

---

* After Eclection split up, Hultgreen adopted the name Georg Kajanus; he was a founding member of Sailor in 1974. Kajanus penned the group's UK Top Ten hits 'A Glass of Champagne' and 'Girls, Girls, Girls'.

jazz group, the Ray Price Quartet. 'Trevor used to joke about us not sounding like the Seekers because we had an Australian girl singer,' says drummer Gerry Conway, who was the last to join Eclection. Conway, then only nineteen, had been recommended to Trevor by British blues champion Alexis Korner; he had played in Korner's short-lived group Free at Last in 1967. 'I think secretly the rest of them were quite worried about that too, and I think she did less lead vocals as a result. They all came from a folk background and didn't want us to be compared to the Seekers, who were pretty unhip.'

Eclection was characterised by its use of three different strong singers up front, Male, Hultgreen and Lucas, and rich multi-part harmonies. With three twelve-string guitarists in the group, it was decided that Trevor should switch to bass, which he had never played before; he was reluctant about the change at first.

The group had already decided on the name Eclection, which had been coined by none other than Joni Mitchell. Michael Rosen's girlfriend Marcie was a close friend of Mitchell's – she is immortalised in the song 'Marcie' on *Song to a Seagull*. 'I believe Michael told Joni about the band's far-flung origins,' says Kajanus, 'and Michael said that Joni exclaimed, "What an eclectic bunch of people you are. Why don't you call yourselves Eclection?" Of course, we all knew that this wasn't a real word, but Eclection did seem to reflect the sum total of the band and its influences rather well.'

Having come together during August 1967, Eclection rehearsed at Bangers, landing an unlikely deal with Elektra Records within months. 'Michael had managed to persuade Jac Holzman to come and see us rehearse. Jac liked our sound, which he described as mid-Atlantic folk rock. When he offered us a deal, we were stunned to be on the same label as the Doors and Love and Tim Buckley.' Holzman was impressed by the band's vocal harmonies

ECLECTION

Elektra publicity shot, 1968. Trevor Lucas is in the back row, far right

in particular and the 'slight out-of-world aspect of their lyrics'. Eclection, along with the Incredible String Band, was one of the few notable British acts signed to Elektra in the sixties.

Eclection's album, simply titled *Eclection*, was released in August 1968. It's something of a mixed bag, although it's considered by many to be a pop-folk classic. Ultimately it's too much of a hybrid of psychedelic, muted folk rock and California sunshine pop that never overcomes its influences. 'Nevertheless', the bright and breezy first single taken from the album, was chosen as the launch song for the opening of Harrods' new 'swinging' department 'The Way In'; it was an airplay hit but nothing more. It was Elektra that edged the group towards a more commercial direction,

revealing its hand by hiring the Bee Gees' producer, Ossie Byrne.*
The resulting album suffers from all the hallmarks and extremes
of post-*Sergeant Pepper* pop ambition, an ornate, baroque pop style
that was very much in vogue.

'We were all influenced by American music of one sort or
another but the direction we followed was more an American folk
pop sound which was very vocal-based,' says Gerry Conway. 'The
opportunity to record happened so quickly that it didn't reflect
what the group was really like once we went on the road. On stage
Trevor had such a strong presence in the group that people looked
upon him as the leader; he did all the talking between songs.'

Within three months of the album's release singer Kerrilee
Male decided to leave, disappointed that she was underused as
a lead vocalist. 'After Kerri left,' says Conway, 'people were regularly coming and going. The last line-up of the group was with
Dorris Henderson,† who Trevor knew from the folk clubs, Poli
Palmer – later in Family – who played vibes and keyboards, and
we even had Gary Boyle on guitar. All fantastic players, but it was
a million miles away from that Elektra album.'

Gary Boyle, now a renowned jazz guitarist – he also played in
Brian Auger's Trinity and with Dusty Springfield – came into the
group when Michael Rosen left. 'It was very song-based but they
let me and Poli have a lot of space to stretch out,' says Boyle.

---

* Ossie Byrne had produced the Bee Gees' first major success in Australia,
'Spicks and Specks', and went on to produce their first international hits in
1967, 'New York Mining Disaster 1941' and 'Massachusetts'.
† The line-up with Dorris Henderson cut only one single, 'Please (Mark
II)', a cover of a song originally by the Californian psychedelic band
Kaleidoscope which Eclection had themselves already recorded with
Kerrilee Male singing.

'Everybody did solo spots in Eclection or had their own featured songs. Trevor had three or four songs [including Joni Mitchell's 'Both Sides Now']. Dorris didn't write so much and would do traditional folk songs like "The House Carpenter" and "One Morning in May", but we never sounded like a folk-rock band.'

For Trevor, that final line-up was the best, but by then Elektra wasn't interested in funding a second album. Speaking about the group ten years later he felt that it was 'a good apprenticeship in electric music [but] I don't think it created anything devastatingly good'. Eclection fizzled out naturally towards the end of 1969, by which time Kajanus says he 'had lost all emotional and musical connection with the group' and its 'hopelessly jazz direction'.

'We did a lot of shows together,' says Richard Thompson. 'We were always on bills with Eclection, Family and Blossomtoes. They were a good live band and very interesting vocally, and like Fairport they were doing something that nobody else was doing, but the big difference was their harmonies, which was something we never explored. Like Fairport, the line-up kept changing after Kerri left.' 'The first line-up was very American-sounding,' says Ashley Hutchings, 'more Mamas and Papas than Jefferson Airplane. We both had girl singers and were cut from similar if not the same cloth. Their one album didn't capture what they were about at all.'

After his marriage broke up, Trevor had been in a relationship with Chris Collins since around spring 1967. Her sister Anne was married to Mike Waterson, and herself a singer; Chris Collins co-wrote two songs on the Watersons' *Bright Phoebus*, including 'Magical Man'. Tod Lloyd, Joe Boyd's original partner in Witchseason, says he, Sandy, Trevor and Chris Collins tried to put a group together for Roy Guest after Sandy left the Strawbs but the combination never went anywhere. All that serves as a reminder is a photo of the four of them in Regent's Park on which the group is named as 'The Original Battersea Heroes'.

Although Trevor and Sandy had known each other since 1966, exactly when they fell for each other isn't certain, but it was some time in late 1968. 'Trevor and Chris Collins decided to have some time apart,' says Elizabeth Hurtt. 'She went off to Ireland, where she realised that Trevor was who she wanted to be with, but in the meantime Trevor had got together with Sandy and they realised they wanted to be together. That would have been around late autumn in 1968.'

One clue to dating the burgeoning relationship is the song 'Now and Then', which Sandy never officially recorded but which was demoed along with 'Autopsy' at Sound Techniques on 30 December 1968, prior to Fairport Convention's *Unhalfbricking* sessions. An unusually subjective lyric, it more than hints that Sandy feels there is something special about her new love; she is certainly fearful that he doesn't feel the same way as she does, writing: 'But when you're gone, perhaps you long to be free.' There are also a number of romanticised sketches of Trevor in her notebook where the draft lyric for 'Now and Then' first appears.

By the beginning of 1969 Trevor had virtually moved into the Stanhope Mews flat Sandy shared with Winnie Whittaker. 'It was always lovely to drop Trevor off at the flat,' says Gary Boyle, 'and if Sandy hadn't been working that day she'd be there and you could just tell there was something special about that relationship.' Plenty of friends saw the change in both Trevor and Sandy as their relationship blossomed: 'When that opportunity came along to join Fairport, I never knew Sandy so happy,' says Gina Glaser. 'That and being with Trevor, who didn't have any of the baggage her earlier boyfriends brought with them.'

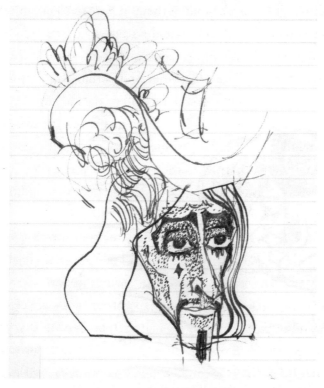

One of Sandy's sketches of Trevor

'When Sandy hooked up with Trevor,' says John Renbourn, 'that did seem like a great match. She finally met somebody who was right for her. He wasn't contorted with intellectual problems about the meaning of folk music or anything like that. He was outgoing, and Sandy was pretty much like that herself. They just hit it off, they were on the same wavelength; irrespective of whether they were both involved in music, I think they would always have been right for each other. I was so pleased for them. Trevor was an easy-going guy and a lot of Sandy's other boyfriends didn't treat her so well.'

'She knew Trevor from around in the folk clubs,' says Linda

Thompson. 'All the girls did. He had a lot of girlfriends. He had a fling with me. It just was the sixties and back then it seemed churlish not to sleep with somebody if they gave you a light for your cigarette. Once they finally got it together, I think it was this great love they had between them. He was a great guy, took care of her. He was a wonderful cook. The first time I can remember tasting really fantastic food was when Trevor used to cook with garlic and herbs. He used to go over to the butcher's in Fulham Road and he'd buy a whole fillet steak and put olives and garlic in it and he made fabulous salads and pasta dishes.'

Stefan Grossman knew both Sandy and Trevor, and had previously occupied the flat in Chipstead Street where Trevor and Sandy moved in together during the summer of 1969: 'Trevor was a playboy, that was the reputation he had, but she was a good-time girl too; they were a well-matched couple. Trevor was another presence on the folk scene; he sang well, he was a good-looking guy and he played solid enough guitar, but Sandy was the gem. She was already grabbing the attention because she had such a beautiful, pure, straight-to-the-heart voice. Trevor wasn't her equal and he knew it, but he could cope with that. It didn't bother him and he was good at handling Sandy's changeability.'

Linda Fitzgerald Moore owned the house on Chipstead Street. She was a photographer and took the first-ever shots of Fotheringay just down the street from the house. 'Trevor was a nice guy and he never had a problem with Sandy being seen as the star, and she never put him down either. She encouraged him but she leaned on him a lot too. I don't think he saw himself as a great guitar player or a great singer – he never purported to be anything like that for himself. He was a much more placid person than Sandy, who was very highly strung. They balanced each other out.'

Trevor was never less than in awe of Sandy, of her voice and particularly her ability with language; he accepted that she was the greater talent. As a result he was always in Sandy's shadow and his own work, both before and after they got together, tends to be unfairly dismissed. That the likes of Martin Carthy, Dave Swarbrick, A. L. Lloyd and Sandy herself recognised Trevor's talent at the very least allows that his own career might well have flourished in the 1970s had things been different.

7 : *Farewell, Farewell*
1969

We were all a little crazy as a result of the accident and it took us a couple of years to reach some equilibrium. It really affected Sandy. She'd escaped the crash but she was just devastated. I think she was haunted by it as much as we were for not having been in the van with us. That was a difficult time of rebuilding and the *Liege & Lief* project was something for us to focus on and it pulled us together as a band because we thought, 'If this is the price for Martin dying, is this what we really want to do for a living?'

RICHARD THOMPSON

I never saw things in terms of any watershed moments until after the crash. We could never make up for the loss of Martin, which did shake our belief for a while. The Royal Festival Hall concert where we launched *Liege & Lief* felt like our moment of rebirth. It was sticking two fingers up at the grim reaper.

SIMON NICOL

It was all in such a short time from what is taken as the first Fairport gig in May 1967 to Sandy joining in May the following year; the accident where Martin died happened in May of '69, all leading to myself and Sandy leaving before the end of that year just as *Liege & Lief* was released.

ASHLEY HUTCHINGS

Ad for Fairport's *Unhalfbricking* album, with Neil and
Edna Denny pictured on the front cover

On 11 May 1969 Fairport played at Mothers in Birmingham, one of the most popular underground venues on the circuit. Eclection were also playing in Birmingham, and Sandy travelled home to London with Trevor. On the way back, just north of Scratchwood services on the M1, Fairport's van veered across the road. Richard Thompson tried to grab the wheel from the group's driver, Harvey Bramham, who had fallen asleep, but the van hit the side barrier and tumbled down an embankment.

After the crash, only Simon Nicol was left inside the vehicle, relatively unscathed. 'Everyone else had gone out either through the doors or the windows. The PA and all the kit had gone out through the back doors. I woke up as the van was careering down the bank. Somehow or other, I wasn't hurled out like the rest of them and, as a result, I was only concussed.'

The rest of the group were scattered over the field where the van landed, the group's guitars, drums and amplifiers thrown everywhere. Thompson, Bramham and Ashley Hutchings were all injured to some degree, but Jeannie Franklin, the young American clothes designer who was Thompson's girlfriend, and Martin Lamble were both dead.

At the time of the crash, Joe Boyd was in the final stages of negotiating Fairport's first American tour, which would have taken in the Fillmore West and was to include their debut at the Newport Folk Festival. It was left to Anthea Joseph at the Witchseason offices to

Fairport tragedy

WHILE returning to London from a gig, at 6 a.m. on Tuesday morning, the mini bus in which most of the members of The Fairport Convention were travelling, skidded off the road near the Mill Hill Service Station. The drummer with the group, Martin Lamble, was killed, and so too was a young American girl, Jeannie Franklin, known as Jeannie The Tailor. Jeannie was well-known in the U.S. for the clothes she made for American groups.

The other members of the Convention, Richard Thompson, Tyger Hutchins and Simon Nicol escaped with cuts and bruises and broken bones. Harvey, their road manager, was the most seriously injured, with a fractured hip and pelvis, it is thought he will have to remain in hospital for three months. Sandy Denny, the group's girl vocalist, was not involved in the crash, as she was travelling in a separate car.

Nothing definite is known concerning the crash. It is thought that the van hit an island in the road, and bounced off, ending up at the bottom of the embankment, a drop of 40 feet.

Fairport Convention was due to star a tour of the States in July. This plan is definitely in jeopardy now. The group have a new album, already completed, that will be released on July 11th.

Top Pops, 17 May 1969

issue the official statement, which read: 'Those poor children. We are all in a state of shock because this tragedy is so unbelievable.'

'We were on the same bill at Mothers,' says Eclection guitarist Gary Boyle, 'and Sandy came back with us. We had a Humber Super Snipe which was pretty roomy, so luckily we could just squeeze one extra person in. It was just so fortunate she came in the car with us; I can still picture Trevor and Sandy snuggled up on the back seat.'

Eclection had a gig the next day in Dagenham and Sandy came along with Trevor – she didn't want to be left alone. 'It was a venue where the stage had wings,' says Boyle, 'and Sandy spent the whole time sitting at the side in floods of tears and I remember her apologising to us because she was so tearful. We played out of our skins that night, I think it was just the emotion of it, and she said afterwards, "I'm really sorry to bring you all down weeping all over the place because the band was so great." And we were just concerned for her. You can imagine the state she was in.'

'Sandy couldn't speak about it,' says Gerry Conway. 'It was unthinkable in that way, that somehow things like that didn't happen to people you knew. For Sandy it was such an incredible fateful moment but one that hung over her as much as the others who were in the crash.'

It was a time when there was a real sense of community among bands, forged, as with folk musicians, by the number of gigs they played and the shared experience they had on the road. 'Everybody in that community was so moved by what happened to Fairport,' says Boyle. 'I think we all felt that given the amount we toured, the distances we travelled, usually in the small hours, the condition of the roads, the state of some of the vans – it felt like an accident that had been waiting to happen to someone. Everyone related to what happened to Fairport. They were such young kids, like school kids really, and, like Eclection, such a tight-knit, friendly bunch of people.'

Linda Thompson (Linda Peters, as she then was) bumped into Sandy and Trevor in a corner shop opposite the Troubadour at four o'clock in the morning after the crash. Somebody had called round to tell Sandy what had happened; they didn't want her finding out about it in the papers. 'She was completely shell-shocked and she and Trevor were in there getting milk or cigarettes or something and she said, "Martin's dead and Jeannie's dead." She was rambling. I didn't know Martin that well but my first thought was that it could have been her in the crash. She and Trevor were already pretty tight but that tightened the knot. I never really heard Sandy say anything about the crash, nor Richard, nor any of the band. We bottled things up back then; stiff upper lip and all that. That's how we were conditioned to react but it's the insouciance of youth, you pick yourself up and you go on.'

Nobody knew what would happen to Fairport, whether they would continue as a group and, if so, how. 'It was a very volatile time,' says Richard Thompson. 'It could easily have been the end for the band. For a while we didn't know if we were going to carry on.'

The album they had finished a month earlier was ready to be released. Joe Boyd had even taken test pressings to America at the time of the crash. 'I was quite convinced that it was Fairport's breakthrough album,' he says. 'If *Holidays* had been a major step beyond the first album, they were now a really great band and they knew it and like all great bands they never stood still. They already had ideas for things they wanted to try out, but the crash put everything on hold and nobody was coercing them to make any decisions about the future.'

'I didn't really know how to deal with it,' said Sandy in 1977. 'Martin's death was a tragedy. He was probably the member of the band I'd got to know least – I think he may have been a bit scared of me. I needed to get away. I wanted to avoid the questions from friends and from the music press. I didn't want to become Fairport's spokesperson. So I went to America.'

Although Sandy had decided to go to Los Angeles, her fear of flying was heightened following the crash. On the morning of the flight she had to leave early to get her health card stamped at her local doctor's surgery, half hoping it would be closed. 'There's nothing to stop me now from going to America,' she wrote in a long essay in her notebook. Joe Boyd and Simon Nicol were already there, so she took the flight, along with Richard Thompson. 'Sandy could imagine the worst happening at any point, which was why it was so hard to be on a plane with her,' says Thompson. 'Flights sitting next to Sandy were torture. White knuckles. We started the flight to Los Angeles and in the first twenty minutes I had a large drink spilt in my lap and I just sat there soaking for hours.' However much she enjoyed the trip on the surface – going to a party at Phil Ochs's house, meeting Mimi Fariña, seeing the 'amazing' John Lee Hooker at the Experience on Sunset Strip, and going to see the film *Monterey Pop* – she was 'missing Trevor awfully'. Sandy makes no mention of playing the Troubadour as a trio with Thompson and Nicol, billed as a Sandy Denny gig and her American debut. Thompson's recollection is almost deliberately vague, but when pushed, he remembers it as a pretty awful experience.

Ashley Hutchings's injuries were more serious than those suffered by Thompson and the others in the crash, and had taken longer to heal. While the others went to America and Nicol, in particular, was involved in readying *Unhalfbricking* for release, Hutchings spent much of his recuperative time in Cecil Sharp House, part of a self-education process of learning more about traditional music. He was obsessed but he wasn't exclusively driving the group towards this goal. If Fairport were to continue to exist, they all needed to find a new repertoire. Yet Sandy for one was uncertain.

'Describing it coldly now makes it sound like emotional black-mail,' said Sandy ten years later, 'but it certainly wasn't. They just made it clear that if I left, Fairport couldn't play any more. They'd already been through that when I joined. Most of the old repertoire from the first album had been dumped in favour of new material. If I left, history would repeat itself.

'I know there was generally a feeling among the boys in the band that Fairport should continue. I discussed it with various friends outside the band. I was actually very slow coming to a final decision. I don't think anyone in Fairport realises how late in the day I made my final decision.'

The folk world was still very much Sandy's other life, her other social scene, and aside from Trevor, she sought comfort in familiar folk haunts and among old friends while she weighed up what to do. 'I think it was Anne Briggs who finally said I ought to carry on. She said, "You have to. Those boys need you. They'd be lost without you."'

So Sandy decided to stick with the boys, and on 6 July 1969 Ashley Hutchings, Richard Thompson and Simon Nicol gathered at Sandy and Trevor's new flat at 20 Chipstead Street, a red-brick Edwardian house in Parsons Green. They had just been told that Island had scheduled *Unhalfbricking* for release in late July and 'Si tu dois partir' was being released as the advance single. They agreed to get back together with the proviso that it would be a fresh start. 'We were all very sensitive people,' says Hutchings. 'We couldn't just get another drummer and try and recreate what we had before, carry on doing those same songs.'

'I'm not sure what we would have done if Sandy had decided to leave,' says Nicol, 'but it seemed as if there was a general assumption that we would continue. The decision had almost been made for us, although nobody actually pressured us. We were all in our own private worlds. We didn't talk about the accident but I think we all felt if we didn't pursue the band, Martin's loss would have been for nothing.'

'Sandy wasn't in the crash,' says Hutchings, 'but she was touched and enormously damaged by what happened. We're all damaged by it and lost in a way, which helps to understand why we had to take that different step, why we had to make *Liege & Lief* and go down that path.'

Although his involvement with Fairport would soon come to an end following his best friend Martin Lamble's death, Kingsley Abbott was still in close contact with them all and was helping Lamble's family with arrangements for the funeral. 'I don't think anybody really had time to stop and take stock, it all happened so quickly, and that's a very apposite thing to point out. Everybody had the capacity for reflection but nobody had the time to reflect.

'They had to reinvent themselves to make sense of it all emotionally. There were such strong emotional attachments within the group as friends that it made the crash even more devastating. It was always different after that, both musically and interpersonally.'

Within three months of the accident, Sandy and Trevor had moved into the Chipstead Street flat together. 'She never forgave herself over the Fairport crash,' says Philippa Clare. 'She had survivor's guilt big time. That was when she and Trevor *really* got together, and because she was with Trevor and not in the van, she never got over that. She went through hell over that. They all still bear the scars.'

'She was rescued by Trevor,' says Bambi Ballard,* who first met

* Writer, art and film historian Bambi Ballard is the daughter of the

Sandy in 1970 and became one of her closest friends, 'by Trevor taking her home instead of travelling with the others. That was what cemented their relationship. There was neediness in Sandy which was far greater than any she ever had before. She had avoided being in the crash thanks to Trevor and because Trevor looked after her it created a dependency on him. The stress of travelling for Sandy was also greater afterwards because she never forgot that terrible crash.'

Joe Boyd feels these events had even wider repercussions on Sandy and clouded her decision-making thereafter. 'There are a series of interlocking feedback loops in Sandy's life at that point,' says Boyd, 'where she was already seriously involved with Trevor, so there was a side of Sandy that was emotionally quite needy after the crash and she had this chance of a relationship and wanted to grab it. It made Sandy more anxious about having a secure emotional life and therefore less willing to take risks. And that may have influenced her to stay with Fairport because that was safe. Although she and Trevor had set up home together, Trevor was still locked into Eclection. So he was going to be off with them and she didn't want to be left alone.

'Eventually Fairport came to me and said they had decided to carry on but were never going to do the same material again, so they had to do a whole new repertoire. *Music from Big Pink* [the debut album by the US–Canadian group the Band] hit London like a ton of bricks that summer and that became the soundtrack

---

novelist Eric Ballard. She became a costume designer in the early seventies for Elkie Brooks, Steeleye Span, Procol Harum and Alex Harvey, among others. She met Sandy in 1970 through Anthea Joseph, and later designed some stage dresses for her. Bambi was married at the time to the *Guardian* and BBC journalist Robin Denselow.

while they were recovering. Musically, so much of what they had done up to then was American in style, looking to Dylan or Joni Mitchell or other songwriters for inspiration and material; the Byrds' music was another touchstone for them. But *Big Pink* kind of said, "Forget it. You're not American, you are never even going to come close to understanding or interpreting this music. Forget about even trying." It put up a wall but at the same time it was inspiring. Jesus, what door has this opened for a real feeling for the roots of their own musical heritage?'

Music from Big Pink had actually been released in July the previous summer, but its impact was a slow burn, fuelled by the Byrds' *Sweetheart of the Rodeo*, the Flying Burrito Brothers' *Gilded Palace of Sin* and Dylan's *Nashville Skyline*, this last released during the month of the crash. '*Big Pink* came as a bit of a shock back in 1968,' says Richard Thompson. 'It seemed to vault over the zeitgeist, back to purer roots – kind of counter-counterculture. The psychedelic bands were playing bits of blues and country, but the Band seemed to have real authority, and a perfect synthesis of Americana styles. And they wore suits! And had short haircuts! It was the perfect antidote to hippie excess and sloppiness – those boys certainly knew how to play on the back of the beat.'

However much the notion of transposing *Music from Big Pink* into an English context was tantalising, whatever door was about to open, Martin Lamble's death effectively closed another on the past. Yet just as the group were moving on, the final album Lamble had completed with them, *Unhalfbricking*, a reminder of that past, was about to be released at the end of July. The title came from a word game called Ghosts that the band played in their spare time: somebody suggests a letter, the next player adds another letter or syllable either before or after it, then the next player adds another, and so on. If challenged, you had to prove that the combination of letters was part of a real word, and it was Sandy who came up with 'Unhalfbricking' when put on the spot. The title was meaningless but somehow apt. The record sleeve was a bold statement too: the striking photograph of Neil and Edna Denny on the front cover was completely unadorned by any graphics.

There was nothing pre-planned about the cover photo, taken by photographer Eric Hayes at the Dennys' home at 9B Arthur Road in Wimbledon. 'We were just playing it by ear,' says Ashley Hutchings, 'although it must have been Sandy who suggested we go there. She certainly wasn't doing it to curry favour with her mum and dad or placate them or anything like that. It was spontaneous and they were really accommodating. Her mother cooked dinner and we all sat round the table in their kitchen, which is the back cover image. It had no significance, the photo wasn't meant as a statement about anything, however much people have tried to read something into it, but it made for a really effective and unusual cover.' Some people also jumped to the conclusion that Sandy was from a particularly wealthy family, judging by the spacious grounds that are the setting for the group in the background. In fact, Neil and Edna only rented the large second-floor flat and had to ask the owner's permission to use the garden.

Unlike the group's previous albums, *Unhalfbricking* went straight into the charts, where it stayed for two months, peaking at number twelve, while the extracted single, 'Si tu dois partir', the most frivolous and throwaway moment on the album, climbed to number twenty-one. The group never had another hit single. 'It's all quite unreal,' says Hutchings, 'because we did almost nothing to promote *Unhalfbricking* in the usual way of things. To some extent we couldn't because some of us were still recuperating physically, let alone mentally. We couldn't return to those songs so we didn't do any radio sessions, and there were certainly no live gigs.'

Having confirmed that Fairport would carry on as a group, Anthea Joseph at Witchseason booked a rehearsal space at Farley House, a Queen Anne mansion in the village of Farley Chamberlayne, near Winchester in Hampshire. She found it through that most gentrified and middle-class of magazines, *The Lady*. The group would stay there for almost three months, through July, August and into September.

The first and perhaps most difficult thing the group had to do was to find a new drummer. Auditions duly took place in a pub back room on Chiswick High Street. The main audition song was Sandy's 'Autopsy', chosen to put the prospective drummers through their paces because of its difficult time signatures. The eventual recruit, Dave Mattacks, doesn't remember Sandy being at the auditions but, as with Sandy's recruitment barely a year before, he was more or less asked to join there and then. Twenty-four hours later Mattacks confessed to Hutchings that he didn't understand the music at all, couldn't tell one tune from another. Mattacks's background was in jazz, including nine months in a Belfast dance band. 'The daunting aspect was that I was utterly unfamiliar with that genre of music,' he says. 'I really was that "deer in the headlights", but my senses were wide open and I knew something good was happening.

'I was dumbfounded with all of them, I'd never met people like this. They all had a profound effect on how I heard music and what I listened to. They were all very bright and their priorities were different from people I'd played with up to that time. Sandy was very effervescent and bubbly and just had the most amazing voice, and I'd not heard singing of that ilk before or singing that good. The depth of her talent as a singer, player and especially as a songwriter did not dawn on me till a few years later.

'She was so welcoming when I came into Fairport. When we did the instrumentals on *Liege & Lief*, I remember hearing Sandy say, "We knew he was good but we didn't know he was that good."'

Mattacks says that his integration into Fairport was made easier because he and Dave Swarbrick were effectively joining the band together. Although Swarbrick had played on the pre-crash session when 'A Sailor's Life' and 'Si tu dois partir' had been recorded, he didn't become a full member of Fairport until he participated in the Farley Chamberlayne rehearsals, having returned to the folk circuit in the months between. Swarbrick had no qualms about joining Fairport: 'I wasn't in two minds at all. I was enthralled by the sound, by Richard, by drums, by the whole electric thing. I still am really. The power available to make a point.'

With Mattacks and Swarbrick on board, the new six-piece Fairport were 'getting it together in the country', by now an almost clichéd process which had begun when the newly formed Traffic went off to a Berkshire cottage in 1967. 'We had never done that before,' says Simon Nicol. 'We had never cohabited, as it were. We all lived locally and we used to book church halls to rehearse in and then go home afterwards. *Liege & Lief* would probably have been a different record if we had tried to record it in London and not gone to Farley Chamberlayne.'

'It was the first time we took ourselves away from the routine of being a working band,' says Ashley Hutchings. 'We'd come down the stairs in the morning, have some breakfast and go into the living room where all the instruments were set up – and play. It's still mind-boggling to me, even though I'm so close to it and have had all these years to get used to it. It is such an incredible beacon.

Everyone and everything contributed, it was a mammoth step.'

'It was an escape from the world,' says Richard Thompson, 'although not from our private thoughts. We were breaking in two new people and I worked on a lot of ideas with Swarb, but the rest of us needed to get the measure of each other again too. It was important to work and play together again, and we did relax, kick a ball about in the gardens, just go for walks or go to the local pub and play darts. Normal everyday things like that. There was no strict regime, no set times when we'd start playing, sometimes after breakfast, sometimes late into the night.'

The surviving members of Fairport have since spoken of the *Liege & Lief* rehearsal period as being magical or euphoric, and there is no evidence that Sandy wasn't as committed and enthusiastic as everybody else, although it meant she was absent from the new home that she had barely begun setting up with Trevor, while his commitments to Eclection kept him away from the Hampshire retreat. The country rehearsals somehow suspended reality and it was only when Fairport became a public band again in September that, for Sandy, the cracks began to appear.

Until then, everybody had assumed that after *Liege & Lief* Fairport would return to the type of material which had characterised *What We Did on Our Holidays* and *Unhalfbricking*. 'At the time,' says Nicol, 'for all of us the whole process of recording *Liege & Lief* and the rehearsals before was the fuel to rebuilding and rebonding the band as a new team. We never doubted the concept but we did see it as a project. It was not supposed to be the doorway to a new world.'

In the middle of this invigorating chapter in Fairport's history, the group found themselves thrust, rather incongruously, into the world of Britain's primary pop TV programme. 'When the single charted,' says Hutchings, 'and we were asked to be on *Top of the Pops*, we didn't take it entirely seriously. We all had mixed feelings about doing it at all – some more than others – but I think we felt we couldn't say no. We were already completely engrossed in the new direction we were heading, so to be performing "Si tu dois partir" on *Top of the Pops* was rather absurd to say the least.'

When Fairport appeared on *Top of the Pops* on 14 August 1969 even the most dedicated fan wouldn't have recognised three of the ensemble: Dave Mattacks was making his public debut with them, miming on a washboard; Dave Swarbrick had at least played on the single, but Witchseason PR Steve Sparks was also on view playing a triangle (which had been Trevor Lucas's role on the recording). Richard Thompson, with his head down, hiding behind his mop of hair, was playing the melodeon. Ashley Hutchings was using a baguette to bow the strings of a huge Perspex double bass, and Sandy stood in the centre with a hand-held mic. The French stereotype was reinforced by some in the group wearing striped shirts, berets and garlands of onions. It was like something off *The Benny Hill Show*. 'It was probably a mistake,' says Hutchings; 'whatever we were aiming for, I think we just looked silly.'

Whatever she felt about it at the time, Sandy was scathing about the experience in print six months later, angrily dismissing both 'Si tu dois partir' and *Top of the Pops* with surprising venom, given that the French translation had been her idea to begin with. 'That was a load of rubbish. The people who bought that record were cheated. If they didn't know us they'd think we were some French group. And the things that went with it – I don't think I'll ever do *Top of the Pops* again – absolute rubbish that single was.'

Two days after appearing on the programme, Sandy was

interviewed by Nick Logan for the *NME*, giving outsiders the first indication of the path Fairport was actually taking. 'The accident taught me that I loved them all,' she said. 'The next album is going to be completely different; it will be based around traditional British folk music to which we may put new words if necessary. We're not making it pop though. In fact it will be almost straight, only electric.' Logan asked her what it sounded like; 'heavy, traditional folk music,' she replied. A week earlier Sandy had told *Disc* that 'we've really been getting into traditional English music'. She had briefly returned from Farley Chamberlayne, the 'mammoth country estate' where the new line-up was rehearsing. 'It may sound amazing, but we put old traditional music with electric instruments and our own words and it really sounds nice . . . though it shouldn't. We're going along a completely different road now. It's really put a new breath of life into us.'

The distractions of promoting their 'hit' single behind them, it was back to reinventing the wheel in the country. 'It helped to bring in that new blood,' says Hutchings. 'DM [Mattacks] played his part, he was a revelation; and Swarb had not actually been part of the group before then, although I'm sure we had already discussed asking him to join before the crash. It's all a little hazy. But once we were that six-piece group, if you took any one person out of that group, it wouldn't have been the same. Everyone had such an important role; *Liege & Lief* might not have turned out at all – let alone the way it did.'

Swarbrick found himself completely drawn to his new bandmates. 'It was very enjoyable and so productive,' he says. 'We certainly put the hours in and it was a perfect environment in which to collaborate and create. The band was cohesive and so special, the chemistry worked and the line-up was sensational. We were all inventing ways to translate folk to rock, none more than DM. Everybody dipped their oar in the water.'

Swarbrick knew Sandy already but had not been aware of just how good she was. 'She stood alone as a singer. I don't think there's been anybody since who can hold a candle to her. She was a one-off. As to what set her apart, how can you quantify a performer that stood and stands somewhere between Piaf and Jupiter?

'Sandy had all the qualities that a singer needs and then some – a great voice, timing, swing, musicality; being a pianist meant that she knew how chords were made up. She knew what note to sing to complement the given melody line. She had great empathy, so she could share the emotion of a phrase with the audience, tell a story, paint a picture, aim the song and so on. She was vulnerable, and that was moving, she could be a girl or a woman, she had a great range too.

'And technically she was great. The tradition has only one kind of improvisation; we call it decoration, she was a master of that, weaving little curly bits and ornamentation and playing around the line, decorating it, beautifying it. The popular conception of improvisation is to use the chord sequence to write alternative melodic sequences or snaps and snatches round it. She had a harmonic education and so was able to draw on that too. And then she could throw her head back and let go. I haven't seen her like since she died.'

Hutchings doesn't feel Sandy was any less committed to the project at the time. 'You couldn't say that Sandy wasn't interested because she wanted to do contemporary songs, because she was very excited about aspects of it as well.' It was always Sandy's way to make light of the dark material she was singing, including her own material, when she was on stage. 'Sandy may not always have given the impression,' says Gina Glaser, 'but traditional music had such a history, and that mattered to her.'

'No matter how dark or serious the song, she'd joke about it in the way she'd introduce it,' agrees Ralph McTell. 'She would almost be in denial of her knowledge and understanding of folk music. It's a defence mechanism, or it's self-deprecating. When you are singing a folk song, you know it's bigger than you because it's been there for hundreds and hundreds of years so you are respectfully approaching it. You approach it in a different way.

'As a singer, it came naturally, though,' says McTell. 'Sandy's decoration, her ornamentation, the little trills and tricks and tremolos, no one really did it as well at that time. If you listen to Shirley Collins or Maddy Prior or any of the other girls who were traditional English singers, none of them did it like Sandy.'

'I was always very serious about the songs,' says Maddy Prior. 'Tim Hart and I spent a lot of time at Cecil Sharp House looking up songs. Martin Carthy always said that we're not on a crusade, but it was a bit of a crusade for me, I have to say. Sandy wasn't a person who was going to spend time looking up stuff, but once she sang she was in the music and she would be lost in the song.'

Ashley Hutchings knew Sandy didn't have Dave Swarbrick's profound knowledge of the songs, or what he calls his own 'almost academic zeal', but, he says, 'she was one of the very, very few there have ever been and certainly the best who could sing traditional folk songs with a rock sensibility. June Tabor can't do it. Maddy can't do it. Shirley Collins can't. The best singers in England have tried and Sandy was the best. She naturally understood how to sing traditional songs and she could translate that into a rock context. Nobody did that better because she was also a very good rock singer.'

The new Fairport ensemble didn't just play traditional songs. The spirit of *Music from Big Pink* encouraged them to delve back into the familiar basement tapes that had been so rewarding on *Unhalfbricking*: 'The emphasis was on traditional material,' says Richard Thompson, 'and that was being driven most purposefully by Ashley and Swarb. And that's not to say Sandy wasn't as fully engaged by it, but we'd also return to familiar territory – Dylan, some old country music, rock 'n' roll standbys. We were figuring out what we were going to do, and we weren't analysing it. Perhaps now when I'm asked I'll say that "we were combining the freedom of rock 'n' roll with the ballad style of folk", or something like that, but that's not how we saw it at the time.'

Thompson's two original contributions are perhaps the most moving on the album. 'Farewell, Farewell' and 'Crazy Man Michael' address the loss they all felt after the crash. Meanwhile, Sandy's sole credit for the album is for the words to the only song she ever collaborated on with Hutchings. 'Come All Ye' joyfully kick-starts the album and the band's radical reboot of the spirit of traditional folk song.

The live shows around *Liege & Lief* – too fitful to be described as a tour – began at the Van Dyke Club in Plymouth on 20 September 1969, a warm-up for the Royal Festival Hall four days later, where Dave Swarbrick and Dave Mattacks had been announced as making their concert debut with Fairport. The date sheet information is sketchy but there were certainly no more than ten live performances in six weeks by the *Liege & Lief* line-up. Alongside all the songs from the album the set list included Dylan's 'Open the Door, Homer' and 'Down in the Flood'. Fairport also threw in a couple of country and western oldies, 'We Need a Whole Lot More of Jesus' (And a Whole Lot Less Rock 'n' Roll)' and 'Just a Little

Talk with Jesus', the latter sung by Swarbrick, with Sandy taking over the violin.

The Festival Hall concert was an emotional return to a venue they had played a year before, almost to the day, but it was particularly nerve-racking for Sandy. Even the more resilient Swarbrick must have had the odd butterfly in his stomach; the audience was full of folkies, after all, many of whom were his and Sandy's friends. 'Did we feel we were making history?' ponders Swarbrick. 'Sometimes, just a little; the sound that was being produced was so exciting for me. To hear a song that I knew from folk clubs take on such power was exhilarating. Nothing like it existed.'

John Renbourn remembers the *Daily Telegraph*'s folk writer Maurice Rosenbaum running for the exit doors 'with his fingers in both ears, saying they were terribly loud', but Sandy delightedly recalled being accosted by A. L. Lloyd afterwards. 'Bert Lloyd was one of the first people backstage to say "it's the most exciting thing I've heard for years." It was pretty special for a while because it was so different. Nobody had thought of doing it before.' The pertinent phrase there is 'for a while'. The doubts Sandy was having and her other underlying fears were now coming to the fore.

In among the sporadic live dates, *Liege & Lief* was recorded at Sound Techniques over six days between 16 October and 1 November. 'The Deserter' and 'Farewell, Farewell' were the first songs recorded, followed three days later by 'Crazy Man Michael'. 'Reynardine' was completed on the 22nd. They took a break from the studio to play dates in Manchester and Redcar on the weekend of 25 and 26 October, before returning on the 29th for a marathon session that yielded four tracks: 'Come All Ye', 'Tam Lin', 'Matty Groves', which they had already started work on, and the 'Lark in the Morning' medley, the first of many combinations of jigs and reels the group would come to record. 'Matty Groves', the song that was the popular apotheosis of Fairport's trailblazing achievement, actually took several days to compile using overdubs and mixing, some of this taking place at Olympic Studios.

Only one traditional track from the sessions, 'Sir Patrick Spens', was not used. A different version was recorded for the subsequent *Full House* album. The Byrds' 'Ballad of Easy Rider' and Richard Fariña's 'The Quiet Joys of Brotherhood' were also set to one side as inappropriate.

Liege & Lief was a triumph all round. It is an undeniable artistic success; above all it's a tremendous ensemble accomplishment and a conceptual album that doesn't buckle under the weight of its intentions. To have completed such a rigorously challenging album in just six days speaks for Fairport's professionalism and instrumental prowess. It also highlights John Wood's skills and Joe Boyd's ability to capture unobtrusively what was 'in the room'. Boyd was familiar with the material from the live shows and having dropped in at Farley Chamberlayne over the summer.

For the first time on a Fairport album only one singer is featured. Sandy rises to the challenge, taking us through every emotion after the stirring 'Come All Ye' sets the scene. The manner in which she conveys the reverse fortunes suffered by the protagonists in 'Matty Groves' and 'The Deserter' is quite astonishing. 'Matty Groves' begins optimistically and ends with the lovers both doomed, while 'The Deserter' goes from sublime sadness to gleeful relish as the condemned man at its heart is saved from the gallows.

Arguably, Sandy's finest vocals are saved for the two Richard Thompson originals, whose content is so poetic and deeply personal in addressing loss, guilt and pain. 'Farewell, Farewell' is almost dreamlike, set to the tune of the traditional 'Willie o'

American press ad for *Liege & Lief*

Winsbury', Sandy's vocal haunting, almost whispered at times. 'Crazy Man Michael', the first songwriting collaboration between Thompson and Swarbrick, opens with a line Sandy might have written herself: 'Within the fire and out upon the sea . . .', delivered with almost unbearable empathy and sensitivity. There is always something mystical about Sandy at her melancholy best, here matched by Thompson's eerie electric guitar.

For Joe Boyd, the impact of *Liege & Lief* was felt immediately after the Royal Festival Hall, though the album wasn't even recorded yet. 'All the signs were that it was going to be something big. Within a week of the Festival Hall we're getting phone calls asking, "Can they come and do this, can they come and do that?" and A&M were up for it as never before and asking, "When can they come to America?" At the same time, Sandy was pointedly moaning that "I don't want to fly, do we really have to do this?" It was classic Sandy; everything she had worked for, everything she wanted was within reach but suddenly she wasn't sure it was what she really wanted.'

John and Beverley Martyn, with Nick Drake opening, had supported Fairport at the Royal Festival Hall. Beverley Martyn was shocked by Sandy's transformation from the sweet girl she'd once met at Les Cousins in 1965, and how demanding she had now become: 'She had turned into the first folk diva. Joe wanted us to tour with Fairport Convention but Sandy put a stop to it. It was as if she really didn't want me around. I was taken aback by her attitude. I think she felt that I was a threat to her crown as the folk singer within the Witchseason hierarchy. When *Stormbringer* came out, she actually phoned me up and gave me a mouthful of abuse. Some time later, she rang me to suggest collaborating on some songs and we invited her down to Hastings, but she never came. She was very changeable. The one or two times I did gig with her or Fairport, she even insisted on knowing in advance what I was going to wear on stage.'

If Beverley Martyn's comments are an indication of Sandy beginning to reach an emotional crossroads, the crux of the problem – as everybody could see – was her relationship with Trevor. 'It was as simple and straightforward to Sandy as carrying on and losing Trevor or jumping ship,' says Simon Nicol. 'And that's what she chose to do. For the first time in her life she had a settled relationship and she didn't want to give it up. I didn't see it coming but I wasn't surprised. I was always fearful of it happening because they were very strongly bonded as a couple and, at the same time, Trevor had a reputation as a "swordsman", which worried her, and they had separate careers taking them in different directions.'

Everybody was aware that Trevor's past reputation made Sandy very insecure about being apart from him. 'She didn't have the confidence to go on the road for a month and know that he'd still be there,' says Boyd. 'This had a big effect on her professional life.' 'Fairport was aware of the conflict over Trevor,' says Thompson, 'and I think we knew at some point it would come to a head. I could always see her and Trevor getting together in a musical partnership. You would hear Sandy and Trevor singing together and it was great – their voices blended really well. And that was something she didn't have in Fairport. We weren't going to bring another guitarist into Fairport, so we weren't going to bring Trevor into the band. As a result, we didn't rule out that at some point she was going to leave. She hit a crisis point; I think the decision when it came was quite sudden.'

'Sandy's career, from that point on,' says Nicol, 'was shaped by that relationship or by her having to make that decision again – because she really, really loved him.'

However much Joe Boyd was concerned about Sandy's issues with travelling and Trevor, there was a third factor he had overlooked: 'What I was the slowest to pick up on was Sandy feeling

like she didn't want to be in a band that did nothing but traditional music. She'd say, "I'm writing songs, where are they going
to go?" Ultimately that could have been resolved; if Sandy hadn't
had the flying anxiety and the Trevor anxiety, she and Richard
could have figured out a way for Fairport to accommodate their
writing, but it didn't last long enough for that to get explored.
Ashley was still discovering things with the zeal of a new convert
that she had been familiar with for years. He would come back
from Cecil Sharp House and say, "I've just discovered this magnificent song," and she would say, "Well, I was singing that when I
was seventeen.'"

For Sandy the high spirits of the rehearsals dissipated during
the live dates, particularly those that followed the recording of the
album, which included a daunting return to Mothers Club on 2
November. The Birmingham gig was traumatic for everyone and
the return journey was almost a silent vigil. Sandy was in tears
throughout. 'Everything seemed to come to a head,' she said later.
'The things I wanted to do with my life – personally and professionally – didn't fit in with staying with Fairport. But I loved the
band and all the guys in it. I loved making music with them. In
fact, I continued to record with them right through my career – if
you just read the credits on my solo albums, it's obvious. But that
night, it got on top of me. The emotion of the gig, the long cold
journey back and wanting to be with Trevor.'

She told Joe Boyd that she didn't want to do the American
tour they had been offered and that she didn't even want to travel
to Denmark for an upcoming TV date. When other members of
Fairport went to pick Sandy up to go to the airport, she simply
wasn't there. She finally arrived the next day for what turned
out to be her and Ashley Hutchings's last performance with the

band, recorded on 7 November at TV-Byen in Gladsaxe, near Copenhagen.

If *Liege & Lief* positioned Sandy on the opposite side of the fence from Ashley Hutchings, Richard Thompson was caught somewhere in the middle. 'She felt her writing was being overlooked after we recorded *Liege & Lief*. I had similar feelings, which grew to a point of my leaving after *Full House*. The balance towards traditional music was tipping over and I didn't always want to do traditional music. It was getting difficult to write for Fairport, and I wanted to develop my own voice, possibly in that style, but to make it contemporary.'

Thompson knew that if he left Fairport after *Liege & Lief*, the band would not survive. He was also energised by the prospect of instrumental adventures, especially trading off with Dave Swarbrick, and by the proposed American tour: 'The dance music was fun, as Fairport had a sort of punk approach to the traditional, but after a year I eventually felt as Sandy must have felt when she left.'

'I certainly didn't fancy the idea of being in a band where it would be hard to have my own songs played because the band was more about traditional songs and instrumentals,' said Sandy in 1977. 'I had several songs which could have been included on *Liege & Lief*, but I knew it wasn't worth putting them forward.'

Ironically, Ashley Hutchings, who had once been the person most fervently driving Fairport to write original material, now felt, like his future wife Shirley Collins, 'Why on earth do you need to write songs when you have this reservoir of great traditional material?' Hutchings thinks that Fairport may have rehearsed 'The Pond and the Stream', and Sandy's notebooks, which are never entirely consistent chronologically, suggest that the songs

'Nothing More' and 'The Sea' may date from when she was still in the group. All three songs, among her very best, found a home on the album she recorded after leaving.

In the midst of the turmoil engulfing her, Sandy met with Joe Boyd. However uncertain she was about Fairport, she also wanted to ask Boyd what future she would have if she left the group. Boyd was caught between wanting her to stay in Fairport and reassuring her that she would have no problem getting a solo deal. He was aware of – and probably excited by – the possibilities of both. In the end, neither scenario worked out. The actual announcement came in the music press on 22 November; it cited 'Sandy's unwillingness to travel' and Hutchings's desire to 'concentrate on traditional folk music'. *Disc* reported that Sandy was to join Eclection and ran a photo of Sandy with Trevor, but this was speculative rather than informed; Eclection had all but broken up at this point anyway.

The release of *Liege & Lief* followed on 2 December. There was never any question of Fairport Convention not continuing: 'After the double blow of Sandy and Ashley leaving,' says Simon Nicol, 'we never thought, "We can't carry on," because we'd overcome the crash and rebuilt the band and made this hugely successful record – not in terms of sales, but as an artistic piece of work. I'm not saying he was the greater loss but Ashley was the key figure in Fairport up to that point. By default he was the captain of the ship; we always expected Ashley to make the decision, if one had to be made. He's always been very good at having the long view in everything that he's done.

'It was a case of finding a new bass player and turning our backs on the idea of a chick singer for a second time. We did consider replacing Sandy but I don't remember us ever acting upon it in any way that suggested we were ever going to try.'

'I wasn't surprised that Sandy left when she did,' says Hutchings. 'The underlying feeling I remember being in the air at that time was a manic feeling. We'd had the crash, we'd not discussed it, in true English-reserve middle-class fashion, we'd brushed it under the carpet and moved on and we didn't have a mass moment of grief, apart from private grief, where it all came out and we talked about it.

'It came out in the songs. Richard wrote "Farewell, Farewell" in particular, but basically we tried to move on and then it started to unravel in a delayed reaction which was sparked by Sandy refusing to go on the flight to Denmark. She was scared stiff of getting on the plane and she got drunk, and she wasn't there when we arrived to pick her up to take her to the airport.'

Hutchings recalls: 'Our reaction was "Well, fuck her, we're going to go by ourselves," and we actually discussed whether this was the end for Sandy: "If she doesn't want to do it, we'll get another singer in. We'll ask her to leave." Then she was bundled on the plane by Anthea Joseph and flew out the next day. And that didn't make everything right and I remember being slightly disappointed that she turned up. We were manic, and I'm sure it was a delayed reaction to the crash. Creating and recording *Liege & Lief* had suspended that moment.

'I don't know why I left Fairport,' continues Hutchings. 'It wasn't to form Steeleye Span, which I did do. After I left the band I had dizzy spells and there was a downward path into a minor break-down that I had. I'm sure Sandy didn't know what she was doing when she left the band either. And if you had asked us both – and this is just my theory – two or three months later, "Would you like to rejoin, would you like to just expunge those last two months since you left, why don't you both get back together again?" I bet we both would have said yes. It's very, very strange.'

None of the band remembers it this way, although Hutchings concedes it might have been said in the heat of the moment after the trip to Denmark, when feelings were on a knife edge, but Linda Thompson recalls Sandy saying that they asked her to leave the group. 'They definitely sacked her. It wasn't told that way. I think they knew she was in a state about it. When they were at the airport and Sandy didn't show up, they could see how it was going to be; she didn't want to tour, certainly not in America, and leave Trevor, and they sacked her, and that flabbergasted her more than anything. "What! Sack me?"'

In years to come, Sandy never spoke about the *Liege & Lief* experience with great enthusiasm – not in the way that she reminisced about Fotheringay or her folk days. She was often dismissive when people said *Liege & Lief* represented her best work. When pushed she would say she liked 'The Deserter' or 'Crazy Man Michael', but she would later state that *Unhalfbricking* was the one she liked best of her Fairport albums and *Full House* her favourite of their other albums. 'I still don't recall that time very clearly,' she said in 1977, 'because it was just after the accident and we lost Martin. Everybody was still in shock and we really didn't know what we were doing. We just sort of did those crazy things and it worked. I know what happened to me; I wanted my own life, which was why I branched out.'

In an *NME* interview in March 1970, the first time she spoke openly about it, Sandy insisted that she had not left Fairport to do 'a big star solo thing'. She said that she hadn't wanted to go to America and had let them down in Copenhagen. 'And they thought I would freak out on them again. So they said it would be better if I left. I was already coming to the same conclusion.' It's an unusually revealing interview. Asked whether she would feature any Fairport songs on the forthcoming tour, she retorts, 'What's the point?' and says she's not too worried about comparisons with her old group: 'Unless they say I should have stayed with Fairport. That would really do me in.'

The press advertisements for *Liege & Lief* described it as 'The first (literally) British Folk Rock LP ever', and above the names of the group they stated: 'Documenting a (very brief) era'. But the reviews were respectful for the most part, rather than unreservedly enthusiastic. They echoed the response of some long-term fans who preferred the Fairport repertoire of old and didn't much care for the direction the group was now taking. At best reviewers found the record worthy and admired what Fairport were attempting, but *Disc* called it 'less accessible and memorable than their previous albums'. *Record Mirror* praised Sandy's vocals but described the album as 'a bit self-indulgent at times'. The *Sounds* reviewer, however, was the first to declare what has since become gospel: that Fairport Convention's renderings of folk songs were 'the most magnetic versions yet conceived'.

Liege & Lief is now almost universally viewed as a landmark album. 'I loved *Liege & Lief*,' says Heather Wood, 'and I still do. Great songs, great arrangements, great people. What could be better? They were doing what we'd been doing for the previous four years. Theirs was just a different approach.' Shirley Collins readily admits it was just outside her field of interest at the time. 'I was always quite happy to listen to unaccompanied old people sing. I didn't need it dressed up except in the way I dressed up the songs with Dolly, without losing the sound of the tradition in it. Sandy, on the other hand, could front an electric band; her voice was that good and that big and that strong. But it was sympathetic as well, and the accompaniments were lovely.

'Traditional songs have always spoken to me more clearly and so totally profoundly that I was completely disinterested in anybody writing their own songs. I lost interest in Anne Briggs when she started writing her own songs – anybody with their foot in both camps I thought was a bit treacherous really – but Sandy's performances of "The Deserter" and "Banks of the Nile" and "A Sailor's Life", they are fantastic. *Liege & Lief* is still a great piece of work. It was the pinnacle of it all.'

Danny Thompson put it more succinctly: 'They took the floor spot, gave it amplifiers, and it swung like the clappers.'

'The thing you can regret that wasn't fully explored', says Joe Boyd, 'was the pop group that was led by Sandy and Richard, the *Unhalfbricking* sequel. Forget *Liege & Lief*, forget folk music, if you took what was "Autopsy", "Meet on the Ledge", that dynamic between Sandy and Richard of writing songs together, or challenging each other to write better and keeping that tight group with Martin, Ashley and Simon, if you can imagine that moving into the future, you can really feel sad about what might have been, even Richard and Sandy singing together. There are few examples where you hear Sandy's and Richard's voices together. And you feel that would have been something they would have figured out in an interesting way, and that's just one of those things that was not to be.'

Richard Thompson echoes those feelings. '*Unhalfbricking* is the better record, a better balanced album, and "A Sailor's Life" – done in one take – is a better recording. That was the start of the process, although *Liege & Lief* has become the landmark album, and rightly so. Once we started, we couldn't go back, and the songs we selected for *Liege & Lief* reflected that decision.'

Sandy played at Les Cousins for the last time in December. In her solo set, *Liege & Lief* was represented only by 'Crazy Man Michael'. She played 'She Moves through the Fair' and 'Who Knows Where the Time Goes?', both of which pre-dated Fairport, and Leonard Cohen's 'Bird on a Wire', a song she had recorded with Fairport for a BBC session. It was a set that touched all bases of her career to date; she wasn't forsaking traditional songs by any means, performing 'Bruton Town' and 'Green Grow the Laurels'. Fittingly, she also played 'Blues Run the Game'. Her set that night featured just one new song, 'The Pond and the Stream', which she would soon record, not as a solo artist but with the new group she was forming with Trevor Lucas.

8 : *Possibly Parsons Green*
1970–1971

All musicians have a group in their lives that's the group they enjoyed playing with the most. That they felt they were being most creative in, most expressive. For all of us in that group, it was Fotheringay.

TREVOR LUCAS, *Juke*, 23 September 1978

There's a general view that I was so against Fotheringay and why was I undermining them on every occasion, and I was. I don't deny it but for very good reasons that people just don't seem to want to know which are at the heart of everything that happens in this world. Somebody's got to pay the bill and Fotheringay was like Greece, it was unsustainable and Sandy was the European bank.

JOE BOYD

I've got no plans for the future but I just hope the future's got some plans for me.

SANDY DENNY, *Sounds*, 24 October 1970

The Pond And The Stream.

Annie wanders on the land ,
She loves the freedom of the air.
She finds a friend iin every place she goes,
There's always a face she knows,
I wish that I was there.

She says " I'm leaving here tomorrow,
To find a new town far away,
She says wont you come too,
you need a break, you'd love to wake up somewhere new,
And find another day.
But I live in the city,
And imagine country scenes,
I live poor among the rich
poor among the rich within four walls
within four walls and out of reach,

Behin a scream.

She smiles as one who loves to smile,
And show that she is free.
                now
Is she thinking that it it's time,
She wandered back again to see her friends and me
We will do live in the city ,
And imagine country scenes,
poor among the rich

Within four

Sandy's lyrics to 'The Pond and the Stream'

Sandy was already putting her new group together with Trevor at the beginning of 1970, using their second-floor flat at 20 Chipstead Street as its base. 'The couple', as many of their friends called them, had now been living there for six months. Trevor had customised and soundproofed the second bedroom as a rehearsal and music room, with enormous Vortex speakers hanging on chains from the ceiling. Sandy was enjoying setting up home for the first time, creating a cosy living room that reflected her taste, with big Chesterfield sofas upholstered in William Morris fabric, hand-sewn fringed covers, shawls and throws, Morris wallpaper, art nouveau posters, and her collection of jardinières, ceramic pots and beaded lamps. A few months later they manoeuvred an upright piano up the stairs and it took pride of place in the living room. 'There'd always be people round the house,' says Stefan Grossman, the flat's previous tenant. 'As you would walk up the stairs there was a sign Trevor put up which said, "Our Home Is Our Office – You Make Appointments at an Office". They wanted people to respect that but nobody did, it was always open house.'

Not least among the occupants were up to four cats – at one point they had three called Ho, Chi and Minh – and Watson the Airedale, whom Sandy and Trevor acquired as a puppy in Chichester that summer. 'He looked remarkably like Trevor, angular features and red hair,' says Richard Thompson. 'When I was still in Fairport in 1970 and we were living at the Angel in Little

Hadham I often used to go and stay at Chipstead Street. Sandy's idea of a good time was getting stoned or getting drunk or both, listening to music and playing Scrabble and Monopoly. There was always lots of stoned Scrabble round at Chipstead Street. It would be classic Sandy, which would dissolve into laughter because she would deliberately put down a word which she knew was wrong.'

When the couple invited *Record Mirror* into their flat that spring, it was clearly staged to present a picture of domestic bliss. Sandy is contentedly sewing cushion covers, a tabby cat by her side, happy discussing feline antics and playfully bickering about her piano skills with Trevor, who tries to rein in the conversation: 'but getting back to the music,' he cuts in, 'we're going to discourage any personality centres in Fotheringay. Sandy was quite upset that most of the press tends to revolve around her. We don't want to present any one person out front. We'd like the band to present itself as a group, a unit.'

Sandy was always unhappy with the fact that she was inevitably the prime focus within the new group – initially called Tiger's Eye. In interviews with the music press which ran in February 1970, she responded angrily and defensively to suggestions that 'she was chasing wealth and solo glory', saying people were 'accusing' her of going solo. It's an odd word to use; why should she feel that a suggestion of going solo was an accusation? It was a dilemma she wrestled with for the remainder of her career: any band she was in was always going to be perceived as *her* project, and she was torn between wanting to be (or feeling she should be) a solo artist and craving the anonymity of just being part of a group.

'The reason I left Fairport was not to go solo,' she told *Music Now* angrily. 'That was silly. That was a load of rubbish. I left Fairport for personal reasons, my personal life was involved. I didn't like going away on long tours and in January we were booked to go to America for two months.' After a barrage of frosty answers the interviewer concludes, 'Wow. I got the message,' adding that 'my advice to Sandy is to relax and concentrate on the most important sentence she uttered during our conversation: "I like having fun."'

In other interviews at the time, Sandy goes to great lengths to explain that the new group is not simply going to be her backing band. Clearly she sought the same collaborative atmosphere that Fairport had achieved. 'I think what changed my mind was seeing Judy Collins one day,' she told *Disc*. 'She was definitely a solo singer who happened to have a good backing group. But that's all they were – a backing group. I thought if you're playing together you might as well be TOGETHER. And look at each other to show you exist.' She also went to see Crosby, Stills, Nash and Young, who 'seemed to have forgotten they had an audience – as though we were incidental. It will be more important to us that the audience enjoys itself.' It was fighting talk ahead of the announcement that the new group was to play its first gig on 16 March, with a Royal Festival Hall headliner a couple of weeks later. They had also officially confirmed the name of the group. 'There is something about the sound of the word Fotheringay that is particularly beautiful,' said Sandy, explaining why they had eventually chosen that name instead of Tiger's Eye. 'We realised afterwards that our albums would be filed under F in record racks, right alongside Fairport.'

Sandy also talked about seeing her old group play the Country Club in West Hampstead at the end of January. She said she felt very nostalgic but had no regrets about leaving. 'I look upon Fairport as the mother group. They've had a lot of people dropping out but they still go on and will be a popular unit for a long time to come.' Her words could not have been more prophetic.

Sandy's decision to form a group rather than go solo was very much against Joe Boyd's wishes, but Boyd could not have been more pleased at how efficiently Fairport Convention had picked up the pieces again. Before they began looking for a new bass player, one or two names were tossed around as replacements for Sandy: A. L. Lloyd, Bob Davenport, Peter Bellamy and Martin Carthy were all considered, however fleetingly. Any suggestion that they ever considered asking Trevor Lucas to join is purely speculative and no 'chick' singers appear to have been considered.

Dave Swarbrick says he was surprised and disappointed when Sandy left Fairport and can offer no insight into why. 'Sandy never told me,' he says, 'and since the convention seemed not to ask directly, I assumed she wanted to go solo. Joe may have done some cherry-picking too. The old enabler! It was hard, of course, but you carry on. Peggy [Dave Pegg] replaced Ashley and we made *Full House*, an album to be really proud of; it was a productive time and the first time that Richard became the lead singer; no grounds for complaint there.'

Incoming bassist Dave Pegg had had a varied history in Birmingham beat groups before joining the Ian Campbell Folk Group. 'There was no discussion about replacing Sandy by the time I came on board,' says Pegg; 'it had been accepted that you can't replace Sandy. You have to go in a different direction when somebody like Sandy leaves, otherwise you are inviting comparison. Nobody could have done the job as well as she did, and that's what they realised.

'The strength of Fairport,' continues Pegg, who has since become the group's mainstay, 'was always that whenever anybody left we either carried on without replacing them or brought somebody into the band from a completely different background, or who played in a completely different way. I fitted those criteria on both counts.'

When the new Fairport line-up debuted at the Hampstead Country Club at the end of January, they played the odd song from *Liege & Lief*, plus a handful of new compositions, including early versions of future Fairport standards 'Sloth' and 'Walk Awhile'. Sandy was there noisily requesting improbable encores from out front. The following month, Fairport began recording the *Full House* album, completed in the US in April. 'Once it happened,' says Boyd, 'the *Full House* band was such a smooth transition. Without Sandy to hold them back, it was like they had been let off the leash: their freedom and the masculinity, the testosterone coming to the fore was something to behold. I remember going to the audition for Peggy, and that was miraculous. The decision to ask him to join was made as quickly and unanimously as when they first heard Sandy.'

Sandy's post-Fairport career went anything but to plan, as far as Boyd was concerned. 'Once I'd accepted the idea that she was leaving Fairport,' says Boyd, 'I sat down with her and said, "OK, Chris Blackwell loves you, Jerry Moss at A&M loves you, but what they want is a solo Sandy Denny record." A&M knew about her going back to Sandy and the Strawbs days, and because they had publishing on "Who Knows Where the Time Goes?", still the only song of Sandy's to have been a hit in America, or anywhere. When Judy Collins recorded it for Elektra it was with David Anderle producing and he was now head of A & R at A&M. So it was all on course to happen. As much as they loved *Liege & Lief*, it was a cult record, a little specialist, but they were happy to have it. Sandy as a solo artist, doing her own songs – they saw her as a potential star.'

At the time Chris Blackwell was in the process of doing a deal with the American record label Capitol to launch Island Records there. Previously Island had only licensed out specific albums in the US. Island had options on any future record of Sandy's, and Boyd knew that if A&M didn't come up with a satisfactory offer, Blackwell would sign her as a solo artist on both sides of the Atlantic. Boyd was also able to exploit a situation – 'I had them by the short and curlies,' he declared – whereby A&M's business affairs lawyer was in a conflict of interest because he also represented Blackwell in setting up Island's US deal. 'So we got a lot of money from A&M for a solo deal for Sandy; it was for £40,000 – twice what they offered for Fairport. Sandy had been saying all along, "I want to form a group with Trevor," but I said, "Hold off," and I thought this would win her round to my way of thinking, but I returned from California to find her and Trevor already in rehearsals with Albert Lee, Pat Donaldson and Gerry Conway.

'I knew that the underlying reason she wanted to form a group with Trevor was so she could be on the road with him and he'd never be out of her sight,' says Boyd. 'She could still have the collaborative relationship and camaraderie of the fixed touring unit with Trevor but she didn't want any part of it being *her* group; she wanted it to be democratic and everyone getting an equal share.'

Boyd suggested to Sandy that Trevor should be musical director of her solo band, stressing that any record had to have Sandy Denny's name on the cover. The deal went through nonetheless. 'So we got her that money and I said, "Can we at least structure it as your group, your deal and your name on the contract?" She refused. It had to be a five-way collaborative deal.' Boyd could only see this as spelling disaster. It not only effectively undermined his authority but also sapped his enthusiasm for the project.

He wanted no part in managing Fotheringay, so they took on Roy Guest as their manager.

Eclection had split up towards the end of 1969, leaving Sandy and Trevor free to form a new group; they immediately recruited Eclection's drummer, Gerry Conway. The idea for the group was to combine some of the elements of Fairport Convention's original folk-rock blend, incorporating some traditional material alongside a more country rock approach. American bands were very much in vogue and visitors to Chipstead Street would usually be treated not only to the Band blaring out of the hi-fi but also to the Janis Joplin-fronted Big Brother and the Holding Company, Captain Beefheart, Buffalo Springfield, the Byrds, the Flying Burrito Brothers, Linda Ronstadt and Crosby, Stills and Young. Sandy and Trevor knew they needed a versatile guitarist and asked Richard Thompson for recommendations. He came up with Albert Lee, very much a guitarist's guitarist.

'I don't think I'd even met Richard at that time,' says Lee, 'although we knew of each other, but he put me forward for the band. They also needed a bass player and I recommended Pat Donaldson,* who I'd known since 1961, and we'd recently been in a country band together called Country Fever, playing pubs to people who weren't really into country. That was in 1968, and around the same time Pat and I were also session players on a record released under the name

---

* Pat Donaldson's first session was in 1962, on Dean Shannon's twist-era reworking of Warren Smith's rockabilly classic 'Ubangi Stomp'. The same year, he joined Albert Lee in a group called Bob Xavier and the Jury. In the mid-sixties Donaldson joined Zoot Money's Big Roll Band, which in turn became the opportunistically psychedelic Dantalian's Chariot in 1967. A year later Donaldson teamed up with Lee again in Country Fever, whose only recordings were eventually released in 1991, credited to Albert Lee, as *Black Claw and Country Fever*.

Poet and the One Man Band. We did a few gigs that never really worked out. We were jobbing musicians, always waiting to see when the next gig or the next session was going to come along.

'It was Trevor who originally called me; the group didn't even have a name and we never played out anywhere, just rehearsing at the flat, mostly the new songs they'd written. I'd been playing R & B for several years with Chris Farlowe and then playing country and rock 'n' roll, so it was a little subdued compared to what I was used to.'

Only weeks into rehearsing with Sandy and Trevor, Lee got an offer to play with Steve Gibbons, whose manager, Tony Secunda, tempted him with the offer of a weekly wage: 'It was more than I'd ever seen before so I ducked out of Sandy's band. There was no ill feeling; I think they knew it wasn't right for me already. I remember Trevor asking me once if I was really into it because there didn't seem a lot for me to do. There wasn't a lot of scope for my style of playing so I bowed out of it and it was Pat who suggested they try Jerry Donahue, who had been brought in as an extra guitar player in Poet and the One Man Band. He was a friend of everybody's because he was a guitar salesman at Selmer's guitar shop on Charing Cross Road.'

New York-born Jerry Donahue, the son of celebrated post-war bandleader Sam Donahue, came to England in 1961 and while studying at colleges in Britain and Germany was in a number of pro and semi-pro groups before his involvement with Poet and the One Man Band. He wasn't sure at first about trying out for Fotheringay. 'I knew Albert didn't feel it was much of a vehicle for his style of playing,' says Donahue, 'so that worried me a little but Pat Donaldson persisted, trying to persuade me to come to rehearsals and meet Sandy and Trevor. He said they wanted a

Joe Boyd (left), of Witchseason Productions, former Fairport Convention singer Sandy Denny and Island boss Chris Blackwell pictured at Sandy's first session at the new Island 16-track studio in Basing Street. She is working on her first album with her new group Fotheringay, for Island release in April. Boyd recently signed a four-year deal with Island giving first option on all Witchseason artists, other than the Incredible String Band.

Island Artists is to book out an exciting new jazz-based progressive band called If, headed by tenor player Dick Morrissey and guitarist Terry Smith. The seven-piece band, which will feature two tenor saxes, is currently rehearsing and will be taking a few mid-week dates until mid-April, when its first album is set for Island release (ILPS 9129). It will then receive a full launch.

Following the re-formation of Traffic, Island Artists is booking the trio out for college and club dates for a five-week period from the beginning of April. The group's new album will be available during that month.

Joe Boyd, Sandy and Chris Blackwell during the first Fotheringay
session at Island's Basing Street Studios

guitarist who wasn't strictly English in his approach and could cover the more country elements in Trevor's writing.'

Donahue had seen Fairport at the Marquee in 1967 and hadn't been too impressed; he'd not heard any of Fairport's albums either, 'but when I finally got down to the rehearsal I was just bowled over when I heard Sandy sing. All it took was the first number we tried out, Gordon Lightfoot's "The Way I Feel"; they loved the guitar part I came up with and I loved their harmony parts. That changed my mind and it changed my life.'

Donahue and Conway paint the same picture of a friendly, laid-back set-up that may ultimately have been the group's undoing. Relying on talent alone, perhaps Fotheringay lacked the purpose-fulness and determination a successful band needs. 'Fotheringay was more of a family than any other band I've been in,' says Donahue. 'We all felt that.' 'Sandy liked to have people around her she could think of as friends,' adds Conway. 'People she could relax with, where she could be herself and be happy around, and she found that with Fotheringay. We spent a lot of time together socially as well.'

The lines between work and play were often blurred. The Chipstead Street flat had already become a social hub, and now it was second home to Fotheringay, but that special rapport had not happened overnight: 'At the beginning of the group I didn't know Pat Donaldson or Jerry Donahue,' said Sandy, 'and we all felt less free to talk about things honestly. It was just a case of getting to know each other properly. I mean there's no real tension now but there was when it started.'

'You had to first gain Sandy's acceptance as a musician,' says Conway, 'but once you did, she really trusted you to do the right thing and you were left to do that. Sandy was no taskmaster. It was an organic process and she never said "do this" or "do that"; it was mostly intuitive. It was more a kind of feeling you got from Sandy when you knew it was right.'

'She was never the boss in Fotheringay,' says Donahue, 'because she always listened to whatever the rest of us contributed musically, while Trevor ran the band logistically. She offered up most of the songs. Trevor was the only other one writing – Sandy really pushed him to write and the way their voices blended was a real hallmark of the Fotheringay sound. It was never just Sandy's band.'

That remained an issue for Joe Boyd, especially her insistence that Trevor should share the focus within the group. Sandy had, however, come up with a series of very strong new songs in 'The Sea', 'Winter Winds', 'Nothing More' and 'The Pond and the Stream'. 'Whenever she presented a song,' says Conway, 'she would be quite coy about it because she desperately wanted approval, she wanted everybody to like what she'd done, which was usually without question, but she needed that reassurance.

'Once she got the piano in the flat, that's how she would introduce her songs to us. She didn't have a great piano technique but her strength was to create beautiful melodies and graceful chords. She worked hard to learn how to play *and* sing, which was something she had never done before. She was a much better musician than she gave herself credit for but she was always very self-effacing about everything.'

With Donahue on the road with country outfit the Tumbleweeds, Fotheringay were only able to rehearse fully for a couple of weeks before their first tour: just five dates but all in concert halls, where they were supported by the Humblebums, then a duo comprising Gerry Rafferty and Billy Connolly, plus Nick Drake as the opening act. With no warm-ups or club dates to prepare them, Fotheringay played well but were often too stiff and uncertain to let go; 'they show promise rather than fulfilment', said Karl Dallas in *The Times*.

Beginning at Birmingham Town Hall on 16 March, they played four shows before sessions got under way at Sound Techniques to record their debut album on the 24th, 26th and 27th. There was a final show at the Royal Festival Hall on 30 March before they

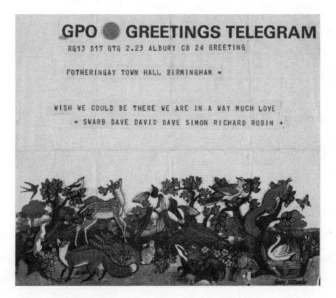

Telegram from Fairport Convention wishing Fotheringay
good luck for their first-ever gig

completed the album on 7 and 14 April. Sandy's reluctance to tour and Donahue's delayed availability meant that Fotheringay was always going to be undercooked. The group's easy-going approach in general meant that nothing was ever rushed, and everybody had their say until a point of consensus was reached. Joe Boyd found such a casual, egalitarian way of going about things – which spilled over into the studio – torturous. He not only liked to be in control but worked best when creating the right ambience in the studio for a group that was well drilled.

Boyd puts it more strongly. 'I know, looking back, I was intolerant. Sandy was the star but she insisted that she and Trevor put together this band; so having got over my shock at the financial structure Sandy insisted upon, I was going to try and put all that to one side and make the best record I possibly can with a band that wasn't fully prepared.'

And against the odds, Fotheringay pulled it off; the eponymous album has more than its share of moments of sheer brilliance. Sandy's singing is arguably her best on record, displaying an undeniable originality, by turns plaintive and sensual, vibrant and grave, intuitive and skilful. As if to confirm the frustrations within Fairport that had encouraged her to leave, she had written more songs for the Fotheringay album than she contributed to Fairport in the whole time she was in the group, and Fotheringay's wonderfully taut arrangement of the traditional 'Banks of the Nile' eclipsed even Fairport's interpretations of traditional material.

Martin Carthy, Shirley Collins and Linda Thompson, among many, cite 'Banks of the Nile' as the consummate Sandy vocal, as does Ashley Hutchings: '"Banks of the Nile", that's the one, and what a one. It's one of Sandy's great performances.'

Although retaining the original verses to this ballad from the

Press ad for the *Fotheringay* album, June 1970

Napoleonic Wars, Fotheringay's less conventional arrangement of 'Banks of the Nile' is based on the version Trevor had recorded on his album *Overlander*. '"Banks of the Nile" was difficult to record,' says Gerry Conway. 'We'd had several goes at it, it just wasn't quite right. It's something that would annoy Joe; we were so relaxed in rehearsals that it carried over into the studio. So we adjourned and went to the pub and we were quite sombre, nobody was saying very much, all trying to work out what we might want to play; then we came back to the studio and it was instantaneous. One take. That was the recording. It was completely unpremeditated.'

Sandy's compositions included two of her great portrait songs: 'The Pond and the Stream' and 'Nothing More'. Richard Thompson is the subject of 'Nothing More', in which Sandy explores the private anguish he suffered after the Fairport crash and the sense that he wouldn't let anyone, including her, get too close to him. 'The Pond and the Stream', written during the *Liege & Lief* rehearsals, places Sandy at the heart of the song as the reluctant traveller wishing she could be freer like her itinerant friend Anne Briggs: 'But I live in the city/And imagine country scenes.' 'She was a lovely lass,' says Briggs, 'and it was very sad that all the pressures of life got too much for her. I had no idea – I thought she was happy – but I was away from all that by then. I'm sure she wasn't envious of me and the way I chose to live, it's just how it happened; she was more reflecting on the way her own life was going.'

'When Annie was around, Sandy used to try and get me to go along and meet her,' says Richard Thompson, 'but Annie would always be a little too worse for wear from drinking. Annie Briggs used to travel a lot.* Sandy found the idea of that quite inspira-

* Anne Briggs was the epitome of an artist who never sought fame. She

tional, wishing she had the freedom of her lifestyle, but Sandy wouldn't have lasted too long without company. Even when she was in London she didn't like being on her own.'

In one of Sandy's notebooks, almost certainly written in 1969, there are three verses to an incomplete song which is also clearly about Briggs:

> How does she bear to have no phone
> to dig the garden all alone
> and smile although she's on her own
> I know she loves someone who lives in Ireland.

The last line is a specific reference to Briggs's boyfriend, Irish musician Johnny Moynihan.

Another high point of the Fotheringay album, 'The Sea' is a beautifully constructed lyric – one of Sandy's best and most overlooked songs – that uses the forecast of a catastrophe in London 'where the sea flows under the doors'. It is still deeply personal:

> You laugh at me on sunny days, but mine's the sleight of hand
> Don't you know I am a joke, a deceiver?
> And I'm waiting on dry land.

By comparison, 'Winter Winds' is delightfully simple, but 'Peace in the End', written with Trevor, has an unusually corny sentiment, however well-intentioned its message. Trevor's 'The Ballad of Ned Kelly', the only song on the album solely attributed

---

effectively retired from singing in 1973, and turned her back on music. She married a forestry worker, and when her husband's job took him to the north of Scotland, they moved to a distant village to raise their two children. Richard Thompson's song 'Beeswing' is inspired by free-spirited artists like Anne Briggs and Vashti Bunyan.

Fortheringay's signatures on signing a release
agreement for the LP with A&M

to him, more than deserves its place; his very own mix of bush
ranger folk and basement tapes Dylan. Anyone who doubts how
well Sandy and Trevor's voices combine need only listen to their
treatment of Gordon Lightfoot's 'The Way I Feel'.

The *Fotheringay* album has aged well and displays a consistency
of content that Sandy rarely equalled, certainly in the light of how
much she struggled to find a balanced musical framework thereafter. It's hard not to conclude that the band broke up too soon and
to wonder what Fotheringay might have accomplished. *Fotheringay*
was released by Island in late June 1970. Its cover painting of the
group by Trevor's sister Marion Appleton reflected Sandy's love of
history, and the Tudors in particular; she is depicted as a courtier
in floral gown. Boyd hated it. In marketing terms it doesn't throw
any focus on Sandy and was too symbolic of the group's all-for-
one-and-one-for-all ethos.

The album spent six weeks in the charts, entering on 11 July
1970 and peaking at number eighteen. Statistically, it was Sandy's

most successful post-Fairport album. Typically, though, Sandy and the other members of Fotheringay failed to promote it; the group had played only one further date (sharing a mouth-watering Roundhouse bill with Fairport and Matthews Southern Comfort on 23 April) since their initial five-date tour three months earlier, and they didn't play again till August. 'We were a little jealous of Fotheringay,' says Dave Pegg; 'we were treading the boards all the time, doing seven gigs to their one. They seemed to have a very easy time of it. Fairport was always a hard-working band.'

Melody Maker's album review said, 'Fotheringay embody the parts of the Fairports I like the best,' and there were similar views expressed elsewhere – all meant as compliments, but they exasperated Sandy. In *Music Now*, she testily comments: 'I'm really amazed that we are compared to Fairport. I don't understand it. This is four different musicians. If the music was the same there would have been no point in leaving Fairport.'

Richard Williams,* who reviewed the album in *Melody Maker*, concluded that Sandy had found 'four musicians who are completely in sympathy and are able to subjugate the power of their playing with the kind of reticence which can produce great music . . . this is the way British music must go.'

'It was a very self-indulgent time,' says Williams, 'and record companies had worked out that you could trust artists to know their audience better than anybody at the record company, but often to their own detriment. Sandy and Fotheringay were allowed that degree of freedom. Fotheringay was a fantastic band but both

---

* Richard Williams was a staff journalist on *Melody Maker* between 1969 and 1973. He went on to become deputy editor, before joining Island Records in an A & R role from 1973 to 1976.

the albums, including the unfinished second one, together they might make one good record. "Banks of the Nile" is, I think, one of the great moments of British music. Better, personally, I would say, than anything Fairport recorded.'

Joe Boyd now feels he should have handed the production of Fotheringay over to somebody else. 'I was not the best person to be producing that band because of the way I felt, but I am very proud of the production of "Banks of the Nile", "The Pond and the Stream", "Winter Winds" and "The Sea", which I think is beautiful.

'They were some of the best things Sandy ever did and the band was good – they are all good, although I was coming in straight from Fairport and at that point – however good they became – Fotheringay was not as good as Fairport. On the face of it, yes, they were a mirror image and there was the chance that it could have been turned into this vehicle that matched Fairport man for man, but they lacked the intensity and the work ethic. And as much her doing as anybody's, Sandy insisted that Trevor had to have "Peace in the End" and "The Ballad of Ned Kelly" on there, and they are OK but they are not at the same level as what she's doing. So I saw the record as flawed.'

Ashley Hutchings feels some sympathy with Fotheringay. His own newly formed group Steeleye Span would often be judged against Fairport. 'Fotheringay did suffer because they weren't Fairport,' he says. 'They are great musicians, and put in some terrific performances, but the group didn't get the recognition it deserved at the time.'

Joe Boyd, however, is still unable to rationalise his initial mis-givings about them. 'Fotheringay was just so alien to the whole Witchseason culture in the way they ran the band. Fairport were lean and mean, they ran a tight ship. There were no flies on

Fairport, their salaries were modest and there was a cushion in the bank. Fotheringay, no, they bought this huge PA system which they called Stonehenge, they bought a Bentley, and I just thought, "What is going on?"'

There's little doubt that there was also a conflict between Boyd and Lucas. Whatever else, their approaches to production were at odds, let alone to life in general – Boyd's cool reserve compared to Trevor's outgoing irrepressible optimism. Boyd's usual partner in the studio, John Wood, wasn't involved in recording the majority of Fotheringay's debut, which was engineered by Jerry Boys. 'There would have been no real common ground between Joe and Trevor in the studio,' Wood told Jim Irvin in 1999. 'They have totally different ideas about making records. Joe's a great believer in people getting on with it and getting something very immediate, the record being a performance. Trevor was obsessed with the deconstruction method, doing things piece by piece.'

Stefan Grossman had arrived in England from New York in 1967.* Joe Boyd was the only person he knew in the country but he soon became good friends with Sandy and Trevor. 'There was competitiveness between Joe and Trevor,' says Grossman. 'Joe would have wanted to control the way the record sounded and Trevor would have voiced his opinion even though Joe was the producer. They were always a little stand-offish towards each other, and Joe really wanted Sandy to make a solo record and not be in a band, and he felt Trevor was complicit in that.'

Boyd's other contention was that Trevor and Fotheringay in

---

* Stefan Grossman used all the Fotheringay musicians on his 1970 album *The Ragtime Cowboy Jew*, Sandy and Trevor Lucas singing on 'My Pretty Little Tune', as well as in the chorus on Grossman's next album, *Those Pleasant Days*.

general were running through Sandy's advance. 'Trevor was a fun guy and outrageous for the times,' says Gerry Conway. 'He'd go feet first – "Let's build a giant PA system," "We're going to drive around in limousines" – and Sandy loved that about him. People might point the finger now and say he was squandering money, but don't forget that Sandy loved to have a good time and she liked her luxuries.

'The PA was his grandest scheme and it was a bit of a folly. It became known as Stonehenge; the idea was to enable us to play more acoustically without it sounding too wimpy, but when you stood next to it you couldn't hear anything coming out of it.' Doon,* Fotheringay's soundman, a friend of Sandy's from way back, had also worked with Eclection. 'Trevor decided we needed these big cabinets,' said Doon, 'so we built this thing – Stonehenge – but then I had to hire a seven-and-a-half-tonne truck because the band's gear was too big to go into a Transit. We never toured enough to cover the costs. I remember once at Oxford we picked up the local taxis coming through the PA because the mic cables were too long.'

Fotheringay's outgoings were never equalled by the money coming in. The group continued to play very little, just the odd festival that summer and then nothing until a couple of UK dates in September. Fotheringay also spent six weeks over the summer at a Farley Chamberlayne-style retreat at Chaffinches Farm, in

* When Doon died in February 2014, Ralph McTell wrote an affectionate obituary: 'It was Trevor Lucas who renamed the former "Gordon Graham" DOON after the way he perceived Doon to pronounce his name. The name stuck and Doon named his small PA company Rig o' Doon. Doon became a total confidant of Sandy; she valued Doon's gentle, non-aggressive stance and many tears were splashed on his shoulders during their long and fruitful creative time.'

Burdham on the Sussex coast. 'They had taken over a month out to rehearse in the country,' says Boyd disparagingly, 'but spent more time on the beach than working on new songs.'

Come September, for the first of two years running readers of *Melody Maker* voted Sandy Best British Female Singer. The poll results were announced on 19 September 1970 with the headline 'Pop Poll Rocked', more a reference to Led Zeppelin toppling the Beatles as Best Group after eight consecutive years than about Sandy winning. The award party was held at the Savoy, where Sandy was photographed with the group and with her arm around Robert Plant, who had been voted Top Male Singer. She told the *Sun* it was strange because '99 per cent of the country have never heard of me', and the paper declared that 'unknown Sandy is our top of the pops'.

'The reality of the *Melody Maker* polls was that you didn't have to get many votes,' says Richard Williams.* 'I can't remember the figures but it would have been hundreds rather than thousands, and in the case of the jazz poll, not even dozens. We were selling two hundred thousand copies a week and folk music was still a core part of *Melody Maker*, but it was a flawed indicator of popularity. Only within a small part of the universe did anybody, including Sandy, believe she was as popular as Dusty or Sandie Shaw, who were winners during the sixties.'

---

* The 1969 winner had been Christine Perfect, with Sandy positioned at six between Lulu and Cilla Black. Sandy topped the poll again in 1971, but in 1972 it was Maggie Bell who won. Sonja Kristina, who had been Sandy's replacement in the Strawbs and was now fronting Curved Air, was second; Sandy had slipped to number three. By 1972 singer-songwriters were now well represented, including Claire Hamill, Bridget St John and Lesley Duncan.

When Sandy was interviewed for the World Service's prestigious *Tomorrow's People* in January 1972, she was asked about the
two poll wins: 'I was utterly amazed when I first won it but when
I won it the second year running, you [could have] knocked me
over with a feather.' What difference did it make to her? the interviewer asked. 'Nothing! I mean, it didn't make any difference at
all. Except that I've got two pieces of quartz.' Yet the awards did
fuel Island Records' belief that Sandy should be a solo artist, and
even in 1977 they were still mentioning the polls in press releases.

Doubts as to whether Fotheringay was the best vehicle for
Sandy were raised by a disastrous Royal Albert Hall concert on 2
October, just two weeks after the *Melody Maker* awards. It would
deflate Sandy's resolve and confidence in the months to come.
The group had asked Elton John to support them and he simply
stole the show. Donaldson, Conway and Donahue had undertaken
a session during the summer to record publishing demos for artists contracted to Boyd's publishing company; the session singers
were Linda Thompson, who was then Boyd's girlfriend, and Elton
John, covering songs by Nick Drake, Mike Heron and John and
Beverley Martyn. 'So we asked Reg [Elton John] to open for us,'
says Donahue, 'and he really did steal the evening. We had drawn
the crowd – it's no mean feat to sell out the Royal Albert Hall –
and Elton was pretty much unknown. It was a turning point for
him and a real disappointment for us. We had to try and put it
behind us but it played on Sandy's nerves; it really knocked her
back.'

Fotheringay had also made the mistake of using the concert to
play new material. 'Even at the Royal Albert Hall, home of the
automatic encore,' wrote Jerry Gilbert in *Sounds*, 'it is dangerous
to reserve the showpiece song, "Banks of the Nile", for the curtain

call. Fotheringay discovered this when audience reaction scarcely invited a return at the end of their set.'

The combined effect of the *Melody Maker* poll success, the Royal Albert Hall fiasco and the rise of the singer-songwriter,* now a distinct phenomenon, provided Joe Boyd and Island Records with the leverage to try to persuade Sandy that this was the right time to make a solo album rather than another with Fotheringay.

'There were always people saying to Sandy, "You should be a solo artist,"' says Conway, 'especially after the *Melody Maker* poll. Then, after we were upstaged by Elton John, they began saying the band wasn't good enough. It wasn't just Joe, but people at Island had definitely swung round to thinking Sandy should get rid of the band and go solo. The pressure was mounting.'

It couldn't come a moment too soon for Boyd. 'I'm dealing with this crazed spendthrift band,' he ranted, even forty years later, 'which is working its way through Sandy's forty grand so fast that it's not going to last the year. And the first record isn't that great, a curate's egg of a record with a corny cover – there's no picture of Sandy other than cartoon-like in an Elizabethan gown on the front – so that detracted from the focus of the band. Sure, the album charted moderately, but they did nothing to sustain that. So of course I'm not feeling positive about Fotheringay and their direction.'

As part of their preparation ahead of recording the second album, Fotheringay played further dates in October, eight in all,

---

* Initially an American phenomenon, the trend took hold in 1970 with albums by James Taylor, Carole King, Joni Mitchell and Neil Young, creating a new wave of sensitive, confessional singer-songwriters for whom the album had become an artistic statement. The movement gathered momentum in 1971, by which time breakthrough British artists Cat Stevens and Elton John had also found massive success in America.

and recorded two BBC sessions in mid-November. The songs they taped for the BBC included Sandy's powerful anti-war song 'John the Gun' and five traditional songs: 'Bold Jack Donahue', 'Eppie Moray', 'Gypsy Davey', 'Wild Mountain Thyme' and 'The Lowlands of Holland', all earmarked for the next album. The selection suggested that Sandy was more than happy to return to some of her favourite traditional songs; another one mooted and demoed was 'Bruton Town'. She had also asked Dave Cousins to write some additional lyrics for 'Two Weeks Last Summer'.

Aside from 'John the Gun', Sandy offered up only one other new song, 'Late November'. Boyd must surely have been concerned and a little perplexed that there were only two Sandy originals lined up for the album he was about to record with Fotheringay, and that she had turned back to the traditional direction which had driven her out of Fairport. A greater worry for him was that Sandy was also relinquishing a lot of the vocals for the songs being put forward. Trevor was taking the lead on the traditional bush ranger's tale 'Bold Jack Donahue' and for much of 'Eppie Moray' and the Dylan cover 'I Don't Believe You', as well as his own two songs, 'Restless' and 'Knights of the Road'.* Effectively Sandy was singing on only half the album. 'It raises the question,' says Boyd,

---

* Trevor Lucas wrote a number of songs with Peter Roche in 1970, and Roche has long been a subject of speculation among fans. Roche edited Corgi's best-selling poetry anthology *Love, Love, Love* in 1967, which includes the work of Pete Brown, Adrian Henri, Roger McGough and Brian Patten, among other contemporary poets, including Roche himself. Trevor confirmed his writing partner was the same Peter Roche in an interview on New South Wales radio station 2NUR in 1985. 'Knights of the Road', 'Restless', 'The Plainsman' and 'Possibly Parsons Green' all later appeared on Fairport Convention albums during Trevor's tenure with the group.

'as to whether democracy is a good thing if she was giving every-body in the band equal weight when she was the undoubted crea-tive force. When we started doing the second Fotheringay album, it just seemed to get harder in the studio, really hard work.'*

More than anyone, Jerry Donahue has carried the torch for Fotheringay, and he and Joe Boyd have often clashed over how well or how badly the sessions went; the two of them argue to this day over how many takes they did for 'John the Gun'. 'We were all so excited by the recording,' says Donahue, 'and it was imme-diately clear how much we'd evolved as a band. The first track we recorded was "Late November" and we took just two takes. It was obvious we were so much tighter as a unit.'

'Even the first album I now think would have gone smoother if I hadn't been around,' says Boyd. 'I have to accept that when it comes to Fotheringay I felt negatively towards them much of the time, and that might have had a negative effect on the recording.'

There is also a back story to the second album sessions, whereby Boyd had been offered a job by Warner Brothers in California and it wasn't just Fotheringay causing him day-to-day grief. 'There were an awful lot of things piling up. Witchseason Productions was getting less and less solvent and becoming dependent on Island to cover the debts. For everyone the process had been demystified and so the relationships changed. I was very proud of the work I'd done as a record producer and felt a little bit miffed that most of the artists were going off their own way and not taking my advice on a lot of things. Sandy was just one case in point.'

* Fotheringay completed five sessions for their second album at Sound Techniques during October, on 17 and 18 November, and in December immediately before the Christmas break.

So when Warner Brothers offered him the opportunity to head part of its film division as Director of Music Services, Boyd went to Chris Blackwell, who was nothing but encouraging: 'Blackwell said he would buy the company, cover the debts, pay everybody's royalties up to date, and I decided it was too good an offer to miss. I felt like something was over, a cycle had concluded, it was time to do something else. Most of the groups seemed to be fairly philosophical about my walking out but Sandy and Nick Drake were the most upset by the idea.'

The smoking gun, as Boyd puts it, came after a disastrous session running up to the Christmas break. During the recording of 'John the Gun' Boyd finally threw up his hands and said, 'Everybody get out of here, I can't take any more of this.' After the aborted session he, Sandy and Trevor went out to dinner. 'Sandy and I both had a lot to drink and she said, "Maybe you're right, I'll break up the group if you'll produce my solo record." And I said, "Sure," and what else was said is unclear but in my mind it was, "I'll take a break from my job in California to produce your solo record," and in her mind it was, "I won't go to California." I'm sure I said something like, "I don't think I can, but that's the only thing right now that's worth considering as a reason to stay."'

In the new year Fotheringay reconvened at Sound Techniques after the Christmas break; in tears, Sandy told the group it was over. Donahue has described it as the worst moment of his life.

'We were mortified when the band split up,' says Conway, 'and Sandy broke down in the control room, saying she had been talked into going solo and she didn't really want to. She said, "There's no way I could say no to the people who have done so much for my career. I've just got to trust Joe." So that was it for all of us.'

The next morning Boyd was asked to meet Sandy and Roy

Guest, Fotheringay's manager, at 11 a.m. 'And that was that famous moment when she said, "When can we start the solo record?" And I said, "I have to go to California and get settled in – so the first moment I can get a week off." And she said, "What, you're still going?" I said, "I've got to go, I've signed the contract and sold Witchseason." It was all agreed.'

When Sandy told him she'd broken up the group, Boyd says his reaction was, 'If the only reason you've broken up the band is because you thought I would stay, then unbreak up the band.' Boyd couldn't see how anything could be so set in stone that it couldn't be changed back. 'My own personal theory,' he says, 'is that on some level the financial issues and possibly the artistic ones had got through to Sandy. I think she was relieved and she didn't want to go back, so I was an appropriate excuse to get this monkey off her back; certainly financially, because the money was running out and Fotheringay wasn't making any money. So I think the misunderstanding we had, or her reading of what was said, provided the opportunity for her to say to them, "I don't want to but I'm leaving the band."'

'She didn't want to do it but she was urged to go solo,' says Donahue. 'She didn't really have a choice, I don't think, so we had to shelve what we were doing.* She knew from the start that

---

* Supervised by Jerry Donahue, *Fotheringay 2* was assembled from the 1970 master tapes with Pat Donaldson and Gerry Conway and finally released in 2008. All Sandy's original vocals were used, although these had in most cases been guide vocals, recorded live with the rhythm section with the intention of replacing them during overdub sessions that never came to pass. 'They are some of her best vocal performances,' says Donahue. 'She was always spontaneous doing guide vocals because the focus was on the band getting it right, not her, so she would sing from the heart without her nerves undermining the performance.'

I'VE ALWAYS KEPT A UNICORN

both Island and A&M always wanted her as a solo artist. And she trusted them and what influenced her decision was that she felt she owed a lot of her high profile to Joe Boyd and people at Island, so she felt like she couldn't say no. In the end she felt there were promises that weren't kept once Joe took up the position at Warner Brothers.'

'I certainly didn't want to go through that again,' said Pat Donaldson in 1989, 'to have somebody pull the plug on you and have absolutely no control. There was no real explanation at all, and now I don't really want to know – I'm happy with the memories of the band. Fortunately, after all that we didn't stop playing with one another or seeing one another. Had it just happened and we'd never seen one another again – then I'd have been mad about it.'

It was *Melody Maker* that broke the news as the cover story on 9 January 1971, with a statement that said Sandy had dissolved the band 'so that she could make her first solo album'. The next part of her statement is more illuminating. 'We weren't a rich band. We couldn't afford to take time off from being on the road since we needed to work to keep going.' Given that Fotheringay so rarely toured, the statement gives some weight to Boyd's argument that Sandy was concerned about the band's finances. The following week, *Sounds* contradicted what had been said the week before: 'Sandy admitted this week that Fotheringay's producer and recording manager had precipitated the break-up of the band.' Roy Guest added that 'we were halfway through the album and Joe just wasn't satisfied, so he stopped it and brought the whole thing to an end'. Guest then adds disingenuously: 'Once the decision was made Sandy, Trevor Lucas and I were quite happy with the result.'

Whatever the disappointments, the Fotheringay musicians all

went on to have successful careers. Gerry Conway concedes that being in Fotheringay might have been too much of a good thing. 'We weren't taking things as seriously as you might when you get older. We really enjoyed being in Fotheringay, all of us, but we should have toured more, and Sandy did have a reluctance to tour; as it was Sandy didn't really step up from where she left off with Fairport. And, of course, Fotheringay wasn't going long enough to evolve or find that next level.

'It was never a case of feeling vindicated after Fotheringay. That never came into it. Fotheringay launched careers for the rest of us; Jerry, Pat and myself were already beginning to make a name for ourselves doing sessions, particularly at Sound Techniques, and that's how I met Cat Stevens.'*

'We all had to move on,' says Donahue, 'but Sandy definitely regretted that decision to split the band and she said it repeatedly in interviews even three or four years later. And none of us stopped working with her on record or live when our commitments allowed.'

'For Sandy to turn round, not just to a band but to her friends,' says Linda Thompson, 'and say, "We're not going to continue," I think that did have a profound effect on her. It was less about Joe leaving for America – that misunderstanding or whatever happened between them. Joe leaving for America is more of a pivotal

---

* Gerry Conway's first sessions with Cat Stevens were for his album *Teaser and the Firecat*. Alongside Elton John, Stevens was the most successful singer-songwriter to come out of Britain. In 1971 he was responsible for almost a quarter of Island's total sales. 'Sandy was just not as driven by success,' says Conway. 'Cat Stevens was completely clued in – very autocratic, so he would control everything and would download instructions to you as a musician. He was incredibly focused, in the best possible way, whereas Sandy – if it felt comfortable, that was enough.'

moment in Joe's mind than it is in anybody else's. I never knew Sandy be too dejected about Joe. She might have gone, "That fucker has fucking gone off to fucking America" – I would have heard her say that but I never heard her break down about it.'

Yet Sandy was never able to let it go, and would bring up the break with Joe and Fotheringay time and time again. Even two years later, in a major *Rolling Stone* interview in May 1973, she laid the blame firmly at 'this person' Joe Boyd's feet. 'They hated us at the [Witchseason] office. They kept saying, "Look, you're not Fairport, you're not the Incredibles, you're nobody."' American readers might have been bemused by the outburst over a group which had made no impact there at all, but an even more damning tirade came a year and a half later, when she and Jerry Donahue were interviewed together for WQAX in Bloomington, Indiana, by Neil Sharrow on 18 October 1974. 'They [Witchseason] had it in for us right from the beginning,' she said almost tearfully, 'and they succeeded in the end in breaking up the band, which was the heartbreaking thing about it. Each of us loved each other a lot; we got on really well, more than is possible to explain.'

She continued: 'He [Boyd] said he would stay in England and not take the offer to join Warner Brothers because "I really think you should be solo." And finally he cracked me that much that I agreed to do it. If he felt so strongly about it then I thought he's got to be right – he led us all into fairly illustrious careers, and I used to know him really well from a long time before – he was a really good friend of mine – I thought, if he says this so often and really is so adamant about it, I thought, OK. And he might have been right but what did he do? He took the job.'

'It definitely damaged my relationship with her,' admits Boyd. 'She felt that I had gone back on my word. We became friends again but certainly I was never as close to her again. I plead guilty to thinking it was the right path for Sandy, and I still feel that. If people think the first Fotheringay record – and the second record that was left unfinished – if people hold those records up as among her best work, then I have to disagree. They were not, at least not in their entirety.

'In a way,' says Boyd reflectively, 'Fotheringay became the template for her albums in the seventies, where you would have four or five great songs and others that were filler material. That's certainly the problem with *The North Star Grassman and the Ravens* that she did next.'

Richard Thompson, who co-produced that album with Sandy, feels the blame for breaking up Fotheringay can't be left solely at Joe Boyd's door. 'It's a shame that it was so messy, the way it was handled, but it was always going to be difficult whenever she made that decision. Joe always felt she should have made a solo record right after she left Fairport, but I don't think she was ready at that point. But Sandy was always going to end up as a solo artist and I think that was the right time for her to take that step – after Fotheringay.'

In the long term, Boyd's leaving for America and not producing Sandy's first solo record was probably less significant than the void he left within Island for the Witchseason acts. 'There wasn't anyone in Island who replaced me,' admits Boyd. 'I was an anomaly within Island; Witchseason wasn't a label deal. If I had just said, "OK, Chris, take over the company, pay me a salary, give me an office in the corner and I'll just carry on looking after these artists, Nick and Sandy, Fairport, Richard." And I think to myself, "Why wasn't that ever an idea?" And the reason was that I was just so exhausted, worn out by exactly this kind of thing. Sandy and Fotheringay, the Incredible String Band was getting out of hand, Nick Drake deciding he'd do this crazy idea of making a record with no accompaniment except himself – which now of course sells twice as many as the other two. I was frazzled by the whole experience. I went to America. That's history.'

Linda Thompson comments: 'Richard and Nick and Sandy were Joe's golden trio – I think that's why it was so hard for Joe before he went to work in America, because he was having problems with all of them at the time. And the Incredible String Band were impossible once they became Scientologists. So I think he felt it was slipping away from him.'

Fotheringay has, over the years, become the 'what if?' moment in Sandy's career. 'I'm guilty of looking through the same rose-coloured glasses,' says Boyd, 'where I think if, after she left Fairport, she had let me do a Sandy Denny solo record with her, then both our lives might have been very different. I might not have gone to LA, it might have been a huge hit and, of course, it might have been a total flop as well.'

We'll never know how much Trevor and Sandy discussed whether or not to pursue Fotheringay during the Christmas break in 1970, although friends said she was constantly changing her mind until she finally confronted the band with the news. After the split in January 1971, Trevor followed a different path to his bandmates and decided to turn his hand to record production. He spent the rest of that year learning the ropes at Island Studios as an in-house engineer and tape operator. 'The rest of us found regular work straight away,' says Gerry Conway, who had adamantly vetoed any idea of Fotheringay carrying on without Sandy, 'either touring or playing sessions. Trevor wanted to stick by Sandy but he always harboured ambitions to go into producing and saw that as the way forward in working with Sandy.' Sandy's own future was secured: she signed to Island as a solo artist on 28 January 1971, two days before Fotheringay's final concert.

The day of the concert, BBC Radio broadcast an hour-long Fotheringay documentary on *Folk on One*. Among those giving testimonials, only Karl Dallas hinted at undisclosed reasons for the split, mentioning 'false friends and real enemies getting between the artist and their music'. Unlike their previous London showcases, Fotheringay's final show, at the Queen Elizabeth Hall on 30 January, was a triumph. It featured all the material they had been recording for the second album, including Sandy's 'John the Gun' and 'Late November'. Long John Baldry, Martin Carthy and Ashley Hutchings all made guest appearances, and Sandy brought down the house when she sang a fitting and emotional 'Let It Be' at the piano as an encore.

Another Sandy original, the sombre 'Wretched Wilbur', was also debuted at the final Fotheringay show. Written soon after the decision to split up the group, it presents a jumble of sketches of past associates, including Ashley Hutchings and Dave Cousins. Its reflections on the passing of the summer, when 'it took so long to see', and the long winter ahead are evocative of the struggles Sandy must have gone through in deciding whether or not to go solo. She was very subdued when interviewed for the *Folk on One* documentary. 'I feel very uncertain about things but I think I'll make a record now and see how it goes for a couple of months.'

9 : *The Queen of Light Took Her Bow*
1971–1972

The future is like the next minute, and the minute after. We don't know what will happen between now and eight o'clock. I can't think a week ahead.

SANDY DENNY, *Petticoat*, 20 February 1971

In Tobias Smollett's eighteenth-century novel *The Expedition of Humphry Clinker*, the character is described by Smollett as being a man without a skin, he was so sensitive to everything and everyone, and I think of Sandy that way sometimes. She was ultra-sensitive to every little thing in the world. She had an incredible imagination. It was as if she lived more vividly than the rest of us. And I think that ability to get right inside a song, inside the persona of a song, was really quite extraordinary.

RICHARD THOMPSON

When I sit down at the piano the words come in their thousands – doomy, metaphorical phrases, minor keys, weird chords – and I can't do a thing about it.

SANDY DENNY, *Sounds*, 8 January 1972

Front cover of Island's press biography for Sandy's first solo album

Sandy as a baby

Sandy and David at Worple
Road

Sandy (*far left*) and her school clique, 1963

Sandy in Trafalgar Square   Early folk club appearance, 1965

Sandy's chalk drawing, with the Strawbs, 1967

Trevor as a child   Trevor playing in London, 1965

Fairport at Farley Chamberlayne, summer 1969 (Eric Hayes)

Sandy and Trevor, Chipstead Street

Trevor and Watson looka-
likes

Sandy and Trevor's wedding group,
September 1973

Fairport backstage in Sydney, 1974

Sandy with Trevor's parents, Melbourne, 1974

Watson standing guard outside The Twistle

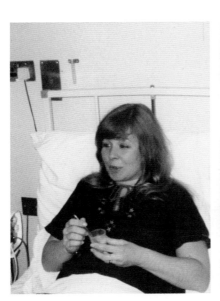

Sandy in hospital after Georgia's birth

Trevor and Georgia

Sandy and Trevor with Neil and Edna Denny

Sandy and Neil

Sandy's VW Beetle

Nigel and Marion with Georgia, Heathrow, 13 April 1978

During Fotheringay's final performance at the end of January 1971, Sandy played three songs she later featured on her debut album. The rest were slow in coming, born out of what Sandy admitted was a depressed state – in one interview she described herself as feeling 'very void' after disbanding Fotheringay. The new recordings eventually spanned almost three months from the first sessions at the beginning of March to wrapping up the title track, 'The North Star Grassman and the Ravens', at the end of May.

Yet before Sandy began work on her debut solo album, she recorded what would become by far her best-selling and best-known vocal performance. Her soaring shared vocal with Robert Plant on Led Zeppelin's 'The Battle of Evermore' is familiar to the thirty-seven million people worldwide who have bought a copy of *Led Zeppelin IV*.

Jimmy Page and Robert Plant were fans of both Fairport Convention and the Incredible String Band, and Page had followed the work and career of Bert Jansch. On *Led Zeppelin*, Page reworked Jansch's arrangement of 'Blackwaterside' as 'Black Mountain Side'. After *Led Zeppelin II*, Page talked about wanting to do more of a 'Pentangle-type thing', which resulted in a more acoustic presence on *Led Zeppelin III*.

Robert Plant and John Bonham both knew Fairport's Dave Pegg from when they were all playing in local Brumbeat bands in the mid-sixties; one of Pegg's bands, the short-lived Way of Life, featured the eighteen-year-old Bonham. Led Zeppelin famously jammed with the *Full House* Fairport Convention at the Troubadour on 4 September 1970, where Thompson and Swarbrick put Page through his paces on a series of furious jigs and reels before they found more familiar ground on 'Hey Joe', 'Morning Dew' and 'Mystery Train'.* The *Melody Maker* Poll Winners bash at the Savoy was just a few weeks later, and there Sandy first met all four members of Led Zeppelin.

'Led Zeppelin's association with Fairport was really strong,' said Plant. 'I was an admirer. When Jimmy Page and I began writing "The Battle of Evermore", it was obvious that it was a two-voice part. The song itself required a response. The other voice would be the rallying cry. To hear Sandy's first vocal response to my first vocal line was amazing. She went into this thing and I looked at Jimmy through the screen in the studio and we both just nodded.' Plant loved the lonesome lyrical quality of Sandy's voice and admired how 'she was able to go from a very deep point in a song to flying up into this beautiful falsetto, this high pitch where she has got absolutely total control'.

Robert Plant once described Sandy as his favourite singer out of all the British girls that ever were. They'd become friends after the *Melody Maker* party; he and Jimmy Page also went along to Fotheringay's ill-fated Royal Albert Hall concert. He said it was the most obvious thing to ask her to sing with him on 'The Battle of Evermore'. 'It was a spectacular moment for both of us,' he said. 'Our worlds joined, we had these great moments, and then we disappeared to wave across crowded rooms as the years went by.'

* This was taped by Joe Boyd and John Wood, who recorded the Troubadour shows for a future live Fairport Convention album (finally released in 1977). The jam with Zeppelin in 1970 was most likely seized by Zeppelin manager Peter Grant and has never even turned up on bootleg.

Led Zeppelin had begun working on their fourth album in December 1970, writing and recording most of *Led Zeppelin IV* using a mobile studio at their own Hampshire country retreat, Headley Grange, where some of their more reflective songs were written in the evenings in front of the fireplace. Robert Plant came up with lyrics for 'The Battle of Evermore' in these quietly conducive conditions at the beginning of January 1971, once describing it as more of a playlet than a song. Jimmy Page then conjured up the musical accompaniment just as spontaneously, almost instinctively, on hearing Plant's lyrics. He explained to *Guitar Player* magazine in 1977: 'On "The Battle of Evermore", a mandolin was lying around . . . I just picked it up, got the chords, and it sort of started happening. I did it more or less straight off.'

In the new year Led Zeppelin switched to Island's Basing Street Studios for overdubs, where Sandy's vocals were recorded within days of Fotheringay's final show at the end of January. Her vocal for 'The Battle of Evermore' was one of the most crucial sessions. 'I approached Sandy . . . and she was up for it,' said Plant. 'I don't think it took more than forty-five minutes. I showed her how to do the long "Oooooh, dance in the dark" so there'd be a vocal tail-in. It was perfect against my bluesy thing.'

Such was the significance of Sandy's contribution that the group felt she should be given her own symbol on the sleeve of the album released in November 1971. 'I hate it being called "Four Symbols",' said John Bonham in October 1978 for Pennine Radio in Bradford. 'In any case it should be five symbols. We made sure Sandy had a rune to credit her appearance. Hers was the double trinity.'* The

---

* Like the symbols representing John Paul Jones and John Bonham, Sandy's symbol was taken from *The Book of Signs* by Rudolf Koch.

symbol consists of three triangles arranged around one inverted triangle.

Sandy invariably made light of any monetary consideration for her involvement on 'The Battle of Evermore'. Following a show with Fairport at the Berkeley Community Theatre on 10 November 1974, she was asked if she was likely to do any further recordings with Led Zeppelin. She laughed and replied, 'They still haven't paid me for the track that I've already done.'

'She never got a penny for that,' said Neil Denny. 'She had that one saved up. Some day she was going to go to Led Zeppelin and say "You owe me."'

'The Battle of Evermore' was unique, the only song Led Zeppelin ever recorded with a guest vocalist.* 'It's unthinkable now,' says Tim Clark, Island's head of marketing at the time, 'but Sandy's recording with Led Zeppelin wasn't seen as that big a deal, not to the extent that it is today. It was never something we exploited in the press. Now it's a bullet point in her career because Zeppelin's stature just grew exponentially after they split up and obviously continues to do so.'

Nor was Sandy asked very often about her Led Zeppelin cameo in interviews; talking about her duet with Plant, all she told *Rolling Stone* in 1973 was: 'We started out soft but I was hoarse by the end, trying to keep up with him.' When Patrick Humphries brought it up in 1977 she was equally matter-of-fact. It was just another

---

* Led Zeppelin rarely played 'The Battle of Evermore' live, but when they did, John Paul Jones sang Sandy's part. In later years, Plant had tremendous success singing with Alison Krauss, and they performed the song in their live shows together. Sandy's role was reinterpreted by British Asian vocalist Najma Akhtar on Page and Plant's *No Quarter* tour in 2013.

day in the office: 'They rang me up and asked me to do it and I thought, "Why not?" I'm game to do anything really; I mean, I did *Tommy* as well. I'm not proud as far as "if it's not folk I don't want to know about it" because I'm not like that at all. I really have a wide appreciation of what I like – if it's good and it appeals to me, that's great because I'm not a snob.'

Sandy performed the fleeting role of the nurse, with just one repeated line – 'It's a boy, Mrs Walker, it's a boy' – in Lou Reizner's 1972 London Symphony Orchestra version of the Who's rock opera *Tommy*. It was not lost on Pete Townshend that Sandy had once been a nurse, although he claimed he had nothing to do with the casting. When the orchestral performances of *Tommy* took place at the Rainbow Theatre in December 1972, Sandy was among the all-star cast, including the Who, Peter Sellers, Steve Winwood, Ringo Starr and Richie Havens. 'I sing one line in *Tommy*,' she said later, 'and this guy calls up and says, "Can you come down to the presentation and pick up your gold record?"'

Sandy did very few sessions over the years but the scope of these certainly bears out her philosophy of 'being game to do anything'. Aside from more predictable contributions for friends like Marc Ellington, Stefan Grossman, Ian Matthews and Richard Thompson, her session work is varied almost to the point of unfathomability: from a soundtrack album recorded with Manfred Mann in the summer of 1970, to *Ribbons of Stainless Steel*, a country album by British wrestling champion Brian Maxine recorded in 1974. She even added vocals to a single with British slapstick comic actor and singer Charlie Drake in 1975, albeit co-written and produced by Peter Gabriel. Manfred Mann had asked her to work on a Danish-made movie about a young, bed-hopping, single-mum stewardess,

The *Swedish Fly Girls* soundtrack album to which Sandy contributed

Swedish Fly Girls,* after doing some jingles with her. 'She was lovely and easy to work with so we used her in the movie,' said Mann.

The only known commercial work that Sandy did was a butter advertisement. After a silky smooth male voice asks, 'Could you really give them anything else but butter?' Sandy's unmistakable voice chimes in, singing, 'We're all a lot better for butter,' over a folksy melody. 'I did a lot more commercials than Sandy,' says Linda Thompson; 'they were the best-paid jobs I did. Sandy kept very quiet about doing them; she dreaded that Richard would find out as she thought he'd really disapprove.'

* The film was originally released under the title *Christa* in 1971, and it played at Cannes and opened in New York. It was then re-released as *Swedish Fly Girls* in 1972, along with the soundtrack album.

None of Sandy's sessions can be seen as calculated career moves, nor motivated by financial incentives. 'She was full of contradictions,' says Richard Thompson. 'She wanted to be successful, she wanted to be popular and usually she believed she was as good as anybody, but she didn't necessarily know how to get from A to B. She made some strange choices but you couldn't tell Sandy what to do. She was very strong-willed but she could doubt herself at times, and that sometimes quashed that confidence and held her back.'

Her broad taste in music, however, reflected the more wilful Sandy who knew her own mind and didn't much care what people thought. It sometimes had its downside. 'The wide sweep of her taste led her to including things on her albums that didn't always work in the context of a whole album,' says Joe Boyd. 'She had an encyclopaedic knowledge of other music, more than her contemporaries, certainly anybody who came out of folk. She loved the 1957 Philippe Koutev *Music of Bulgaria*, this was fifteen years before anyone thought of reviving it; she knew rock 'n' roll and country music; she was very open-minded.'

Richard Thompson also recalls Sandy's wide-ranging record collection. 'There wasn't too much folk, but Aretha Franklin, Billie Holiday, early Neil Young . . . some rock 'n' roll, Buddy Holly, the Everly Brothers, Rick Nelson. She really liked the Beatles. When she was growing up she heard a real cross-section of music on the radio, which was typical of the generation that listened under the bedclothes to Radio Luxembourg and to *Saturday Club*, which would feature everything from the Joe Loss Dance Band to Alma Cogan to the Pretty Things.'

'She wasn't at all snobbish in what she liked,' says Bambi Ballard. 'I despised Queen but Sandy loved them. "Queen," she said, "you're wrong. This is a fabulous band."' Sandy also mixed socially with some of Britain's biggest 1970s rock musicians – Robert Plant, Pete Townshend, Keith Moon, Rod Stewart, Marc Bolan, Elton John, Freddie Mercury, and Island label-mates such as Cat Stevens, Traffic and Free – although Linda Thompson says, 'She didn't fraternise that much with rock stars. It's been exaggerated over the years. We used to go to the Speakeasy all the time and you'd bump into the great and the good of the day. She had a fling with Frank Zappa but it never lasted. Others were unrequited, like Pete Townshend and Richard [Thompson]. She was mad about him; it was never reciprocated. She was very ahead of her time in open relationships. Like a lot of brilliant people she didn't stick to conventions; they didn't mean much to her, considering – or because – she was brought up in a conventional household.'

Sandy's 'fling' with Zappa dated back to when he was in London recording *Late Night Line-Up* for the BBC in 1968. 'Frank was really good fun, very intelligent but a fantastic person,' says Linda Thompson. 'It's funny, he looked very like Trevor – it was before they got together. Trevor had red hair, Frank had black hair, but Trev had that famous Zappa-style moustache and beard. Sandy had crushes on a lot of people, didn't we all? Usually that was as far as it went; men and women, dogs and cats all fell in love with Sandy.'

'Sandy was never a "sweet little innocent",' says Philippa Clare. 'There was one time we were round my table at the Hyde Park Mansions flat, which was known as "the safe house" because nothing was ever repeated. And she said, "Let's make a list of all our lovers," but my list was so appallingly lacking and Sandy's list went on for pages. "Man on beach in Spain". I said, "Didn't you even know his name?" She said, "No, he didn't tell me, but he was fun."'

There were two sides to her personality: the good-time Sandy and the private Sandy who would shut herself away to write the dark, introspective songs which set the tone for her debut album *The North Star Grassman and the Ravens*. 'If you are going to have thoughts as profound and dark as she conveyed in her songs,' says Gerry Conway, 'you are going to need the opposite as a release. You couldn't just be in that one world without having to escape from it some of the time. On stage she could pour her heart into a song at the piano, then break out into laughter straight afterwards. She was full of opposites. Looking back I think she was more at ease in that serious side, rather than the light-hearted. She tried to laugh it off. She was so mature for what she was writing at that age, her songs could really touch you.'

The contradictions in Sandy's persona are inherent to the singer-songwriter; the songwriter may be intensely private but the singer – both on and off stage – is a public figure. The paradoxes were there for all to see in performance: 'She used to get very nervous before we went on stage,' says Jerry Donahue, 'but once she was there she'd just get lost in the song – drowned in the music – and when she stopped singing she'd realise there was an audience there, and she'd get silly and awkward, she'd trip over. She broke my foot pedal once or twice.' 'There were certainly two Sandys,' says Ashley Hutchings. 'That was reflected in her particular stagecraft, and it was very endearing and lovable. She was always tripping up on stage, tripping over leads, fumbling with microphones, and then she would open her mouth and it was just heaven.'

That contrast between the flippant, garrulous Sandy and the more despairing nature of her writing was something Ian Whiteman*

---

* Ian Whiteman was a member of mod favourites the Action in 1967, and then Mighty Baby in 1968–9. Over the next few years he did session

observed in the studio environment too; he barely knew Sandy but was brought in by Richard Thompson to play piano for the *North Star Grassman* recordings. 'I wouldn't say the sessions were easy-going, although the people were; everything was done in a few takes but often continuing right into the night. We'd take a break on each session in an Indian restaurant on Westbourne Grove, where Sandy would finish off a couple of bottles of Mateus Rosé. You wouldn't have guessed we were recording such melancholy songs if you'd been in the Indian restaurant in the evening.'

The North Star Grassman and the Ravens was the album Joe Boyd would have produced but for the circumstances that led to Fotheringay's split. Sandy chose to produce the album herself with Richard Thompson, who had left Fairport in January. They were originally going to work with producer Andy Johns but instead they turned to John Wood. 'Did you ever miss Joe Boyd in an artistic role?' Sandy was asked two years later. With typical insouciance, she replied: 'I dunno. I just kind of plodded on, really. I don't remember it specifically, but yes, it was a bit higgledy-piggledy after he left, but it sorted itself out. I mean afterwards, Richard and John and I just said, "Let's have a bash at doing this record," and it was a very laid-back album to say the least. But at least it was a try.'

Thompson says it ended up too much like producing by committee. 'It was a new experience to all of us,' he says, 'even John Wood to some extent. We were all used to working with Joe as producer, and John had something of a love–hate relationship with Joe in the studio. John tended to speak his mind to Joe – their

work on keyboards for Island and with folk artists wanting electric backing; his many credits included working with John Martyn, Richard and Linda Thompson, Shelagh McDonald, Marc Bolan, Steve Winwood, Rick Gretch and George Harrison.

way of working was quite antagonistic towards each other, but it got results. Sandy and I were musicians first and that created a different series of relationships between the three of us which didn't bring out our best as producers. Some of the production decisions weren't always right.'

Thompson doesn't think he was strong enough to dictate direction, especially as Sandy could be exasperating in the studio. 'I was too hands-off and she would sometimes float through the recording process without really trying. To some extent you had to hold a gun to her head to get her to sing. She'd postpone the real performance until the absolute eleventh hour, at which point she'd be on the money. So it was a bit of a muddle really. And I think that was a hangover from Fotheringay. With Fairport we recorded quickly and finished batches of songs in a day and there were very few overdubs.'

It was Thompson who selected the musicians: Fotheringay's Trevor Lucas, Jerry Donahue, Pat Donaldson and Gerry Conway all feature. 'Late November' was retrieved from the unfinished Fotheringay album, with Thompson adding guitar plus a new vocal by Sandy. The other aborted Fotheringay song, 'John the Gun', was re-recorded, and featured some of folk's finest in Robin and Barry Dransfield and Royston Wood. 'Generally, each track was all done on the day,' says Ian Whiteman, 'and it would be quite relaxed to begin with.' Then, once Sandy was ready, he describes the process as: 'Chord sheets, one rehearsal and then a take, so it was quite intense; very few takes, if I remember right. It was hard to tell how confident Sandy was in the studio. She was commanding when she sang. You can tell that from the record.

'John Wood just sat in the control room but Richard and Sandy would talk us through and organise and then "One, two, three, four" and the tape was rolling. It was a fairly spontaneous event, although there were some difficult chords to sort out. *North Star* is a very melancholic album and like so much folk music it's nostalgic for an olde English/Irish/Scottish vanished world. It was an out-of-time experience and the atmosphere on the album reflects that – a bit doom and gloom.'

The ever-modest Richard Thompson feels he didn't serve her too well. 'I wish I had been more focused, more experienced. I should have been more vocal at the time – especially in terms of arrangements. I think they could have been better thought out. We brought Harry Robinson in to do some string arrangements, and they were too big in terms of the number of pieces in the orchestra and they were a bit overriding at times.'

It was John Wood who recommended arranger Harry Robinson to Sandy; he had already done a fine job on Nick Drake's 'River Man'.* Robinson added strings to 'Next Time Around' and 'Wretched Wilbur', but Sandy's comment to *Sounds* suggests she wasn't entirely happy with the results. 'John Wood is a terrible string freak,' she said ahead of the final mixes; 'if I leave it just to him to mix it will come back swamped with strings.'

A recurring feature of Sandy's songwriting was her preference

---

* Harry Robinson went on to provide string arrangements on all of Sandy's solo albums. He has a most eclectic CV. He was the leader of the chart-topping Lord Rockingham's XI in the 1950s and arranger for Jack Good's TV shows, including *Oh Boy!* and *Shindig!*; he also arranged Billy Fury's early singles. To others, he is best known for writing and orchestrating a number of classic scores for Hammer Films. He met John Wood through the Children's Film Foundation. The strings on Sandy's albums – she would describe them as putting on a fur coat – are often an issue with fans and critics alike, although they do have their admirers. 'I actually loved them,' says Ian Whiteman. '"Next Time Around" is very majestic. It made the piano kind of float on the orchestra.'

for slow tempos. 'Sandy used to have a metronome at home with the piano,' says Thompson, 'and I don't know where the idea came from, possibly from Trevor, but she would set the metronome faster and play along to try and create songs at a faster tempo. It was an exercise to try and break that habit. She was just an instinctive musician. When it came to writing she'd sit at the piano and be lost in this swirl of music, and that's what came out, sad, melancholic songs. It has its limitations, especially if you are producing a record.'

'Yes, a lot of the things I write are slow,' Sandy said in 1973, 'because I find it difficult to play the piano fast and I think that restricts me a bit, but even so I don't mind that very much because I really don't like to be disturbed by my music – I like to take it easy.'

A cloud of melancholy hangs over much of *The North Star Grassman and the Ravens*, although the first songs recorded – on 11 and 14 March at Sound Techniques – were not Sandy's originals, as was often the case when she began work on an album. Sandy completed the haunting, traditional 'Blackwaterside' and an unconvincing Brenda Lee cover in those preliminary sessions, and recording then continued at intervals during April and through to the end of May at Island Studios.

Thompson feels Brenda Lee's 'Let's Jump the Broomstick' didn't really fit on the album. 'It was there to give the album some variety but it didn't make for a whole. I wish I had thought it was my place to say something.' There was a second cover that also finally made the cut. Dipping back into the reservoir of songs from the *Liege & Lief* era, Sandy and Richard Thompson swap vocals on Dylan's after-the-deluge romp 'Down in the Flood', a near-permanent fixture in Sandy's set list over the years.

It's Sandy's eight original songs that make the case for *The North Star Grassman and the Ravens* being by far the most underrated of her albums, often unfairly dismissed as part Fotheringay and part *What We Did on Our Holidays*-era Fairport. 'I think the album's great musically,' Sandy told *Sounds*, 'and if you are in sympathy with the musicians you can't go terribly wrong. I'd rather be pleased with the album and I'd rather it didn't sell than there was anything wrong with it and it sold really well.' Sandy's final comment would eventually come back to haunt her; her debut album's commercial failure resulted in her cultivating a more user-friendly approach in subsequent recordings. Yet it's the most magical and mystical of Sandy's solo albums and the only one to convey a cohesive, if forsaken, mood. Despite its sustained slow pace, *The North Star Grassman and the Ravens* is the only album on which Sandy steadfastly stands her ground – usually by the seashore or the riverbank – and invites her audience to come to her.

The album had tentatively been called *Slapstick Tragedies*: 'Instead of slapstick comedies, I thought of tragedies because I'm no comedian in my music,' she explained in May 1971. 'Most of my songs seem pretty traumatic, pretty serious. I can't sing happy songs.' *The North Star Grassman and the Ravens* usually finds the 'tragic' Sandy landlocked on a beach while others sail out upon the sea, frequently drifting towards disaster under autumnal or wintry skies. There is something disquieting about the album's key tracks – 'The Sea Captain', 'Late November' and the title track, which may have been inspired by the death of a friend of Sandy's, a sometime merchant seaman known as Tigger who lived at Stanhope Street for a while.* The notion of watching somebody depart on

* This is suggested by Philip Ward in *Sandy Denny: Reflections on Her Music*, published in 2011, which contains extensive analysis of her songwriting and a chapter about 'Tigger', whom Sandy met through Heather Wood.

Press ad for *The North Star Grassman and the Ravens*

their final journey is certainly conjured up by the song's brooding, atmospheric accompaniment. 'I loved playing the "North Star" track itself,' says Ian Whiteman, 'which opens with the sea and a ghostly bell and the pipe organ. That's Stevie Winwood's pipe organ, which was parked in the studio. This was before the days of synthesizers. That was certainly Sandy's sensitive inner landscape, although she didn't actually verbalise whatever anguish she was experiencing. Performers like Sandy and Nick Drake were pained and tragic figures and the pain is all in the music, which is why it communicates so well.'

'Sandy was so fascinated by words relating to the sea,' says Bambi Ballard, 'and the smell of the sea and the light of the moon over the water, that kind of language which was part of the Celtic folk tradition and a seafaring tradition. Her favourite writer was Joseph Conrad; I was a Captain Marryat fan, she liked C. S. Forrester's Hornblower series and Patrick O'Brian's *Master and Commander*. She was well read.'*

Sandy would be defensive in interviews when asked whether the sea was too recurrent an image in her work. 'No, I don't think so, except that I like the sea. I mean, don't you?' On stage she would laugh it off. Introducing 'The Sea Captain' at a date in York in 1972, she says, 'This is a song about the sea. Sometimes I sing "The Sea"; they are both the same song really.' Sandy's version of 'Blackwaterside' inhabits the same world; she even subtly changes the final line for a more apocalyptic effect. 'Blackwaterside' would be the last complete traditional song Sandy recorded for any of her albums. It had a strong connection

---

* Sandy had a good grounding in the classics – Austen, Dickens, Shakespeare – as befits an O-level English Literature student, and according to various friends she also liked the historical fiction of Georgette Heyer and Mary Renault; on a lighter note she enjoyed Agatha Christie and P. G. Wodehouse, whose stories she liked to read aloud to Trevor.

to Sandy's past, barely four years after she left the world of folk clubs.

It's a retrospective thread she carries into a series of portraits on *The North Star Grassman*, highlighted by 'Next Time Around', which is evidently about Jackson C. Frank. Few realised at the time that her former boyfriend was its subject. Sandy loved doing crosswords and 'Next Time Around' is the most cryptic song she ever wrote, but once you penetrate the code – as with so many of Sandy's songs – the clues begin to mount up: 'And do you still live there in Buffalo?' where Frank was born; 'Who wrote me a dialogue set in tune?' alluding to his song 'Dialogue'. If these are simple to decipher, there are more veiled references to the fire Frank was trapped in as a child and to his later mental illness. Lines three and four could easily be four across and six down in a crossword: 'The house it was built by a man in some rhyme' – referring to 'The House that Jack Built' – followed by 'But whatever came of his talented son?' There is even a reference to 'Theo the sailor', alluding to Theo Johnson. 'A couple of my songs may be fantasy,' she explained in an interview that year, 'but a lot of my songs are about people. They are about situations that have occurred but you have to be clever to find out what they are all about. I don't really want people to know what I'm talking about. And that's what I'm trying to do, give somebody something and at the same time enjoy myself. And I wouldn't be enjoying myself if I was singing about my last affair or something.' It's a revealing comment. It's no surprise that Sandy admits to being evasive, but it's enlightening to discover how much she enjoyed the process of teasing people as to what her songs were about.

Joe Boyd and John Martyn have been suggested as being among the characters in 'The Optimist'. Beverley Martyn offers a clue to this. 'The line in the song "There's a tale which says he was pursued by an assassin" sounds very much like John Martyn. John was a hash smoker, where the word "assassin" is said to derive from; that was Sandy's way of saying what she knew about the time when John – in a fit of jealousy – went up to the Witchseason offices wielding a hatchet to attack Joe.' When Sandy introduced 'The Optimist' at the Lincoln Festival in July 1971 she described it as being about a terrible thing which might not have happened 'if, like me, you turned a different corner at a different time'. Is it too simplistic to see that as a reference to the decision she made to leave Fotheringay?

'Sandy obfuscated as a writer,' says Richard Thompson. 'She never wanted to give too much away. It's only years later you figure what some of those songs are about, reading other people's interpretations. "Oh, this one's about Jackson Frank or about Pete Townshend." She didn't always want to come out and say what she felt. I think later she got more comfortable with that.'

The two recordings on *The North Star Grassman and the Ravens* that were reworked from the aborted Fotheringay sessions are both quite magnificent. 'Late November' is a lyrically twisted song often thought to be a reference to the time when Sandy left Fairport. It mixes elements from a dream she had in February 1969, before the 'ill-fated day' of the Fairport crash, and a bizarre real-life incident that occurred some months later. In the eight-page transcription of the dream – almost a premonition – which she neatly recorded in one of her notebooks the next day, 21 February, Sandy is at the wheel of the Fairport van driving along hazardous icy roads. 'I was driving down a very steep hill and I was rather scared of what the consequences might be as we were going very fast, so I handed the wheel to Harvey [Bramham] . . .' The dream continues with Sandy encountering a herd of 'sacred' cows and finding strange objects that resemble parts of internal organs, which she is told by the cows 'are all that is left of the human race'.

Months later, as Sandy described in detail in *Rolling Stone* in May 1973, on her way back from St Andrews in Scotland she stopped at a beach to take her Airedale terrier, Watson, for a walk, only to discover it was the same beach as in her earlier dream. While on the beach she witnessed a jet pilot come out of nowhere and seemingly disappear, perhaps crashing into the sea. The resulting lyric conjures up a twilight zone between reality and imagination: 'The pilot he flew all across the sky and woke me.'

By comparison, the forceful and forthright 'John the Gun', featuring one of Sandy's most acute melody lines, is a rare message song* which manages to combine a traditional phrasing as its lyrical bedrock with a powerful contemporary theme and a towering vocal performance. Sandy stamps her authority on the song right from its evocative opening lines:

> My shadow follows me
> Wherever I should chance to go, John the Gun did say.

The final song on the album, 'Crazy Lady Blues', might easily be autobiographical, although many of Sandy's friends thought otherwise. Linda Thompson says: 'She didn't usually let on, but Sandy did tell me she wrote it about me. Her songs were often a

---

* 'John the Gun', Fotheringay's 'Peace in the End' and 'One More Chance' on *Rising for the Moon* all contain an anti-war declaration. 'John the Gun' is one of the few of Sandy Denny's songs which Richard Thompson has performed live; versions can be found on his fan club cassette *Doom and Gloom II (Over My Dead Body)* (1991) and with Fairport Convention live at Cropredy in 1984 on *From Past Archives* (1992).

mix of people she knew. I take it as a compliment, it's such a great song – and it could just as easily have been about herself.'

'Anthea Joseph was convinced "Crazy Lady Blues" was about her,' says Bambi Ballard. 'I think that has to be about me. Linda says it's about her. Don't we all? It's Sandy saying that "the ladies that I like are crazy". It's a composite of all of her girlfriends and herself. There's a quality of "The Lady Is a Tramp" about it.'

Sandy was 'very eccentric', says Ballard. 'One time she and I went shopping together and we went into a sex shop on Tottenham Court Road, which in those days was just not done. We went in and we were looking at these things and saying, "Well, is that all?" And the shopkeeper comes up and says, "Would you like to come to the back room?" which obviously had the big dildos. And we were just about to buy something and Sandy says, "I'm famous, suppose somebody writes about this?" She panicked and said, "Let's get out of here." We were having fun, we were bored looking at fabrics and thought we'd go and look at dildos – and suddenly there was this moment when she became aware of her surroundings – a moment of "What am I doing in here? I might get recognised." So we rushed across the street and bought two saris. She knew that somehow "Sandy in a sex shop" would have come out.'

On 24 July 1971 Sandy appeared at the Lincoln Festival, on a bill that featured the Byrds, James Taylor, Tom Paxton and Buffy Sainte-Marie, as well as old friends Pentangle, Steeleye Span, Martin Carthy and Ralph McTell. She premiered much of her forthcoming debut album, backed by the self-appointed Happy Blunderers. The group, whose one and only appearance it was, comprised past, present and future members of Fairport Convention – Richard Thompson and Gerry Conway, who had been involved in the album recordings, plus Dave Pegg. As a further part of the advance promotion, Sandy did two solo sessions for the BBC: *Sounds of the Seventies* on radio, and *One in Ten* on TV in September 1971. It's the only footage of Sandy solo which survives,* and it shows her sedately but persuasively performing the album's title track, 'Crazy Lady Blues' and 'Late November', either on the guitar or piano.

The North Star Grassman and the Ravens was released in September 1971, coinciding with Sandy winning the *Melody Maker* Best British Female Singer award for the second time. It was her only solo album to grace the UK Top Forty LP charts, lasting just two weeks, and peaking at number thirty-one on 2 October 1971. Its mysteriously seductive cover art shows a thoughtful Sandy sitting in an apothecary's shop (dimly lit, although it's bright and sunny through the window), surrounded by jars of herbs and spices. It's the most fitting and beguiling of any of her solo album sleeves, presenting Sandy as an alchemist on what was her most experimental and, at times, otherworldly album.

Sandy's debut didn't follow the pattern of open, tell-all, slickly produced albums that were selling by the truckload in America. It provoked a surprisingly muted reaction among fans and was passed over critically. 'I was pleased when I heard that Richard was producing her solo record,' says Joe Boyd. 'It was good but not as

---

* The ten-minute film is included in the box set *Sandy Denny at the BBC*. Apart from a snippet of Fairport performing 'White Dress' on LWT's *The London Weekend Show* in August 1975, the only other footage of Sandy in circulation is Fotheringay's appearance on German TV's *Beat Club* in August 1970. They perform 'Gypsy Davey', with Sandy's lead vocal, and 'Too Much of Nothing', sung by Trevor. 'John the Gun' and 'Nothing More' were recorded but not broadcast.

Sandy with Rod Stewart celebrating winning *Melody Maker*'s Best
British Female and Male Singer awards, September 1971

transcendentally wonderful as I would have imagined a collaboration between Sandy and Richard to have been. It just didn't glow
as it should have. And because it wasn't a commercial album, her
solo career didn't pick up or gather any momentum going forward.'

The official launch for *The North Star Grassman and the Ravens*
was a concert at the Queen Elizabeth Hall on 10 September. In

the *Guardian* that day, previewing the show, Robin Denselow described Sandy as the one serious contender in Britain for an internationally acclaimed female rock star. He goes on to describe her as: 'A chubby cheerful girl of twenty-three who lives with a massive dog, an Australian and three cats in Fulham and looks as if she would be most at home making cups of tea.' It was just the kind of journalistic stereotyping she hated. Sandy is happy chatting away but tenses up once her music is mentioned: 'Ambitious? No. Yes. Well, I just plod. It just happens.' Nor will she discuss why she left Fairport and why Fotheringay split up. She's a little more forthcoming about her songs: 'They are biographical. About ten people can understand them. I just take a story and whittle it down to essentials. I wouldn't write songs if they didn't mean something to me, but I'm not prepared to tell everyone about my private life like Joni Mitchell does. I like to be a bit more elusive than that.'

Asked about the forthcoming concert, she's almost blasé about how unprepared she is, performing without Conway (on tour with Cat Stevens) and Thompson (in the US with Ian Matthews). Instead, she drafted in Dave Mattacks from Fairport and former Fotheringay guitarist Jerry Donahue to join Dave Pegg. The end result was an inconsistent, sloppy performance where nerves got the better of her. Only the back-to-trad encores, an unaccompanied 'Lowlands of Holland' and a pared-down 'Wild Mountain Thyme' with Donahue, saved the day.

In what would be a recurring pattern, the erratic Queen Elizabeth Hall concert was the only one to coincide with the release of the *North Star* album. When Sandy returned to the stage in the UK a month later to play fifteen dates, she had the benefit of a commanding, cohesive band comprising Richard Thompson,

Pat Donaldson and drummer Timi Donald,* a Sound Techniques session regular renowned for his laid-back approach. It was a line-up she would tour with regularly over the next twelve months and who would play on much of her next album. *The North Star Grassman and the Ravens* was already becoming a more distant memory.

*

Trevor Lucas was conspicuously absent from Sandy's recording and live work during 1971. He took no part in her live shows at all, adding only some acoustic guitar and backing vocals to three tracks on the *North Star* album, including the two held-over Fotheringay songs. Trevor was close enough at hand, though, usually in Island's Basing Street Studios and, as per any apprenticeship, learning the job by working on anything and everything that came along. He is not always credited but he was certainly the assistant engineer on three albums that year, two of which were for Island: Bronco's *Ace of Sunlight* and Luther Grosvenor's *Under Open Skies* – he adds vocal harmonies to both. His oddest credited job was as an assistant engineer on Dr Z's *Three Parts to My Soul*. Produced by Nirvana's Patrick Campbell-Lyons, the Dr Z album is

* Timi Donald had been in various Glasgow-based groups in the 1960s before forming Blue in 1973 with two ex-members of fellow Scottish group the Poets. Donald was very much part of the extended Fairport/Sound Techniques family – seemingly interchangeable with Dave Mattacks and Gerry Conway – and can be heard on records by Richard Thompson, Sandy Denny, Ian Matthews, Andy Roberts and John Martyn. John Wood: 'His greatest attribute was that he never played anything superficial; he also had that great laid-back feel, which was very unusual for someone in the UK.'

a kind of shambolic orchestral garage rock and now one of the rarest of the original swirl-label Vertigo releases. Trevor's only credit as a musician that year was as a featured artist on A. L. Lloyd's *The Great Australian Legend*, returning to his roots singing the lead vocal on three songs, including 'Banks of the Condamine' and a powerfully sung 'Streets of Forbes', elegantly backed by Dave Swarbrick.

Trevor's first job as a producer was a very different proposition: an ad hoc collection of Fotheringay and Fairport extended family members gathered together to record an album of rock 'n' roll covers. The idea came to him while watching Fairport at the Rainbow Theatre on 27 November 1971. At the close, Sandy and Richard Thompson joined the group for a series of rock 'n' roll and Band-inspired country rock encores on what was Simon Nicol's final tour with the group (for the time being at least).*

Recorded during the second week of December, *Rock On* by the Bunch was only the second album to be made at the newly opened Manor Studios,† run by Richard Branson. The first fully residential studio in England, it was situated in the village of Shipton-on-Cherwell, near Oxford. The album, which warranted advance features throughout the weekly music press in December, saw journalists visiting the studios, where they found the atmosphere relaxed and convivial, Watson happily pootling round the control room, while Sandy threw paper darts at one of the photographers.

* The two of them guested with Fairport again at Cecil Sharp House on 3 December, where, despite the setting, the same rock 'n' roll encores closed the show. The songs ranged from 'The Weight' and 'Country Pie' to old rockers from the Jerry Lee Lewis and Chuck Berry songbook.
† The Bonzo Dog Band's reunion album *Let's Make Up and Be Friendly* had been the first to test the facilities at the Manor.

By the evening a party vibe prevailed. So much lager was con-
sumed that Trevor contrived a curtain out of the ring pulls from
the cans: 'It was just one long and fabulous party,' says Philippa
Clare. 'There was a lot of creaking round the floorboards at the
Manor, but that was accepted. I was lying in my bed and in comes
Trevor stark naked and next door was Sandy. Trevor goes, "What
d'ya reckon?" and I go, "Fuck off, my best friend's next door."'

Behind the scenes, Trevor pulled everything together, eventually persuading Island to fund the album after initial scepti-
cism. In the grand manner of Trevor's schemes, it was leaked that
Jerry Lee Lewis was going to take part, 'but he wanted too much
bread'; everybody else did it for love. Other rumoured no-shows
included session giants Bobby Keyes and Jim Price, as well as
Steve Winwood and Chris Wood from Traffic, but it was the more
simplistic idea of folkies playing rock 'n' roll that prevailed. A year
on from the break-up of Fotheringay (all of whom were present at
the Manor), *Rock On* was true to the spirit of the group. Trevor
unassumingly described it as 'a really nice fun record that people
can just dig for what it is'.

Sandy sings five tracks, including an Everly Brothers duet with
Linda Thompson; Richard Thompson is lead vocalist on four;
Trevor sings 'Don't Be Cruel'; and even Ashley Hutchings takes
a rare vocal spot on Chuck Berry's 'Nadine'. Sandy's best performances are on three covers from the pen of her childhood hero
and one of rock 'n' roll's first singer-songwriters, Buddy Holly:
'Learning the Game', 'That'll Be the Day' and 'Love's Made a Fool
of You'. 'Sandy and I sang together on "When Will I Be Loved",'
says Linda Thompson. 'It was finished at Island's studios, where
some of the vocals were added. The party carried on; Richard was
incredibly drunk and on his knees. Sandy was the only one in

decent shape that night. We had a bit of a clash over who was going to sing the harmony but I said, "Come on, you can sing higher than me." It was good fun.'

The sober Richard Thompson now sees it as a bit of a throwaway. 'Conceptually, Fairport, Ashley and myself and Sandy were developing a more fragile style of music that nobody else was particularly interested in, a British Folk Rock idea that had a logical development to it, although we all presented it our own way. *Morris On* was rather more true to what we were doing. *Rock On* was rather a retro step. I'm not sure it was lasting enough as a record but Sandy did sing really well on the Buddy Holly songs.'

Concurrently with the *Rock On* overdubs at Island, Thompson was getting down to the serious business of recording his solo debut album at Sound Techniques during January. Having accumulated an idiosyncratic amalgam of ideas and songs, he looked no further than the rhythm section he'd recently been touring with when he recorded *Henry the Human Fly*. It features Sandy as well as Pat Donaldson and Timi Donald; she appears on four songs, contributing measured piano beneath Thompson's reverberating guitar on the pessimistic 'Painted Ladies', and providing harmonies with Linda (Peters, as she then was) on 'The Angels Took My Racehorse Away', 'Cold Feet' and 'Twisted'. Hearing Thompson drawing inspiration from the folk tradition may have influenced Sandy's mindset. In her next series of songs she too often used the language and identifiable vocal inflections of folk as she attempted to cast off the sorrowful mood which had dominated *The North Star Grassman and the Ravens*.

10 : *The Lady*
1972

After Joe left, Sandy was cut adrift a little. The people at Island didn't really see what was great about her, beyond how great a singer she was. She was caught between wanting a 'hands off' approach and floundering around looking for people to give her direction. When it came to the *Sandy* album, she was clearer about what she wanted and Trevor was definitely giving it a greater sense of direction. He did a very good, balanced job on that.

RICHARD THOMPSON

It would piss me off that Island couldn't sell *Sandy* but we couldn't press enough copies of Cat Stevens' *Teaser and the Firecat*.

FRED CANTRELL, head of sales at Island Records in the 1970s

The Lady

The lady she had a silver tongue
For to sing she said,
And maybe that's all.
Wait for the dawn, and we will
        have that song.
When it ends it will seem
That we hear silence fall.

The lady she had a golden heart;
For to love she said,
And she did not lie.
Wait for the dawn and we'll watch
        for the sun.
As we turn it will seem
to arise in the sky.

We heard that song while watching
        the skies,
Oh the sound it rang,
So clear through the cold,
Then silence fell and the sun
        did arise
On a beautiful morning of silver and
        gold.

Sandy's handwritten lyric for 'The Lady' from the inner
gatefold to the *Sandy* album

In February 1972, a year since Fotheringay had played their final concert, Sandy undertook two week-long residencies in the US – backed by Richard Thompson, Pat Donaldson and Timi Donald – first at the Bitter End in New York, then at the Troubadour in Los Angeles. The same band then performed a series of UK dates during April and May, interspersed with recording Sandy's next album. Thompson remembers the tours and recordings during 1972 particularly fondly: 'It was a really happy time in Sandy's life; if I think of the times I knew Sandy, that seemed to be when she was the most balanced. More calm and secure than she had seemed in Fairport.'

Tragically, only bootleg tapes survive of this fine band in action, in which Sandy's in great voice, interacting seamlessly with a dazzling, intuitive group of musicians, chatting and giggling with the audience. The emphasis is on songs from *The North Star Grassman and the Ravens*, which sound dramatic but a lot less imposing live, with a couple from *Rock On*, and Sandy gives in to pressure to play 'Matty Groves'. There's also a strong contingent of other traditional material, including 'Bruton Town', which was a contender for the new album, 'Maid of Constant Sorrow' and two songs performed unaccompanied and joyously by the entire ensemble, 'Reynard the Fox' and 'The Rigs of Time', the latter learnt off Shirley Collins's *Sweet Primroses*. They introduced only one new song during the American trip, 'Listen Listen', although Sandy had declared in advance she would use the dates to break in new material.

The combination of a more self-assured Sandy, an energised Thompson, the extrovert bass player Donaldson and the no-frills drummer Donald resulted in a group she described as 'fantastic' and one that was getting better all the time. History, however, was repeating itself, as Sandy once again found herself wanting to hang on to her new group against the wishes of her latest manager, Steve O'Rourke,* who had taken her on after she parted company with Roy Guest following Fotheringay's break-up. O'Rourke advised her she needed to be projected as a solo artist and that she neither needed nor could afford a band. As a result she dismissed him and for the rest of the year effectively managed herself, however contrary it was to her character to be so organised. 'I've got to cope with it myself,' she told the NME in April. 'It isn't an easy job but I'm prepared to do it because I believe in it. I can understand their point of view but I *really* like to be with a band.' It was a sensitive issue. She had walked away from Fotheringay barely a year before and still harboured regrets and recriminations. 'It's only now,' she said the same month, 'after all this time that I realise how stupid it all was. That's quite an admission really but it was so numbing at the time that I didn't really think about it for ages afterwards.'

'You could never tell her what to do,' says Gerry Conway. 'So she was tough to manage, and didn't always make the best moves or the ones other people advised her to do; if she thought an idea was crap, she just wouldn't entertain it.'

---

* O'Rourke managed post-Syd Barrett Pink Floyd and went on to mastermind the release of *The Dark Side of the Moon* in 1973.

Sandy had already spent three days at Island Studios in mid-November 1971, where she recorded 'Quiet Joys of Brotherhood', one of the forthcoming album's undoubted highlights. She was returning to the words of Richard Fariña's song, which had been discarded during the *Liege & Lief* recordings, where the accompaniment was an almost growling dirge; Sandy now set the words to a traditional Irish melody, 'My Lagan Love'. She later explained that A. L. Lloyd had first given her the song but told her he didn't care for the words, so she was pleased to find Fariña's poeticism fitted it so well. It's a wonderful creation, her multitracked voice enhanced by the graceful, unadorned sound of Dave Swarbrick's solo violin. 'I've got some really discordant harmonies,' she said. 'I've been very much influenced by some of those Eastern European groups like the Bulgarian State Ensemble. I've tried to capture some of the starkness of the singing in those groups.'

Recording proper began less well at the Manor in early March 1972, where John Wood later grumbled that the sessions were too ill-disciplined and from which only two songs, 'Bushes and Briars' and 'Sweet Rosemary', were kept. There were two tracks which weren't resumed when sessions resumed the following month: Anne Briggs's 'Go Your Way My Love' and Sandy's own 'After Halloween', which she would return to a few years later. 'Sweet Rosemary' is written and performed very much in a traditional style, but borders on cliché as the girl of the title gathers flowers ahead of her wedding day; 'Bushes and Briars' was written while Sandy was at the Manor – most likely during the *Rock On* sessions, after she had come across an empty church in the local village during a Sunday walk and observed the vicar giving the service to a phantom congregation.

Before returning to her own album, Sandy was asked to

contribute to the music for Peter Elford's short film *Pass of Arms*,* which appears to have engaged her creatively more than most of her extracurricular sessions. Its medieval setting and chivalric theme are very much the stuff of folk music. Recorded in spring 1972 at Basing Street and Sound Techniques and released later that summer, the soundtrack seven-inch single features Sandy's performances of 'Man of Iron' and 'Here in Silence', written by Don Fraser and Elford, with a string arrangement by the Incredible String Band's Mike Heron. Sandy is said to have helped considerably in fashioning these tracks in the studio. The single is given additional gravitas by the inclusion of Wilfred Owen's poem 'Strange Meeting', read by Christopher Logue.

The bulk of her own album's songs, featuring the band she was so adamant about retaining, were then completed at Sound Techniques and Island Studios in four or five sessions between the end of April and late May, when string arrangements by Harry Robinson were also added. The final take was a cover of Bob Dylan's 'Tomorrow Is a Long Time'.

Lyrically, the yearning opener 'It'll Take a Long Time' would not have been out of place on *The North Star Grassman and the Ravens*, but here the treatment is very different: specifically, the cosmic sound of the Flying Burrito Brothers' *Gilded Palace of Sin*; it even features Sneaky Pete Kleinow on pedal steel guitar. The tapes were flown to Los Angeles, where Joe Boyd organised the overdubs.

It was a sure sign that Trevor was putting his authority on the album as producer. Elsewhere, *Sandy* – as the album came

---

* *Pass of Arms* was Peter Elford's only film as director. He is credited as production manager or location manager on numerous TV productions and films through the 1980s and '90s, including *The Long Good Friday*, *The Final Conflict* and *King Ralph*.

to be called – is graced by gloriously accessible melodies like 'Listen, Listen' and 'The Lady', which brilliantly capture her self-deprecating, humorous and outgoing personality. Unfortunately, Harry Robinson's overly lush veneer undermines one of her most captivating songs, with its charmingly self-mocking opening lines: 'The lady she had a silver tongue. For to sing she said, And maybe that's all.' Up until its completion, the working title for the album had been *The Lady*, Trevor's nickname for Sandy.

The most consistent and satisfying of her solo albums,* *Sandy* also includes the most accomplished of her traditional-sounding narrative songs, 'It Suits Me Well', which touches on similar themes to 'The Pond and the Stream'. Introducing the song at a concert in the Netherlands in June 1973, Sandy explained that she'd written the song after she and Trevor saw a news item on television about landowners evicting gypsies from their land. Its main subject, Jan the Gypsy, is a traveller, his own man, who has almost always lived in a caravan (as Anne Briggs was doing around this time) but is content:

> That the living it is hard oh
> But it suits me well.

'The Music Weaver', which Sandy wrote in America when she was feeling lonely, is simple and autobiographical – 'about how far you always are from where you want to be'. Not so much sad as nostalgic, it was a theme which would dominate her next album.

---

* Only 'For Nobody to Hear' is out of place; it features an incongruous brass arrangement by Allen Toussaint tacked on later and recorded at his Sea-Saint studio in New Orleans. Island occasionally used Toussaint to give a lift to recordings by the likes of Jess Roden, Robert Palmer and Frankie Miller during the 1970s.

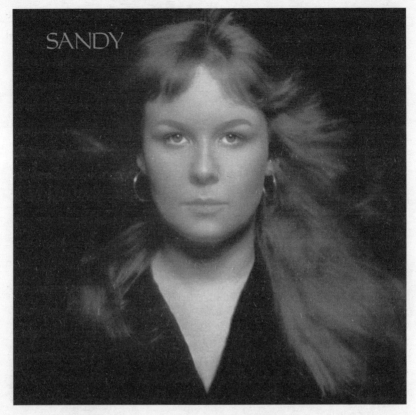

David Bailey's photo on the cover of Sandy's second
solo album, September 1972

Sandy was clearly more engaging and less intense than its pre-
decessor. Though still broadly in folk mode, Trevor, who must take
considerable credit, had modernised and integrated the sound, helping make it Sandy's most cohesive musical statement as a singer-
songwriter. Released in September 1972, it was the album which
Island thought would bring about a commercial breakthrough.
It was issued in a gatefold sleeve featuring a cover photograph of
Sandy by the best-known photographer of the day, David Bailey.

'We were unstinting at Island in believing in Sandy's great

potential,' says Tim Clark, the label's head of marketing at the time. 'Just the fact that we asked David Bailey to take a beautiful picture of her for the *Sandy* album is a measure of that. I don't think she took much persuading. We saw the Bailey shoot as a definite boost to get the album noticed. We were still trying to put across Sandy as who she was, but it was trying to move her beyond that folk audience. I thought it was a really beautiful shot of her and it showed our intent.'

Some within Island felt it was a marketing exercise that back-fired. 'The David Bailey session was just to add a bit of glamour,' says Fred Cantrell, then Island's head of sales. 'Was she into that? Not really. There was no sense of desperation. We realised we had a total genius on our hands but the question was how to channel it. The *Sandy* album was her best shot; after that we began won-dering: where are we going wrong?'

'We did feel very confident when Trevor took over the produc-tion and he did a very good job on the *Sandy* album,' says David Betteridge, Chris Blackwell's second-in-command. 'Island did have considerable chart success with so-called underground acts or fringe acts, so we were utterly confident that we would break Sandy with this album. The shoot with David Bailey reflected that confidence. We knew we had to reposition her but she still pro-jected herself as very much the folk singer, certainly in the way she dressed. So it rather sent out mixed signals.'

'She had a very folk look, she was never styled,' says Sandy's friend, photographer Linda Fitzgerald Moore. 'She could have worn clothes to suit her figure better but the clothes she tended to wear – kaftans, smock dresses and big frocks – didn't always bring out your best features. Trevor would try and smarten her up but she would never listen. I think she wanted to be Janis Joplin, she saw a parallel there; Janis was somebody who had made it in spite of the way she looked and gave off an air of not giving a damn. Sandy was more self-conscious though.'

In 1970 Prudence Glynn, fashion editor of *The Times*, spoke to Sandy about her taste in clothes. Sandy projects an image, says Glynn in the resulting article, 'which is entirely suitable for a folk singer. Most of Sandy's clothes are bought in second-hand markets or the antique stall.' Contemporary photos provide further evidence of Sandy's fondness for floral-print midi dresses, often bought in flea markets. 'If I go into a shop I can't get anything that fits me and I get so brought down,' she told Glynn, who comments that 'Sandy Denny is not misshapen, indeed she is the most engaging shape, but is not the skinny prototype of the modern boutique customer.' So being photographed by Bailey, whose work helped propagate sixties fashion, was always going to make her uneasy.

'The Bailey session . . . that was awful,' says Philippa Clare. 'It was, "Come on, love, just do it." "Can't you just get it together, love?" It was a fucking three-day nightmare because she just hated herself; it was such a mistake to put her through that. I understand why Island wanted Bailey, it was a statement which they were making, not Sandy. It freaked her out before, during and afterwards.' Bambi Ballard remembers it differently, recalling that Sandy got on with Bailey and that she did get a buzz out of being photographed by him. If anything, she was more nervous waiting to see the results.

A relieved Sandy went to visit Bambi the night she first saw prints from the Bailey session and eased the tension by uncorking several bottles of wine. Then Bambi was treated to a unique preview: 'We were a little pissed but that night she played all those wonderful songs from the *Sandy* album to me, the entire album, privately at the Howff on Primrose Hill. We went there about one

One of Sandy's sketches

in the morning and Roy Guest, who ran the Howff, was leaving and said, "Just slam the door when you leave." And she just sat down and started to play but she kept stopping in the middle of a song and saying, "Shall I go on, are you enjoying it?" She was singing them just for me but between each song she'd ask, "Do you really want to hear any more?" I had to encourage her to carry on and of course it was wonderful, I was in tears. She really *needed* the praise; she was not just seeking praise. Sandy always needed a lot of reassurance, as if it was something she'd been starved of.'

By contrast, the official launch for *Sandy* saw her return to the Queen Elizabeth Hall on 6 September 1972, sharing the bill with John Martyn. It was yet another London showcase where stage fright gradually enveloped her. The concert had started well, with

Dave Swarbrick joining her early on for a crowd-pleasing, poised 'Quiet Joys of Brotherhood', but her confidence soon dissipated to a point where she later felt it necessary to apologise in the press for making the audience wonder if she was going to get through to the end.

Reviews and reactions to *Sandy* were almost universally positive. The album was seen as far more coherent, lucid and better constructed than *The North Star Grassman and the Ravens*, despite some carping in the folk press about the strings and clichéd folk lyrics. 'Listen, Listen' was even single of the week on Tony Blackburn's BBC Radio 1 breakfast show. Yet, once again, Sandy found her album struggling to sell. *Sandy* wasn't even rewarded with the cursory chart appearances that *The North Star Grassman* and *Fotheringay* had received.

Linda Thompson says Sandy was horrified by the Radio 1 accolade: 'We were all such snobs about the charts.' 'I remember the feeling of panic,' said Sandy a year later, 'thinking, what on earth am I going to do if I get in the charts? I mean, could I go on *Top of the Pops*? Anyway, the single got nowhere and the panic passed.'

It was a typically perverse reaction: profound disappointment that *Sandy* sold poorly combined with relief that the single didn't chart, which was then still the most likely way to boost sales and reach a wider audience. 'She was devastated after that,' says Linda Thompson, 'because her records didn't sell millions. Richard was the same; he was desolate when *Henry the Human Fly* sold so poorly.* They were young and very ambitious. However

* Richard Thompson's *Henry the Human Fly*, released in June 1972, had been poorly received; it was the first critical backlash in his career. He now relishes the fact that it is the worst-selling record by any arm of Warner Brothers in the US.

much you are an artist first, you want people to buy your records.

'After the *Sandy* album, it got her down that her popularity didn't suddenly increase in leaps and bounds, and that was the start of her really fretting about the way her career was going. Things only escalated after that. People like me or Martin Carthy or Norma Waterson would think, "What are you on about? This is folk music."'

Sandy played a handful of shows with the band in October, the last in Brighton on 11 October 1972, after which they all went their separate ways. Richard Thompson was moving on anyway to pursue his career as part of a duo with Linda, but Sandy could no longer afford to pay a band out of her own pocket, as she had been warned. For the next twelve months she went on the road with no other musical accompaniment than her own guitar or piano. 'She was always the centre of attention but she didn't enjoy being solo,' says Jerry Donahue. 'From the outside it probably doesn't seem to be that different but she felt she couldn't command the stage on her own, quite wrongly, of course. She was mesmerising but she lacked confidence when she wasn't surrounded by the guys in the band. So that was a tough call for her.'

To add insult to injury, since finishing the *Sandy* album Trevor had been called in by Fairport as producer and went on to join the group: he played his first gig with them in Germany on 16 September, just as *Sandy* was released. Fairport Convention had been in disarray at the start of 1972, with only Dave Swarbrick and Dave Pegg left to try and piece together an album. 'We were struggling,' says Pegg. 'We had dumped half of what we'd been recording. Trevor was big friends with Swarb and we heard what he had done on Sandy's album, so we brought him in initially for his production skills. His joining the band just happened and then he suggested we bring Jerry Donahue in; Trevor had been stuck in one studio or another for over a year and was itching to get out on the road again.'

To represent the new line-up on the piecemeal *Rosie*, two Trevor Lucas songs were even taken from the abandoned Fotheringay album sessions, 'Knights of the Road' and 'The Plainsman'. In another turnaround, Dave Mattacks returned to Fairport, reinstating a more 'classic' line-up. Swarbrick, Pegg and Mattacks were all old hands, with Trevor playing rhythm guitar and sharing vocal duties with Swarbrick, plus a strong lead guitarist in Jerry Donahue, the first since Richard Thompson had left. Fairport's new line-up was officially announced in October 1972, coinciding with publicity and reviews for the double compilation LP *History of Fairport Convention*.

It was poor timing all round for Sandy. Her second solo album had barely been released and was sinking fast, just as Island was heavily promoting a 'best of' by her old group – whose line-up now included her boyfriend. This would have far-reaching repercussions. Sandy could see that she and Trevor would soon be spending months apart. Her touring was always sporadic but she knew that a fully functioning Fairport would take to the road with a vengeance. Nor were her fears unfounded. 'I toured with Fairport at the end of 1973,' says Marc Brierley. 'Sandy was as miserable as hell because Trevor was away from home. She was back in the flat and scared Trevor was off shagging somebody else, and he was, of course. I was happily married and always went back to the hotel straight after the show, and she'd phone me there in the evenings. I'd try and console her and reassure her that he had just gone out with the lads but she knew what was really going on. That was Trevor's reputation.'

The overriding and increasing dilemma for Sandy and those

close to her at Island was that her new album had seriously under-performed. 'We all recognised what a wonderful singer Sandy was,' says David Betteridge, 'but I often feel we failed to take her in a direction where she could have been more successful here and in America. She could have developed – or been developed – into something really, really special and successful but we never figured out the right strategy. It was the failure of the *Sandy* album where we started to wonder, "What do we have to do?"' Sandy felt much the same, as she almost flippantly told *Beat Magazine*: 'It didn't do as well as it should have done. I was really disappointed as we worked very hard on it. I thought everybody would say, "Oh what a nice change, it's coming along after all."'

In a quiet end to the year, Sandy joined Fairport Convention on stage at Kingston Polytechnic in their final show before Christmas for an encore of the trusty 'Down in the Flood'. All that was left for her that month was to start thinking about her next album. It was Trevor's idea to put her in a classical environment when she recorded a new song on 3 December, just her, seated at a twelve-foot Bechstein concert grand in Walthamstow Assembly Hall, a venue often used for concert recordings by the BBC.

Sandy delivers an opulent, stark performance of 'No End', which she later said began as a piece about her earliest days on the road with Fairport, when touring with a group was a completely new experience for her. What she recorded that day was, quite unfathomably, completely re-recorded later for the next album; yet it's a towering, extraordinarily moving performance. Sandy sounds positively jolly, laughing and joking between takes, however despondent she must have felt, and belying the mood of the song. Sandy's description of 'No End' hints that she is in two minds about what to do next. 'It's the story of two friends, one a person who loved to travel, and the other one to paint. They persuade each other back to their respective vocations. A strange song perhaps, but we all lose our zest for life sometimes, don't we? Let's hope it's never for long.'

11 : *Things We'll Always Hold Dear*
1973–1974

None of the other British female singers were under the same pressure as Sandy; there was nobody of her ilk that you can remotely say comes close to her for the quality of her singing, construction of the song, lyrics; she was a giant. And all eyes were on America, so she was always measured against Joni and Carole King and James Taylor, who sold massive amounts of records, which Sandy never did.

JOE BOYD

As a matter of fact, I'm a bit numb about the way things are going at the moment.

SANDY DENNY, *Melody Maker*, 15 September 1973

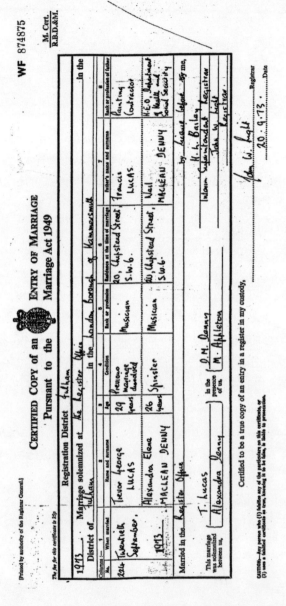

Sandy and Trevor's marriage certificate, 20 September 1973

From the beginning of the 1970s a number of singer-songwriters came to prominence in Britain, especially women, who often had just one song that proved to be commercial – Jaki Whitren's 'Give Her the Day'* or Linda Lewis's 'Rock a Doodle Do', for example; purely in terms of hits, you can argue that Britain's most successful female singer-songwriter was Lynsey de Paul. Sandy's songs were very slow burners; there were no simple hooks to them, so she never even had that one hit.

At the same time other British female singer-songwriters were conspicuously emerging, whose work, like Sandy's, was more focused towards albums, notably Bridget St John, Lesley Duncan, Claire Hamill and Joan Armatrading. Joni Mitchell provided the benchmark against which everybody was measured, and it was Sandy who was seen as Britain's answer to Joni. 'Compared to the rest of us,' says Shelagh McDonald,† 'Sandy was the closest we

---

* The largely acoustic backing on Jaki Whitren's sole album, *Raw but Tender*, comes from original Fotheringay members Albert Lee, Pat Donaldson and Jerry Conway. Linda Lewis was another who performed at Les Cousins, although her five-octave range meant that she was more often heard as a soul singer, fronting soul/rock band the Ferris Wheel in 1969 before the best of her solo albums, *Say No More*, in 1971, and *Lark*, in 1972, on Reprise, plus 1973's *Fathom's Deep* for Raft.
† Shelagh McDonald was described by Karl Dallas as 'the new Sandy Denny' after Sandy left the folk world behind to join Fairport. She released the *Shelagh McDonald Album* in 1970 and *Stargazer* in 1971, before

had over here. And that's a lot to live up to because, let alone Joni Mitchell, people tended to see American performers or writers generally as better, certainly when it came to folk musicians or singer-songwriters. We were taken for granted whereas visiting Americans always got the acclaim. Sandy was a totally British voice, and one of the most original voices this country has ever produced. People accept that now but when she was alive she wasn't so appreciated.'

Bridget St John's debut, entirely her own compositions, was released in 1969. Her career flourished after she was introduced to John Peel; she became a regular on his radio show and was the first signing to his Dandelion label. *Ask Me No Questions* was the first of three albums for the label; gentle, late-night, melancholy songs which draw comparisons with Nico and Nick Drake. She and Sandy knew each other, usually through shared gigs: 'I still remember feeling I was "the new girl",' says St John, actually a few months older. 'Sandy was already somewhat of a veteran in my eyes.' Peel's support gave St John instant credibility and enabled her quietly to build a cult following. 'Sandy was certainly under the spotlight far more than I ever was,' she says. 'I was under John Peel's protective umbrella, which meant I had total control over the songs on my first album and the cover artwork – and who could have wanted a more supportive producer than John Peel? There was no commercial pressure, whereas much more was expected of

---

going AWOL for the next forty years. Almost entirely self-written, each of McDonald's albums features one traditional song. *Stargazer*'s 'Dowie Dens of Yarrow' carves out her own original take on folk rock, and across her two albums folk rock's finest session men are out in force, including Richard and Danny Thompson, Ian Whiteman, Andy Roberts and the Fotheringay rhythm section.

Sandy.' St John feels she was fortunate to be able to sidestep the folk tag which stuck with Sandy: '"Folk singer" carries too much baggage with it,' she says.

Claire Hamill came out of nowhere to be signed to Island in 1972 by Chris Blackwell himself. She and Sandy met just once, literally in passing when Sandy was coming down the stairs from Blackwell's office in Basing Street. 'I was younger than Sandy by seven years, sixteen when I signed to Island. I was also coming from the north-east and had no background in the London-centred sixties folk scene. I was much more influenced by Joni Mitchell's music and I was signed as a singer-songwriter. That's what was in vogue.'

Hamill clinched a deal at a time when labels began seeking out British counterparts to American girl singers such as Carly Simon, Judee Sill, Dory Previn, Bonnie Raitt and Linda Ronstadt, all winning plaudits if not necessarily selling records over here. 'I was signed on the basis of Joni Mitchell being a success. Chris was looking for something similar which might cross over into pop and I just happened to be there with a bunch of songs and clutching a guitar. I recorded Joni's "Urge for Going" on my first album, which was to try and position me.'

Part of Hamill's appeal to Island was that she was completely unknown. 'It was harder for Sandy and the other acts that had come through Witchseason; they were so much part of the Island family by then that they had also become part of the furniture. Sandy was imprinted on people's consciousness as a folk singer, and as the singer with Fairport, which I don't think she ever successfully shook off.'

After two well-received albums, *One House Left Standing* – featuring John Martyn, Terry Reid, David Lindley and various members of Free – and *October*, Hamill failed to get sufficient recognition. Island sent her out on the road with top rock acts before trying to push her unsuccessfully towards pop.* 'They tried to find a formula but female singer-songwriters were never a phenomenon in Britain that could be marketed. All of us came from different music backgrounds – pop, folk, rock, R & B. Very few consistently had hit records, and that was still the only way to get noticed in the early seventies.'

Lesley Duncan had a very different history from the rest. She had been pumping out pop singles since 1963, but was simultaneously working as a session singer and songwriter through the sixties.† It was soon after Elton John recorded her composition 'Love Song' on *Tumbleweed Connection* that she was snapped up by CBS to record the first and strongest of her five albums, *Sing Children Sing* in 1971, which featured him on piano and the core of musicians who would soon play on his *Madman across the Water*. The album was a critical success and she even sang the title track on *Top of the Pops*, but wider success eluded her. In 1976 she dropped out and went to live in Cornwall, commenting that she was no longer interested in 'chasing stardom'. 'She could have been a British Carole King,' says Hamill, 'but she didn't push herself as a performer and she did what a lot of us do. She got married and settled for domesticity later in the seventies, which is where I've been for the last thirty years.'

* Claire Hamill left Island voluntarily and became the first signing to Ray Davies's Konk Records in 1974.
† As a session singer, Lesley Duncan's many highlights include her back-up vocals on countless Dusty Springfield sessions from 1964 onwards, as well as for the likes of Donovan ('Goo Goo Barabajagal') and Pink Floyd (*The Dark Side of the Moon*), and on the original recording of *Jesus Christ Superstar* and four of Elton John's early albums.

Joan Armatrading was another who broke the mould. She made her debut in 1972 and was the only other British female singer-songwriter to be successful internationally during Sandy's lifetime.* 'I was never a folk singer or drawn to that,' explains Armatrading. 'I'm singing only because I write. I never wanted to be a singer. I did it the other way round to most people who started out in folk clubs wanting to be Bob Dylan or Joan Baez. I was a songwriter first but once they heard my songs everyone wanted me to sing them. So I ended up becoming this other thing, a singer-songwriter – and have been for forty years.'

Both Dave Mattacks and Jerry Donahue played on Armatrading's seventies albums. 'Sandy was always a little typecast as a folk singer,' says Donahue. 'It was easier for somebody like Joan to come along who didn't have that history. Joan was a striking, sensitive black woman writing very direct, expressive pop songs. She fitted no recognisable image, which is what made her so noticeable.' Armatrading claims she didn't know Sandy's work at all; Sandy, on the other hand, is known to have grumbled when their diaries occasionally clashed about how Joan Armatrading stole her band.

Like Sandy, Maddy Prior had moved from playing folk clubs to fronting a folk-rock band, Steeleye Span, which enjoyed greater and more consistent commercial success than either Sandy or Fairport in the 1970s.† 'There was nothing like the energy of

* Joan Armatrading achieved her breakthrough with her self-titled third album, in 1976. The single 'Love and Affection' became her only UK Top Ten hit and struck the same strong emotional chord worldwide. *Joan Armatrading* was the first of four albums produced for her by Glyn Johns; it was recorded soon after he had produced Fairport Convention's *Rising for the Moon*.
† Steeleye Span had a surprise Christmas hit with 'Gaudete' in 1973, and 'All Around My Hat' reached number five in November 1975. In between,

fronting a full-on band,' says Prior. 'There hadn't been electric bands with girl singers at the front singing folk songs. Nobody had done that before Sandy. We were quite different from the pop world that had gone before but I saw that as a challenge, whether it was appearing on *Top of the Pops* or playing stadium shows in America. It was no big deal being a woman either; I didn't feel in any way that I was a female singer fronting a band – I was a singer fronting a band. You became one of the boys. It's like John Martyn said to me, "You're just another great mate to go and have a drink with," and you were treated like another bloke. However it appeared on the surface I'm not sure Sandy was as comfortable with that.'

Prior never had the same responsibilities as Sandy. She wasn't writing songs; Steeleye's staple was always traditional material and the overall load was very much shared with Ashley Hutchings, Tim Hart, Rick Kemp and Martin Carthy in the early line-ups. Sandy, by contrast, had a lot more on her plate than just singing.

'Sandy laughed a lot. Sandy was funny,' says Prior. 'She was very witty and could be quite devastating. You didn't want to be in her line of fire and I think people assumed she was always in charge, but she wasn't. We were both nervous before going on stage. She was always the centre of attention, whether it was just her or as part of a band, so the pressure was constant. It wasn't till Kate Bush that you had somebody where it took a year to make an album, a year to sell it and a year to write the next one; we were required to put albums out as fast as we could.'

Now We Are Six, produced by Jethro Tull's Ian Anderson, *Commoner's Crown* and *All Around My Hat*, produced by the Wombles' musical mastermind Mike Batt, were all Top Twenty albums for the group.

As 1973 dawned, Sandy was feeling deflated and unsure of herself. After all, here was an artist who rarely found the ideal circumstances for the expression of her art. 'It was always a struggle,' says Joe Boyd, 'and people didn't really see that side of her.'

At the end of 1972 Stephen Holden had said in *Rolling Stone* that '*Sandy* is the year's finest album by an English singer.' He concluded that 'if this doesn't do it for her, nothing can'. She also had the backing of A&M and was now expected to promote the album in the US. All this convinced her to agree to a lengthy tour, even though this time it would be just her, going solo.

In truth, there was little to keep her at home since Trevor was committed to being on the road with Fairport Convention, already more or less fully booked till the summer. In mid-January 1973 Fairport embarked on thirty-two UK dates to promote the patchwork *Rosie*, followed by a sprawling world tour, beginning in the US, where Sandy joined them on stage at a free concert on 10 May at the foot of the Hollywood sign; they in turn joined her on stage at the Troubadour the following week. The decision had already been made that Trevor would produce Sandy's third solo album, which would get under way at A&M Studios in Los Angeles when their respective tours aligned.

One particular idea would have saved Sandy from having to play solo and prevented Trevor being on the loose with Fairport: reforming Fotheringay. 'At the start of the year,' Jerry Donahue remembers, 'just before Fairport went out on tour, Sandy, Trevor, Gerry Conway, Pat Donaldson and me, all of us from Fotheringay went out and had dinner. Pat, Gerry and Sandy wanted to restart the band, and I said, "What do you think, Trevor?" It was a definite proposal and he said, "I'll do whatever you do." I was really happy in Fairport, as was Trevor, which is why he deferred to me.

It was very unfair of him really. I'd just joined, Dave Mattacks was back in the band and Swarb had taught me all those fiddle tunes; it was all so new to me and very exciting. It was just too hard to walk away from. Any other time, I would have jumped at it. In retrospect,' he adds ruefully, 'I wish I'd gone the other way. Maybe things would have turned out differently.'

Sandy maintained a very low profile in the first few months of 1973, with recording put to one side and no dates until a six-week solo American tour. This began on 2 April at the Philharmonic Hall, New York, where she opened for Randy Newman, moving on to Toronto's Massey Hall, Rutherford, New Jersey and Boston. Shows with Loggins and Messina in Washington DC and on the West Coast followed, before playing support to Steve Miller in Philadelphia and Shawn Phillips in Detroit and Chicago. She played some shows of her own towards the end of the month, as well as her week-long stint at the Troubadour, beginning on 13 May.

She wasn't entirely alone on the American tour, taking her friend Miranda Ward with her as travelling companion. Sandy had first met Ward through Joe Boyd when she was still on the folk circuit and the two had much in common, including a similar professional middle-class family background. Sandy's brother David was also there as tour manager; by the summer, he was managing her with Trevor under their newly formed Luny Management. Bringing in her brother was yet another example of Sandy preferring to work with people she knew and trusted but who were often completely untried.

David Denny's marriage had recently broken up after five years and Sandy wanted to help him out. 'She picked him up when he was in a very low state,' explained their father. 'He was so upset that his marriage had gone wrong and Sandy brought him into the music business. He took a year's sabbatical from Taylor Woodrow, where he'd been working since he graduated in 1967. I was annoyed at this because I knew he'd never go back to engineering – and he didn't – but I think it saved his sanity.'

Management issues had dogged Sandy in the two years since Joe Boyd had gone to America. 'Trevor and David were well-meaning,' says Martin Satterthwaite, then head of Island's field promotions, 'but they didn't have the clout of the strong management that, say, Roxy Music had with EG, where the record company didn't have to worry too much because they knew the management was steering the group. Island was there to put the records out and actually looked to management to keep them on their toes. Sandy and Fairport were always allowed to drift along.' A more astute manager might perhaps have advised her against doing such a long tour, which her American agency projected would barely break even. Writing to David Denny on arrival, they calculated that her earnings for the tour would be $8,050, but the expenses for three people were estimated at $8,149.

Before leaving for the US, Sandy spoke to Steve Peacock at *Sounds*; she was clearly ruminating over the rigours of touring that lay ahead and the fact that she would be apart from Trevor for so long. 'I don't want anyone saying, "Ah poor Sandy," because it's just something you either choose to do or you don't; and if you do it you have to become strong and get yourself together. It's when I'm sitting in hotel rooms on my own I tend to get a bit morose, but I think I'm going to be a bit better off this time. I think I'm getting a bit more mature about it.' However she couches the language, her greatest concern is what Trevor might be getting up to: 'Men have different ways of entertaining themselves on the road, and no way could I get into entertaining myself *that* way. Women get very emotionally attracted to people, blokes have the ability to entertain themselves for an evening and then forget about it.'

Such are the thoughts at the heart of the more subjective songs Sandy had written or would complete by the end of the American tour. She was playing solo but, unlike her folk days, mostly at the piano. She was also playing huge concert halls to audiences who didn't know who she was and who were there for the headline act. Towards the end of the tour, at a 3,500-seater in Berkeley where she was supporting Loggins and Messina, she played only one number before walking off because the crowd failed to settle down. Her usual set drew entirely on post-Fairport material, including a new, typically morose hotel-room-written song, 'At the End of the Day'. She would later introduce it by saying: 'Anyone who has ever been away from home for a long time and has felt a little homesick will understand the sentiment behind this song.'

Interviewed by *Rolling Stone* after the Berkeley show incident

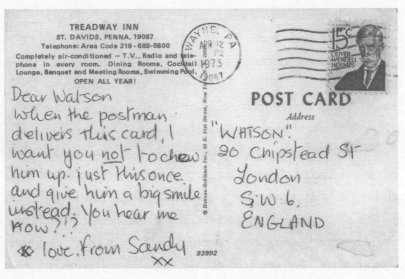

Sandy's postcard to Watson during her solo tour in the US, April 1973

304

she said that next time she would bring a group or rejoin the ready-made group she was about to record with in Los Angeles. 'She has been asked to rejoin Fairport,' reported *Rolling Stone*, 'and because several of the Fotheringay people are now in Fairport, she will do it, although probably not till later this year.' Between 5 and 7 May Sandy and Fairport went into the A&M studios in Los Angeles, where they recorded four songs: 'Friends', 'Solo', 'At the End of the Day' and a new version of 'No End'. A fifth song, 'What Is True', was also begun at these sessions, another soul-searching lyric written late into the night; it would eventually be recorded for Fairport's *Rising for the Moon*.

Sandy flew home after her Troubadour residency ended on 13 May, while Fairport travelled to Australia for their first shows in Trevor's home country, beginning three days later in Perth. Their parting inspired her to write a somewhat hackneyed new song, 'Dark the Night', on the plane journey back, with a plea of 'Oh to be with you'. Fairport returned home in late May but their relentless schedule soon trundled on; they played dates and festivals in Holland, Denmark and Finland, and further UK shows during June. The group had already begun working on their ninth album, fitting in sessions during June, July and going into August, when sessions for Sandy's third album also resumed at Sound Techniques. Both albums were being produced by Trevor with John Wood.

With half the year gone and half an album recorded, Sandy was low in spirits and short on songs. Sitting in hotel rooms or languishing at home while Trevor was away had done little to lift her gloom about the way her career had stalled. At Sound Techniques, Sandy returned to one of her earliest songs, 'Carnival', although it retained only one line from the version she had penned back in 1966. It was the next batch of songs, however, which determined the direction that the new album would take: her own 'Like an Old Fashioned Waltz' and two swing-era favourites, the Inkspots' 'Whispering Grass' and Fats Waller's take on 'Until the Real Thing Comes Along', which Sandy knew from her family's record collection. The idea of recording the Fats Waller song 'came up quite accidentally', says John Wood. 'We were sitting around somewhere and Fats came into the conversation, and she just started singing the song and it grew from there. We decided to record it, partly because she wasn't writing an awful lot of material at the time.'

To set the mood, a few old friends were recruited, including Danny Thompson – the only time he played on one of Sandy's albums – Diz Disley and pianist Ian Armitt (a veteran Soho jazz player who worked with Humphrey Lyttelton, Chris Barber, Long John Baldry and Alexis Korner). The nostalgic mood generated by these songs and the liberal application of sweeping strings or brass arrangements would soon colour the entire album. 'Like an Old Fashioned Waltz', the final song written for the album, confirmed the tone. 'I'd started a waltz rhythm on the piano and I couldn't get out of it,' Sandy explained. 'It was supposed to evoke an idea about Fred Astaire and Ginger Rogers dancing round a completely deserted ballroom with a spotlight on them. That's why the actual orchestration on that – which Harry Robinson did – really works. I don't say everything he's done has come off, not the way I wanted it. That one does, he really got the feeling from it.'

Sandy is said to have been elated by the album when she delivered it to Island at the beginning of September. *Like an Old Fashioned Waltz*, more than any of her solo albums, emphatically demonstrates her versatility as a singer; but it's the third of her albums in a row to change character from the one which preceded it. This time the album is dominated by its sentimental under-current: gentle, melodic piano, rich strings and barely a trace of her British folk roots. 'I think this one is simpler and more roman-tic than the last,' she told Karl Dallas in September. 'It's more direct, I know I always say that about every album, but I'm a bit of an old softie at the moment. I'm going to have to get myself some boxing gloves.'

Ironically, most of the original material would have created a cohesive, if one-dimensional, singer-songwriter album, but because of the way the album is sequenced, the two covers jar with the more contemplative songs either side. The effect is to diminish Sandy's most personal artistic statement to date. As it is, the album is profoundly moving, but it could have been truly devastating.

There is nothing evasive or cryptic about songs such as 'Solo' and 'Friends'. Sandy would describe 'Solo', which opens the album, as 'a song which depicts the knowledge we all have inside, which is that nobody can live your life for you'. It's one of her greatest compositions, with a gorgeous melody, and impeccably sung; lyri-cally it combines her selfless wit with a compelling, profound hon-esty.* Bambi Ballard remembers talking to Sandy about the song: 'It works on so many levels. It's utterly moving but laced with Sandy's offbeat humour. The battle of the sexes is part of what goes into Sandy's writing – the anguish of relationships. Sandy was very able to put this kind of suffering across. It's all coming from inside. It's never direct. Sandy doesn't wear her heart on her

---

* When Judy Collins played the Royal Albert Hall in October 1973 she played 'Solo', which she said she had learnt from Sandy two days before. She has never recorded the song.

sleeve; it's about that realisation that not everything happens the way you want it to, so you have to develop an inner strength and take control of your own life. Alas and alack, Sandy wasn't always able to do this.'

Although it doesn't walk the same emotional high wire, 'Friends' is a rare portrait song to which Sandy revealed the answer: Joe Boyd says she told him it was written about Pete Townshend. Sandy wrote the song after being rejected by Townshend while Trevor was away with Fairport before the American tour. 'My love is not here, my love is away,' she sings. Townshend told Clinton Heylin about the specific encounter at Chipstead Street that inspired the song: 'I kissed her, but she insisted I should stay all night, otherwise I couldn't touch her. I took my driver's presence as an excuse and left. I was married and very rarely unfaithful to my wife at the time. Sandy rang me later and told me she'd written me a song.'

Like an Old Fashioned Waltz is another flawed album, marred by a couple of weak, uninspired songs in 'Carnival' and 'Dark the Night', and by the romantic mood which softens the impact of some of the darker material. 'It's easy to blame Trevor for allowing Sandy to indulge that nostalgic/pop side of her taste,' says Joe Boyd, 'but Sandy was hard to say no to and it takes a strong personality to do that.' After her disappointments over the *Sandy* album, Richard Thompson feels that Sandy lacked confidence in her own judgement and was reconsidering her approach. 'When you have a very original artist like Sandy,' says Thompson, 'it's less about pressure from outside – and that may well have come later – but she was feeling pressure from within. And the tendency is to move towards the middle of the road, which is a mistake. *Like an Old Fashioned Waltz* went too far in that direction.' Others disagreed. Danny Thompson described *Like an Old Fashioned Waltz* as a magic album. 'Her voice is stunning and mature. "Solo" is incredible. She had that same quality as Richard, when she wrote a song you thought it was an old folk classic. You can lie about your image but you can't lie about your music if you're sincere about it. I don't think she thought, "I'm going to write something really deep and heavy," it was just her being very truthful.'

Circumstances had kept Sandy and Trevor apart for long stretches of the year so far, but now the pressures of working together in the studio during August, when Trevor was simultaneously immersed in a Fairport album, resulted in the couple hitting a rocky patch. Away from the studio, they spent much of their time separately. Both of them were known to have had brief affairs elsewhere. Sandy remained at Chipstead Street, while Trevor invariably stayed at his sister's flat on Talgarth Road or was holed up at Philippa Clare's Hyde Park Mansions flat, always something of a refuge for stray folk musicians.

In interviews before the scheduled October release of *Like an Old Fashioned Waltz*, Sandy sounds deflated and indecisive. 'You have to think things are going to look up tomorrow,' she told *Sounds*' Jerry Gilbert, a regular confidant in the music press. Speaking to Karl Dallas, she said: 'Apart from writing, I do a lot of thinking. Trying to find out if I have any enthusiasm under that lazy façade.' Is it just a façade? asks Dallas. 'Well that's what I'm trying to find out.'

The recurring question that Sandy was dodging in all the interviews was whether she was going to rejoin Fairport Convention. When on 3 September she gave a masterful solo performance at the Howff, previewing the new songs, she effectively put the issue to one side, at least for the time being. Roy Guest had no doubts that she should remain solo: 'I couldn't ever convince her that she didn't need other musicians. She felt the sound was better with the texture of other musicians, but that wasn't true. She was wonderful on her own, especially in the seventies. I think she was a bit overwhelmed by the paraphernalia of touring with a group and it was very much a boys' thing, whereas Sandy had the ability to be a completely solo artist. She was a great singer and she didn't know it, and she was a really nice person but she didn't know that either.'

The Howff performance was a rare triumph for a London showcase. 'She would have been terrified,' says Linda Thompson. 'Sandy had a strong sense of self like all great artists; they either think they are the best thing in the world, or the lowest of the low. That's the template for somebody like Sandy.' Al Stewart hadn't seen her play since she left Fairport in 1969: 'She had terrible stage fright on a scale I'd never seen her experience before when she played the Howff. She almost had to be pushed on stage. She sang "Solo" and it was astonishing, the first time most of us heard that song; that night she was wonderful. It was remarkable considering how much she had to be coaxed to go on stage.'

Sandy was lost in the music throughout the entire performance. The reviews were the best she ever had, typified by Robin Denselow's assessment in the *Daily Telegraph*: 'It was one of those happenings that critics dream of but rarely experience, when a good but hitherto erratic singer suddenly takes off, carrying her audience with her, on the kind of trip that singing is really all about. It was, in fact, Sandy Denny's moment of truth . . . there were glimpses of depth which few other singers have revealed to us.'*

* It was a moment that was also captured: recorded by John Wood on Ronnie Lane's Mobile Studio with a view to releasing an acoustic 'best of' called *Sandy Denny Solo*. The tapes have since gone missing, presumed wiped.

Wedding congratulations from John and Beverley Martyn

What should have been a career-defining moment turned into a personal milestone. An emotional, tearful Sandy had left the Howff in a cab with Trevor, and not only were they reconciled but they made the surprise decision to get married. Cynics suggested they got back together because they couldn't decide what to do with the dog, Watson; others thought it was done to save the relationship, but on 20 September 1973 Trevor Lucas married Sandy Denny at the Fulham registry office. Her father refused to attend, although Edna Denny was present, and it was Sandy's brother David who gave her away; he and Trevor's sister Marion were witnesses. Trevor wore a dark suit and an open-necked red checked shirt; Sandy wore a dyed green floral-print dress she got from a flea market. The press later reported that 'Fairport singer marries', referring to Sandy rather than Trevor, the current Fairport singer.

The couple then had to make their way to Plymouth in the afternoon as Fairport had a TV show to do the next morning. 'Danny Thompson came along, he had been best man,' says Dave

Pegg. 'We were all party animals, as was Danny in those days, and the two of us had a gin-drinking competition. Danny refused to buy a ticket for the train but he got away with it both there and back by staying in the restaurant car. That was the wedding reception – in a railway restaurant car; they tried to kick us out because they wanted to serve the second sitting, so we all ordered a second set of meals in order that we could carry on drinking.'

Sandy revealed her thoughts about marriage a few months later in an article in the *Hamilton Times* in New Zealand headlined 'The Feminine Touch'. She said that her relationship with Trevor was better since they had got married – 'so there must be something in it'. She added: 'I think it's important for Trevor to be able to say "I've got a wife at home", not just "the bird". There are enough separations in a marriage like ours and I feel that if you can avoid those long periods apart whenever possible, then you should. Let's face it there are enough strains without adding to them.

'That's why I see marriage as a romantic thing,' she continued. 'It's such a tremendous gesture on the part of a man, much more so than a woman.' In a more flippant moment three years later she said: 'Trevor finally decided to make an honest woman of me. Sadly, it didn't work the other way round.'

Island had originally scheduled *Like an Old Fashioned Waltz* for release in October 1973, the same month as Fairport Convention's latest, *Nine*. On the face of it, it was poor timing, but as it turned out there was no conflict of interest because Sandy's album was inexplicably pushed back by Island. *Nine* was duly released, the label coming up with a clever and positive marketing line: 'Schubert didn't quite make it, but Fairport have just completed their ninth.' 'It was something of a comeback album,' says Dave Pegg, 'and a really underrated Fairport album. The *Nine* album gets forgotten because it's seen as a stepping stone for Sandy rejoining the band. I think that five-man line-up, had it stuck together, would have gone on to do greater things.'

The delay in Sandy's album release was prompted by the advance single, 'Whispering Grass', sinking without trace. A letter to Sandy's American representatives dated 27 October 1973 from David Denny explained that the album was being put back to 18 January 1974 so they could 'set it up properly', and suggested a February release in the US, with a view to Sandy touring there in the spring. This confirms that Sandy hadn't committed to joining Fairport at this stage.

Ahead of the projected January release in the UK, Sandy did the rounds of press and radio promotion, which included a handful of solo British dates in November and a couple of BBC sessions. The session she did for John Peel on 14 November, broadcast a month later, previewed four of its songs: the two swing-era covers, which hardly suited Peel's programming, 'Dark the Night' and 'Solo'. The last two featured Pat Donaldson, guitarist Hughie Burns and drummer William A. Murray, although the proposed new line-up never played again. A characteristically cheery interview with Peel was pre-recorded in November and broadcast on 6 January: Peel wished Sandy a happy birthday and they chatted about the album due for release the following week. Embarrassingly, though, Island had already taken the decision to delay the album until the spring.

Two of the shows Sandy did in November in Brighton and Manchester were with Bert Jansch, who had seen little of her during the past five years. He was then living on a remote farm in Wales with his second wife, Heather, although they separated at the end of 1973. He felt that Sandy was quite desperate at the time

and surprisingly downcast. 'We were both at loose ends. Pentangle
had broken up and we had all gone our separate ways; from playing
big concert halls and festivals we had managed to work our way
back down to playing clubs again. That didn't worry me. I never
thought too much about the future,* but Sandy was troubled by
the uncertainty of what lay ahead for her. I was never interested in
being famous, and never interested in anyone who was or wanted
to be famous, but Sandy was somebody who was caught in the
middle. She wasn't bothered by success but others expected it of
her and it wasn't coming.'

The uncertainty Jansch observed in Sandy was fuelled by what
she saw as Island's lack of commitment and understanding, at a
point when Fairport were soon to be heading off to the Far East
and Australasia after the Christmas holidays. To add insult to
injury, with *Like an Old Fashioned Waltz* sitting on Island's shelf
and slipping back to 1974, her only 'new' album in 1973 had been
the six-year-old Sandy and the Strawbs' *All Our Own Work*, which
had finally been released that May and sold a reputed sixty-five
thousand copies.

Island Records was a very different label in 1974 from the one
Sandy had signed to five years before as a member of Fairport. 'The
Witchseason acts were almost the last vestiges of the old spirit
of Island,' says Richard Williams. 'Joe Boyd had been involved

* The following year Jansch found himself signed to Charisma Records,
then home to Genesis, Van der Graaf Generator, Lindisfarne and Monty
Python. He released *LA Turnaround* in September 1974, produced by
Mike Nesmith, and, even by Jansch's high standards, it's one of his richest
and most laid-back albums. A year later Charisma packed Jansch off to
Los Angeles to record *Santa Barbara Honeymoon*, before their enthusiasm
waned, and his third album for the label, *A Rare Conundrum*, ended up on
the shelf for a year before release.

in every aspect of their careers – manager, producer, publisher, everything; it was an anti-trust nightmare, you would have to say, but it worked. It was a protected environment where nothing unrealistic was expected of those acts. Roxy Music were very much a symbol of the new but the big change was the move from the old Basing Street offices to St Peter's Square, which was another universe.* I joined Island pretty much the month after they'd moved there and my first decision was whether I wanted six of the £400 chairs or the £600 chairs, which shocked me.'

Muff Winwood, who had played bass in the Spencer Davis Group alongside his brother Steve, headed up the A & R department and was looking forward. Marc Brierley tells how he was offered a three-album deal by David Betteridge towards the end of 1973, but Winwood then withdrew the offer, saying he was no longer interested in signing low-volume singer-songwriters. True to his word, Winwood's next major signing was eccentric American glam-rock duo Sparks, now living in England. 'I am not sure that Muff Winwood was ever too enthusiastic about any of the Witchseason acts,' said John Wood in 2014. 'He was certainly never that enthused about Richard and Linda or Nick Drake.'

Richard Thompson says he doesn't ever recall speaking to Winwood and had no regular contact with anybody at Island: 'Chris Blackwell definitely loved Sandy but when the whole folk-rock thing was handed over to Island Records after Joe left, I don't think they really knew what to do with any of us. *I Want to See*

---

* Island moved at the end of 1973 from its funky home in a former church at 8–10 Basing Street in Notting Hill, where it had been based since 1969, to the plush residential St Peter's Square in Hammersmith, taking up quarters in the converted Royal Chiswick Laundry building.

the Bright Lights Tonight sat on the shelf for over a year awaiting release.'*

Blackwell, once Sandy's greatest ally at the label, was now spending more and more time away from London, usually in Los Angeles or Jamaica. The game-changing deal for him had been signing Bob Marley and the Wailers in 1972. Following the heavily promoted release of *Catch a Fire* in April 1973, Marley's career had gone from strength to strength. As Barney Hoskyns observed: '*Catch a Fire* set the world alight but *Burnin'* got it blazing.'

Burnin' had been released in November, while the fate of Sandy's third album was still dangling in mid-air. With Blackwell otherwise engaged, it was left to David Betteridge to run the company. 'Increasingly,' says Betteridge, 'when it came to Sandy there would be a collective record company groan as to what do we do? You had an artist who was obviously becoming more unstable and was slightly confused in herself about her music, and you had a record company who recognised her talent but was failing to develop her. Island was going in too many different directions, so the folkier acts were left rather in no-man's-land.'

'When I joined,' says Williams, '*Like an Old Fashioned Waltz* hadn't been released and nobody knew quite what to do with Sandy, but there was still a sense that she could be the biggest female artist in the country irrespective of category. Island was a company that was growing, in retrospect, disconcertingly quickly, and its ambitions were growing. When you have success you want more, and because Sandy obviously had very broad taste in music,

* It was Richard Williams who brought about the eventual release of *I Want to See the Bright Lights Tonight* in April 1974; it had been gathering dust on Island's shelves until he revisited the mixes.

it made her vulnerable to trying to chase a more commercial approach.'

Betteridge believed *Like an Old Fashioned Waltz* was a clear indication that Sandy was trying to take a more accessible direction in her songwriting. 'We were happy that she recorded the two jazz standards but perhaps "Whispering Grass" wasn't the best choice as the first single. She was still perceived more as a folk singer, probably still best known as the singer with Fairport Convention, the group which she was now being linked with once again. Her core fans may well have been confused.'

*

Back in May 1973, when Sandy told *Rolling Stone* she thought she would eventually rejoin Fairport, no invitation to join the group had actually been made. 'When we recorded the four songs with Sandy in Los Angeles, there was a real chemistry between us as musicians,' says Jerry Donahue. 'That was the first time we really thought about asking her to join the band but it remained an open question for the rest of the year. Her new album, the one we were recording with her, was scheduled for October and that was her priority. I don't think she'd have rejoined Fairport had it all gone well with her solo albums. She really couldn't understand why *Like an Old Fashioned Waltz* was delayed and that certainly made her feel insecure about being a solo artist.'

Donahue had no doubts about Sandy joining the band again, nor could Dave Pegg see it as anything but beneficial: 'The *Nine* line-up was a monster instrumentally and it was so eclectic, but for me it would have been crazy not to bring Sandy back, especially with her being such a prolific songwriter.' Dave Mattacks was more circumspect: 'Sandy rejoining was a wonderful idea on paper but my reservations were unfortunately proved right. Sandy had a vision for her music; she started to realise it with Fotheringay and her solo recordings and I couldn't see the Fairport musical dynamic adapting to her. She probably thought it was a good idea to be with Trevor and "the chaps". We all did, arguably without thinking it through properly.'

Dave Swarbrick completely rejects suggestions that he was particularly hesitant about Sandy's return. 'Why me?' he asked, in reaction to comments in the 2012 book *Fairport by Fairport*. 'Everyone was uncertain, including Sandy. I wasn't anything but pleased to be able to work with her again. She improved the group tenfold. Despite all that has been said about Sandy and me and our relationship, I was, with the exception of Trevor, the closest to her.'

'To begin with Sandy only joined us on stage a few times,' says Pegg, 'which she did on and off until that became a more regular thing by the end of the year.' Her appearances were restricted to encores, but even these were stretching beyond the usual romp through 'Down in the Flood'. When she guested with Fairport at the Rainbow Theatre on 15 December 1973 and the following night at Fairfield Hall, Croydon, both shows were opportunely recorded.

Although Sandy decided to go on tour with Fairport when they went to the Far East just after Christmas, she still hadn't made her mind up to rejoin the group, but circumstances were increasingly influencing the choice she would eventually make. 'I felt disillusioned,' she said. 'I'd be stuck at home without Trevor. I decided to go with them.' She told Australian publication *Go Set* that she wouldn't have actually gone on tour with Fairport 'if it

Dear Friends, I am pleased to be here in Tokyo, shortly before the release of this, my third solo album, as it enables me to explain a little to you about the songs. I do hope you enjoy the album as much as I have enjoyed my stay here. I also want to tell you that the feeling of some of these songs, hopefully will evoke some of the romance of the Thirties, for these are also time when a touch of the romantic, may be just what we need. Don't you agree?

Solo A song which depicts, I think, that knowledge we all have inside, which is, that nobody can live your life for you. But at the same time, let's try to help one another, all the same.

Like An Old Fashioned Waltz. Being a romantic at heart which I indicated before, I tried to capture the magic of an old Hollywood movie. Two dancers alone in an enormous deserted ballroom. But where does the orchestra hide? Notice when the strings come in!

Whispering Grass. When I was young, my parents used to possess many of the old Inkspots recordings, this is one of my very favourites of these. I always promised myself that one day I would record it. So here it is!

Friends. This is about some people I know and love. Even with their faults and all.

Carnival. When I wrote this song, and when I sing it now it was, and is, a creation of imagery. Like when the summer is gone, and all the laughter and frivolities which go with the summer have mellowed, all at once the autumn is with us, albeit beautiful just the same.

Dark The Night. About love lost perhaps, and being alone with your memories, wishing that things may have been different, if you had your time again.

At The End Of The Day. Anyone who has ever been away from home for a long time, and has felt a little homesick, will understand the sentiment behind this song. I wrote it on the plane journey home, after an extensive tour of the United States.

Until The Real Thing Comes Along. Once again, a which I loved as a child. When I first heard it, it was sung by a wonderful black Pianist-Singer, Fats Waller-master of the keyboard, as is the pianist on this rendering of the song-Ian Armit. We recorded it as closely to the aforementioned recording by Fats, as possible.

No End. The story of two friends, one a person who loved to travel and the other one who to paint. They persuade each other back into their respective vocations, a strange song perhaps, but we all lose our zest for life at times don't we? Let's hope it's never for long!

Many of the names of the musicians I know you will recognise. They are all very fine people, and it's my thanks to them.
It is my hope that I will see you all again soon.

Love From

Sandy Denny

X

Sandy's programme notes for a concert in Tokyo, January 1974

hadn't been for the fact that the album release was late. I decided that the gigs I had on hold for myself were a bit superfluous.'

It was no coincidence that Sandy committed to rejoining Fairport after Island decided to push *Like an Old Fashioned Waltz* back yet again, into the spring. 'It was early in January,' says Donahue. 'I remember that Trev and I were in our New Otani Hotel Japanese dressing gowns at the time. I popped briefly across the hall to their room and asked him what she had decided. His reply, to my delight, was that she was indeed coming on board.' No official

319

announcement was made at this point as the tour moved from Tokyo to New Zealand for a couple of shows and then on to Australia, where on 25 and 26 January 1974 Fairport Convention became the first rock group to play Sydney Opera House. Sandy was billed as a guest, the poster claiming she was 'the world's No. 1 Female Singer'. She sang on six numbers, also playing piano and adding harmony vocals on other songs in Fairport's twenty-strong set list.

By the time the group began a residency in Los Angeles at the Troubadour which ran from 28 January to 3 February 1974, Sandy's contributions on stage – including the still unreleased 'Solo' and 'Like an Old Fashioned Waltz' – had doubled. The Troubadour shows witnessed a renewed energy and enthusiasm in the band, who were now a more fully integrated ensemble. They played some songs they never went back to: Sandy and Dave Swarbrick rolled back the years on a spellbinding 'She Moves through the Fair', they belted out Dylan's 'Knockin' on Heaven's Door', and Sandy and Trevor sang Richard Thompson's 'Down Where the Drunkards Roll'. Some of the Troubadour shows were recorded but the group couldn't afford to pay Wally Heider's studio, which provided the facilities, so the tapes languished.*

It was only after the band returned to the UK that, on Valentine's Day 1974, the NME officially confirmed that Sandy had rejoined Fairport Convention. 'It was ironic, really,' she said in 1977. 'One of my main reasons for leaving Fairport in the first place was that I had wanted to be able to spend more time with Trevor. Then

---

* The Troubadour recordings would dribble out in the 1990s and the tracks featuring Sandy were collected for the complete box set, *Sandy Denny*, in 2010. The full Troubadour set was eventually released in 2013 as a bonus disc to the *Rising for the Moon* reissue.

he was asked to join Fairport. So I ended up back in the band for exactly the same reason as I had left it.'

Over at Island, the news came as no surprise but it was coolly rather than ecstatically welcomed. 'If I remember correctly,' says Richard Williams, 'there was a sense of relief when she rejoined Fairport. They were a known quantity; it was an easier thing to focus on. Fairport had become very boring by themselves, solid instrumentally but too many jigs and reels, no songs and no songwriter to speak of since Richard left. Dave Swarbrick wasn't somebody to build a band around. On the face of it Sandy solved that problem within Fairport.'

Neither David Betteridge nor Tim Clark can today explain why Sandy's album still awaited release: 'I'm surprised that *Like an Old Fashioned Waltz* was delayed for so long,' says Clark. 'If we as a label were more focused on other acts coming through, it comes back to the benefits of having good strong management, which Sandy always lacked. Good management makes sure all these different strands are coordinated properly and record companies, certainly back then, only did one aspect of it – we put out records. Once the first single flopped, and with the Christmas schedules looming, I can see why we would have pushed it back to January. It seems rather more unfathomable that it wasn't released until June.'

As with the *Sandy* album, no expense was spared in dressing *Like an Old Fashioned Waltz* in a striking gatefold jacket. 'There was a lot more thought going into art direction,' says Williams, 'to try and give her greater appeal. This time it was Gered Mankowitz, but the *Old Fashioned Waltz* sleeve rather chintzified her. Just like David Bailey's *Sandy* sleeve, it didn't give a helpful impression of who she really was.'

With Sandy back in the band, it was business as usual for

Fairport as one tour followed another till the summer. They went to Scandinavia at the beginning of April, followed by a tour of the eastern seaboard of the US which wound up in Washington on 18 May. Sandy would return home to find that *Like an Old Fashioned Waltz* was finally being scheduled for release in June, nine months after it had been delivered to Island.

There was no promotion to speak of. Sandy talked about doing a concert with a full orchestra, which was never going to be financially viable; she did no solo shows, nor any radio sessions to coincide with its release. Everybody involved with the long-anticipated album seems to have shown a surprising, almost contemptuous indifference towards the long-anticipated album. Fairport Convention, meanwhile, played a string of dates in June and the prestigious Pop Proms on 7 July, just as the *Fairport Live Convention* album was about to hit the shops. When Fairport recorded a Peel Session on 16 July they featured nothing from *Like an Old Fashioned Waltz*. To all intents and purposes, Sandy's third solo album had been unceremoniously buried by all concerned.

'Typically for Sandy, having never toured enough to support her own albums,' says Joe Boyd, 'when she finally ended up touring a lot, she was back in Fairport, and it was just as *Like an Old Fashioned Waltz* finally came out and people didn't understand what was going on.'

Like an Old Fashioned Waltz charted at 197 in Billboard. It was the first and only time any of her solo albums scraped into the US charts, reflecting the impact of her American touring on her own and with Fairport. In the UK it failed to chart at all.

Fairport Live Convention was released in July 1974; it was retitled *A Moveable Feast* in the US. Three of the tracks, including 'Down in the Flood', had been recorded either at the Rainbow Theatre

Ad for the North American release of the retitled *Fairport Live Convention* or Fairfield Hall, Croydon, back in December; the rest came from the two historic shows at the Sydney Opera House. It was Fairport's first live album but it didn't really do anybody justice. Sandy 'wasn't really bedded into the group by the Sydney Opera House gig', says Dave Pegg, 'so it meant the recordings from those gigs were neither one thing nor the other. We were winging it to some extent and it was more a bridge between one line-up and the next.'

Sandy's sketches of Watson

On the domestic front, Sandy and Trevor gave up the Chipstead Street flat and, during July 1974, moved to Byfield in Northamptonshire, close to Cropredy, where Dave Swarbrick had been the first of the Fairporters to settle, followed by Dave Pegg and his wife Chris. The village of Byfield was a far cry from the hurly-burly of the city life Sandy and Trevor were used to. 'When you move to a small village like Cropredy,' says Chris Pegg, 'you are a bit of an outsider. Dave and Swarb knew everybody who went to the pub and, because we had kids, I knew everybody who went to the school, so we had it covered between us. Sandy and Trevor moved to Byfield, which was another village about six miles away, so we all saw each other regularly, but they had no circle of friends outside the band.'

Sandy had often talked about wanting to live in the country and about having a garden. The Twistle – the address was 41 The Twistle, but the name was applied to the picture-book cottage as well as the road – was almost idyllic, but most of their friends thought she and Trevor would soon hanker after city life again. 'My sense of it was that it was more Sandy's idea to move to the country,' says Nigel Osborne; 'she did have this romanticised idea of it and she liked the idea of the band all living close together. Trevor wasn't against that. I'm not sure he felt one way or the other but he liked living in Chipstead Street and they were at the centre of things there. It was a kind of hub for everybody they knew. It was a decision they made which wasn't thought through and once things began to go wrong in their relationship – and, pretty much simultaneously, within Fairport – they were stuck there and it was easier for Trevor to get away. Sandy was cut adrift and that wasn't good for her mental state.' Sandy would live in the rural surrounds of Byfield for the rest of her short life.

12 : A Curse on the House of Fairport
1974–1975

Sandy was mesmerising. Pete Townshend put his finger on it: no vibrato at all. The expressiveness of her voice, the wonderful songs, and the problem for all of us was that she was endlessly forgivable. She only had to open her mouth and sing and the synchronised weeping would start. Her tragedy was that she never really understood how well loved she was both by the punters and the band and other musicians.

BRUCE ROWLAND

Once, at the Troubadour in Los Angeles, Fairport played three shows in one night – and Sandy happened to fall off stage. Just like that. But the audience, who were fantastic, just caught her and stood her back up. And she didn't miss a note.

TREVOR LUCAS, *Ram*, February 1989

Island Records invites you to attend a
dinner-reception in honour of

FAIRPORT CONVENTION

at the

Meridiana Restaurant (upstairs)
169 Fulham Road (entrance off Pond Place)
London SW3 on Wednesday, June 4th

6 to 10:00 pm.

ADMITS TWO

Invite to the media launch for Fairport's *Rising for the Moon*

When Sandy was asked by Australian paper *Go Set* if she thought there was a curse on Fairport, she said yes; she even suggested they change the name, although they wouldn't countenance it: 'It's like do or die, the band have gone through so much but they decided to have another bash. Why not? I just think that I need them and they need me.'

Buoyed by Sandy's return, Fairport had come home from their tour of the Far East and Australasia in February 1974 only to discover they'd hit rock bottom financially. 'Things just got worse with each succeeding line-up,' Dave Pegg told *NME*, 'until everything was going wrong, and no one could play; our business just got totally screwed up and nearly put an end to us.* Although we earned a lot of money, we also incurred a pile of debts which weren't being paid off.'

The debts had mounted during January and February 1974 as the band travelled from Tokyo to Australia and New Zealand, then to North America and back home: 'We ended up owing the travel

---

* After Joe Boyd left for California in 1971, Fairport were managed by Philip Sterling Wall, a successful businessman friend of Dave Swarbrick. He managed the group until they returned from their shambolic Far Eastern, Australasian and American travels in February 1974. David Denny then took over in 1974–5. 'It's the way they used to operate,' says Chris Pegg. 'The professional side of it wasn't Fairport's forte. It was an old mates' society; it was more important that somebody fitted in rather than knew what they were doing.'

agency far more than we made,' says Jerry Donahue, 'because all the luggage – which included the entire back line (guitars, drums, amps, the lot) – was sent not as freight but as excess baggage. Our arrival home after two months was soon followed by a travel debt of around £25,000.'

Chris Blackwell agreed to absorb all their debts, leaving them free of their fears of insolvency and able to focus on recording their first studio album since Sandy's return to the fold. Without Blackwell's backing, Fairport would not have survived, but the debt had merely been transferred: 'We owed thousands to Island because the world tour had backfired,' says Dave Swarbrick. 'The Piper turned up at rehearsals in the shape of a bailiff; Island took care of the bill, we had then to take care of Island.' Everybody knew that the next album was crucial to the band remaining on Island and, after all the disappointments, even maintaining their own resolve to carry on. Dave Mattacks almost left the band for the second time but was persuaded to stay. A new song written by Sandy, 'Rising for the Moon', which Fairport had debuted on the Peel Session of 14 July 1974, became something of a template for the album: a traditional-sounding composition presented in a contemporary and, in theory, more marketable setting.

With this end in mind, the group also decided they needed to bring in a producer from outside the Fairport family. That was fine by Trevor, the present incumbent, who was beginning to feel the strain of multitasking within the group – he was de facto Sandy's personal manager as well. Trevor suggested they approach Glyn Johns, whose CV as a producer and engineer was second to none; among the acts he had worked with were the Rolling Stones, the Who, the Steve Miller Band, the Beatles, Led Zeppelin, Eric Clapton, the Faces, Paul McCartney and the Eagles.

'Trev had done a great job in the studio,' says Jerry Donahue. '*Nine* is a very underrated Fairport record, but we all thought we needed to try something different to make that breakthrough and it was getting harder for Trevor, he had a lot on his plate. Island was excited by the prospect as well. When I joined, Fairport had been on Island's books for five years, and although they had stuck with the band, we were no longer a priority.'

Island certainly thought an album with Johns might reverse Fairport's fortunes both financially and artistically and, at the same time, reposition Sandy after the relative failures of her three solo albums. 'The Island way was that we always considered the artist knew best,' says Tim Clark, 'and it was the band's idea to approach Glyn Johns. We saw it as a positive step. Glyn wouldn't have come cheap but Chris Blackwell had a good relationship with him. [Johns had been the engineer on Traffic's second, and a number of Spooky Tooth albums.] We may have been idealistic at Island but Chris was a very good businessman. Glyn Johns was a really successful producer and anything he attached his name to was going to attract interest.'

Sandy was as eager as anybody about the prospect of working with Johns and knew Trevor was beginning to walk on eggshells around the others in the group. She didn't know Johns but was friendly with many of the major rock acts who had worked with him; she had also worked with his brother Andy. 'Sandy was always very reluctant to bring in anybody from outside her circle who might have a wider perspective,' says Richard Thompson. 'Working with Glyn Johns is a rare exception. Much as having that extended family around her was a good thing, in that it gave her the security she needed, you can get too comfortable. Glyn was the right person to produce Fairport and, coming from outside the camp, Glyn would have seen her potential too.'

The question was, would Johns take the job? 'We didn't think he'd be interested,' says Dave Pegg. 'Glyn took his time to decide whether he wanted to work with Fairport. You're only as good as your latest hit, after all, and he'd had lots and we'd had none. We weren't a successful band if you look at Glyn's track record; we weren't even a successful band in terms of Island.'

Johns was aware of Fairport but didn't know any of their albums, nor had he met them before going along to a rehearsal, but he was immediately impressed by their musicianship. 'I enjoyed working with them enormously,' says Johns. 'They were very easy to work with. They had made a lot of records with the same producer or the same type of producer; it's good for any artist to make a change. It can get a bit stale and the way I work in the studio was very different, a lot less laid-back than they were used to.'

In reality, Johns wasn't that different from John Wood. 'My attitude was always that a recording studio should be more like a factory than a hangout,' Wood told Jim Wirth. But Wood was the devil they knew and Fairport were no longer the disciplined unit which completed albums in days rather than weeks.

'They certainly responded in a good way,' Johns says, 'that's very obvious from listening to the record. I remember being tremendously impressed with all of them but particularly with Sandy, who I thought was astonishing, but a rather sad character, quite disturbing really.'

Johns also made it clear that the group were not to rely on covers, traditional material or any set instrumental pieces. 'That was understood from the start,' he says. 'As a result, quite possibly Fairport fans didn't like it. It was a different-sounding record for Fairport.' Explaining the decision, Sandy told *Sounds* that

'Steeleye are the masters at digging up the old material. We could do that but the group want to move on taking their roots with them.'

Johns is, however, quick to deny that Island told him this album was the last chance saloon for Fairport: 'I don't have any memory of anybody telling me it was make or break or there being any particular expectation from Island, but it wouldn't have made any difference to the way I made the record. I remember they were happy with it.

'I never did pre-production. We'd always work it out in the studio. If you over-rehearse you lose the adrenalin rush you get when you first come up with a part and it all gels together; I like to capture that in the studio. It was all done with their approval. Nothing was rammed down their necks and nothing was done without their being enthusiastic about it. They were very much party to the new sound.'

Fairport were aware that Johns came with a reputation as a hard taskmaster, and whether out of respect or trepidation the group knew they would have to knuckle down. 'There wasn't any conflict in the studio because you either did it Glyn's way or not at all,' says Pegg. 'He put the fear of God up me to start with. But it was one of the best times I've had in a studio, very disciplined, which was not necessarily the Fairport way.'

'Glyn is more hands-on,' says Dave Mattacks. 'He also has a strong personality and will tell all and sundry when something's not good. He'll also tell and praise you when it's working and he makes everything sound great. Interestingly, a lot like John Wood.'

The first recording sessions took place in December 1974 at Olympic Studios, where, in the weeks up to Christmas, they recorded three songs written by Sandy: 'Rising for the Moon', 'One

More Chance' and 'Dawn', written with Donahue. They tackled two of Trevor's songs: 'Restless', dating back to Fotheringay days, and 'Tears', which was released as a B-side to 'White Dress', an uplifting, romantic song written especially by Dave Swarbrick for Sandy to sing. Johns says 'White Dress' is one of his favourite songs ever, at least as Sandy performed it.

'One More Chance' and 'Rising for the Moon', both demoed over the summer, are two of the album's other highlights. 'Rising for the Moon' is a perfect opening track, a real call to arms. 'It's definitely a road song,' said Sandy, 'it's about being a musician. Everyone else gets up and prepares for the day. A musician gets up and prepares for going on stage at night. The fiddle riff that Swarb created always reminds me of the sound of the road under your wheels as you travel endless miles from gig to gig.'

More than anything else on the album, the closing song, 'One More Chance', showed just how good Fairport with Sandy could be, and what Glyn Johns could draw out of them collectively with a classic song. 'One More Chance' can be taken as Sandy's stirring cry for peace or as a thinly disguised plea to her husband, cased in some of the most thrilling instrumental work Fairport have ever recorded. It's one of Sandy's last great vocals on record, mature and fragile as she implores:

> Is it too late to change the way we're bound to go?
> Is it too late? There's surely one of us must know.

'He really could get the best out of people,' says Dave Pegg. '"One More Chance" – that's the second take, certainly vocally, and Sandy would always say, "I can do better than that," and he'd say, "OK, you've got one more take." She got upset with Glyn a few times but that's the way Glyn is. She always got very nervous before doing a vocal in the studio. John Wood could push her too but she was used to him.'

Fairport broke off from recording in January 1975, when they did a TV show in the Netherlands and other Dutch and European dates before returning to Olympic on 5 February. But when they resumed, it was with a new drummer. Having been back in the band since October 1973, Dave Mattacks now decided to leave again. 'Glyn fell out with DM, which is why he left,' says Dave Pegg. 'Glyn was a perfectionist and he insisted on doing things his way, and eventually DM reached breaking point.' Both parties now make light of it. 'I know nothing about Dave leaving or why,' says Johns. 'It wouldn't have been anything to do with me. I can only remember being surprised at Dave having left, and disappointed. I was a big fan and we got on really well.' Mattacks at

Melody Maker news clip following Dave Mattacks's
departure from Fairport, January 1975

least admits to a certain disagreement: 'I love Glyn; we did have a wee falling out towards the end of the recording but that's not why I left. I got tired of earning £100 a week and feeling, post-Joe Boyd's management, that we weren't going anywhere. I was also doing a lot of very enjoyable session work, without the stress of being in what was basically a struggling band.'

Fairport's immediate reaction was to try and increase the Fotheringay quotient within the group but Gerry Conway was still tied up with Cat Stevens. According to Dave Pegg, thirty-two drummers were auditioned before the group eventually agreed on Glyn Johns's recommendation, Bruce Rowland. He had been the drummer with Joe Cocker's Grease Band and Ronnie Lane's Slim Chance; both had worked with Johns. 'There was some friction after Bruce came in,' says Pegg, 'but that was because he was a different kind of drummer; we were all so used to DM. Bruce was thrown straight in at the deep end. He knew Glyn, which would have helped him, but it's always tough being the new boy.'

Before joining, like Johns Rowland did his homework and listened to the back catalogue. He concluded: 'There was no getting away from the fact that Sandy just reached inside you – it was so perfect and her lyrics were just wonderful.'

Rowland remembers: 'DM once said to me that when he was first asked to join the band all the tunes sounded the same to him, and I knew exactly what he meant. They did to me too. DM had defined electric folk as far as the drums went and I was really stepping into the shoes of a legend.

'Glyn told me, "There won't be any airy-fairy folk bullshit, it's a commercial album." He played me what they'd done, about half the album by then, and it's fair to say I was floored, but at the back of my head was a little voice saying, "If this wasn't called

Fairport you'd have a hit album." I thought they had anchored themselves by making it a Fairport Convention album.'

Rowland's first rehearsal could easily have sent him running; it was in a bleak room, with awful acoustics and 'seriously bad vibes', but he had only committed to doing the recording sessions. Sandy and Trevor arrived late and had clearly been arguing. 'Peggy had Sandy in tears,' says Rowland, 'because there was a Derek and Clive album out and Sandy hadn't heard the album so she didn't know the punchlines. At one point she was complaining that nobody was listening to her, and Peggy said, "I'll tell you who listens to you – no fucker, that's who." So she burst into tears. I soon got used to that happening.'

Aside from breaking in a new drummer, Fairport and Sandy in particular were facing the familiar problem of a lack of material, and this time they had no option of turning to folk or contemporary covers. The songs they recorded during February to complete the album were a real mixed bag. 'I thought it was important that it was all original material,' says Johns, 'and, to be fair, not all of it was wonderful. There are a couple of tracks on there that aren't very good at all. That's normally the case. Trevor's song "Iron Lion" and Peggy and Swarb's "Night Time Girl", a country hoedown, are awful. It's political, it's normal in any band where there are two or three other writers that you try and involve them all and give them at least one each.'

'Glyn would say we needed an up-tempo song,' says Pegg. '"Go and write one and come back tomorrow," which is why you get "Night Time Girl", which is throwaway. Me, Swarb and Sandy got that together overnight in the hotel room. We didn't have songs to play with and that was tough on Sandy; we all looked to her to come up with the goods.' Johns's recalcitrance over covers rather backfired. At the time Fairport were playing a rousing version of 'All Along the Watchtower' in their set. Its inclusion would have certainly enriched the album's content and kept fans on side.

Only Dave Swarbrick's charming waltz 'White Dress' holds up among the group contributions, and in the final sequence seven of the eleven tracks on *Rising for the Moon* were either written or co-written by Sandy. It's surprising that Sandy's own traditional-sounding 'The King and Queen of England', demoed for Fairport during the previous winter, wasn't considered. It's not one of her most original lyrics and is in Sandy's stock 3/4 time, but compared to 'Night Time Girl' it's a masterpiece. She did, however, rework two songs from her past: 'After Halloween', from the *Sandy* sessions, and the revised 'What Is True', briefly rehearsed in LA during the sessions she did with Fairport for *Like an Old Fashioned Waltz*.

The only new song Sandy came up with after the January break was one of her great portraits in song, 'Stranger to Himself', and it's one of her sharpest lyrics. 'It's very much a song about Swarbrick,' she explained. 'The first time I was in Fairport, I had barely time to get to know him; I was pretty much in awe of him because he had come with a great reputation from the folk scene. The second time I joined, I was around him a lot more. When you are on tour, you tend to live in each other's pocket a bit. I began to realise what a complex and odd character he was. Someone – it could have been Peggy – remarked that no one really knew who Swarb was; in fact, he doubted if he even knew himself. That's what inspired the song, which began as a series of images.'

Swarbrick has since said that he was flattered by the song, although he thinks that some of the lyrics might also have been applied to Sandy herself. His nickname for Sandy was Boadicea and he wrote his own tribute to her, 'Boadicea', on his 1983 album *Flittin'*: 'All woman, totally English, irrepressible and invincible.'

The irrepressible Sandy was known for being lackadaisical in the studio, and Johns was not renowned for his patience. 'Glyn never left anyone in any doubt as to who was in charge and that things were going to be done his way,' says Rowland, 'and Glyn is a genius. He never failed, as far as I'm aware, to get the best out of his artists, including Sandy. Glyn did come close to bullying her and he would look at me and give me his "not one fucking word" glare. And it ended in smiles.

'When Sandy was doing her vocals Glyn didn't so much tell her what to do but he left her in no doubt as to what he didn't like. He handled her like a riding master. He was never bashful or reticent, he was just absolutely positive, and Sandy would have liked him to be a little gentler but she didn't burst into tears once – and she got on and did it. He just waited till she could see it for herself.'

Johns found this one aspect of Sandy's studio craft well to his liking: 'Sandy was a one-take wonder,' he says, although Sandy herself would often feel she could do better. 'There's absolutely no need to do anything more than once in my view if it's right the first time – and that was my memory. Not every time, of course.

'Her extraordinary delivery was based on folk music, which is a totally different animal to the commercial sound that most people were used to hearing. Her roots were folk and she never really left those roots whatever she wrote, not in my experience anyway. That held her back from crossing over to that pop audience. And *Rising for the Moon* was a Fairport Convention record, not a Sandy Denny record. That's a big difference. She wasn't glamorous either; she really didn't fit the bill for being a pop singer. Basically, she was too good. And there weren't too many other female singers writing their own songs, whether in pop or folk.

'Sandy was such a sad girl and really very lonely, it always seemed to me. She actually made a massive pass at me, which was slightly embarrassing and, again, very sad. I felt very sorry for her and for how lonely she was.'*

Philippa Clare saw a lot of Sandy at that time and agrees that she was very depressed. 'Sandy was always on the edge. She might have held it together in the studio but she'd come round to my flat in tears, and I'd say, "You're a grown-up, just stick it out." Sandy was so freaked by people. Glyn wasn't somebody she knew and she liked working with him, but she was scared rigid. So scared, and she felt Glyn was like a tyrant in the chair; and that's her feelings, not facts. The rest of them might have responded to working with somebody new but Sandy liked to be around people she felt safe with. And I think she felt so overloaded making that record, the pressure was on her, more so than if it was her own record and worrying that she was good enough to carry the load.'

Echoing Johns's own thoughts, Richard Thompson thinks it would have been more stimulating had Johns produced a Sandy record as opposed to one by Fairport. '*Rising for the Moon* is a bit of both,' he says, 'so it's inevitably compromised, but it is a really good record; there are some good songs all round and Glyn doesn't take any shit from anybody, and that was important. For me that's

---

* Glyn Johns says he never saw Sandy or the other members of Fairport again after they finished the album. 'I only saw Jerry Donahue and Dave Mattacks because I used them. It wasn't uncommon. I was working seven days a week with different people. My life at that time was one record after the next. I didn't socialise much with anybody and,' he says, laughing, 'a lot of the people I worked with didn't want to see me again anyway. I don't think that was the case with Fairport. Our paths just never crossed.'

one of the most successful of Sandy's records, let alone Fairport records, for getting performances out of her. Glyn was able to drive her harder, more than I was able to.'

Sandy's low spirits weren't only attributable to the stress of recording *Rising for the Moon*. Living in the country was proving to be far less idyllic than it had seemed six months earlier, which is painfully apparent from some distressing, self-critical entries in her notebooks. Most likely dating from around January 1975, these passages follow her lyrics to 'Stranger to Himself' and 'What Is True', handwritten during the break between sessions. In a letter to herself, she asks: 'Dear Sandy, Where did it all begin? This need to hide away?'

The letter continues: 'When you are there with the one who loves you, you want to get away somewhere, yet no one else is quite the same when you do, so you run hell for leather home to him and swear to yourself you'll never leave again.

'I wish I was a real musician. I wish I could just sit and play anything going. Consequently rehearsals get me down but for millions of reasons not just that.' She concludes: 'But mostly I'm LAZY. I know I am.'

A list of questions that appears on the next page is even more anguished. She answers only a few of them, but they not only encapsulate that moment in time, they delineate everything that would eat away at her for the remainder of her life.

Am I happy in the country?
Do I enjoy my job?
Is there anything I haven't done which is bugging me?
Am I musically up to my own standards? NO!
Am I in love with my husband?
Is the business side getting me down?
Am I writing well?

341

Am I writing enough?
If anything what do I need to inspire me?
Do I rely on other people?
Am I a great singer?
Am I talented? Yes.
Do I need to lose weight?!? Yes.
And guess who is going to solve all these problems.
ME!
Ain't I great? Yes!!!!!

*

Aside from joining Richard and Linda Thompson on stage at the Queen Elizabeth Hall in April to sing 'When Will I Be Loved', in the months between finishing recording *Rising for the Moon* in February and its release in mid-June things were quiet, if not blissful, on the home front.

On its release, Island gave *Rising for the Moon* the biggest push of any Fairport album of the seventies. '*Rising for the Moon* was a very classy album and definitely bore the imprint of Glyn Johns,' says Brian Blevins, then Island's head of press. 'It was the one that we put a lot of promotional heft behind. I organised a dinner for them with the press and radio producers and broadcasters at the Meridian Restaurant in Fulham, a rooftop affair. Fairport was a band where more sweat than money was usually put behind them. Island did both for *Rising for the Moon*.'

Fred Cantrell was less convinced by the record: 'Bringing in Glyn Johns was a mistake in hindsight; the direction he took them in alienated hardcore fans; they were confused by that record. It was an attempt to broaden their appeal to commercial radio but it didn't connect with radio producers.' However much

Island, and the group, had hoped that the Glyn Johns touch would help Fairport win over a new audience, it neither brought them new fans nor appeased the faithful. In the UK its chart position of fifty-two didn't justify the expense of hiring Johns and the increased promotional spend. In the US it fared better: *Rising for the Moon* reached number 143, by far the group's most successful American album. It remains the highest American chart position for Fairport, Sandy or any of the Witchseason acts.

Bruce Rowland perceptively pinpoints why *Rising for the Moon* stands apart from any other Fairport album. 'It's the first album and only Fairport record that counts as product. Whether you think that's a good thing or not is another matter.' For Fairport fans it was not a good thing. '*Rising for the Moon* shifted too far away from our template, and successfully so for the most part,' says Jerry Donahue, 'but some of the fans felt it moved too far from that traditional platform. It wasn't that there were too many of Sandy's songs, but Fairport had long been viewed as a folk act, so they missed the instrumental tunes and traditional emphasis. The problem for folk acts was that their fans never wanted them to change too much.'

Misunderstood in its day, the rationale behind *Rising for the Moon* seems far less calculated now than it did at the time; it holds up well and Sandy's songs include some of her finest. The album is mostly let down by the compromise of three or four poor songs written by others in the group. *Rising for the Moon* was a fascinating experiment in attempting to use Sandy's songwriting and the arrangements to create a sound that would appeal to FM radio; its relative popularity in the US suggests it was, at least, partially successful. Ahead of its release in June 1975, Trevor Lucas described the direction as 'soft rock', telling *Sounds* that the Fotheringay side of the line-up was coming to the fore.

Two years later Sandy drew an interesting comparison with Fleetwood Mac's *Rumours*, which had only been released in February 1977 and is far slicker in production but was conceived, she feels, along the same lines as *Rising for the Moon*. 'I saw an article that talked about AOR [album-oriented rock] acts tending to produce introspective work, songs about themselves and the inner workings of a band. *Rumours* is the obvious example, but also Joni Mitchell's songs, or Crosby, Stills and Nash, or *Hotel California*. *Rising for the Moon* fits right into that state of mind – you don't have to dig too deep to find which songs were inspired by relationships within the band. It happened in our live sets, too; a song like "Solo" fitted well into Fairport, partly because it was very obviously about band members past and present.'

Rising for the Moon was largely well received in the press. The *Sunday Times* felt that Fairport were 'at their versatile peak'. *Sounds* said the album 'bore witness to a new found confidence and self-assurance', and Robin Denselow in the *Guardian* wrote that Sandy's 'superb singing and songwriting has apparently galvanised her colleagues: the new album is their best for six years and it ought to re-establish the Fairports as a significant British band'. Colin Irwin in *Melody Maker* thought it was too much a Sandy Denny record with backing musicians. He touched a nerve. Due to be interviewed by Irwin the day his review appeared, Sandy walked out of the Island offices after reading his appraisal, just as he was arriving.

'It did become much more of a Sandy album,' agrees Dave Pegg. 'If you've got Sandy in the band you're going to use her. You want her to do the lead vocals and she came up with most of the songs, so the dreadful result is that you become a backing band. Perhaps that was inevitable – any band Sandy's in, you to want to make the most of her talent. I'm sure that's what Island wanted, even if it wasn't said upfront.'

The band had launched the album with a concert at the Royal Albert Hall on 10 June but played no other UK shows over the summer. Mindful of Fotheringay's disastrous show at the Royal Albert Hall, before introducing any of the new songs the group set things up with a string of Fairport oldies: 'Hexhamshire Lass', 'Brilliancy Medley', 'Sloth', 'Rosie', 'Walk Awhile', 'Tam Lin', 'Who Knows Where the Time Goes?', even reaching back to 'Mr Lacey' from *What We Did on Our Holidays*. Sandy's solo recordings included 'Quiet Joys of Brotherhood', 'It'll Take a Long Time', 'Listen, Listen' and a new song she dedicated to her father, 'No More Sad Refrains'. They played the best of the *Rising for the Moon* material and delivered a truly great band performance, with Sandy in superb voice despite her usual anxiety before a major London show.

'She really suffered so much with nerves,' says Bambi Ballard. 'The concert at the Royal Albert Hall, she couldn't go on unless I went with her. I ended up sitting under the piano and every so often she'd put her hand down and I'd squeeze it and she'd carry on.'

Ballard says of Fairport's other members: 'They hated being thought of as her backing band, and that fed her insecurities. They were using Sandy because they knew how much they needed her songs but they were always too ego-driven [to admit it]. However laid-back they liked to appear to be, there was always a slightly stressful sense within Fairport. Backstage, they'd be going, "For God's sake, pull yourself together, Sandy."'

As the man in charge of Island's regional sales team, Martin Satterthwaite was close to Fairport, spending much time with them on the road. 'When Sandy came back into Fairport,' he says, 'she had lost that sense of enjoyment she used to have. She never wanted to be out front, the leader of the band, but she was sometimes uncertain of her role. She went from tagging along and getting up for encores to being centre stage doing her own intense songs, but a little sidelined at other times. Fairport's core audience was there as much to see Swarb as her and would get off on his fiddle pieces. It was two or three bands in one and they never looked entirely unified on stage. There was always a certain amount of jockeying for position.'

That competition came to the fore when Fairport left for a series of American dates in September to promote the new album. It started poorly when the proposed schedule of interviews and promotion didn't happen. Instead, most of the band partied; Sandy began drinking a great deal, as well as enthusiastically sampling prime Los Angeles cocaine. 'The band was always divided between those who liked a drink and those who took drugs,' says Dave Pegg, himself in the drinking camp. 'Sandy and Trevor were the ones who did both.' The effect on her singing was starting to show in performances. In New York, where the tour began on 23 September, she had put so much strain on her voice that she needed hospital treatment.

In present-day interviews, the remaining Fairport members tend to play down their concerns about Sandy's drinking at that time. 'There's no doubt that Sandy knew she had a problem, and it was a bloody big problem with her drinking,' says Marc Brierley. 'As a group Fairport were almost all heavy drinkers – mostly fine wines and beer – but not before going on stage and not first thing in the morning, and Sandy was hitting the spirits first thing. My wife and I were very close to Peggy and his wife Chris, and they were worried that she was so alcohol-dependent. I was on the way to becoming a transcendental meditation teacher at the time and Peggy and Chris learnt TM at our house in Birmingham. We spoke to Sandy about how it could help with her alcohol problems, which she acknowledged. So I gave her the introductory talk, and she said, "I absolutely, definitely want to learn how to meditate if it can help control my drinking." She said she wanted to learn as soon as she got to California. I arranged for the TM teachers to meet her off the plane and they arranged for her to have the instruction. But she never turned up. She just got back into the old routine.'

'Her singing was always spot on,' says Dave Pegg today (although he wasn't always so complimentary), 'even if she'd had a few too many. The problem was that she didn't believe it. Most evenings she would come off and say, "I was really crap tonight, it was terrible," very self-effacing; it was always, "I'm too fat, I can't sing – everybody loves Joni Mitchell, or Linda Ronstadt or Kate McGarrigle, and my songs aren't as good as theirs." And you would go, "No, no, you were great."' Sandy was, perhaps, more honest than her bandmates about her erratic presentation and acknowledged this with customary internalisation, occasionally adapting the words to 'Solo' to sing, 'I've always kept a unicorn and I *hardly ever* sing out of tune,' instead of 'never', often addressed pointedly towards certain members of the band.

'Sandy drank, yes. She liked to drink,' said Trevor in his last-ever interview. 'She liked the effect of alcohol, the feeling of being drunk – which is always dangerous. And she was one of those people whose bodies don't metabolise alcohol very well, so the first drink really had the effect of the last drink.'

'Trevor could handle his drugs and drinks better than Sandy,' says Linda Thompson. 'He just had that sort of constitution.

347

Sandy liked go-faster drugs and she got heavily into cocaine in America after she had rejoined Fairport in 1974, and it didn't stop back home. Other times it was tranquillisers and sleeping pills. A real cocktail of uppers and downers. They'd smoke a joint first thing in the morning – wake and bake, they called it. All stuff that made you paranoid and caused heavy mood swings, which Sandy had anyway, in spades.'

'Drinking was an integral part of Fairport's lifestyle,' says Chris Pegg. 'Nobody was ever sober, or that's how it seemed from the outside. Trevor and Sandy took a lot of different drugs. The others may have smoked dope but Trev and Sandy were taking coke, and that just blunted the reality of the situation. They did amyl nitrate too, and that hardly keeps you stable.'

Nor did it help Sandy's equilibrium that she never lost her fear of flying. 'She used to take beta blockers before getting on an aeroplane,' says Ralph McTell, 'and Fairport, when Sandy came back in the band, were always on and off planes and crossing time zones. It was the most she ever toured and travelled. Her rejoining Fairport may not have been the best thing for her. The living is hard enough without numbing yourself to get on a plane the next day. So Sandy was always on the edge of something.'

At the start of the campaign for *Rising for the Moon*, Fairport had hired Jo Lustig as manager specifically to take care of the business. Lustig had already proved himself, not least in managing Pentangle and Steeleye Span. He replaced David Denny, who had been interim manager since the group returned from their financially crippling 1974 tour. But the curse of Fairport struck again and the usually dependable Lustig made a mess of the arrangements on the American tour. 'It was a hard tour from the outset,' says Dave Pegg. 'We'd turn up to gigs and find they were cancelled because contracts hadn't been signed. The combination of all these things going wrong led to squabbles and fallings out. That was a permanent undercurrent. Sandy became increasingly insecure and was often depressed. It felt like there was either a row going on or one that was brewing. There'd still be some great shows; we could always put all that behind us when we got up on stage.'

It was a new experience for Bruce Rowland, who, against his better judgement, decided to join Fairport full-time and remained with the group until its 'farewell' tour in 1979. 'The American tour was appallingly organised,' says Rowland, 'and there was a lot of tension, particularly between Sandy and Trevor and Swarb, and the rest of us were onlookers to all this and it got you down. It was very intense, there would be flashpoints, and I had no idea of the politics behind all this but what I did know was that the banter was absolutely world-class. What I didn't know was that there were times when it was OK to laugh and times when it definitely wasn't. Sandy could be vicious towards people but that's when she was at her funniest, unless you were on the receiving end.'

Rowland offers the perfect example: 'She and Trev went to this party and, as they enter, sitting on a sofa is the archetypal stick-thin pretty blonde with very straight, long blonde hair. And pretty blondes were Sandy's bête noire. Sandy was wearing a big fur coat and carrying a Gladstone bag made out of carpet material. The coat must have weighed thirty kilos. And she takes it off, swings it round and dumps it on top of this girl, who is crushed by the weight of it. Sandy waits for her to emerge, knowing perfectly well what she's done, helps the poor girl up into the sitting position and says in her poshest voice, "I'm so sorry, I thought you were a hat stand."'

'Swarb was very close to Sandy,' says Chris Pegg, 'and he understood a lot of things that went straight over my head. After Trevor, he was closest to her, but Trevor and Swarb were good mates from way back and having Sandy around did come between that male bonding thing. Between Trevor, Swarb and Sandy it was always very volatile. Arguments would flare up over nothing.'

'Sandy and Swarb did have a feisty relationship,' says Rowland, 'but there was a lot of love between the two of them and a lot of understanding. He was hit very, very hard when she died. Sandy was lachrymose in spades and she would make me cry when she would sing. I saw Swarb once – she did something that was spontaneous, a little vocal trick, and when it happened in a very quiet part of the song, I heard Trevor go "Aaahhh," and I looked up at Swarb and we both had tears in our eyes. She could do that.

'Sandy could be difficult and exasperating and would invite disapproval so she could cry and get drunk. She would be maudlin, spiteful and then suddenly sociable from one minute to the next – you never knew what to expect. What made Trevor invaluable was that Sandy would play endless mind games with you and take you to the brink of making her cry, but Trevor was just that little bit better than her at that, and he made her laugh. And he kept her in a very good place to work. I liked Trevor enormously. He was the best of friends and awesomely amoral – he made no bones about it.'

For all the old hands in Fairport, the curse was coming round again. 'We couldn't believe it,' says Pegg, 'it was the same old story and when we got back home at the end of it we came away with no money. After the English tour which followed I remember collecting my receipt from the office and it came to £300, which represented over two months' work.

350

'We all thought Jo Lustig would make a difference because he'd had so much success as a manager, mostly with other folk acts. So we all lost faith because nothing had changed. It was another fine mess. That's why Jerry left, and then Sandy and Trev. We had such hopes at the start of the year but by the end of 1975 the band was falling apart.'

'Good management is crucial,' says Donahue. 'Fairport and Sandy suffered through the seventies as a result. None of us were very good at making the right decision. When David [Denny] came in, he did a good job but he didn't have the experience of Jo Lustig, which is why we brought Jo in; but he messed up like all the rest. Instead of "manager", Danny [Thompson] used to refer to him as "the damager". He was right. The last American tour was the beginning of the end for me.'

Jerry Donahue saw the band through a month of dates back home during October, followed by some European dates, before he announced he was leaving and returning home to America. The *Rising for the Moon* line-up's final performance was recorded for Dutch TV on 17 December 1975; by the time it was shown in January half the group had gone. 'We knew Island was never going to commit to the group in such a way again,' says Donahue. 'After we recorded the album with Glyn, and Jo came on board, I thought, mistakenly, there's nothing to stop us now. The stress was beginning to mount for everybody. I had only seen the upside of Sandy in Fotheringay, not the tears and tantrums. I only saw that when she rejoined Fairport, and it was very worrying. I really felt for her.'

Sandy's second tenure in Fairport escalated the process of her emotional unravelling, particularly during and following the American tour that September. She had rejoined Fairport for the wrong reasons, and the rest of the group went along with it with the same clouded judgement and false optimism. Sandy was certainly not in the right mindset at the time: her own album delayed, her resentment building at being let down by Island, tagging along and more or less falling involuntarily into Fairport again. The hope and expectation of what that line-up might achieve was simply never realised and *Rising for the Moon*, a valiant effort, was not the hoped-for commercial turnaround for either Sandy or the group. 1975 was a year when Fairport fragmented and Sandy was unhinged by the combination of relentless touring, massive exhaustion and personal conflicts with those she was closest to in the band, all exaggerated by prolonged drink and drug intake.

'The second time I was with Fairport wasn't mind-boggling at all,' said Sandy in 1977. 'It wasn't a total catastrophe but it could have been better, but I think everybody had just about had it at that point. Fairport were in dreadful financial straits; it was a depressing situation that we couldn't do anything about, we were working and all the money was going straight into a hole.

FAIRPORT SPLIT UP

FAIRPORT CONVENTION have finally and irrevocably broken up — and that is official! The band's future has been in doubt for some time, and speculation regarding a split was heightened when three members of the group — Dave Swarbrick, Bob Pegg and Bruce Rowlands — recently started gigging on their own, aided by former Fairport member Simon Nicol. But the final break came with the news this week that Sandy Denny and Trevor Lucas have left Convention.

The split was also hastened by Jerry Donahue's decision to settle in the United States whence he has been commuting to this country to work with Fairport. Now he will live permanently in Los Angeles, where he will work as a session musician.

Sandy Denny will shortly be starting work on a new album, produced by her husband Trevor

Lucas, who — it is understood — also plans a solo recording career. Swarbrick, Pegg and Rowlands are in the process of forming a new group, together with two other musicians whose names cannot yet be revealed (although it is known that Simon Nicol in not one of them), but they have not yet decided upon a name for the new outfit.

SANDY DENNY

NME news story confirming Jerry Donahue, Sandy and Trevor had left Fairport

I'm not ashamed of it but it just didn't spark off the way it might have done.' Not even counting when she played and recorded with Fairport unofficially in 1973, Sandy's second stint in Fairport Convention lasted two years, from January 1974 to the end of 1975, longer than she spent in Fairport the first time around. It wasn't until 14 February 1976 that it was announced in the press that Sandy, Trevor and Jerry Donahue had left Fairport, two years to the day since *NME* confirmed that she had officially rejoined the group.

As a newcomer to the camp at the start of 1975, Bruce Rowland has an insightful overview of the year he spent with Sandy in Fairport. 'I find *Rising for the Moon* such a joyful and uplifting album,' he says. 'It's one of Glyn's, so the sound and the production are brilliant. It's timeless, as you'd expect – and the material speaks for itself. In the context of the chemistry of that band, the combination of those ferocious egos, it has a sad piquancy and beautiful piquancy because it's a swansong if you think about it – both for Sandy and for Fairport. It never got better.

'Fairport is an extraordinary entity, although it's creaked a few times – it's like one of Richard Thompson's songs, "We Sing Hallelujah", from *I Want to See the Bright Lights*.'

> A man is like a rusty wheel
> On a rusty cart.
> He sings his song as he rattles along
> And then he falls apart.

13 : *All Our Days*
1976–1977

I don't think she ever got comfortable, however remarkable, and whatever great timing and poise she had as a vocalist. In a similar but obviously different way to Janis Joplin, the gift was so powerful – living around that gift is tough. The more brilliant the gift, the more life is fragile around it.

ROBERT PLANT, *Uncut*, October 2010

I don't want to write miserable songs. Do you know how I feel after I've written a miserable sad song? Something that's really hit me and hurt me; I feel terrible. I go and sit down and I'm really upset by it. I always write on my own. I tend to think of sad things and so I write songs that make me feel even sadder. I sit down and I write something and it moves me to tears almost. I'm fed up with feeling like that. Why do I have to put myself through it?

SANDY DENNY, *Melody Maker*, 16 July 1977

Georgia, though you sleep so
soundly now,
When autumn leaves are
falling to the ground
You'll reach to catch them
with your tiny hands
and gaze in wonderment
as only babies can.
How I long to to see you wake
and smile
My beautiful most precious
child.

Sandy's poem for her daughter Georgia, September 1977

After Sandy and Trevor left Fairport Convention at the end of 1975, they had no plans for the foreseeable future. Both had spent much of the time since moving to Byfield either touring or in the studio. Now they had an opportunity to live the normal, stable domestic life that Sandy always said she wanted. In December Sandy demoed a batch of new songs at home, mostly written during the final months of the crumbling Fairport. She had played the oldest of these, 'No More Sad Refrains', at the Royal Albert Hall back in June. The title alone brought a wave of incredulous laughter from the audience. 'Can you believe that?' she asked. The phrase proved to be anything but prophetic, at a time when Sandy was generating her most prolific and personal outpouring of songs yet.

As well as 'No More Sad Refrains', she made demo tapes of 'Full Moon', 'Take Me Away', 'Still Waters Run Deep' and the autumnal 'All Our Days', an attempt at reconciliation with the past, eloquently channelled through the passing of the seasons. It's Sandy at her most purely poetic, absorbed by 'memories for saving all our days'. Much of what she wrote that winter is dominated by her attempts to confront the volatile nature of her relationship with Trevor and, at least to begin with, the songs are tinged with optimism. 'Full Moon' expresses hope:

> Our lives will be so different from now on,
> Each and every good time will be long.

'Take Me Away' simply asks: 'If not for you how would I keep going?'

Almost overnight Sandy had gone from the demands of travelling and touring with a group who were often at each other's throats to a more sedentary life in a small country village, but the only people she knew nearby were those same members of Fairport. The adjustment wasn't easy and the songs she wrote in the early months of 1976 have a fundamental sense of despair fuelled by persistent bouts of insomnia. 'The darkness it grows and *the lady* she does not sleep' is a line from 'Still Waters Run Deep', written early in 1975; it's full of self-loathing and feelings of isolation.

> She has a thorn in her side, a chip on her shoulder,
> Some heartache to hide, a lot of people to scold her.
> No one comes near to set her free,
> They all live in fear, thinking it's no place to be.

The most telling line from the twice-acclaimed Best British Female Singer of the early 1970s is 'Queen of her kind but she doesn't wear the crown.'

'When she left Fairport none of us at Island thought it was a bad move,' says Fred Cantrell, one of the few close friends left within the depleted Island camp. 'We knew there were clashes within the band and organisationally it was a mess. Sandy ended up thinking they were holding her back. She went from constantly being on the road to mostly being at home or in the studio. She suddenly had too much time to dwell on what was going wrong in her career or with Trevor or whatever else was troubling her overactive mind. She would walk into the offices and she looked so down. She would perk up – but only briefly. She wanted to be happy more than anything else and she wasn't, and I don't think she was ever happy again.'

Since going to America, Joe Boyd now only saw Sandy a few times a year and was saddened by the change in her. 'I know she started tooting powder, got thin and thinner, and she never seemed very happy. When I saw her she seemed a little desperate at times.'

It certainly wasn't a particularly happy Christmas that year. Nigel Osborne and Marion Appleton spent Christmas at Byfield and outside pub hours were confined to the cottage: 'David [Denny] had brought two cases of his own favourite wine, Black Tower, as I recall, and he wouldn't share it with anybody,' says Osborne. 'He just sat in the corner being miserable. Sandy had a strop at one point and she stomped off. She'd been drinking brandy all day and Watson was under the piano in the corner, where he usually slept. She crawled under the piano and tried to cuddle up with Watson, who promptly got up and walked away, and she burst into tears and screamed, "Even the dog doesn't want to be with me."'

More out of curiosity than desperation, Sandy briefly succumbed to the wiles of Scientology, having signed up initially, according to Linda Thompson, because she fancied the guy at the local centre. 'Trevor went crazy when he found out she joined,' says Chris Pegg. 'He discovered that she paid them an awful lot of money. They tried to lie about it but he went through the bank statements and got every penny back. Although Trevor was dyslexic, he was very good with numbers and figures.'

'Sandy didn't do things by halves and could be impulsive,' says Bruce Rowland, 'and she got seriously hooked into Scientology not long after leaving Fairport. The thing that made her drop it was the truth machine; they connect you to some sort of lie detector, and that eventually freaked her out. She agreed to give them her piano, the Steinway, although luckily they never came to collect it. She promised it to them because they convinced her that having that piano was holding her back. Absolute bullshit. And Trev said, "Over my dead body." He went down there and wrecked the place. I was only upset that he didn't take me with him.'

During March, Sandy demoed another batch of emotionally charged songs: 'Take Away the Load', 'I'm a Dreamer', 'By the Time It Gets Dark' and 'One Way Donkey Ride'. 'By the Time It Gets Dark' is mock-hopeful in its tone about her and Trevor's increasingly troubled relationship, while 'I'm a Dreamer' is more ambiguous: it would be one of the high points of the album she would soon begin recording. 'It's my imagination,' she sings with flickering resolve, 'when I get low/And the truth is I don't think I'll ever go'. 'One Way Donkey Ride', which she later said was her favourite off the album, is another song about crippling uncertainty, unusually morose, as much about her frustrations in her career as her wavering marriage.

> No one is given the map to their dreams,
> All we can do is to trace it,
> See where we go to,
> Know where we've been,
> Build up the courage to face it.

The recurring refrain 'God bless the poor ones . . .' marks a rare use of religious imagery in Sandy's writing.

The feelings poured out in her songs are echoed in Sandy's messy and often frenzied notebooks of the time. The content veers from declarations of love towards Trevor and a longing for him to be by her side, to anger, despair and scorn. 'My dearest one,' she writes in 1976, 'I hope you are well. I worked till five in the morning just to make you realise I meant what I said about trying hard. I think it is the best song I've ever written, maybe because I feel I know all the feelings in the song. It takes a lifetime usually, but maybe I'm just lucky.' The song that follows is not her best, nor would she ever record it, although it became the title track of Thea Gilmore's *Don't Stop Singing*.*

With considerably more vitriol towards her absent taskmaster of a husband she writes elsewhere: 'No Deal/I won't write a song about the one I love even if he is a shitbag. I can't rhyme when I'm upset.' Another letter to Trevor, torn out of a notepad and now almost too faded to read, begins: 'My darling Trevor, I never write to you. I wish I was like you and was with you always. Sometimes I feel that I am so far away, but perhaps the reason we stay together is that we are so different. After all these years I treasure your love as something that occurs only once in life the way it has for me.'

Yet the notebooks and scraps of songs also suggest an affair or affairs Sandy was having. There are hints in the lyrics of 'London', another song later recorded by Thea Gilmore, while 'Makes Me Think of You', which Sandy wouldn't demo for another year, is arguably the most explicit depiction of her troubled marriage. The song concludes:

> The albums strewn without their clothes
> Gather among the grooves.
> The only one I play is *Blue*,
> It makes me think of you.

* In 2010 Thea Gilmore was chosen from a shortlist of female singer-songwriters to write melodies for Sandy's abandoned lyrics and works in progress, mostly dating from the last few years of her life. Gilmore's album, *Don't Stop Singing*, was released by Island Records in November 2011. The extracted single, 'London', was playlisted at BBC Radio 2 but was never a substantial hit.

This is Sandy wearing her heart on her sleeve for once on the last original song she committed to tape, an acute expression of pure emotion worthy of Joni Mitchell. *Blue* had been the album which consolidated Mitchell's reputation as the queen of the Californian singer-songwriters, and to this day its honesty and vulnerability still resonate. Sandy often spoke of her dislike for Mitchell's explicit approach, usually after her own evasive style had been panned: 'Joni Mitchell, you know what her songs are about,' was a typical comment she made in 1971, the year *Blue* was released. 'She really is a bit of an open book. I don't really want people to know what I'm talking about.'

Sandy was often compared to Mitchell: she was the British counterpart but she was in no way as commercially or critically successful. The two actually had much in common. Both were caught between ambition, creativity and emotional needs, and a major impetus for both artists' work was a desire to settle down with a man and a longing for love. In the last years of her life Sandy's writing was moving towards the self-examination that underpins Joni Mitchell's work in the 1970s, and perhaps never more so than in 'Makes Me Think of You'.

*

In February 1976 Island confirmed they wanted another album from Sandy. Fairport Convention had also been given a reprieve; they were back to the core duo of Dave Swarbrick and Dave Pegg, but with Bruce Rowland supervising the recording. They were completing their album, *Gottle o' Gear*, in the month before Sandy was due to begin recording.

The remaining trio brought in friends such as Martin Carthy,

Robert Palmer and Simon Nicol, who soon decided to rejoin the band. *Gottle o' Gear*, released in May 1976, was not their finest hour. Dave Pegg described it as 'a bit after the Lord Mayor's show' and it was their last album for Island. Sandy's 'Take Away the Load' was one of the high points, retitled 'Sandy's Song'.

Sandy was more prepared than usual to begin recording again. It was the first time in her solo recording career that she didn't have to come up with songs at the last minute. She had amassed a cache of songs that was almost enough for two albums and which could easily have been cherry-picked to create an absorbing and deeply personal album. With a surfeit of songs, it was all the more puzzling that she then chose to record so many covers during the stop–start sessions between April and June 1976.

The new album was to be produced once again by Trevor, with John Wood, and began with great purpose at Island Studios in a productive burst between 23 April and 2 May. On the first day of the sessions Sandy cut 'One Way Donkey Ride', recorded in one take, James Carr's 'Losing Game', a song she knew from *The Last of the Red Hot Burritos*, and Richard Thompson's 'For Shame of Doing Wrong', from Richard and Linda's *Pour Down like Silver*. It was the only Thompson song she ever recorded, its repeated refrain, 'I wish I was a fool for you' (as she also retitles the song), almost deliberately taunting her husband sitting in the control booth. In that first week she also cut six of the eight songs previously demoed, so that they had already recorded enough material for an album.

Then on 2 May Sandy switched from Island Studios to CBS Studios, where 'All Our Days' was recorded, an eight-minute orchestral tribute – virtually a mini-cantata – in the English pastoral style of Vaughan Williams and Delius, but with elements of Hungarian-born Miklós Rózsa's classic Hollywood soundtracks. As well as the officially released version, Sandy and Trevor sang with a thirty-piece choir, creating a 'High Church' choral arrangement of the song. This was originally intended to be a reprise at the close of the original album, but was never used. 'All Our Days' is by far the fullest expression of Sandy's classical influences. The music was arranged and conducted by Harry Robinson; Sandy later said how pleased she was with his contribution.

'I was there when Sandy was singing with the orchestra,' says Jerry Donahue. 'That's how we were still doing it then, completely live; she was spellbinding. She made a real effort. She dressed up, wore a favourite floral dress and sang wonderfully. If she is over-stretching at times in later months on some of the *Rendezvous* recordings, here she showed she still had the power in her voice to be able to rise above an entire orchestra.'

The other orchestral session, this time at Island's Basing Street Studios, was no less remarkable. It yielded finished versions of 'I'm a Dreamer', 'Full Moon' and 'No More Sad Refrains', all cut live in one day. John Wood later recalled the sessions: 'We decided we would record three titles completely live with Sandy playing the piano with the rhythm section and the strings. We did it in Basing Street 1; on "I'm a Dreamer", there's one point where the strings go to a solo, and I just whacked the string mics up in the mix and you get this fantastic drum sound because it's all blasting round the studio. It sounds great – I love it! Not only that, but after three hours we had eighty-five per cent of the recording finished.' Yet, as Jerry Donahue remembers, she later re-recorded those vocals: 'I can't believe Trevor let the originals go or perhaps Sandy wasn't happy with them. When she did them again she was too conscious of herself and holding the notes longer than she needed to. She was trying too hard to display her technique for dramatic effect rather than singing from the heart as she did first time.'

It was symptomatic of the indecision and equivocation that set in when recording resumed in June. Sandy recorded 'Still Waters Run Deep' and one from the old Fotheringay repertoire, 'Silver Threads and Golden Needles', followed by a new song, 'Gold Dust', that tried too hard to fashion an FM-radio-friendly, adult-rock sound; Sandy's vocal inflections are also unusually reminiscent of Joni Mitchell. A cover of Little Feat's 'Easy to Slip', cut from the same cloth, was recorded at this time. Further sessions stretching into July were then taken up with extensive mixing and overdubs, largely at Trevor's behest. He was doing such protracted overdubs that it was almost as if he was subconsciously trying to bury the sentiments of the songs.

The vocal overdubs, which unusually brought in back-up singers Sue and Sunny as well as Claire Torry, and the instrumental overdubs continued to pile up even on songs that wouldn't make the final cut, including 'By the Time It Gets Dark' and 'Full Moon', where Dave Swarbrick's lovely original solo was replaced by a clarinet solo courtesy of Sandy's old Capricorn Club chum Acker Bilk. Two of the covers, 'Losing Game' and 'Easy to Slip', were discarded.

John Wood's optimism and enthusiasm were now reversed. He describes Sandy's black moods: 'She wouldn't turn up, or turn up very late. Trevor would be trying to cajole her into doing things that she wasn't so keen on. She was not in control of herself.'

Her voice was noticeably different too, much less rootsy, less folky than on previous recordings and a lot huskier at times, especially on the tracks recorded after 2 May. This may have been an intentional shift towards a more rock sound but Sandy's prolonged smoking and drinking was taking its toll. Even her father, usually in denial about his daughter's excesses, observed years later: 'I felt Sandy was losing it and I think she was losing it because of drink.'

'I think, to her credit,' says Jerry Donahue, 'she was trying out new directions as a writer but she hadn't quite mastered them vocally, and the arrangements and the production, instead of providing the right backdrop, overpowered the songs and stretched her even further. I think she and Trevor felt under pressure to ring the changes. It should have been a good album; it's far from her best but if you divorce the songs from the treatments and the arrangements, you can see she still had some great songs. It has the feel of being a transitional album, working towards something different in terms of Sandy's writing but, tragically, it ended up being Sandy's last.'

There's no doubt Sandy was trying to reposition herself: 'I've got my own way of singing,' she said a year later. 'I don't sound like anybody else as far as I know but I started by singing in folk clubs. It's an odd trip to be labelled a folk singer. I wish they'd knock off the folk bit because it's misleading. I'm not writing in the folk style and I haven't done for a long time and I wish people would wake up and knock all these labels on the head because it gets a bit boring after a while.' After the string-laden, lush *Like an Old Fashioned Waltz*, Sandy and Trevor's approach to its follow-up found them trying too hard to 'knock off the folk bit', and not just vocally. The emphasis shifts away from an organic folk sound to a more contemporary rock style; this is evident in their bringing in former Fleetwood Mac guitarist Bob Weston and adopting a fuller keyboard sound courtesy of Steve Winwood and American keyboardist John 'Rabbit' Bundrick, who had made such an impact on the Wailers' *Catch a Fire* and had done countless sessions for Island. Jamaican reggae musician Junior Murvin was even drafted in on the original, later rejected recording of 'Gold Dust'.

'They lost their way as the recordings went on,' says Donahue. 'Trevor was trying too hard to be creative and keep up with the times. It's a fifty–fifty album at best.' John Wood certainly felt Sandy was floundering to find an acceptable way forward, describing the album as almost schizophrenic at times and far less distinguished than her earlier work. 'She'd not had the commercial success that everybody thought she'd have,' said Wood to Jim Irvin, 'particularly in America; so it was a difficult record to make.'

Overall, the recordings present too many jumbled ideas and different styles and they suffer from an inability to leave well alone. Trevor is usually blamed for this, but Sandy had become progressively less sure of herself once the sessions stretched into June and July. One of her notebooks, dating from that summer, offers a clear indication of this in a particularly lengthy diatribe, taking up twelve pages in lurid green ink, sparked by a disagreement with Island over money she was expecting. The tone is a combination of bitterness and intense soul-searching, often almost incomprehensible. She veers from feelings of being 'tricked by one's own innocence' to an admission that she is 'impetuous and inconstant', 'guided by naïve, sudden impulsive whims' and 'not being able to make a decision'. She talks about being 'zombie-esque' and 'sheepish', 'easily led' and 'easily persuaded' but 'without any deep conviction'. 'Capricorn,' her birth sign, she scrawls, 'epitomises this quality, hence the adjective capricious' – the last word is underlined.

Sandy is clearly worried about her future after a long series of commercial failures and she doubts whether Island still have faith in her. She is confused as to where she stands and annoyed that she hasn't been true to herself, incensed about being 'ingratiating', 'grovelling' and 'obsequious . . . perhaps with a view to one's own future well-being'. It's a frenzied, enraged rant that gives a frightening insight into her general state of mind. Sandy was running scared. What she calls a 'cowardly defection or desertion of one's own beliefs and ideals' and 'cow towing [sic] to the new power in order to promote oneself and survive' goes a long way to explaining the degree of compromise she felt she had made and which marred an unfocused album.

There is no real evidence or admission on their part that anybody at Island was trying to influence proceedings. 'She was always very much left to her own devices,' maintains David Betteridge. 'That was Island's way. We only became involved when it was time to put the record out. In hindsight, perhaps she didn't have the right support from any of us. It was a case of us thinking she didn't need our advice and direction, and, in truth, she probably wouldn't have taken it anyway.'

'There was no A & R person within Island giving her direction,' says Tim Clark, 'and we had faith in Trevor, although I'm not sure who else we could have brought in to produce Sandy at that time; she could be a real handful, a real, real handful. As Sandy's husband, Trevor had a lot more on his shoulders than just being the producer.'

Sandy's fourth solo album was delivered to Island in July and scheduled for release in October under the title *Gold Dust*; the front cover artwork was a striking but unappealing line drawing of Sandy by Marion Appleton in which she looks almost manic. Sandy talked about wanting to take an eight-piece band on the road in the autumn that was to include familiar touring companions Pat Donaldson, Jerry Donahue and Dave Mattacks, who all played on the album, alongside guitarist Andy Roberts and keyboard player 'Rabbit' Bundrick, but plans were shelved when Island once again put the record on hold.

Marion Appleton's cover drawing for the abandoned *Gold Dust* album

Tim Clark, who had been made MD at Island, says the delay was mainly caused by financial problems at the label, although he was aware of the personal issues Sandy was having, which may well have influenced their decision to push the album back. 'We had made an unfortunate investment in a factory and pressing plant, which made sense until we lost manufacturing rights for Virgin, Chrysalis and EG, so we had to sell the factory and we didn't get a very good price for it. At one point we had to do a licence deal with EMI just to stay in business. For those of us that had been independent for the best part of ten years, it was very traumatic.'

'I wasn't aware that she was breaking down the way she was,' says Brian Blevins, Island's head of press. 'It was only much later I found out and it was a real surprise to hear about the extent of Sandy's drug use and heavy drinking. I never saw that side of her. If other people at Island were privy to that sort of thing, there was an almost unspoken agreement which was very much like the code that groups have of "what happens on the road stays on the road". Privacy was more respected back then.'

It was at this time that Sandy came up with the idea of recording an album of covers with Maddy Prior and Elkie Brooks, to be co-ordinated and managed by Bambi Ballard, who made the suggestion to Blevins. With one album already on hold, it's hard not to see this as Sandy's attempt, however ambivalent, 'to create a situation whereby one is promoted in some way', as she had written in her notebook.

'Sandy and Bambi were great mates,' says Maddy Prior. 'Bambi made outfits for me and Tim Hart, so I knew her too. I knew Elkie a bit and we did all meet up but it never went as far as rehearsing or anything remotely concrete. If Island considered looking at the trio concept, it was because they didn't really know what to do with Sandy; but I had already started working with June Tabor. It wasn't something I ever really considered. I can see how it might have worked. I can also see why it wouldn't. Sandy was not a calm presence.'

In any event, Brooks wasn't available, as she was tied to another label. And soon Sandy had something else on her mind. In January 1977 she found out she was pregnant.

Sandy had always wanted to have a baby and it wasn't the first time she had been pregnant. In his 2014 autobiography, *Exorcising Ghosts*, Dave Cousins tells how when they were recording together in Copenhagen, she confided in him that she had had an abortion when she was seventeen and that the doctor had told her that, as a result, she could never have children. He thinks that the despondency she felt following the abortion contributed to 'her irascibility, her frustrations, and her melancholy'.

However speculative his opinion might be, there's no reason to doubt what she told him, although at seventeen she would still have been at school.

Beverley Martyn recalls an incident soon after her first child was born, not long after Sandy had joined Fairport. Beverley and Sandy met at a friend's house: 'I had taken the baby in the carry cot and Sandy saw the baby and immediately ran into the toilet crying. I waited for her to come out and I said, "What's the matter?" and she said, "I just lost a baby." I took that to mean a miscarriage.'

Once she and Trevor married, friends say that Sandy wanted a baby even more, but that she had at least one further abortion because Trevor felt it wasn't the right time and she needed to put her career first. 'Sandy wanted a child but nobody wanted her to have one,' said Neil Denny. 'Eventually she said she was going to have one and everyone was annoyed because it was going to upset their schedules.' It was another cause of friction between Sandy and Trevor, particularly in the months after the split from Fairport when they were no longer constantly on the road, until they eventually decided to go ahead with the pregnancy in 1977.

'She used to say to Dave, "You're lucky to have children,"' says Chris Pegg. 'He would say, "Well, you come and babysit for us." She and Trevor wanted the idea of that family stability but they wanted the other life as well. I used to get cross with Sandy, watching her drinking heavily and taking all sorts of drugs when she was pregnant. You have to make a serious lifestyle change when you have kids.

'You just couldn't imagine Sandy staying at home, taking the kids to school, that kind of normality. Sandy wasn't practical. She would come round to ours if they had mice in the house or if the dog had fleas and say, "What do I do?" Trevor was a buffer zone between Sandy and the outside world. He was very good for Sandy but he wasn't always there for her. I always felt she lived in a slightly different world to the rest of us.'

This unease with everyday life was something Trevor later observed about Sandy: 'There were so many contradictions to her. She could get on quite well meeting Princess Margaret – she'd chat away quite happily, without any kind of self-consciousness at all. Yet put her in a supermarket, and expect her to talk to the checkout girl, and she'd be a bundle of nerves. She had real difficulties in relating to people at times.'

'It's hard to explain Trevor and Sandy's relationship by saying it was open or whatever cliché from that time,' says Bruce Rowland. 'It comes back to their being in a relationship where they were trapped by the circumstances of what they did and the lifestyle that went with it. It played on Sandy's mind a little; I don't think she was as upfront about it as Trevor was in how anxious she felt. Each would choose to turn a blind eye to each other's affairs and flings, but Sandy was more fearful of the outcome and feared that Trevor would eventually leave her for somebody else.'

'They fancied each other rotten at the beginning,' says Bambi Ballard, 'but however much Sandy might have felt "I've got to get out of this relationship" towards the end of her life, it's not easy to break away. And of course Sandy wanted the relationship to end all relationships. She couldn't have that, and I think that's why she got pregnant, largely because she was frightened of losing Trevor.'

While some friends suggested Sandy and Trevor both felt that having a baby would save their marriage, it seemed to others that Trevor finally relented because he thought it might halt his wife's descent into drinking and substance abuse. Ultimately it resulted in neither outcome.

Sandy's pregnancy wasn't going to upset Island's schedules; her album was still on hold when the news came out. The practical move might have been to rush the album out so that Sandy would be better able to promote it during the early stages of her pregnancy. Instead, the decision was made to revisit the album and make one or two changes. The title was switched from *Gold Dust* to *Rendezvous* and, more contentiously, the decision was made to record a cover of Elton John's 'Candle in the Wind', which soon became the lead single off the album.

'Island really had no idea how to market Sandy,' says Richard Williams, who by now had left the label, 'beyond the need to have a hit record as the only way to launch an album by an artist who was really quite passé. It's not insignificant that she covered "Candle in the Wind". Elton John was exactly the kind of artist every record label was looking for – somebody who came out of that scene from the sixties and who suddenly found this vast audience. Sandy most likely went along with it not quite believing in it but thinking, "Well, if they think it's the way to go, I'll do it."'

Sandy later said she was playing the song at home on the piano and Trevor suggested they record it. 'I still had pangs about whether I should or not, and eventually when I did it, I was glad that I did.' Years later Trevor insisted that he had given in to pressure from Island because they so desperately wanted a hit. In 1985 he told New South Wales radio station 2NUR that Island wanted Sandy to be a bopper and record pop songs. 'She would love to have had hits but only on her own terms. They asked us to record "Candle in the Wind", which Sandy liked as a song but [had] never considered recording. We felt a little let down by the songs we left off the album to accommodate that.'

Ralph McTell recalls Trevor thinking it was a particularly apt song for Sandy. 'She was a six-hundred-pound gorilla, which is what Tony Curtis said when he was asked about Marilyn Monroe after she died. Trevor could see the parallels between them. Sandy was just like Marilyn: she was wildly unpredictable, she was insecure, she was doing drugs, she was frequently drunk on stage.'

Richard Thompson came out of self-imposed exile to play guitar on the track, Dave Pegg and Dave Mattacks were also on hand and successful Scottish chart duo Benny Gallagher and Graham Lyle provided back-up to one of Sandy's poorest ever vocals. Harry Robinson then added the familiar finishing touch, dousing it in strings. 'Candle in the Wind' was recorded in February and immediately slated for the album. 'Still Waters Run Deep' made way for it in the running order, ending up as the B-side to 'Candle in the Wind' when it was released in early May to herald Sandy's new album.

The single was heavily promoted, pitched to press and radio as a comeback by Sandy, with reminders of her *Melody Maker* Best British Female Singer honour from six years earlier. Sandy made all the right noises in radio interviews: 'This time we've deliberately included some things you'll be able to play, even a couple of familiar oldies, like the Elton John song. It's something we started doing on my last album with Fairport – making it more radio-friendly.' She joked about the album coming up for its first birthday but more or less admitted she was struggling to rekindle the excitement she had felt when it was first delivered to Island.

Since that first burst of activity back in April 1976, when virtually the entire album had been recorded in a two-week period, just about every move in completing *Rendezvous* was open to question. What could have been a strong, well-balanced album, with some impressive songs exploring new directions for Sandy, had become the proverbial mixed bag. The undoubted highlights – 'I Wish

We searched for everything
Keeping what we would win
Orchids (or) tiny flowers
Wooden huts or ivory towers
Centuries or hours.

Dark, are the winter days,
Holy in many ways.
Vaults of time, unshaken
Whilst through them we are
                            taken,
Sleeping forests wake
Ice melts on the lake
Birds begin in making their way
            back home.

Sandy's draft lyrics to 'All Our Days'

I Was a Fool for You', 'One Way Donkey Ride', 'I'm a Dreamer'
and the impressive, elegiac 'All Our Days' – are weighed down by
the overwrought 'Candle in the Wind', the cluttered California-
rock pastiche of a reworked 'Gold Dust' and, on what should have
been safe ground, a dreary, ill-advised brass-band arrangement on
a lacklustre 'Silver Threads and Golden Needles'.

Trevor is often singled out for blame because of the overbearing
production, but Ralph McTell firmly believes he only had Sandy's
best interests at heart. In 1985 Trevor even described *Rendezvous* as
his favourite of Sandy's albums. McTell is aghast at any suggestion

that Trevor might have had the wrong intentions, though he concedes that his judgement was poor. 'They went through some bad times and some people suspected [Trevor] of Machiavellian machinations, but no, he had a deep belief that she could cross over. And Sandy wanted that too.'

'I find this about a lot of artists I have worked with over the years,' says Joe Boyd. 'They have a certain audience and if you try and satisfy your audience and do it well, you have a chance to break out of that and reach other people. If you try and go directly to reach that wider audience, you are in danger of losing the core. When you get to *Rendezvous* that's exactly what she is doing, and she is second-guessing. You can tell she was backed into a corner.'

Rendezvous was not the album to relaunch an artist who had done nothing for eighteen months; it was scrappy and unconvincing, with a cover better suited to melodramatic power ballads. In the summer of 1977 its content and design was completely out of step with the current musical climate. It was met with a mixture of indifference and muted praise from the press faithful, and was overshadowed on its release by the uproar over the release of the Sex Pistols' 'God Save the Queen'. 'The punk thing was very scary for anybody signed earlier in the seventies,' says Claire Hamill, 'because you didn't know the impact it was going to have. If you were from an earlier era – and I was the same age as Joe Strummer – you were made to feel you were all washed up.* It would have been tough for Sandy; it's like being told, "We don't want your kind of music any more."'

Sandy must have wondered if Island didn't feel the same way.

---

* Bambi Ballard recalled that Joe Strummer came round to visit her on one occasion in 1977 and just missed bumping into Sandy. Strummer was deeply disappointed at not meeting her because he was such an admirer.

She'd been let down, once again, by her label's dithering over the release date; it can have done little for her self-esteem that, for the second time in a row, they had chosen to flag up her latest album with a cover rather than one of her own songs. Her songwriting spree from the year before had virtually dried up. 'Gold Dust' was the last original song she had recorded, now almost a year ago. When Sandy returned to the familiar Basing Street Studios on 20 May 1977, just days before *Rendezvous* was released, the session proved to be her last ever studio recording. She recorded the song 'Moments' by Bryn Haworth;* he had played it to Sandy when he toured with Fairport in 1975 and he didn't even know she had recorded it. 'Moments' is a song Sandy might almost have written herself, and the lyrics would soon take on a greater significance:

> Time moves slowly and it goes so fast
> And who knows how long the days will last.

'Moments' was intended as the B-side to a single release of 'I'm a Dreamer' but, in the end, Island decided to cut their losses; they couldn't see the point of releasing another single by Sandy and the track went unreleased until it appeared on the first of Trevor's *Attic Tracks* compilations in 1988.

'Privately we knew Sandy was in a bad way,' says Tim Clark. 'Publicly she was treading water, she hadn't toured in a year and a half, and then she couldn't tour because she was pregnant. I

---

* Bryn Haworth was an Island artist who had recently been dropped after two fine albums, *Let the Days Go By* (1974) and *Sunny Side of the Street* (1975). He eventually recorded 'Moments' on his third album, *Grand Arrival*, released by A&M after Sandy's death. Haworth toured with Fairport in 1975; they often encored with his ironic, upbeat song 'Pick Me Up' on their final American tour. The only official outing for the song by Fairport is on Dave Pegg's *A Box of Pegg's*.

think at that point we had lost the plot between us all.' 'We were friends,' says David Betteridge, 'and I hope I was a sympathetic shoulder. I liked her a lot. I think cocaine contributed to her downfall and she just became increasingly downhearted and distrustful. She went from the drinking culture of the folk world and smoking pot to taking cocaine. Smoking pot's one thing, cocaine is a whole different thing. It gives people a false perspective. I saw what it did to far too many people, but there was no close watcher when she needed help the most.

'In the end,' Betteridge says, with great candour, 'Sandy finished up – in the nicest sense of the word – in our second division because there were other things that were coming through. It was easier to break something that was new, and we didn't know what to do with her.' In America, that was made abundantly clear: *Rendezvous* was her only album that failed to secure a release over there.

'Sandy felt let down,' says Gerry Conway, 'but she also felt she had let people down in the way her life was going. And her life and music were entwined. If her life was going badly, the music was too – and the other way round.'

The situation was not improving on the home front, lacking the sense of meaningful purpose that her career had once provided. With the album repeatedly pushed back and eventually sinking without trace, the familiar pattern of the couple's life went from bad to worse. 'The lifestyle was taking its toll on Sandy,' says Chris Pegg. 'The drinking and drug-taking was constant and got worse after she came back into Fairport. For the others it was something you did while you were on tour but you stopped when you got home. Sandy and Trevor didn't stop when they came off tour. They fought constantly about something he said or she hadn't said, but when you're both off your face nothing is logical.'

Trevor was increasingly looking for reasons to get away, a situation that was tougher on the pregnant Sandy, who was trapped in the country while he was off who knows where. Whether stuck at home or out on a bender, Sandy had not stopped drinking heavily and taking drugs, illegal or otherwise; she was reliant on sleeping pills prescribed by a tame London doctor. 'In that last couple of years,' says Nigel Osborne, 'there were times when nobody knew where Trevor was. He would say he was going back to Byfield and he didn't, he would stay at Marion's overnight but then he'd stay somewhere else, the assumption being with one of his lady friends. He'd have bouts of responsibility. He would nag Sandy about drinking and taking drugs while she was pregnant, but he never stopped and then he'd disappear again.'

Sandy had plenty of warnings from medical staff when she went for check-ups but she took no notice and even took to skipping antenatal appointments rather than be admonished. 'She'd wanted a baby for ages,' says Linda Thompson, 'but she couldn't handle the reality of it. When she was pregnant she said to me, "Do you think cocaine would hurt the baby?" And I said, "Sandy, you haven't been doing cocaine, have you?" And she said, "Yeah, just a little." Usually when you have a baby you wake up and think, "I can't do that any more." That usually sobers people up, if not before then once the baby is born; that finally makes them stop and think about how they are living, but not Sandy.'

Some two months before the baby was due, Colin Irwin went to Byfield to interview Sandy for *Melody Maker*. It was an odd time for her to be talking to the press. *Rendezvous* was already history and even though Sandy was beginning to think about an autumn tour, it was still only June. The article presents a picture of false contentment, with the heavily pregnant Sandy seated on an overstuffed sofa at home. 'I wasn't at all au fait with what was going on in her private life,' says Irwin. 'I found her very up, very positive. She certainly didn't come across like a woman who was falling apart at the seams. If it was an act, it was a good one, although we now know differently.'

Rendezvous had underperformed on every level and Sandy had been out of the public eye for a year and a half since leaving Fairport, but in interviews she could usually put a positive spin on a situation. 'I really needed a break from the business,' she told Irwin. 'I've been in it up to my eyes for over ten years, virtually non-stop, though people don't realise it because I'm not hitting the headlines every day. It's taken me since last summer to get back to some sort of sanity, something I didn't even realise I'd lost. Now I feel I can renew my old enthusiasm.'

'Sandy Denny Pregnant' was the unfortunate headline on Irwin's piece, which ran several days after Sandy had been taken into hospital in Oxford. There, Georgia Rose MacLean Lucas was born on 12 July 1977, almost two months prematurely. She was named Georgia after Trevor heard the Hoagy Carmichael song 'Georgia on My Mind' driving back from the hospital after she was born. Rose, he wisecracked, would be handy if she ever became a stripper.

Georgia had been brought into the world by Caesarean section at the John Radcliffe Hospital. She weighed around three and a half pounds at birth and was immediately put in an incubator. It was uncertain for a while whether she would survive. It was only after doctors understood how dependent Sandy was on alcohol and drugs, and that she was in withdrawal, that they were able to treat both her and Georgia correctly. They had to 'detox' the baby to begin with, and she remained in hospital care for almost two months until she reached a healthy weight. Sandy was discharged within weeks, after which she made the near-thirty-mile trip to Oxford daily to breastfeed Georgia until she was moved to a hospital in Banbury, just fourteen miles away. Georgia was finally allowed home at the beginning of September.

Once Georgia was home, Sandy tried to be a responsible mother, but the experience of full-time motherhood was something she wasn't prepared for. She felt even more trapped, which made her all the more fearful that she wouldn't be able to cope. As the months went by Sandy felt more isolated and helpless – at times she almost hibernated with Georgia. 'She was a city girl and always very London-centric,' says Ralph McTell, 'and living away from London was a mistake at what was a very difficult time for her after Georgia was born. It meant that usually, for one of [Sandy and Trevor] to be in London, the other was back in the country holding the baby. It was like a rota system.'

Both parents had attacks of responsibility, but Trevor would veer from being overly protective to disappearing because he couldn't cope with the situation at home. 'Once Georgia was born,' says Chris Pegg, 'Trevor became the responsible daddy. He was tall and had big hands and that baby never left his hands or his shoulder. He would walk round with her all the time. She was so tiny she'd fit into his hand.' Yet Bambi Ballard would often hear from Sandy that Trevor was away somewhere in London. 'What legitimate reason did he have to leave her alone all the time with the child if he was *that* responsible? It was always much easier for Trevor to get away on so-called business, and more so once Georgia was born.'

The well-meaning Trevor even bought another Airedale puppy, which they called Daphne, so Watson wouldn't be put out after the baby was born. 'It wasn't the smartest idea,' says Osborne, 'but, typical Trevor, he thought it was for the best.'

Written just weeks after Georgia came home, one of Sandy's final poems is a heartfelt declaration of love, neatly scripted in one of her notebooks and surrounded by hearts:

Georgia, though you sleep so soundly now,
When autumn leaves are falling to the ground
You'll reach to catch them with your tiny hands
And gaze in wonderment as only babies can.
I long to see you wake and smile,
My beautiful most precious child.

14 : *Stranger to Herself*
1977–1978

I love flowers, I congratulate them often – Watson thinks I've cracked. I feel better in the garden; even the weeds are OK if you give them a wink and say 'Watch out. I've got my eye on you.'

SANDY DENNY, notebook entry, 1977

She wasn't well. The baby had an impact on her. Looking back I think she was suffering from some kind of postnatal problem. I very much regret that it wasn't picked up by me. She was drinking and taking coke and smoking dope. She wasn't happy in her marriage; it wasn't going anywhere but down. I think suspicion ate her. I feel as if she left mid-sentence and I mourn her leaving almost daily.

DAVE SWARBRICK

I miss her terribly. I'm sure everybody says that. I don't know anybody that I still miss except Sandy. She was just amazing. So full of life and it was sad to see her go downhill. She could be just the worst but you just forgave her. She was so talented and you did make special consideration for that because she was special.

LINDA THOMPSON

No use knocking on my door
I don't think I live ~~there~~ here
          any more.
I live in the past you see I
think of last time we were
          friends ~~together~~ there
Before you ~~fell in love~~ went away with
          her.

All my letters lay ~~once~~ ~~a~~ unopened
~~I think the a noone~~
~~There was no one home~~
~~along with raisters~~ ~~and~~ tokens
          along with calling cards and
~~what is the need to~~
I cannot read you see I~~I~~
think of the need to be by you
                    now
if I could only move somehow

Sandy's draft lyrics to 'Makes Me Think of You', the last
song she ever demoed

Coming just two months after Georgia was born, Island's timing in dropping Sandy appears heartless, but it was hardly surprising. Sandy's deal was up and *Rendezvous* alone was unrecouped to the tune of £35,000. Chris Blackwell did sweeten the pill by paying off the mortgage on the Twistle house, which he had originally guaranteed.

Sandy wasn't alone in being dismissed by the label. 'Island was right to can us all,' says Linda Thompson. 'We all had such a good run. Richard and I were on Island for six years and I never felt bad when we were let go. Island had no expectations for us. We were prestige acts and time has proved that. Richard and I never tried to be in the least bit commercial. Neither did John Martyn. Sandy they had hopes for and she didn't have the courage of her convictions. When you heard her sing "Banks of the Nile", that was an absolutely incomparable vocal, instead of her singing "Whispering Grass" or "Candle in the Wind". That direction didn't work for her, and being dumped by Island was another blow at a time when she was already in a complete state.'

By 1977 Chris Blackwell's ambition for Island Records had expanded even wider; now his vision for the label led to heavy investment in building Compass Point Studios in the Bahamas as a recording home for his and other artists. The decision would be fully justified over the next few years by the array of major artists who recorded there, but to begin with the enterprise stretched

Island financially to the point where it had to streamline its roster. John Martyn, signed by Blackwell ten years before, was one of the very few artists from the 1960s who remained on the label, and the only one who had started out in folk.*

'She was lost,' says Philippa Clare. 'Chris Blackwell was always wonderful with Sandy but as Island grew bigger his priorities lay elsewhere so he wasn't around for Sandy, and then he had to let her go. Island could no longer afford to subsidise people like Sandy or Fairport. That hit her hard.'

'By the time she was dropped I was gone,' says David Betteridge, 'along with most of the people within Island that she knew well. I saw her several times during that year and she was not in great shape. I think the decision taken at that particular stage was because Sandy was no longer capable of performing satisfactorily and she no longer fitted what had become a commercial machine. Sandy was never driven to be successful, and that was becoming more imperative.'

Sandy once said, 'I'm told I have a success neurosis because I'm so frightened of success. So if I find myself in the limelight, it's not because I've been working towards it.' It was a viewpoint that went with the laissez-faire approach Island once took. 'When Sandy came to Island,' says Tim Clark, 'the ethos was "art for art's sake", and it was almost by accident that some of the artists on the

---

* Since signing Roxy Music in 1973, Island's focus had been on new signings such as Sparks, John Cale, Nico and Kevin Ayers, although of these only Sparks were consistently commercially successful. They fared better with the spin-off careers of Bryan Ferry, Jim Capaldi, Robert Palmer and Bad Company, featuring two ex-Free members. In Bob Marley's slip-stream there was also a continued investment in reggae, notably albums by Burning Spear, Toots and the Maytals, Lee 'Scratch' Perry and Junior Murvin, as well as home-grown reggae acts such as Aswad and Steel Pulse.

label were successful. There wasn't that necessity to be successful; if it happened, it happened. In Sandy's case it didn't.

'I was managing director but I really don't remember the exact circumstances of her being dropped. Chris would have spoken to her personally. We were very aware of the difficulties she was having in her life and it was difficult to make a case for committing further to somebody in her situation. With all the experience I have now, I think we might have acted differently and I hope that we might have helped more than we did – personally and professionally.'

In an interview for *Audio* magazine in 1987 Chris Blackwell mirrored those feelings. 'Joe Boyd sold me his company and we inherited all these acts. I'm afraid we weren't really able to continue what he had done. I wasn't that much value to any of those artists I inherited. Like, I don't think I was much help in guiding Sandy Denny or Fairport or any of them.' In 2013 I asked Blackwell if he still thought the same. 'Yes, for sure,' he replied, 'sadly!'

'I was no replacement for Joe,' says Blackwell. 'I simply did not have the feel for those artists so I was really not much help in their difficult times. I was saddened that Sandy didn't enjoy the commercial success she so deserved, but commercial success is not an exact science.'

Even without the backing of a label, Sandy was still going ahead with her autumn tour and Roy Guest agreed to act in a managerial capacity as well as being her agent. In a letter from his company, Evolution Theatrical Management, dated 27 October he outlined that 'the current tour was to be used as a re-entry for Sandy into the concert arena', since she hadn't played live since leaving Fairport two years earlier and had not undertaken a solo tour in twice that time. Guest added that 'we plan an April tour which will be undertaken with the support and co-operation of a record company after we have negotiated a new deal for Sandy'.

Guest was also promoting a tour for Tom Paxton and he took Sandy along to a lunch with Paxton in Oxford. Paxton recalls: 'She was not in good shape, frankly; she'd obviously had a few before arriving. She seemed very unhappy and a bit bitter. Not a great lunch. I must say that I love the recordings she did of my songs and I wish I could have known her in better times.'

Billed as *Sandy Denny and Friends*, Sandy's dates ran from 6 to 27 November. Beginning and ending with shows at London's Royalty Theatre, the tour ambitiously took in nine other major concert halls across the UK. Island still contributed towards advertising costs and allowed use of the Island Mobile Unit for a recording that was to be made at the final London show. Georgia came along with a nanny, Denise, a former midwife who was married to one of Fairport's road crew.

After such a long break, it was soon clear that the grand scale of the tour was a mistake and some dates were poorly attended. Unwisely, Sandy was responsible for paying the musicians. She didn't skimp, putting together a top-notch band comprising the ever-dependable Pat Donaldson and Dave Mattacks, alongside Trevor and former Renaissance guitarist Rob Hendry, plus one of the UK's top steel guitarists, Pete Wilsher. The tour was always going to test Sandy's levels of endurance as she played an unstinting seventeen-song set most nights that showed great faith in *Rendezvous*. Songs such as 'Gold Dust' and 'Take Me Away' were transformed by more sympathetic readings, while *Rising for the Moon*'s 'One More Chance' was given an epic arrangement that enthusiastically brought down the curtain each night. They would return to play 'Who Knows Where the Time Goes?' as an encore, a tender, protracted version, with an almost spoken vocal at times.

The well-balanced set list stretched back to Fotheringay and *The North Star Grassman and the Ravens*, including the rarely played 'Wretched Wilbur' and 'Nothing More', but there were no early Fairport crowd-pleasers and nothing traditional. 'If I have to sing "Matty Groves" one more time, I'll throw myself out of a window,' she said before the tour. The band crafted a sound not dissimilar to Fotheringay's, in which the steel guitar effectively enhanced the atmosphere on early songs such as 'The Sea' and 'The North Star Grassman and the Ravens' and gave real substance to a country-tinged cover of Bob Dylan's 'Tomorrow Is a Long Time'.

The greater concern was over Sandy's voice, although, on listening to tapes from the tour, it sounds far better than poor notices at the time reflected. She was having fun too, laughing and joking with Trevor and Dave Mattacks in particular and talking warmly about having Georgia on the road with them. 'I always hope she'll still be awake after the show so I can say goodnight,' she tells noisily responsive fans in Birmingham, always a Fairport stronghold. 'I haven't enjoyed myself so much in years,' she hoots gleefully at the end of the night. There, midway through the tour, she's clearly nursing a cold. 'I made up a concoction of freshly squeezed lemons, honey and brandy, heated and put in vacuum flasks,' said Miranda Ward, who was on hand throughout the tour. 'Judging by the state of her voice that last afternoon it was a miracle that she did the gig.'

That the last show was recorded was down to an eleventh-hour contract, for a £6,000 facility fee, signed only two days before between Guest's Evolution Theatrical Management and Marcel Rodd from Saga Records, whose company now owned B&C

Records. Karl Dallas had put Sandy back in touch with Rodd, who jumped at the chance to get her onto his label again. 'I remember somebody saying, "We're going to record it tonight,"' says Dave Mattacks, 'and all the musicians went, "OK." She delivered on that show and throughout the last tour; there were a couple of hairy moments, but her performance was usually excellent. "Solo" was always a highlight. I have fond memories of those dates. It was all very sociable; vast quantities of tea and sticky buns. Sandy liked strong-brewed tea. I was the one with the sweet tooth in the outfit, and she was too.'

Linda Thompson was less impressed: 'Her singing wasn't good on that last London date and she looked awful, she looked so unwell. I was with Richard and Ashley, we were all shocked. Her voice was really shot by the end.'

The live recording from the Royalty turned out to be another blow for Sandy. The proposed live album would have given her breathing space while a new deal was being sought. John Wood had been brought in to supervise the recording, but when the tapes were played back, there was what Dallas describes as a nasty whistle right across every track. As a result, Rodd refused to pay for them and the album was ditched. The tapes remained unheard until 1990.*

---

* Nine of the soundboard tracks from the Royalty were eventually released in Australia in March 1990 as volume three of the cassette-only *Attic Tracks* series. The Royalty tracks were sourced from tapes that had been in Trevor's possession; there are no glaring technical problems, but after going through the reels for the 2010 box set, Andrew Batt confirmed that on other tracks entire guitar parts are missing and there is a ringing hiss through much of it. The Royalty concert was released in May 1998 under the title *Gold Dust*, with some of the offending guitar parts re-recorded by Jerry Donahue and backing vocals added, sung by Simon Nicol and Chris Leslie.

The low turnout at some of the dates and the problems with the Royalty recordings severely dampened Sandy's enthusiasm as her further career plans now dissolved. She had left it too long to tour again and too many of her old fans stayed away. 'We were all so naïve and unbusinesslike, it was like we led a charmed life,' says Maddy Prior. 'We just went from day to day. There was no plan in any of this, we just bumbled along. You knew this wasn't a proper job but we were all very passionate about the music. Sandy never lost that passion, but after she left Fairport in 1975 she dropped out for two years, and that caught up with her when she toured again. It didn't go well.'

'Sandy, she was always a bit of a wild card,' says Ralph McTell. 'She comes from a time when we all felt we were indestructible, and of course none of us are, and Sandy lived pretty hard, did what the boys did, that's fair to say. If the boys drank a lot, Sandy drank a lot; if the boys did marching powder, so did Sandy. But what held everybody together was the passion with which we all believed in music. The music was so important to us, but after Fairport hadn't worked out and the disappointments with *Rendezvous* some of that intensity about the music had gone for her. That tour was the last straw. That's when she really started losing it.'

The tour had provided a positive focus but with the live album abandoned and no new deal forthcoming, there was nothing to hold Sandy together or to save her faltering relationship with Trevor. Increasingly there were fewer people Sandy trusted and could turn to; her brother David was now living and working in the US and she had become more distant from her parents, who saw little of their grandchild. 'Sandy never entirely cut herself adrift from Neil and Edna,' says Nigel Osborne. 'She always kept in touch, but Trevor certainly came between them because he wasn't good enough or intelligent enough in their eyes. He came from a trade, he was certainly not from a professional or academic background, which Edna would have liked, and he embodied the world of music, even though Sandy had taken that path long before she met him. They weren't so blinkered that they couldn't see what was happening to Sandy. It was easier to blame Trevor than face up to the truth about how Sandy was losing her grip. She wasn't in great shape and that was hard to disguise.'

As far as Neil Denny was concerned, Sandy's downhill trajectory dated from when she got together with Trevor. 'She met Trevor Lucas, then she formed Fotheringay, which was a bit of a mess – nobody was boss – Sandy wasn't capable of bossing. I really do think that her music suffered from her association with Trevor Lucas – because he wasn't up to her standard – and I think there was a bit of a decline. And, of course, he was now producing her records. We never really thought she was doing what she should have been doing.'

Trevor's folks were more tolerant towards their daughter-in-law but they were still confounded by her. 'Frank and Ada were very easy-going,' says Osborne, who spent time with them on trips to Australia with Trevor's sister Marion. Frank and Ada Lucas also came to the UK several times, including a long holiday in July 1975. 'They were confused by Sandy and how much she always had to be the centre of attention. They couldn't really see why everybody put up with the way she behaved and how she always got her own way. They found the shambolic nature of her and Trevor's lifestyle hard to understand, whatever veneer of organisation Trevor tried to maintain. What they saw was how demanding Sandy was and Trevor running around after her, and they didn't think that was right. Then Watson would slobber over Frank's neat slacks or

Sandy would tip wine over somebody. Everybody else was so used to how clumsy she could be. It's the way she was. Glasses were always being knocked over; wine would end up in your lap or coffee down the back of the sofa. And she'd leave lighted cigarettes all over the place, there were burn marks on the edges of every piece of furniture.' The only exception was Sandy's cherished Steinway piano.

'They were madly in love,' says Jerry Donahue. 'As long as I knew them there was nothing Trevor wouldn't have done for Sandy. It was a tumultuous relationship. They would part company for days and they had regular spats but would always come back to each other. They were suspicious of what the other one was getting up to. Sometimes it was without foundation, but often for good reason. Anyone on the outside world would see it as a relationship that was unworkable.'

Sandy's friends had learnt to be forgiving but she was beginning to test everybody's tolerance. 'She would provoke – push people to the very limit at times,' says Ralph McTell, 'which sounds like she was a nasty person, but she wasn't – people would take it because they loved her. I don't know anyone who didn't love her.'

'She was very close to Richard,' says Linda Thompson, 'but we weren't around when she really started going downhill in 1976. I had two kids under five and I had already stopped doing those mad things we used to do. Richard and I had become Muslims and were living a quiet, devout life, though we were hardly like Keith Moon or Ozzy to begin with.* When we went into the commune Sandy

* Having quit music at the end of 1975 following the release of their devotional album *Pour Down Like Silver*, Richard and Linda Thompson discreetly pursued their faith, joining a remote religious community the following year. As a result, they saw little of Sandy until they moved back to London in 1977.

thought we were nuts; we must have been an awful poker-up-the-arse couple to her for a couple of years, very disapproving.'

'It was as if a barrier had come between us,' says Richard Thompson, 'and not just geographical. In the last years of her life she wasn't in a great state. Mood swings off the scale. Having a baby was something she'd absolutely longed for as long as I'd known her – it was a very strong physical urge to have a child – but she was never going to be equipped for motherhood. She was not responsible. And a stoned Sandy was even less responsible. Sandy was seriously abusing substances and drink, and you can't do that and be a mother.'

'Trevor would tell me that he'd come home and the baby wasn't fed and was crying and Sandy was passed out,' says Linda. 'Moving to the country was a disaster. I went there quite a few times when she was pregnant and after the baby was born, but they were cut off from everybody and the only people she socialised with were people in the pub and Fairport.'

'Trevor told me how he returned home one time and he went to Georgia's room to kiss her goodnight and she wasn't in her crib,' says Donahue. 'And he looked everywhere. He woke Sandy, who was in bed in a drunken stupor. She'd gone out, spent the whole day drinking at the pub and returned and left Georgia in the car. And you have to wonder how she got home in the state she was in.'

'We all tried hard to encourage her to straighten herself out but she'd never listen,' says Chris Pegg. 'Personally, I was always reminded of that line in "Solo": "But I can't communicate with you/And I guess I never will." She was always more comfortable with the boys in the band and she knew they would never give her a hard time about how she was behaving.'

Sandy would regularly drive the six miles of country lanes from The Twistle to Cropredy, where she stood a good chance of seeing somebody from the Fairport camp in one of the two pubs, the Red Lion and the Brasenose Arms. If no one was around, she'd just sit at the bar on her own and wouldn't leave. She was barred on more than one occasion. 'The baby would be in the car outside in its cot,' says Chris Pegg, 'and she would leave the dog looking after the baby, so the landlord would call and ask Dave to come and fetch her. We tried once to get the baby out of the car but the dog wouldn't let us.

'She wouldn't be fit to drive. She had a bright orange Beetle with green hubs and the locals knew to stand clear when they saw it coming. The car hit a ditch so many times and, if Trevor or none of the band was around, one of the local farmers would be called out to haul it out.'

Bruce Rowland thinks a lot of Sandy's behaviour was actually manipulative. 'I was staying at Swarb's and she phoned for help late one night, so I drove out there and the car was in the ditch but very carefully parked, just one wheel carefully embedded in the ditch, and Georgia was in the car. So I took the carry cot and put it in my car and drove the fifty or sixty yards to where they lived. And the door was open and I brought Georgia in and Sandy's there in her dressing gown, three parts cut, but seemingly together rather than hysterical. She said, "I can't cope, I can't do this on my own." Then I realised what she's done: she's taken Georgia home, fed her, changed her, got her in her night things and taken her back to the car and driven it into the ditch, before coming back home and phoning. She knew I'd rumbled her.'

If Rowland's reading is correct, it was another sign of Sandy's increasing desperation. 'She couldn't cope with motherhood,' says

Ralph McTell. 'I was round at Peggy's house soon after Georgia was born and when Sandy was holding the baby the women in the room were all on the edge of their seats, as if she was going to drop her at any moment and they were poised ready to catch her. Sandy and motherhood was a catastrophe waiting to happen.'

'She used to phone Linda in the middle of the night,' says Richard Thompson, 'and say, "I think the baby's stopped breathing," or "She won't stop crying, she's got diarrhoea, what do I do?" If she was teething, it was life-threatening; everything became larger than life, just as Sandy was larger than life.'

Sandy continued to unravel while those around her wondered what they could do. Those closest (certainly those in nearby Cropredy) had all learnt from experience and usually kept their heads down. 'If you gave her an inch,' says Rowland, 'you were trapped. She could really make you feel bad about ignoring her. I could understand why the rest of the band were exasperated by her behaviour and they all knew the only person who could really handle Sandy was Trevor.' For Dave Pegg, the alarm bells had been getting louder since the end of the November tour: 'Even being close friends you never really know what's going on between two people,' he says. 'You only see what they present to the outside world and you can't get in the middle of that. When Georgia was born Sandy was over the moon, but it didn't resolve the problems she and Trev were having.

'They were opposites,' says Pegg perceptively. 'Trevor was always up, even if it was just on the outside, but Sandy would get these fits of depression. Whereas there always used to be something that would bring her out of it, it took more and more for her to be happy, and in the end nothing would.'

'Sandy could be really, really difficult and hard to love at times,' says McTell. 'She could be unreliable, abusive, violent, very loud; the last time she was at my place she was wondering where Trevor was and was so drunk she took the dustbin lid outside and banged it in the road, crashed through the window, fell down the stairs; she was a nightmare, just out of control. I calmed her down enough to get her to sleep on the settee, but by the time I got up she'd gone and left the car parked halfway in the middle of the road.'

'I think with Sandy,' says Linda Thompson, 'and with Nick Drake – I think they were much more in charge than people think. They were both dejected souls. Nick was obviously mentally ill and Sandy, she was manic – she was up, up, up or in the depths of despair. I don't think it was people deserting her so much as that she was rudderless. And you can't drink like that and do the amount of drugs that she was doing and not have your brain go, you really can't.'

Beverley Martyn saw little of Sandy during the 1970s, but can draw parallels with her own larger-than-life husband. 'She was a human being,' she says. 'She had weight problems, she didn't think very much of herself and she could be funny and she could be spiteful, she could be very needy, she could be a nightmare – there's nothing wrong with that, that's what we are. Thing was, she didn't hide anything, she acted it out. The saddest thing is that she didn't live long enough to bring up her daughter. She was like John, she was self-destructive. John was hard to live with, hard to deal with; you wouldn't want to live with either of them. I left it for so long with John because I had children. I thought the baby would save Sandy's life, that she would get her shit together. I gave up everything for my children, my music. And people forgot about me. It's a selfless thing being a mother.'

At the beginning of 1978, Sandy also had to face the fact that her income was drying up and debts were mounting. 'They had always lived beyond their means,' says Nigel Osborne. 'Trevor was notorious for going off and buying fancy jeans, shirts, boots, having brocade jackets handmade. It would always be the best wine in the fanciest restaurants. She liked shopping at Fortnum and Mason's. That never stopped, as far as I remember, whether they were on the uppers or not. They were both as bad as each other, although Trevor was probably more culpable.'

Plans to take Georgia to Australia to meet her grandparents had to be scrapped because they couldn't afford the trip. In the new year, the vultures were circling. Alongside tax demands and overdue VAT payments, among Sandy and Trevor's papers is a letter from solicitors acting for the Musicians' Union on behalf of Dave Mattacks, Pat Donaldson, Rob Hendry and Pete Wilsher regarding the November 1977 tour. None of their cheques was met when presented for payment. Also dated March 1978 is a letter from Savill's estate agents, who had first been approached back in January, about instructions to view 41 The Twistle, for sale at a price in the region of £25,000. Nobody I spoke to was aware that Sandy and Trevor were considering selling the cottage or knew exactly what they had planned for the future. It's likely that they needed the valuation to raise a loan. They even spoke implausibly about converting the adjoining barn where Fairport rehearsed into a studio.

Sandy also talked about the possibility that she, or she and Trevor, might live and work in America for a while and record with American musicians, but with no new deal, or even the likelihood of one, there was nobody to fund it. Sandy was popular in the US, particularly in California, and had loyal high-profile fans there, such as Glenn Frey and Don Henley of the Eagles, Lowell

George and Randy Newman; Bruce Johnston of the Beach Boys wanted to produce her. It could have been the clean break Sandy needed, to a place where the market was still more sympathetic towards singer-songwriters and the direction *Rendezvous* had been aiming for. 'Sandy was highly thought of among that California scene but I don't think she made as much of that as she could,' says Albert Lee, who had moved to Los Angeles in 1973 to join Emmylou Harris's Hot Band. 'Emmylou was very impressed when I told her I had a brief spell playing with Sandy in Fotheringay.'

Echoing the exhortation popularised by American author Horace Greeley, one of Sandy's final notebooks includes several incomplete variations on a poem or lyric which begins 'Go West young woman/You need to change'. It continues variously: 'With your idle hands the devil gains', 'You need a visa for heaven and God doesn't have an embassy here' and, more pointedly, 'Smile and leave the losers behind'. Elsewhere, an increasingly desperate Sandy writes: 'There must be something I like about the few friends I have – or is there?'

'Go West young woman' is one of many scraps and snippets of potential new songs but Sandy had not submitted any new material nor demoed anything in a year, so there was no publishing money coming in either. Her publishing deal was structured so that she was paid £1,000 per song on delivery, usually in batches of four or five new compositions. There are a number of fevered songs in her notebooks, the most startling of which, later recorded by Thea Gilmore, is 'Long Time Gone'. Its candour is frightening as Sandy pours out her innermost feelings and appears to be close to the end of her tether, while conceding that only she can take charge of her life: 'I just have to realise that I'm my own best friend.' The song is full of resignation, recrimination and desperation:

> Got me a bottle of wine
> I don't want to drink
> Get me out of my mind
> I don't want to think . . .

But it's the repeated refrain of 'But if I don't get there before I die/I just ain't gonna die' that resonates so much; however low she had become, she had not given up yet.

Towards the end of March Sandy took Georgia to visit her parents at their cottage in Mullion in Cornwall. It would be the last time they saw her. They weren't happy that Sandy cut short her stay, but she had agreed to give a concert at the village hall in Byfield on 1 April, as a fundraiser for the local school. When Neil and Edna suggested they could look after Georgia, Sandy said she couldn't leave her with them because, in Neil's recollection, 'Trevor would go mad'.

It was during that visit that Sandy fell down the stairs onto a stone floor, gashing her head. The incident has since become one of the many during the last month of Sandy's life which are open to speculation.

When Jim Irvin's brilliantly incisive appraisal of Sandy's life and work appeared in *Mojo* in June 1998, it was the first major assessment of her career in twenty years. Irvin later explained that he had omitted certain things he'd been told out of considera-tion for Neil Denny because they cast Edna in a poor light. After Neil's death the following year, however, Irvin revealed: 'Sandy told friends afterwards that, even though she was in some pain, her mother had refused to take her to hospital because she didn't want to be seen with a drunken daughter.'

Much hearsay surrounds Sandy's final weeks, and while this story fits what is known of Edna Denny's sense of propriety, it's still questionable, just as we can only speculate as to how much the accident contributed to the chain of events leading to Sandy's death three weeks later. Even if Edna had been embarrassed by her daughter's state at the time of the fall, she could still have sought medical help later, but Sandy did not see a doctor at any time after Neil took her home to Byfield on 31 March.

Neil Denny never commented publicly about the incident, but two weeks later he spoke to his daughter for the last time: 'She was doing a crossword,' he said, 'and called me on the phone to ask my help. It was in the *Observer*. I remember the answer was "three-line whip". She said something like, "Oh, you are clever, Daddy."'

On 1 April 1978 Sandy gave her final public performance to around 120 people at the village hall in Byfield. It was largely unplanned. Eyewitness Nigel Schofield remembers her being nervous but typically good-humoured, starting 'Silver Threads and Golden Needles' before cutting it short, giggling and saying, 'That's not going to work, is it, playing it on my own?' What she played that night was a fitting cross-section of her life's work, including 'Solo', 'She Moves through the Fair', 'Crazy Man Michael' (after which she wished Dave Swarbrick a happy birthday for the following week), 'Quiet Joys of Brotherhood', 'Tomorrow Is a Long Time' and 'When Will I Be Loved'. She ended the set, almost inevitably, with 'Who Knows Where the Time Goes?'.

Some time in the next two weeks, Sandy fell downstairs again, this time at The Twistle. Trevor knew about the fall and certainly mentioned it to his sister Marion. Whether he was there when it happened, or whether she had Georgia in her arms at the time, is not known, but Sandy falling downstairs was a far from uncommon occurrence. 'She fell down our stairs, she fell down everybody's stairs,' says Chris Pegg. 'If there were three stairs, she would fall down them. She'd fall off stools. It was her party piece. It was no surprise that that was the way she was going to go, or that sort of accident would contribute to it.

'Sandy lived in terror of my seven-year-old son. She was really frightened of him because he would play tricks on her, like put worms on the kitchen table; and he was coming downstairs once and she fell behind him and took him with her. That was the fear we had for Georgia, never that she would harm Georgia deliberately. She was so accident-prone.'

'There are bits of the jigsaw I've gone over and over,' says Ralph McTell. 'Sandy's party trick was falling downstairs and it became known as Sandy's party piece. She certainly did it in my house and it could be a very dramatic gesture, like self-harming. She could do it without hurting herself usually but I had a feeling there would be one time too many.' Nigel Osborne also witnessed her 'party piece' on various occasions. 'I've seen her go down the stairs at Byfield; it was a very narrow stairway in the cottage, going up to the two rooms on the next floor.'

It may be that this fall, following the one in Cornwall – which had left Sandy with a visible cut, so he would have known about it – triggered Trevor's decision to take Georgia to Australia. On Thursday 13 April he boarded a flight to Melbourne, taking his daughter with him. Whether Sandy knew Trevor had gone, and whether he was planning on coming back, are questions of considerable uncertainty.

'It was no snap decision,' says Nigel Osborne, who drove Trevor to the airport with Marion. 'He'd been wrestling with this for at least a month, maybe longer, before he took the baby away; I was a party to several conversations he had with Marion about it. He wasn't intending on coming back, that's what he told us.

He bought a one-way ticket to Melbourne. He sold one of the cars [the Austin Princess, not Sandy's runaround VW] without Sandy's knowledge in order to raise the money for the flight. I don't know if Trevor was hoping Sandy would shape up and get her act together and he'd come back with Georgia. It might have been at the back of his mind, but his plan was definitely to look for work in Australia.'

'Trevor was always saying he was leaving,' says Chris Pegg, 'but this was the one time he did and it was about the baby, not about Sandy. The baby was at risk, and had to be taken somewhere that was safe. I've got great respect for Trev for doing that and he knew what people would say about him, even if Sandy hadn't died. That took a lot of courage.'

Trevor had told Sandy he was taking Georgia to London to visit his sister, and it wasn't until she noticed that some of his clothes were missing that she started to ring round the usual suspects. 'Marion had a lot of calls from Sandy that weekend,' says Nigel Osborne. Sandy even tracked down and rang Nigel's parents to try and reach Marion. 'She just left the answer machine on over the weekend rather than be confronted by Sandy and lie to her.'

On that evening of 13 April Miranda Ward, who hadn't seen Sandy in a while, responded to her call and drove up to Byfield to pick her up. The two old friends spent the weekend at Ward's flat in Barnes, in southwest London. Trevor had already rung Ward, but as she told Jim Irvin: 'Trevor didn't tell me where he was going. I got to Sandy's on Thursday night and brought her back to London. She was convinced I knew where Trevor was. We had a great weekend; we did a lot of reminiscing and a lot of talking. She was being very stoical and strong; she was not going to grovel or get hysterical but she was convinced I knew where he was. I was the one who was getting hysterical, and after she'd gone to bed every night I was frantically ringing everybody to say, "Where the fuck is Trevor?" And they were all denying that they knew anything about where Trevor was.

'On the Monday I was ringing the same people to tell them that Sandy was in a coma. And none of them would tell me where Trevor was. But some of them knew.'

It eventually came to light that a number of Sandy's friends had known about Trevor's departure, including Bruce Rowland and Dave Swarbrick. 'Trevor rang me up,' says Philippa Clare, 'and Trevor never cried, and he was in floods of tears. He was in bits. And he said, "I've told her I'm leaving, I'm going to take the kid and I'm going to Australia to introduce her to my folks, and when I get back she's got to shape up."

'He was coming back and she knew,' Clare believes. 'He was going to give Sandy a few weeks to get herself together. When Sandy rang me from Miranda's that weekend for help she said to me, "I know why Trevor's gone: I'm such a mess, I need help."'

Linda Thompson had also been taken into Trevor's confidence. 'I felt for Trevor at the end. Trevor told me he was taking Georgia away and he said, "Sandy will be calling you," which she did. I'm sure she knew that Trevor had gone to Australia but by then she wasn't taking too much in; by that time her brain was in free fall. She was just gone. She wasn't quite the full shilling any more. I don't think he thought, "Maybe she'll shape up." His baby was in danger and in that situation you don't think about her and you don't think about you. You just say, "I've got to get this kid out of harm's way." I'm surprised he let it go for as long as he did. He didn't know what to do, and I didn't say "Do this" or "Don't do this" – he's telling me things that had happened and that Georgia could have been dead. Sandy was gone. She wasn't really there any more.'

As Joe Boyd points out, in a way it was irrelevant whether Trevor intended to come back or not: 'Because whatever his intentions were, Sandy imagined that she might never see them again. The birth of Georgia had pulled Trevor together in a way, so he was trying to be more responsible towards Georgia. It's hard, because I was never hugely fond of Trevor. I didn't view him as a benign force in Sandy's life, but Sandy was not an easy person and it's clear that she did not handle motherhood well.'

In the immediate aftermath of Sandy's death, says Martin Carthy, 'there were a lot of people who hated Trevor's guts and wanted someone to blame. Sandy was ill. It's not a question of apportioning blame. It was a heartbreaking thing for him to do. Sandy's drinking problem was a big secret for a long time. Nobody realised the extent of it, certainly outside of close personal friends or people who saw her regularly. I didn't know the seriousness of the problem first hand. Trevor wasn't always responsible, but he was always a responsible person. Trevor always looked after Sandy, right down the line. He could have a good time with anybody but when it came to a thing like that he looked after his baby daughter. Sandy was out of control and it was a very, very brave thing to do.'

Opinion has since swung around, but Trevor was ostracised for a long time afterwards. Along with Miranda Ward, he was made the scapegoat by many. Bambi Ballard is one of the few of Sandy's friends who still has no sympathy for Trevor's actions. 'She was over the moon with the baby but when she rang me on the last time that I spoke to her [a few days before Sandy was taken to hospital], Trevor hadn't been there all day. They had a very democratically planned relationship; she certainly didn't think he had left her.' Ballard scoffs at the idea that Trevor feared for the baby's safety, and feels that the secretive way he left may have sent Sandy over the edge.

'Trevor once told me that he'd reached a point where he didn't feel he had the same sense of commitment to Sandy any more,' says his third wife, Elizabeth Hurtt. 'He felt it was Georgia who had to come first, because Georgia couldn't look after herself at all. He had these two dependants but he could only cope with one of them. He said he was no longer "in love" with Sandy, which is not the same as not loving her. He just loved his daughter more. His fear was never that Sandy would do anything on purpose to harm Georgia, but she had crashed the car in a ditch more than once with Georgia in the back and she was always falling down-stairs. Sandy had become a danger to herself, so if she had a child with her, the child wasn't safe.'

Miranda Ward would also find her actions questioned follow-ing Sandy's death. While we have only her own account of what happened, she was the one who was there for and with Sandy that last weekend, and she has been condemned by others ever since, largely because it was in her flat that Sandy was eventually discov-ered in a coma.

In *No More Sad Refrains* Clinton Heylin has carefully pieced together Sandy's last weekend, using extracts from Miranda Ward's diary of the time. Ward says that Sandy was neither drinking exces-sively nor taking drugs other than prescription or over-the-counter painkillers and some Valium. Sandy was suffering recurring head-aches and on the Sunday Ward rang her local GP and made an appointment for Monday afternoon. Aside from the headaches, she says, they decided Sandy should tell the doctor about her alcohol problem and admit that 'once she started she found it very difficult to stop'. The diary entry continues: 'She was hopeful about doctor, wanted to try, I said I could only help her to help herself.' Ward's feeling is that Trevor taking Georgia away had shaken Sandy into thinking she needed to address her problems.

The chain of events on Monday 17 April is more a matter of record. Apparently Sandy got up at five in the morning and woke Ward to ask for more painkillers. When Ward left at 8 a.m. to go to Mayfield School in Wandsworth, where she taught, Sandy was asleep again; Ward left her a long note, with her numbers at school, contacts for friends and general household instructions, adding that she'd be back in time for the doctor's appointment. At 1.30 p.m. Steven Walker, a local gardener who was taking care of the dogs back in Byfield, called the flat and spoke to Sandy. It was at around 3 p.m. that Ward was telephoned at the school and told that Sandy had been found unconscious by Jon Cole,* a musician friend whom she had asked to look in. When Cole arrived, Sandy was unconscious at the foot of the stairs between the bathroom door and the stairs to the upper bedrooms. He phoned immediately for an ambulance. Sandy was rushed to the nearby Queen Mary's Hospital, Roehampton, where she remained in a coma.

On Wednesday 19th she was transferred to the Atkinson Morley Hospital in Wimbledon, which specialised in brain injuries. There she had surgery but it failed to improve her condition. David Denny arrived that day, having flown back from the US, where he was tour-managing Parliament/Funkadelic.

Neil Denny was convinced that during that weekend 'Sandy was drugged because she never attempted to communicate with

---

* Jon Cole was the guitarist and singer in the group the Movies.

her mother'. However, as he rightly points out, 'The trouble was that when she fell, there was no one in the house and she lay there for three or four hours at the bottom of the stairs, and the doctors said that was the fatal time, she hadn't been revived.' In fact, it was more likely two hours at most, but the point is still valid.

It was within a few days of arriving at his parents' house in Melbourne that Trevor received a phone call from Bruce Rowland. 'It fell to me to tell him about Sandy's accident,' says Rowland, 'because a PC from Barnes police station phoned me up, maybe because I was one of the first numbers in Sandy's book. So I phoned Trevor and I just told him Sandy was in a coma. After Trev told him what had happened, Frank, his dad, pulled the skirting board off the wall and gave him his savings which were stashed there, and Trevor was on the plane to England within hours of my call. Trevor knew he was going to get it in the neck for taking Georgia but he [came back] anyway, and I admired him for it.'

Nigel Osborne picked Trevor up from the airport and took him to the hospital. 'Trevor was asked for permission to turn off the life-support machine, and that was on the day he got back. The consultant told him she was not going to improve, that she was brain-dead.' In the end, Sandy Denny died naturally at 7.50 p.m. on Friday 21 April, without ever having regained consciousness, just ten minutes before the hospital was going to turn off her life-support machine.

The funeral took place at Putney Vale Cemetery the following Thursday, 27 April 1978, on a gusty day, with around fifty of Sandy's close family and friends attending. Her favourite psalm was read, 'The Lord is my shepherd', and then a piper, arranged by Trevor, played the traditional lament 'The Flowers of the Forest' while Sandy's body was lowered into the ground.

The inscription on her gravestone is headed 'The Lady', followed by 'Alexandra Elene MacLean Lucas (Sandy Denny) 6.1.47–21.4.78'.

'I was the only one who was standing with Trevor at the funeral,' says Osborne. 'Marion didn't attend and everybody else stood on the other side of the grave, and everybody was staring, glowering in some cases, at Trevor. The atmosphere was eventually broken by Richard Thompson, who came across and made this rather strange mystic comment to Trevor [about] how he mustn't feel bad and it was meant to be. And although what he said was a little pompous in that sense, it was a personal moment, putting his hand on Trevor's shoulder, and he had the grace to do that.'*

'I don't mean to romanticise,' says Linda Thompson, 'but I am a believer in fate or destiny. She had such an amazing life and such an amazing talent and she left some wonderful songs and that might have been all that was meant to be. And Richard did say something like that at the funeral – something to the effect that she was never meant to write anything more, which upset some people. But we were both like that at the time. I still feel like that.

'Sandy wasn't daft. Part of her went to the country just to finish the job. It was the same with Nick Drake. I never feel with either of them that it was the biggest tragedy, "How could that have happened?" It was patently obvious to everybody and it was patently

---

* 'That's All, Amen, Close the Door' appears on Richard Thompson's 1999 album *Mock Tudor*, recorded when interest in Sandy was building twenty years after her death. Although Thompson has never specified that he wrote this song about Sandy, the lyrics appear to echo his sentiments that day at the funeral.

obvious to them. That's their destiny. What Nick and Sandy left behind is amazing, and I don't think he had much of a will to live at the end. I don't think that Sandy did either.'

Following a coroner's inquest, the death certificate issued for Sandy on 12 May 1978 cited 'Traumatic mid-brain haemorrhage. Accidental.' The verdict, as reported, was that her death was as a result of a fall at Miranda Ward's house. No evidence of suspicious circumstances was reported at the inquest, nor any significant levels of drugs or alcohol in her body.

Although he had been half a world away in Australia, Trevor was called to give evidence. The agreed story was that he had taken Georgia to Australia to visit his parents; Miranda Ward wasn't called, nor was her statement read, even though she could have given the true reason for Trevor's being in Australia.

After the inquest, some of Sandy's family and friends blamed Ward for contributing towards her death. There was speculation as to whether the weekend she spent with Sandy was as innocuous as she claimed, particularly in terms of drug and alcohol intake. Ward feels that the story that was circulated to the press, repeated to this day, gives an inaccurate impression that Sandy died after falling down the stairs at her flat. Ward's contention is that Sandy did not fall downstairs but collapsed at the foot of the staircase, which is certainly consistent with the position of her body and with the fact that boxes of books and newspapers on the stairs were undisturbed.

Ward told Jim Irvin her own theory about Sandy's collapse: 'I used to decant drinks and Sandy had finished about three-quarters of a pint of gin in the drinks cabinet in the drawing room. In the blood rush from the drink she'd felt sick and taken Andrews salts [there is evidence of this], had vomited, cleaned the loo up and coming out of the loo had fallen at the bottom of the staircase, grabbed hold of the curtain, the curtain rail was bent and the curtain was partly wrapped around her.' It's also possible that Sandy simply collapsed as a result of gradual, residual bleeding in her brain following her previous falls.

Trevor Lucas was also branded as culpable at the time, although, with some exceptions, opinions have since changed. David Denny slammed the door in his face at Miranda Ward's flat, where he, Neil and Edna were staying during Sandy's last few days. 'There was a whole army of people who wouldn't even answer the phone to Trevor,' says Chris Pegg. 'He really took the brunt of it. He couldn't walk down the street at home; the villagers blamed him, as did a lot of people who thought she died because Trevor left.' Trevor rarely returned to Byfield, preferring to remain in London, staying with Philippa Clare.

Trevor and David were reconciled the following July, says Elizabeth Hurtt. They ran into each other in Camden, at a gig where Iain Matthews was playing: 'We went along and David was there, and he and Trevor went off together. The next day Trevor said that they'd had a good talk and cleared the air about a lot of things.'

Neil and Edna Denny were less forgiving. There was even an issue over the gravestone which Trevor had organised at Putney Vale. 'He didn't put anything on the headstone – no affection or memory, anything,' said Neil, still angry twenty years later. 'Eventually we had the surround made and I had to sign a waiver that if the owner of the grave objected I would have to pay for its removal. I had no rights on the grave. When my son died and I got his ashes we got the site behind the grave, so they're all together. My parents' ashes were in Putney Vale. I've got five people there, including my wife, and I shall be the sixth.'

The inscription which Neil Denny organised, at the base of a low wall around the grave, reads: 'Fondly remembered by Mummy, Daddy, Brother David and Baby Georgia.' There is no mention of Trevor.

Neil's bitterness was heightened by the lack of contact regarding Sandy's possessions and by the fact that all communication thereafter was through a solicitor. 'That's the situation and I feel very bitter about Trevor Lucas, and in my view, I feel he's responsible, not only for Sandy's death but he's responsible for my wife's death.'

In the next three years Neil Denny suffered the further losses of his son and his wife. David Denny died in a car crash in the Rocky Mountains in Colorado on 15 December 1980.* Neil flew to the US as soon as he heard about the accident. 'I was in Denver about half past nine and I saw him that night. He opened his eyes and whether he saw me I don't know. The next morning I was going in to see him but he was dead. I came home and my wife was in a terrible state – we both were. My wife never got over it. She died in April. She had cancer of the throat and I think it was the trauma – the shock that caused it.' Edna Denny died nearly three years to the day after her daughter, 23 April 1981. Neil Denny died on 20 August 1999.

---

* After Sandy's death, David Denny had returned to the US, where he became production manager for major rock concert promoter Barry Fey's Feyline Presentations. Alongside his sporting and academic achievements, the King's College School's Old Boys Register records that David 'went to the USA to assist his sister in the entertainment business and worked as Designer and Stage Manager for the Parliament/Funkadelic Touring Extravaganza'. Following his death, a David Denny Scholarship for students in technical Theatre Art was established in 1981 at the University of Colorado.

In the High Court of Justice

The District Probate Registry at OXFORD

BE IT KNOWN that ALEXANDRA ELENE MACLEAN.LUCAS otherwise ALEXANDRA ELENE
MACLEAN DENNY otherwise SANDY DENNY of West View 41 The Twistle
Byfield near Daventry Northamptonshire

died on the 19th day of April 19 78

domiciled in England and Wales

intestate

AND BE IT FURTHER KNOWN that at the date hereunder written Letters of Administration of all the estate which by law devolves to and vests in the personal representative of the said intestate were granted by the High Court of Justice at the said Registry to

TREVOR GEORGE LUCAS of West View aforesaid

And it is hereby certified that an Inland Revenue account has been delivered wherein it is shown that the gross value of the said estate in the United Kingdom (exclusive of what the said deceased may have been possessed of or entitled to as a trustee and not beneficially) amounts to £ 14000.00 and that the net value of the estate amounts to £8035.00

Dated the 25th day of September, 19 78

District Registrar.

Admon. Extracted by Whitehorns & Haines 36 The Green Banbury Oxon DR6
WH

Register of Probate following Sandy's death

'Neil and Edna did not really approve of Trevor but they didn't entirely cut him out during Sandy's lifetime,' says Elizabeth Hurtt. 'The particular antagonism that's been expressed came after Sandy died. When it comes to Neil it's totally understandable, when you take into consideration the age and the class he grew up in, and then in the space of three years he lost his wife, his daughter and his son – and his only brother. So it's a huge burden of grief to handle and one of the classic defence mechanisms is to be angry and to look for someone to blame, and Trevor was a sitting duck.'

Trevor returned to Australia four months after Sandy's death, following the sale of The Twistle and settlement of her estate, which, after tax, was valued at £8,035. In the months between, he sang backing vocals on 'Died for Love' on Richard and Linda Thompson's *First Light* and also on Julie Covington's self-titled album, produced by Joe Boyd, which includes a cover of Sandy's then unreleased song 'By the Time It Gets Dark'. Both albums were released in 1978.

Trevor came back to Britain a year later and married Elizabeth Hurtt on 18 July 1979 at Marylebone Registry Office. They had met again, by chance, at Philippa Clare's the previous summer. Dave Pegg was his best man. They returned to Melbourne two weeks later, where Georgia was brought up, along with Trevor and Elizabeth's son Clancy, who was born in March 1981.

On his return to Australia Trevor started a film production company, Andromeda Productions. He was the company's music consultant but was also learning the ropes in film production. He continued to work in the music industry in Australia and produced successful albums by Goanna, the Bushwackers and Redgum, as well as working on a number of film scores and in film and TV pro-duction. In 1982 and 1985 Trevor was a special guest at Cropredy, reuniting Fairport Convention's *Nine* line-up.

Ralph McTell, who was another guest for that 1985 Cropredy get-together, vividly remembers something Trevor told him. 'He was mixing all the old tapes and playing a track over and over and he was deep into the track and talking to the engineer and suddenly a voice that came from the speakers said, "Is that all right then?" and he said, "Yes, love," and it was Sandy. They'd left the tape running and Trevor answered as if she was still there. And when he told me that story his eyes filled up with tears. You can't switch that on.'

In an interview with *Ram* magazine before Christmas 1988, Trevor spoke freely to the press about Sandy for the first time. It turned out to be his last interview; Trevor died of heart failure in his sleep on 3 February 1989. 'If she came into a room, a party, she was immediately the centre of attention – partly, I suppose, because of who she was: she was always incredibly respected, even back in the early days, just by virtue of her voice. But it was something more than that – she had a charisma about her, a style that people were automatically drawn to. It was amazing to watch at times.'

15 : *In a Lonely Moment*
1947–1978

Denny was less a folk-singer than a singer who meant to
defeat time, and that may be why, in her strongest moments,
no female singer of the last ten years could touch her. As
with Van Morrison on *Astral Weeks* or *Veedon Fleece*, no one
else could go where she went.

GREIL MARCUS, *Rolling Stone*, 15 June 1978

Melody Maker cover, 29 April 1978. Still overshadowed by Bob Marley . . .

In the obituaries that followed Sandy's death nobody tried to conceal the fact that her career had been in decline, although in most of the tributes, exemplified by *Melody Maker*, she was remembered as 'unquestionably the finest female singer produced by the British folk scene'. *Melody Maker* editor Ray Coleman thought it right to commemorate her life and career as the cover story the following week, but Colin Irwin's piece didn't pull its punches: 'Sandy's loss is made even more sickening by the fact that her full potential and commercial possibilities were never fully realised. Part of it was undeniably her own fault – she was a compelling personality of extreme sensitivity with a notorious inability to organize herself and guide her career to logical triumph.'

The most eloquent tribute appeared in *Rolling Stone*, where Greil Marcus wrote that her finest music 'has not dated in any manner, unlike much of the best music of the late '60s and early '70s. She sang about serfs and noblemen with the naturalism of a woman describing everyday life, and she sang about everyday life as if from the perspective of a woman a thousand years gone.'

It's Sandy's unflinching, emotional singing that Marcus singles out for praise, yet the songs he cites, with the exception of 'Who Knows Where the Time Goes?', are not Sandy's own compositions or from her solo albums: Dylan's 'I'll Keep It with Mine', Richard Thompson's 'Genesis Hall' and 'Meet on the Ledge', Led Zeppelin's 'The Battle of Evermore' and Fairport's traditional staples 'A Sailor's Life', 'Tam Lin' and 'Matty Groves'.

It was completely in keeping with the prevailing view that Sandy Denny was always regarded as a singer first and foremost and, as Irwin's tribute reflects, her songwriting 'was a bonus we had no right to anticipate'.

In the mid-sixties Sandy chose the path of an art-school folk troubadour while Britain was in the midst of a golden age of pop music, when girl singers as different as Dusty Springfield, Cilla Black, Sandie Shaw, Lulu and Petula Clark held their own against the boys and the predominant group sound. Yet the songs they recorded were usually provided by professional songwriters, and there was almost certainly a producer or A & R man calling the shots. By contrast, today's British pop music contains a more than healthy proportion of female artists writing and performing their own songs, often fronting their own groups: Lily Allen, Bat for Lashes, Imogen Heap, Florence Welch, K. T. Tunstall and Alison Goldfrapp, for example. The reference point for the more unconventional of these is usually Kate Bush, while for those brandishing a post-punk attitude it's likely that Siouxsie Sioux inspired them in some way; both these artists' first recordings appeared in 1978.*

Understandably, given Bush's enigmatic but enduring creative success, her name is cited more often, but it was Sandy who paved the way for others to follow; Bush name-checks her on 1980's *Never for Ever*.† Yet today Sandy's influence is still largely con-

---

* Kate Bush's debut, mostly recorded the previous year, was released in March 1978, when 'Wuthering Heights' still held the number-one spot. Siouxsie and the Banshees' debut album, *The Scream*, was released in November that year.
† Sandy Denny's name occurs in Kate Bush's song 'Blow Away (For Bill)', aptly coupled with that of her first pop crush, Buddy Holly.

fined to folk, a genre from which, at least in Britain, only Laura Marling might be considered a major breakthrough act. When the *Sunday Express* wrote about Sandy in 2007, she was described as 'the Amy Winehouse of her day', but measured only in terms of her 'insecurities and a slide into addiction which saw her talent and reputation overshadowed by tales of excess'.

Sandy became a folk singer rather than attempt to emulate the sixties stereotype of the pop dolly bird she was always so disparaging about. 'They just find a little starlet,' she said. 'Never mind if the song means anything or not. If it's recorded well enough it becomes a hit. I really don't agree with that outlook. It's so mercenary. It wouldn't be beyond the realms of possibility for me to get a hit single, go into the studio and record it and have a big hit. It's something I've never done and I don't want to either.'

However much Sandy disdained or was scared of pop success, she effectively provides the bridge between manufactured sixties pop and the era of the singer-songwriter or the sensitive solo singer of the early seventies. In Britain, most of her contemporaries came directly out of folk: Anne Briggs, Shirley Collins, Beverley Martyn, Bridget St John and Linda Thompson. Sandy was the only one of these fully in the public gaze and, as the unwitting flag-bearer, it was always tough on her.

'The pressure of being successful in the music world was intense for women at that time,' says Julie Felix. 'Sandy was like Dusty Springfield because she was unique; in her case because she wrote her own songs and wanted to be taken for who she was. She had come out of folk and became a star with Fairport, and there was a real anticipation that she would succeed commercially to a far greater degree than she ever did. Dusty was a reluctant star, and a much bigger star, of course, but she had some really hard times in her life after the sixties. Dusty didn't write but she chose what songs to record and could be very demanding in the studio. She called the shots, which women weren't supposed to do – so she was called a bitch.

'It was a particularly difficult transition for folk singers to be thrown into the mainstream as Sandy was and I was – and when the spotlight moved on we were left wondering what we were supposed to do. Sandy struggled with that in the last few years of her life. She was always a little down on herself, outwardly feisty but inwardly insecure, and she became more so.'

Sandy's range as a writer was not broad; her best-known and most significant compositions almost all follow a pattern of slow-paced, bleak and/or reflective ballads, often with allusive and poetic imagery. Such an approach was never going to bring about a major breakthrough single. 'Who Knows Where the Time Goes?' is still the only song written by Sandy to have become a hit, albeit for Judy Collins,* and only in the US, not on home turf. It is almost certainly the only song of hers that casual fans can name. Sandy rarely spoke about her signature song, and usually only when pressed. 'It was one of my first songs,' she said frostily to *Sounds*' Jerry Gilbert in 1973, 'and I just wish people would listen to some of the other ones, although some people still maintain it's the best song I've ever written. They can't all be wrong, although I don't agree with them.'

The eighties was a tough decade for Sandy's contemporaries from the late sixties and early seventies; most no longer enjoyed

* Judy Collins says, 'Sandy was marvellous. We became friends and we always had fun together. I never saw her perform but she spent time at my home and in my studio. She died on 21 April 1978, one day after I put down the alcohol.' Collins entered a rehabilitation programme in Pennsylvania in 1978 and has maintained her sobriety ever since.

the cushioning of the major record deals they'd become used to and were back playing folk clubs and smaller venues. At the time of her death, that was a downhill path Sandy looked almost certain to follow. As it was, her work was in danger of being completely overlooked until the timely, thoughtfully compiled four-LP box set *Who Knows Where the Time Goes?* was released by Island at the end of 1985. It was carefully assembled by Trevor Lucas and Joe Boyd; Trevor's memos from the time show how much he tried to ensure that it included the songs she herself would have chosen. The selection brilliantly encapsulated Sandy's career, featuring many of her classic performances and greatest songs. Only four previously unreleased songs were included among the unheard live performances, demos and BBC recordings that make up around half the selected tracks. Box sets weren't routine in 1985,* and its run of 3,500 copies was quickly devoured, but it was a dozen years too soon to stoke the fires of a genuine reappraisal beyond her most faithful fans.

When Richard Thompson provided the foreword to Pamela Winters's unpublished biography of Sandy Denny, *No Thought of Leaving*, in 1999, he was almost angry about her lack even of cult success.† 'Her records don't fit the current formats, don't send the programmers into paroxysms, don't have listeners voting in. She couldn't be considered for '60s and '70s hit nostalgia: she never had hits. Rock album stations? Never sold enough albums. Even Nick Drake sneaks into the odd easy listening show; the music lulling and deceiving, something romantic for a cult to cling to.'

---

* The first Bob Dylan box set, *Biograph*, was released the same month.
† Thompson's foreword is reprinted in the booklet for *A Boxful of Treasures* (2004).

Sandy's music was, however, finally being reassessed and introduced to a new generation.

The careers of many major artists were now being methodi-
cally revisited, and Sandy's was no exception. In her case, though,
it was a particularly rewarding exercise; notably, Strange Fruit's
enthralling 1997 release, *The BBC Sessions 1971–1973*, which
swelled to become the four-disc *Sandy Denny at the BBC* ten
years later. *Gold Dust*, Jerry Donahue's long-awaited but conten-
tious recreation of her final concert at the Royalty Theatre, was
released the following year. Expanded CD releases of all her solo
and related albums followed; even the Saga albums with Alex
Campbell and Johnny Silvo were dusted down.

In 2004 Fledg'ling Records' five-CD *A Boxful of Treasures*
proved to be the real eye-opener, enlightening us with an entire
disc's worth of revelatory, previously unheard home recordings
and demos. These unadorned recordings send shivers down the
spine; her unguarded performances are spellbinding. When the
all-encompassing nineteen-CD set simply titled *Sandy Denny* was
released in 2010, it brought to light another fifty unreleased performances, collecting together all her home recordings between
1965 and 1978.*

Now we can all judge Sandy's life's work for ourselves, from
her initial sketchy demos of 'Who Knows Where the Time Goes?'
through to her harrowing parting shot, 'Makes Me Think of You'.
Almost every classic song she wrote is accessible as a bare-bones
demo, most revealingly those for *Rendezvous*, which one reviewer

---

* The *Sandy Denny* box set sold out on pre-orders alone. In 2012 a
well-chosen four-disc highlights package was released, *The Notes and the
Words: A Collection of Demos and Rarities*.

felt provided 'a corrective to the notion that Denny's creativity was in irreversible decline'.

Comparisons with Nick Drake are inevitable, but Drake has reached a far wider audience than Sandy, and not just through a 1999 Volkswagen TV commercial which featured 'Pink Moon'. 'Sandy and Nick regarded each other with respect but from a distance,' says Joe Boyd. 'Sandy couldn't relate to Nick, and Nick was as reticent towards her as he was towards most people. They were both English to the core, but what might seem a nuance of difference between suburban middle-class and rural/colonial middle-class is actually a chasm.'

It is widely agreed that Nick Drake's music hasn't aged, partly because his understated singing is so in tune with the times – far more so than Sandy's more assertive approach. Drake's more private life and doomed-youth career trajectory are also perhaps easier to relate to and more appealing than Sandy's turbulent rock 'n' roll lifestyle. Unlike Drake's quietly engaging voice, Sandy's strength, power and technique still don't send radio programmers into paroxysms, even though no vocalist operating in the same sphere comes close to singing as she did. Rachel Unthank may have been kidding when asked about Sandy for the 2010 box set but, in a comment worthy of the lady herself, she said: 'Don't listen to her! You'll realise that the rest of us are wasting your time.' Sandy was a hard act to follow. The dominant trend now is a gossamer, buoyant singing style and a simpler deconstruction of traditional music which has seen Vashti Bunyan become a far more achievable role model among present-day female singers.*

---

* Vashti Bunyan's 'Just a Diamond Day' was another song which came to public awareness via an advertisement, for T-Mobile in 2006. It was taken

'At her best, she was the best,' says Shirley Collins, never one to throw compliments about lightly. 'Nobody quite came up to that standard and Sandy's recordings with Fairport still give me goosebumps. It was timeless really. What Sandy was doing, what Fairport were doing, it just wasn't what I was interested in, but when I finally listened to *Liege & Lief* I was blown away by it. I played it non-stop once I heard it. They can't be held responsible for the imitators, who rather paled by comparison. When other singers try to sing like Sandy they throw their voices at top lines rather than just singing them. It just sounds wrong when they try and introduce that into an English traditional song; Sandy was the only person who could do that and make it sound right.'

Perhaps more than any other, the factor that must be understood in Sandy's brilliant but exasperating career is that she was irrevocably identified as the singer with Fairport Convention. As everyone who has ever been in the group has found, you can leave Fairport but you can never entirely escape its clutches. Over forty years after leaving the group, and having made over forty albums in a richly varied career, Richard Thompson is still commonly defined as the guitarist in Fairport and his music – like Sandy's – is invariably and misleadingly filed under 'folk'.

Joe Boyd is correct in saying that she never made that one classic album, but Sandy's solo work was never entirely able to break free of associations with her more familiar recordings with Fairport in 1968 and 1969. Yet the Fotheringay album simply gets better with each passing year, and *The North Star Grassman and the*

---

from her Joe Boyd-produced album *Just a Diamond Day*, released in 1970, which features Simon Nicol and Dave Swarbrick from Fairport, Robin Williamson of the Incredible String Band and string arrangements by Robert Kirby.

Ravens and *Sandy* are both near masterworks representing the two sides of Sandy she could never reconcile, one haunted, the other haunting and beguiling.

Towards the end of her life Sandy was plagued by the pursuit of the commercial success that had long eluded her, although she craved it less than those who wanted it for her. She increasingly lacked confidence in her actions and her judgement became more contrary and wayward. Despite her reputation and extraordinary talent, at the time of her death she was unknown to so many.

In the wake of the cool reception given to *The North Star Grassman and the Ravens*, her first, purest and most evocative solo album, Sandy spoke poignantly in an interview for the BBC World Service: 'I just want to communicate to more people. I communicate to a lot of people but it's not enough yet. And it's not purely from a mercenary point of view. I just want to, that is my ambition. I want to be happy. I want to be happy in my work. But it's all happening in a very slow way and if we've got time left in this world, perhaps I'll get there one day.'

In the end, however, she was unable to defeat time.

> I've always lived in a mansion
> on the other side of the moon.
> I've always kept a unicorn
> and I never sing out of tune.
> I could tell you that the grass is really greener
> on the other side of the hill,
> But I can't communicate with you
> and I guess I never will.
>
> We've all gone – solo.
> We all play – solo.
> Ain't life a solo.

Acknowledgements

A lot of people have been extraordinarily helpful over the past four years in preparing and writing this book.

Colin Davies deserves particular mention just for being there more than anything, always at the end of a phone in Wimbledon. We'd not met before I started on the book and I now consider him a true friend. His interviews with Neil Denny were utterly invaluable; I also plundered his archive and address book mercilessly.

Jim Irvin, Andrew Batt, Colin Harper, Patrick Humphries and Nigel Schofield were also enormously helpful and generous with their time, expertise and further source material.

About four years ago I rang Simon Benham, whom I'd met once before at a book launch, and said: 'I don't know if you remember me but . . . do you think anybody would be interested in a book on Sandy Denny?' He made one phone call and that was that. Since then he too has been a true friend.

At Faber and Faber, I'd like to thank Lee Brackstone for taking that call and saying yes, Dave Watkins for patiently guiding me through the book at every stage and keeping me on track, Eleanor Rees for her wonderful editing skills, and Ian Bahrami for typesetting and proofreading.

My wife Sara has had to put up with me being elated, becoming depressed and generally being stressed while completing the book and, let's face it, for being that way for the last twenty years or more. What can I say that is anywhere near enough?

Interviews: only a couple of people declined to be interviewed about Sandy, one or two others proved elusive or unresponsive. My sincere thanks to everybody who did speak to me, some with great candour, some with too much candour, and almost all with a mixture of joy and sadness in talking about Sandy. There were one or two people I interviewed before researching this book but whose comments were relevant to the story. Thanks one and all: Kingsley Abbott, Joan Armatrading, Bambi Ballard, David Betteridge, Chris Blackwell, Brian Blevins, Joe Boyd, Gary Boyle, Marcus Brierley, Anne Briggs, Diana Cadman (née King), Fred Cantrell, Martin Carthy, Philippa Clare, Tim Clark, Geoff Clarke, Judy Collins, Shirley Collins, Gerry Conway, Dave Cousins, Jerry Donahue, Judy Dyble, Julie Felix, Linda Fitzgerald Moore, Gina Glaser, Stefan Grossman, Claire Hamill, Mike Heron, Elizabeth Hurtt, Ashley Hutchings, Colin Irwin, Bert Jansch, Glyn Johns, Wizz Jones, Georg Kajanus, John Kay, Sonja Kristina, Albert Lee, Shelagh McDonald, Roger McGuinn, Jacqui McShee, Ralph McTell, Manfred Mann, Beverley Martyn, John Martyn, Dave Mattacks, Iain Matthews, David Moses, Simon Nicol, Nigel Osborne, Tom Paxton, Chris Pegg, Dave Pegg, Frankie Post (née King), Mike Post, Duffy Power, Maddy Prior, John Renbourn, Dave Richards, Andy Roberts, Bruce Rowland, Bridget St John, Martin Satterthwaite, Al Stewart, Dave Swarbrick, Linda Thompson, Richard Thompson, Rachel Unthank, Dave Waite, Ian Whiteman, Richard Williams, Heather Wood, Martyn Wyndham-Read.

Thanks also to the following for help in arranging interviews or providing source material, or in some cases for their encouragement or inspiration: Richard Allison, Sue Armstrong, Christine Atkins, Tony Bacon, Jeff Barrett, Stuart Batsford, Max Bell, Joe

Black, Cally, Michael Chapman, Declan Colgan, Mark Cooper, Phil Cooper, Julian Cope, Nigel Cross, Ted Cummings, Karl Dallas, David Denny, Robin Denselow, Jason Draper, Bill Drummond, Daryl Easlea, Andy Farquarson, Bob Harris, Jac Holzman, Stevie Horton, Ken Hunt, Danny Jackson, Michael Jackson, Loren Jansch, Andrew Lynn, Will McCarthy, Dave Mann, Jon Mills, Andy Morten, Richard Morton Jack, Peter Muir, Brian New, Andrew Oldham, Mark Pavey, Peter Purnell, John Reed, The Sethman, Harriet Simm, Phil Smee, James Soars, Terry Staunton, David Suff, Jamie Taylor, Arwell Williams, Martin Williams, Jim Wirth, Rob Young.

Warlock Music Ltd; 'Late November' © 1971 Warlock Music Ltd; 'Next Time Around' © 1971 Warlock Music Ltd; 'It Suits Me Well' © 1972 Warlock Music Ltd; 'The Lady' © 1972 Warlock Music Ltd; 'Solo' © 1973 Warlock Music Ltd
Words and music by Richard Thompson: 'We Sing Hallelujah' © 1974 Warlock Music Ltd

For the following, all words and music by Sandy Denny. © Jardinière-Music (NS). All rights administrated by Intersong Music Ltd. All rights reserved: 'One More Chance'; 'Full Moon'; 'Take Me Away'; 'Still Waters Run Deep'; 'I'm a Dreamer'; 'One Way Donkey Ride'; 'All Our Days'

The majority of the photos and images were provided by Elizabeth Hurtt, Administrator for the Estates of Sandy Denny and Trevor Lucas; thanks also to David Denny, Colin Davies, Mike Post, Richard Morton Jack, Andrew Batt and Phil Smee.

Thanks too to Eric Hayes for permission to reproduce in the plate section the photograph of Fairport Convention during the recording of *Liege & Lief* (© Eric Hayes).

Sources

All quotations from Neil Denny are taken from Colin Davies's series of interviews with him. Unless otherwise stated, quotations from Danny Thompson, John Wood and Miranda Ward are from transcripts kindly given to me by Jim Irvin. Thanks also to Patrick Humphries for the transcript of his interview with Sandy in March 1977, which was later published in *Hokey Pokey*, and to Nigel Schofield for his revealing interviews with Sandy as recorded in the book *Fairport by Fairport*.

All other interviews, unless credited below, were undertaken by the author.

CHAPTER ONE

8 'he's dead, he's dead . . . Buddy Holly's dead', Pamela Winters, *No Thought of Leaving*, 1999
10 'hated school, every minute of it', *Petticoat*, 20 February 1971
16 'I've always had a very straight background', *Petticoat*, 20 February 1971
23 'The first time I ever stood up on stage my mouth went all dry', *Disc & Music Echo*, 7 October 1972

CHAPTER TWO

30 'To understand Sandy', *Ram*, 25 January 1989
40 'When everybody used to go down the Cousins', Patrick Humphries interview, March 1977
41 'It was far cooler', *Ram*, 25 January 1989
47 'I think that my first songwriting influences', *NME*, 15 January 1972
48 'She was a nurse at the time', Pamela Winters, *No Thought of Leaving*, 1999, reprinted in *A Boxful of Treasures*, 2004

433

51 'When I first met Sandy Denny', *Dirty Linen*, April/May 1995
56 'It was throughout my year at college', *Tomorrow's People*, January 1972, BBC World Service
58 'I met, and followed around for a while', Eric Clapton, *Eric Clapton: The Autobiography*, Century, 2007
60 'Some critics have called it folksy', *Record Mirror*, August 1974
64 'Sandy was quieter and more serious', Pamela Winters, *No Thought of Leaving*, 1999
64 'Whenever I sing "The Sea"', *Melody Maker*, 27 June 1970
66 '"Fotheringay" came out of my interest in Mary Queen of Scots', Nigel Schofield, *Fairport by Fairport*, Rocket 88, 2012

CHAPTER THREE
69 'Sandy Denny has the sort of rich, soaring voice', *Melody Maker*, 17 December 1966
73 'My friends all thought I was stupid', *Petticoat*, 20 February 1971
77 'Alex's friends include Sandy Denny', *Gramophone*, September 1967
78 'the only British girl folk singer', *Gramophone*, February 1968

CHAPTER FOUR
108 'I'm collecting material together', *Melody Maker*, 23 September 1967
113 'There was nowhere to go', Brian Hinton and Geoff Wall, *Ashley Hutchings: The Guvnor and the Rise of Folk Rock*, Helter Skelter, 2002
114 'a ramshackle, happy-go-lucky', Colin Harper, *Dazzling Stranger*, 2000
116 'It always seems so phoney', *Petticoat*, 20 February 1971
117 'Somehow I don't look like a dolly-bird singer', *Petticoat*, 20 February 1971

CHAPTER FIVE
122 'I would say there was a special atmosphere', Brian Hinton and Geoff Wall, *Ashley Hutchings*, 2002

132 'does a mixture of country and western', *Melody Maker*, June 1968

132 'I wanted to do something more with my voice', *Melody Maker*, 27 July 1968

133 'I always sang with my eyes shut', *A Boxful of Treasures*, 2004

134 'We think of ourselves as a folk-based band', *Beat Instrumental*, November 1968

143 'I wanted to leave', *Zigzag*, September 1976

143 'The first time we did "A Sailor's Life"', Patrick Humphries, *Richard Thompson, Strange Affair*, Virgin Books, 1996

143 'I'd been singing "A Sailor's Life"', Nigel Schofield, *Fairport by Fairport*, 2012

145 'I have regrets about leaving', *Zigzag*, September 1976

149 'I wasn't involved in the rock arrangement at all', Nigel Schofield, *Fairport by Fairport*, 2012

CHAPTER SIX

158 'He had a deep, rich, pleasant voice', *Remembering Traynor's: A Collaborative Folk History*, July 2009

162 'must be one of the few singers', *Melody Maker*, 2 April 1966

162 'his Australian repertoire', *Melody Maker*, 27 August 1966

163 'In the film *Don't Look Back*', *Remembering Traynor's: A Collaborative Folk History*, July 2009

166 'a very underground flower power group', *The Age*, 2 September 1978

171 'a good apprenticeship in electric music', *The Age*, 2 September 1978

CHAPTER SEVEN

182 'I didn't really know how to deal with it', Nigel Schofield, *Fairport by Fairport*, 2012

184 'Describing it coldly', Nigel Schofield, *Fairport by Fairport*, 2012

189 'I was dumbfounded', Jim Irvin interview, 1998

192 'That was a load of rubbish', *Record Mirror*, 4 April 1970

193 'The accident taught me', *NME*, August 1969

193 'we've really been getting into traditional English music', *Disc & Music Echo*, August 1969

197 'Bert Lloyd was one of the first', Patrick Humphries interview, 1977

202 'Ashley was still discovering things', Brian Hinton and Geoff Wall, *Ashley Hutchings*, 2002

202 'Everything seemed to come to a head', Nigel Schofield, *Fairport by Fairport*, 2012

203 'I certainly didn't fancy the idea', Nigel Schofield, *Fairport by Fairport*, 2012

206 'I still don't recall that time', Patrick Humphries interview, 1977

206 'And they thought I would freak out', *NME*, 14 March 1970

208 'They took the floor spot', *Folk Britannica*, BBC4, February 2006

CHAPTER EIGHT

214 'we're going to discourage any personality centres', *Record Mirror*, 4 April 1970

214 'The reason I left Fairport', *Music Now*, 14 February 1970

215 'I think what changed my mind', *Disc & Music Echo*, 24 January 1970

215 'There is something about the sound', Nigel Schofield, *Fairport by Fairport*, 2012

215 'I look upon Fairport as the mother group', *NME*, 14 March 1970

222 'At the beginning of the group', *Sounds*, 24 October 1970

229 'Fotheringay embody the parts', *Melody Maker*, June 1970

229 'I'm really amazed', *Music Now*, 18 July 1970

233 'unknown Sandy is our top of the pops', *Sun*, 16 September 1970

234 'I was utterly amazed', *Tomorrow's People*, BBC World Service, January 1972

234 'Even at the Royal Albert Hall', *Sounds*, October 1970

240 'We weren't a rich band', *Melody Maker*, 9 January 1971

240 'Sandy admitted this week', *Sounds*, 16 January 1971

242 'They hated us', *Rolling Stone*, May 1973

242 'They had it in for us', WQAX, Bloomington, Indiana, 18 October 1974

245 'I feel very uncertain', BBC *Folk on One*, 30 January 1971

CHAPTER NINE

249 'very void', *NME*, 15 January 1972

250 'Led Zeppelin's association with Fairport', *Sandy Denny* box set, 2010

250 'It was a spectacular moment for both of us', *Sandy Denny* box set, 2010

251 'On "The Battle of Evermore"', *Guitar Player*, 1977

251 'I approached Sandy', 'The Power and the Glory: Led Zeppelin and the making of IV', Barney Hoskyns, *Rock's Backpages*, July 2006

252 'They still haven't paid me', britrockbythebay.blogspot.co.uk/ 2011/04/fairport-convention-with-sandy-denny.html

252 'We started out soft', *Rolling Stone*, May 1973

253 'They rang me up and asked me to do it', Patrick Humphries interview, March 1977

253 'I sing one line in *Tommy*', *Tomorrow's People*, BBC World Service, January 1972

258 'I dunno. I just kind of plodded on', *Sounds*, 8 September 1973

260 'John Wood is a terrible string freak', *Sounds*, 3 July 1971

261 'Yes, a lot of the things I write are slow', *Sounds*, 8 September 1973

262 'I think the album's great musically', *Sounds*, 3 July 1971

262 'Instead of slapstick comedies', *Melody Maker*, May 1971

264 'No, I don't think so', *NME*, 15 January 1972

265 'A couple of my songs may be fantasy', *Screen 'n' Heard*, January 1973

271 'A chubby cheerful girl of twenty-three', *Guardian*, 10 September 1971

272 'His greatest attribute', Jim Wirth, 2014

274 'a really nice fun record', *NME*, 25 December 1971

275 'Conceptually, Fairport, Ashley and myself and Sandy', Patrick Humphries, *Richard Thompson, Strange Affair*, 1996

CHAPTER TEN

280 'I've got to cope with it myself', *NME*, 5 April 1972
280 'It's only now, after all this time', *Sounds*, April 1972
281 'I've got some really discordant harmonies', *Melody Maker*, 2 September 1972
286 'which is entirely suitable for a folk singer', *The Times*, 2 June 1970
288 'I remember the feeling of panic', *NME*, 15 September 1973
291 'It didn't do as well', *Beat Magazine*, November 1972
291 'It's the story of two friends', Sandy's notes for a show in Tokyo, January 1974

CHAPTER ELEVEN

301 '*Sandy* is the year's finest album', *Rolling Stone*, December 1972
303 'I don't want anyone saying', *Sounds*, 31 March 1973
305 'She has been asked to rejoin Fairport', *Rolling Stone*, May 1973
306 'I'd started a waltz rhythm', Patrick Humphries interview, 1977
307 'I think this one is simpler', *Melody Maker*, 15 September 1973
308 'I kissed her', Clinton Heylin, *No More Sad Refrains*, Helter Skelter, 2000
309 'You have to think things', *Sounds*, 8 September 1973
309 'Apart from writing, I do a lot of thinking', *Melody Maker*, 15 September 1973
309 'I couldn't ever convince her', *Sandy Denny Tenth Anniversary Special*, BBC Radio 2, April 1988
310 'It was one of those happenings', *Daily Telegraph*, 3 September 1973
312 'I think it's important for Trevor', *Hamilton Times* (New Zealand), 23 January 1974
312 'Trevor finally decided to make an honest woman of me', Nigel Schofield, *Fairport by Fairport*, 2012
315 'I am not sure that Muff Winwood', Jim Wirth, 2014
316 '*Catch a Fire* set the world alight', Barney Hoskyns, *Uncut*, January 2005

318 'if it hadn't been for the fact', *Go Set*, 29 June 1974

320 'It was ironic, really', Nigel Schofield, *Fairport by Fairport*, 2012

CHAPTER TWELVE

329 'It's like do or die', *Go Set*, 29 June 1974

329 'Things just got worse', *NME*, 28 September 1974

332 'My attitude was always that a recording studio', Jim Wirth, 2014

334 'It's definitely a road song', Nigel Schofield, *Fairport by Fairport*, 2012

338 'It's very much a song about Swarbrick', Nigel Schofield, *Fairport by Fairport*, 2012

344 'I saw an article', Nigel Schofield, *Fairport by Fairport*, 2012

347 'Sandy drank, yes', *Ram*, 25 January 1989

352 'The second time I was with Fairport', Patrick Humphries interview, 1977

CHAPTER THIRTEEN

364 'We decided we would record three titles', *Sound on Sound*, November 2011

366 'I've got my own way of singing', Patrick Humphries interview, 1977

370 'her irascibility, her frustrations', Dave Cousins, *Exorcising Ghosts*, Witchwood Media, 2014

372 'There were so many contradictions to her', *Ram*, 25 January 1989

373 'I still had pangs', Patrick Humphries interview, 1977

374 'This time we've deliberately included', Nigel Schofield, *Fairport by Fairport*, 2012

380 'I really needed a break from the business', *Melody Maker*, 16 July 1977

CHAPTER FOURTEEN

386 'I'm told I have a success neurosis', *Petticoat*, 20 February 1971

387 'Joe Boyd sold me his company', *Audio Magazine*, February 1987

389 'If I have to sing "Matty Groves"', *Melody Maker*, 12 November 1977
406 'they decided Sandy should tell the doctor', Clinton Heylin, *No More Sad Refrains*, 2000
415 'If she came into a room', *Ram*, 25 January 1989

CHAPTER FIFTEEN
419 'unquestionably the finest female singer', *Melody Maker*, 6 May 1978
419 'has not dated in any manner', *Rolling Stone*, 15 June 1978
420 'was a bonus we had no right to anticipate', *Melody Maker*, 6 May 1978
421 'the Amy Winehouse of her day', *Sunday Express*, 28 October 2007
421 'They just find a little starlet', *Petticoat*, 20 February 1971
421 'It wouldn't be beyond the realms of possibility', *Screen 'n' Heard*, January 1973
422 'It was one of my first songs', *Sounds*, 8 September 1973
423 'Her records don't fit the current formats', Pamela Winters, *No Thought of Leaving*, 1999, reprinted in *A Boxful of Treasures*, 2004
425 'a corrective to the notion', *Uncut*, December 2011
425 'Sandy and Nick regarded each other', Joe Boyd, *White Bicycles*, Serpent's Tail, 2005
427 'I just want to communicate to more people', *Tomorrow's People*, BBC World Service, January 1972

Further Reading

Between 1998 and 2000, three major appraisals of Sandy Denny's life and career were undertaken by Jim Irvin, Pamela Winters and Clinton Heylin. They have all been invaluable to me in writing this book; the authors can only be applauded for their vision in writing about Sandy Denny when she was less a cult figure than an almost forgotten one. Since then, an awful lot more has been written in newspaper and magazine articles and there have been two BBC radio documentaries, a songbook and an *Under Review* DVD, but only one further book analysing Sandy's work, written by Philip Ward in 2011.

This short list includes just some of the many books about folk music or folk rock, various related biographies and a handful of reference books, all of which have been well thumbed by me over the years.

Maartin Allcock, *The Complete Sandy Denny Songbook*, Squiggle Records, 2005
Clinton Heylin, *No More Sad Refrains*, Helter Skelter, 2000
Jim Irvin, *Angel of Avalon*, Mojo, 1998. An updated version appears in Jim's anthology *Wildflowers: Sandy Denny, Joni Mitchell and Kate Bush*, Silver Hutchins, 2014
Philip Ward, *Sandy Denny: Reflections on Her Music*, Matador, 2011
Pamela Winters, *No Thought of Leaving*, 1999

J. P. Bean, *Singing from the Floor*, Faber and Faber, 2014
Joe Boyd, *White Bicycles*, Serpent's Tail, 2007
Shirley Collins, *America Over the Water*, SAF Publishing, 2007
Dave Cousins, *Exorcising Ghosts*, Witchwood Media, 2014
Colin Harper, *Dazzling Stranger: Bert Jansch and the British Folk and Blues Revival*, Bloomsbury, 2000

Brian Hinton and Geoff Wall, *Ashley Hutchings: The Guvnor & the Rise of Folk Rock*, Helter Skelter, 2002

Patrick Humphries, *Meet on the Ledge: A History of Fairport Convention*, Eel Pie, 1982

Patrick Humphries, *Nick Drake: The Biography*, Bloomsbury, 1998

Patrick Humphries, *Richard Thompson: Strange Affair*, Virgin Books, 1996

Neville Judd, *Al Stewart: The True Life Adventures of a Folk Rock Troubadour*, Helter Skelter, 2002

Dave Laing, Karl Dallas, Robin Denselow and Robert Shelton, *The Electric Muse*, Methuen, 1975

Jeanette Leech, *Seasons They Change*, Jawbone, 2010

Richard Morton Jack, ed., *Galactic Ramble*, Foxcote Books, 2009

Chris Salewicz, ed., *Keep on Running: The Story of Island Records*, Universe Publishing, 2010

Nigel Schofield, *Fairport by Fairport*, Rocket 88, 2012

Martin C. Strong, *The Great Folk Discography*, Vol. 1, Polygon, 2010

Britta Sweers, *Electric Folk*, Oxford University Press, 2005

Rob Young, *Electric Eden*, Faber and Faber, 2010

Playlist

The playlist contains all Sandy Denny's primary releases during her lifetime, highlighted in bold, plus all her sessions for others, which are indicated ***. I've also included recordings that might be seen as influences, records Sandy is known to have liked, and sources of key covers, as well as recordings and sessions by Trevor Lucas.

To give further context the list includes selected releases – often identifying debut albums only – by Sandy Denny's friends, rivals and contemporaries in the UK and the USA, with specific reference to Island Records' roster and to artists and titles mentioned in the text, as well as certain trends which had an impact on her life and career.

Bearing in mind that forty-to-fifty-year-old release dates are notoriously hard to pinpoint, and that very few sources and discographies actually correlate, I've tried not to be too wildly speculative.

Family favourites and early influences

1937 Fats Waller, 'Until the Real Thing Comes Along'.

1940 The Inkspots, 'Whispering Grass'. This and Fats Waller's song were covered on *Like an Old Fashioned Waltz*.

— Beethoven: *Moonlight, Pathétique and Appassionata Sonatas*, played by Joseph Cooper, World Record Club. The Moonlight sonata was one of Sandy's piano practice pieces, which she also played at a school recital.

1955 Philip Koutev and the Ensemble of the Bulgarian Republic, *Music of Bulgaria*, Nonesuch. One of Sandy's favourite records, it influenced her multitracked harmonies on 'Quiet Joys of Brotherhood'.

1956 Ewan MacColl and A. L. Lloyd, *The English and Scottish*

Popular Ballads (The Child Ballads), Vols *1 and 2*.

1958 The Johnny Otis Show, 'Willie and the Hand Jive'.

1959/60 Buddy Holly, *The Buddy Holly Story*, Vols *1 and 2*, Coral. Includes 'That'll Be the Day' and 'Learning the Game'.

1960 The Everly Brothers, *The Fabulous Style of the Everly Brothers*, Cadence. Includes 'When Will I Be Loved'. The above rock 'n' roll songs were sung by Sandy on *Rock On*.

— Joan Baez, *Joan Baez*, Vanguard. This was the debut album by the teenage Baez, comprising traditional folk ballads from British and American sources. On her fourth album, *Joan Baez in Concert, Part 2*, in 1963 she included two Dylan songs, as well as Pete Seeger's 'We Shall Overcome'.

1961 Brenda Lee, 'Let's Jump the Broomstick'. Covered on *The North Star Grassman and the Ravens*.

1962 The Springfields, *Silver Threads and Golden Needles*, Philips. Recorded for the unfinished Fotheringay album; eventually recorded for *Rendezvous*.

1963 Bob Dylan, *The Freewheelin' Bob Dylan*, CBS. The album which launched an unstoppable cult following; a year after release it topped the UK album charts in May 1964.

— The Countrymen, *The Countrymen*, Piccadilly.

— The Ian Campbell Folk Group, *This Is the Ian Campbell Folk Group*, Transatlantic. This was the group's album debut after releasing a couple of EPs for Topic in 1962. The Ian Campbell Folk Group always presented their own particular brand of folk, favouring British traditional music as well as showing a strong commitment to contemporary writers. The group were also out-standing vocally and instrumentally; in many ways they were precursors to Fairport Convention, not least because the line-up included fiddler Dave Swarbrick.

1964

MARCH Bob Dylan, *The Times They Are a-Changin'*, CBS. *Unhalfbricking*'s 'Percy's Song' was originally an outtake from

Dylan's 1963 album sessions.

JULY The Beatles, *A Hard Day's Night*, Parlophone. Roger
McGuinn: 'I noticed that the Beatles were doing folk music
chord changes in their songs, probably because of their skiffle
background. They were also doing a lot of fourths and fifths
harmonies, which up to that point in time had been exclusively
Appalachian. There was so much going on in those songs that
sounded so simple on the surface. They'd borrow stuff from Celtic
folk but then mix up with influences like the Everly Brothers.
It was astonishingly creative. But it was those folk music chord
changes that inspired me to do what I was doing in the Byrds.'

— The Animals, 'House of the Rising Sun', Columbia. Ground-
breaking No. 1 hit on both sides of the Atlantic. Singer Eric
Burdon says he first came across it sung by local Tyneside folk
singer Johnny Handle; others in the group cite Dylan's eponymous 1962 debut album.

AUGUST Trevor Lucas, *See That My Grave Is Kept Clean*, East.
Debut album recorded that month, spanning traditional folk
blues, contemporary songs by Shel Silverstein and Bob Dylan
and a couple of outback standards, 'Bluey Brink' and 'The Flash
Stockman'.

SEPTEMBER Bob Dylan, *Another Side of Bob Dylan*, CBS. Includes
'It Ain't Me Babe', among Sandy's first home demo recordings.

NOVEMBER Tom Paxton, *Ramblin' Boy*, Elektra. His debut album
includes the ubiquitous 'The Last Thing on My Mind', which
Sandy recorded on *Sandy and Johnny*.

DECEMBER Shirley Collins & Davy Graham, *Folk Roots, New
Routes*, Decca. An unlikely coupling and a remarkable, ageless
fusion of English, European and Eastern elements, including folk
standards 'Nottamun Town' and 'Reynardine'.

— Anne Briggs, *The Hazards of Love* EP, Topic. Her first recordings,
much praised by A. L. Lloyd, with whom she collaborated on
other Topic recordings, including Lloyd's conceptual *The Bird in
the Bush*, 1965.

1965

APRIL Bob Dylan, *Bringing It All Back Home*, CBS. 'If You Gotta Go' was a session outtake; the fully electric, Chuck Berry-influenced 'Subterranean Homesick Blues' was one of five hit singles in the UK that year.

— Richard Fariña, *Celebrations for a Grey Day*, Vanguard. Debut album including 'Reno, Nevada', one of Fairport's most incendiary early covers, recorded only for a John Peel session.

— Bert Jansch, *Bert Jansch*, Transatlantic. High-impact debut album; Jansch's version of Davy Graham's 'Angie' was mandatory for aspiring acoustic guitarists. It's also a credible early British singer-songwriter collection, including 'Strolling Down the Highway' and one of the first anti-drug songs, 'Needle of Death'.

MAY Paul Simon, *The Paul Simon Songbook*, Columbia/CBS. His London-recorded solo debut.

JUNE Marianne Faithfull, *Come My Way*, Decca. An unadulterated folk album which was simultaneously released with the more pop-orientated *Marianne Faithfull*. Faithfull recorded Sandy's 'Crazy Lady Blues' in 1971 on her *Rich Kid Blues* album, which remained unreleased until 1984. Her career was revived after she signed to Island in 1979 and released *Broken English*.

— Fred Neil, *Bleecker and MacDougal*, Elektra. Includes 'A Little Bit of Rain', one of Sandy's home demo recordings in 1966.

JULY The Seekers, *The Seekers*, EMI/Columbia. UK debut by the folk quartet and first internationally successful Australian act.

AUGUST The Byrds, *Mr Tambourine Man*, CBS. The Byrds can justly claim to be the most significant originators of folk rock, and continued to release innovative albums throughout the 1960s.

SEPTEMBER Martin Carthy, *Martin Carthy*, Fontana. Debut album featuring an unlisted Dave Swarbrick; contains his radical take on 'Scarborough Fair' and the no less astonishing 'Lovely Joan'.

OCTOBER Donovan, *Fairytale*, Pye. The third and best of Donovan's gentle folk albums, on which he overcomes a derivative style that owes as much to Bert Jansch as Bob Dylan. He didn't impress

the folk establishment but broadened folk music's appeal to pop
audiences.

— Julie Felix, *The Second Album*, Decca. Felix not only helped
popularise folk music but used musicians such as Martin Carthy,
Dave Swarbrick, John Renbourn and Trevor Lucas to accompany
her on record and on stage.

— Alex Campbell, *In Copenhagen*, Polydor. A rare major-label
release; includes his best-known song, 'Been on the Road'.

— Manfred Mann, 'If You Gotta Go', HMV. Later covered by
Fairport, albeit in French; their only hit single.

NOVEMBER The Watersons, *Frost and Fire*, Topic. Norma, her
brother Mike and sister Lal (Elaine), plus second cousin John
Harrison, were an all-singing act from Hull who flew the flag
for traditional British folk. *Frost and Fire* was their debut album
proper, a compelling seasonal collection of songs.

DECEMBER Joan Baez, *Farewell Angelina*, Vanguard. Her third Top
Ten album of the year; she inspired many young girls to become
folk singers and can be credited as a conduit to traditional
material.

— Jackson C. Frank, *Jackson C. Frank*, Columbia/CBS. His sole
album, produced by Paul Simon, includes 'Blues Run the Game',
'You Never Wanted Me' and 'Milk and Honey', all covered by his
sometime girlfriend Sandy Denny.

— Theo Johnson, Roger Evans, Dave Shelley and the Barge
Group, *Hootenanny at the Barge*, Summit.

1966

JANUARY Simon and Garfunkel, *Sounds of Silence*, CBS. Recorded
in New York after Paul Simon's second sojourn in Britain;
includes the Brit-folk instrumental staple 'Angie'. Jackson C.
Frank's 'Blues Run the Game' was an outtake from the same
December 1965 sessions.

MARCH Gordon Lightfoot, *Lightfoot*, United Artists. Includes 'The
Way I Feel', covered by Fotheringay.

— Eric Anderson, *'Bout Changes 'n' Things*, Vanguard. Includes 'Close the Door Lightly When You Go' and 'Violets of Dawn', which both figured in Fairport's early repertoire and were recorded for BBC sessions.

— Judy Collins, 'I'll Keep It with Mine', Elektra. Allegedly written by Dylan with her in mind; also recorded by Nico for *Chelsea Girl*, Verve, October 1967. Memorably sung by Sandy on Fairport's *What We Did on Our Holidays*.

MAY The Mamas and the Papas, *If You Can Believe Your Eyes and Ears*, Dunhill. Glorious folk-pop album; John Phillips's songs and the group's exhilarating harmonies influenced the direction Dave Cousins took with Sandy and the Strawbs.

— Martin Carthy, *Second Album*, Fontana. Dave Swarbrick is credited this time, marking the birth of one of folk's great duos.

JUNE The Incredible String Band, *The Incredible String Band*, Elektra. Debut album produced by Joe Boyd, recorded at Sound Techniques with engineer John Wood.

— The Young Tradition, *The Young Tradition*, Transatlantic. Debut album by the flamboyant trio; they gave traditional folk an authentic facelift.

JULY Trevor Lucas, *Overlander*, Reality. His only UK solo album, now ultra-rare and commanding a £700 price tag; includes 'Banks of the Condamine' aka 'Banks of the Nile'.

AUGUST Jim and Jean, *Changes*, Verve Forecast. Includes 'One Sure Thing', which was covered by Fairport on their debut album and remained in the repertoire for a few months after Sandy joined.

SEPTEMBER Bert Jansch and John Renbourn, *Bert and John*, Transatlantic. Revelatory guitar interplay; includes 'Soho' and one of Jansch's collaborations with Anne Briggs, 'The Time Has Come', both covered on Sandy's early home demos.

— John Renbourn, *Another Monday*, Transatlantic. Prefaced Pentangle in more ways than one, including an early Elizabethan foray; also features a virtually unknown Jacqui McShee.

— Bert Jansch, *Jack Orion*, Transatlantic. Jansch's bold album of almost entirely traditional material includes 'Blackwaterside', which Sandy sang in folk clubs and eventually recorded on *The North Star Grassman and the Ravens*.

— Paul McNeill, *Traditionally at the Troubadour*, Decca. Features Trevor Lucas on twelve-string.

DECEMBER Judy Collins, *In My Life*, Elektra. Recorded at Sound Techniques; an unlisted Trevor Lucas plays twelve-string guitar.

— Simon and Garfunkel, *Parsley, Sage, Rosemary and Thyme*, CBS. Includes 'Scarborough Fair', which Simon learnt from Martin Carthy; 'Homeward Bound' was written at Warrington railway station.

— Roy Harper, *The Sophisticated Beggar*, Strike. Debut album for an independent imprint. Harper's next, *Come Out Fighting Genghis Smith*, was for CBS. Another Cousins regular who befriended Sandy and was close to Jackson C. Frank, Harper remains on the fringes of folk and rock and helped establish folk's more underground presence.

1967

FEBRUARY Jefferson Airplane, *Surrealistic Pillow*, RCA. American Top Ten hits 'Somebody to Love' and 'White Rabbit' helped put the San Francisco music scene on the map. The Airplane embodied the Summer of Love; early on, Fairport played 'Plastic Fantastic Lover' in their set.

— Dorris Henderson, *Watch the Stars*, Fontana. Her second album with John Renbourn, a novel mix of Appalachian folk, gospel, Billie Holiday's 'God Bless the Child' and a song written with Anne Briggs, 'Mosaic Patterns'.

MAY Shirley Collins, *Sweet Primroses*, Topic. Wonderful, minimalist, gloomy, traditional fare. She had recorded her debut, *Sweet England*, back in 1959.

JUNE The Beatles, *Sergeant Pepper's Lonely Hearts Club Band*, Parlophone.

JULY The Incredible String Band, *The 5000 Spirits or The Layers of the Onion*, Elektra. It laid down the marker for what became

known as acid folk. Paul McCartney said it was his album of the
year.

— Bert Jansch, *Nicola*, Transatlantic. Includes the Anne Briggs
co-write 'Go Your Way My Love', which Sandy demoed in 1966.

— **Sandy Denny and the Strawbs, *All Our Own Work*,** recorded
in Copenhagen during the second half of the month.

AUGUST **Alex Campbell, *Alex Campbell and His Friends*, Eros/
Saga.**

— **Sandy Denny and Johnny Silvo, *Sandy and Johnny*, Eros/
Saga.**

SPRING–LATE AUTUMN Bob Dylan and the Band, *The Basement
Tapes*. Selected songs were in circulation as publishing demos,
including 'Million Dollar Bash', 'Too Much of Nothing' and
'Crash on the Levee' aka 'Down in the Flood', recorded by Sandy
with Fairport (on *Unhalfbricking*), on Fotheringay's debut and on
The North Star Grassman respectively.

*** AUGUST **Sandy Denny and Alex Campbell, 19 *Rupert Street*,**
home tape from 5 August at Campbell's Glasgow home, released
by Witchwood Media in 2011.

OCTOBER Tim Buckley, *Goodbye and Hello*, Elektra. Includes
'Morning Glory', which Fairport played during the auditions
where Sandy joined.

— John Martyn, *London Conversation*, Island. His debut album,
produced by one of folk's most colourful small-time operators,
Theo Johnson, and supervised by Chris Blackwell, who signed
Martyn directly to Island.

NOVEMBER A. L. Lloyd, *Leviathan! Ballads and Songs of the Whaling
Trade*, Topic. Featuring Dave Swarbrick, Martin Carthy, Trevor
Lucas and Martyn Wyndham-Read.

— Al Stewart, *Bedsitter Images*, CBS. His debut album, dominated
by well-observed romantic tales.

— The Merry-Go-Round, *The Merry-Go-Round*, A&M. Includes
Emitt Rhodes's 'Time Will Show the Wiser', which opens
Fairport's debut album.

DECEMBER Leonard Cohen, *The Songs of Leonard Cohen*, CBS.

Includes 'Suzanne', which was transformed after Sandy joined Fairport and, for many, definitively captured her and Ian Matthews singing together; only ever recorded for John Peel's *Top Gear*.

— Traffic, *Mr Fantasy*, Island. Traffic was built around Steve Winwood after he left the Spencer Davis Group. All the Spencer Davis recordings had been licensed by Chris Blackwell to the Fontana label from 1964 onwards, when Island was a production company.

— Dave Swarbrick with Diz Disley and Martin Carthy, *Rags, Reels and Airs*, Bounty. Produced by Joe Boyd; virtuoso playing which introduced some of the fiddle tunes Swarbrick brought to Fairport's repertoire in the 1970s.

— Richard Rodney Bennett, *Far From the Madding Crowd*, original soundtrack, MGM. Features performances by Trevor Lucas, Dave Swarbrick and Isla Cameron; Swarbrick appears in the film as the fiddler during the barn dance scene.

1968

JANUARY Shirley Collins, *The Power of the True Love Knot*, Polydor. A flawed departure from her previous, sparer recordings, this was produced by Joe Boyd.

FEBRUARY Ralph McTell, *Eight Frames a Second*, Transatlantic. McTell followed the well-trodden bohemian path, busking in Europe and living in Cornwall, and has always been a skilful ragtime guitar picker and blues interpreter, the backbone of his early albums. A much maligned songwriter; 'Streets of London' has overshadowed his career since becoming a surprise Christmas hit in 1974.

MARCH The Incredible String Band, *The Hangman's Beautiful Daughter*, Elektra. Something of a must-have hip accessory in underground circles, it was an unlikely Top Five album.

MAY Johnny Cash, *At Folsom Prison*, CBS. Ian Matthews sang 'I Still Miss Someone' during his last few months in Fairport. Along with 'Tried So Hard' from Gene Clark's first post-Byrds album, both of which were recorded for the BBC in December 1968, it anticipates the country rock direction he followed in Matthews Southern Comfort.

— Strawbs, *Strawbs*, A&M. The group's debut album release: intelligent, well-structured, well-produced songs that still had one foot in folk but set the platform for a more grandiose rock sound to come.

JUNE Fairport Convention, *Fairport Convention*, Track. The debut album, produced by Joe Boyd and featuring Judy Dyble, who was replaced by Sandy Denny just two weeks before it was released.

— Pentangle, *Pentangle*, Transatlantic. Tentative debut album; it fails to live up to the group's lofty individual reputations.

— Joni Mitchell, *Song to a Seagull*, Reprise. Her debut album, which includes 'Night in the City', recorded for Sandy's second BBC session with Fairport in June 1968.

. JULY The Band, *Music from Big Pink*, Capitol. The Band's debut was an immediate critical success and a slow burner in the way it fundamentally influenced musicians, most famously George Harrison and Eric Clapton, to rethink their musical strategies. Its impact on Fairport was profound.

— Eclection, *Eclection*, Elektra. Eclection enabled Trevor Lucas to put his 'professional Australian' reputation and repertoire behind him; the multinational, multi-talented group were popular on the underground/college circuit over the next two years.

AUGUST Sweeney's Men, *Sweeney's Men*, Transatlantic. The group's debut album was a turntable favourite at Farley Chamberlayne. All but one of its songs is traditional and the melody for 'Willie o' Winsbury' was used to underpin Richard Thompson's 'Farewell, Farewell'.

SEPTEMBER The Byrds, *Sweetheart of the Rodeo*, CBS. Alongside the Band's *Big Pink*, this influenced Fairport's mindset towards a new approach to traditional music.

*** OCTOBER The Young Tradition, *Galleries*, Transatlantic. Sandy is credited on the track 'Interlude: The Pembroke Unique

Ensemble' but, explains Heather Wood, 'That was just a bit of tape of Sandy playing piano which was lying around the studio from someone else's session – not even sure whose. We were not in the studio together.'

— The Ian Campbell Folk Group, *The Circle Game*, Transatlantic. The year following Dave Swarbrick's departure, Dave Pegg joined from Birmingham beat group the Uglys; his only recordings with Campbell.

NOVEMBER Richard and Mimi Fariña, *Memories*, Vanguard. Includes 'The Quiet Joys of Brotherhood', one of the highlights of the *Sandy* album.

— Marc Brierley, *Welcome to the Citadel*, CBS. His charming chamber folk debut album; he had released a more conventional folk EP for Transatlantic in 1966.

— Jethro Tull, *This Was*, Island. Debut album.

— Free, *Tons of Sobs*, Island. Debut album.

— Mott the Hoople, *Mott the Hoople*, Island. Debut album. Three significant releases by Island in the same month; all three groups became part of Island's bedrock over the next few years. (Fairport's debut for the label had also originally been scheduled for November.)

DECEMBER Judy Collins, *Who Knows Where the Time Goes*, Elektra; Sandy's most famous song also appeared on the B-side of Collins's US hit single 'Both Sides Now'.

— Pentangle, *Sweet Child*, Transatlantic. Part studio, part live double LP that brilliantly delineates Pentangle's blend of acoustic folk, jazz and rock.

1969

JANUARY **Fairport Convention, *What We Did on Our Holidays*, Island.** Sandy's recording debut with Fairport and the group's first for Island Records.

— Al Stewart, *Love Chronicles*, CBS. Alongside Jimmy Page, Fairport's Simon Nicol, Martin Lamble and Richard Thompson appear under the pseudonyms Simon Breckenridge, Martin Francis and Marvyn Prestwick. Ashley S. Hutchings appeared as himself. One of the first great British singer-songwriter albums, too often unjustly overlooked.

FEBRUARY Led Zeppelin, *Led Zeppelin*, Atlantic. Debut album.

MARCH Leonard Cohen, *Songs from a Room*, CBS. Includes 'Bird on a Wire', already in Fairport's repertoire, recorded for the BBC in December 1968.

— Flying Burrito Brothers, *Gilded Palace of Sin*, A&M. Debut album.

APRIL Poet and the One Man Band, *Poet and the One Man Band*, Verve. Debut album by the group, which included Albert Lee, Pat Donaldson and, later, Jerry Donahue; all soon became members of Fotheringay.

MAY Crosby, Stills and Nash, *Crosby, Stills and Nash*, Atlantic. Debut album.

JUNE Shirley and Dolly Collins, *Anthems in Eden*, Harvest. The Collins sisters found themselves part of the underground, even sharing bills with label-mates the Edgar Broughton Band. The highlight is a compelling suite of songs with medieval instrumentation courtesy of the Early Music Consort.

JULY Dr Strangely Strange, *Kip of the Serenes*, Island. Debut album by the Irish group who are, unfairly although not unsurprisingly, commonly labelled as Incredible String Band clones. Robin Williamson brought them to Witchseason and Joe Boyd duly produced them.

AUGUST **Fairport Convention, *Unhalfbricking*, Island.**

— Jethro Tull, *Stand Up*, Island. The group's second album and the first Island album to reach No. 1; the group soon left Island for its new affiliate label, Chrysalis.

— Bridget St John, *Ask Me No Questions*, Dandelion. Debut album.

SEPTEMBER Nick Drake, *Five Leaves Left*, Island. His debut album, which made virtually no impact at the time; nor did the two albums which followed.

OCTOBER Pentangle, *Basket of Light*, Transatlantic. Like Fairport,

Pentangle had just one hit single, 'Light Flight', taken from this album. 'There was never any comparison or rivalry with Fairport,' explained Bert Jansch. 'People today assume there must have been. Neither band was exclusively folk-based. We played acoustic instruments; they were more an electric band. We were never on the same bill; we were doing concert halls and they were playing clubs and universities, so our paths never really crossed.'

— Joni Mitchell, *Clouds*, Reprise. 'Chelsea Morning' and 'I Don't Know Where I Stand' were both covered on Fairport's debut album. 'I Don't Know Where I Stand' was one of the few songs held over when Sandy joined; she sang it on her first Peel session with the group.

— King Crimson, *In the Court of the Crimson King*, Island. Debut album; lit the fire under the entire progressive genre.

DECEMBER **Fairport Convention, *Liege & Lief*, Island.**

— *** Strawbs, *Strawberry Music Sampler*, a publishing demo of which only ninety-nine copies were pressed; it includes Sandy Denny and the Strawbs' version of 'Who Knows Where the Time Goes?', which was still unreleased at the time. On the sampler Sandy also sang lead vocal on 'Sail Away to the Sea' and 'Two Weeks Last Summer' from the Copenhagen sessions.

1970

JANUARY Matthews Southern Comfort, *Matthews' Southern Comfort*, Uni. Essentially Matthews's solo debut album; Fairport's Thompson, Nicol and Hutchings all play on the record.

— Martin Carthy and Dave Swarbrick, *Prince Heathen*, Fontana. Swarbrick's final album with Carthy before joining Fairport; the two resumed their partnership in later years.

FEBRUARY John and Beverley Martyn, *Stormbringer!*, Island. Duo's debut and the start of an astonishing run of impeccable recordings by John Martyn, first with Beverley, then solo from *Bless the Weather* through to 1975's *Sunday's Child*.

— Trader Horne, *Morning Way*, Dawn. After singing briefly with pre-King Crimson Giles, Giles and Fripp, Judy Dyble's post-Fairport recording career began with Jackie McAuley in the charmingly ethereal duo Trader Horne. Still shaken by her enforced exit from Fairport, she left Trader Horne soon after their sole album was released and retired to the English countryside to raise a family. Thirty years later she returned to music.

APRIL Trees, *The Garden of Jane Delawney*, CBS. Trees' two albums, this and *On the Shore*, February 1971, occupy the same ground as both pre- and post-*Liege & Lief* Fairport. Generally, they inject a spikier, more psychedelic feel and a heavier guitar sound, and singer Celia Humphris has a more clipped, higher-pitched voice than Sandy Denny's.

MAY James Taylor, *Sweet Baby James*, Warner Bros. Along with Carole King's *Tapestry* and Joni Mitchell's early work, Taylor epitomised the transition from folk to a new era of tell-all singer-songerwriters, especially after the success of 'Fire and Rain'. Taylor's introspective stylistic approach became the blue-print for the elite Laurel Canyon set, which included members of major rock acts such as Crosby, Stills, Nash and Young and the Eagles.

JUNE **Fotheringay, *Fotheringay*, Island.**

— Steeleye Span, *Hark the Village Wait*, RCA. Steeleye inherited Fairport's tendency to change personnel at will and their debut featured a criminally short-lived line-up in which the voices of Tim Hart and Maddy Prior, Gay and Terry Woods were consistently stunning.

JULY Fairport Convention, *Full House*, Island. Dave Pegg's first with the group and arguably Fairport's peak as an instrumental unit. Nor is it reliant on traditional material; 'Sloth' and 'Walk Awhile' are classic originals.

— Cat Stevens, *Mona Bone Jakon*, Island. Label debut with which Stevens reinvented himself as a singer-songwriter following an earlier string of catchy pop hits; he would become Island's biggest-selling artist worldwide over the next few years.

— Free, *Fire and Water*, Island. Includes 'All Right Now'; validates

Free's hard-earned transition from solid blues band to rock.

— Traffic, *John Barleycorn Must Die*, Island. The group which facilitated Island's move into progressive rock, Traffic had broken up the year before but reformed in early 1970. The title track is a rare and exceptional foray into folk.

— Elton John and Linda Peters, *The Warlock Sampler*. Recorded as a showcase for Witchseason's publishing arm; an ultra-rare pressing in which Elton John sings four Nick Drake songs and, with Linda, three by John Martyn and two by the Incredible String Band's Mike Heron. Gerry Conway, Pat Donaldson and Jerry Donahue from Fotheringay provide backing.

— Jade, *Fly on Strangewings*, DJM. Former Countryman Dave Waite began performing in folk clubs as a duo with singer-writer Marian Segal. Expanding to a trio they recorded this overlooked album, highlighted by Segal's singing, which, almost inevitably, invited comparison with Sandy.

AUGUST Martyn Wyndham-Read, *Ned Kelly and That Gang*, Trailer. UK debut album after he returned from Australia, drawing on his vast repertoire of Australian songs, including 'The Wild Colonial Boy' and 'Moreton Bay'.

OCTOBER **Sandy Denny, *It's Sandy Denny*, Mooncrest.** Compilation of her lead vocals from *Alex Campbell and His Friends* and *Sandy and Johnny*. However, '3.10 to Yuma', 'Pretty Polly', 'Milk and Honey', 'The Last Thing on My Mind' and 'Make Me a Pallet on Your Floor' are re-recorded, alternate versions appearing here for the first time. This was later re-released as *The Original Sandy Denny* by B&C in 1978 with slight changes, notably adding a previously unreleased version of Tom Paxton's 'My Ramblin' Boy' from the sessions, and with liner notes by Marcel Rodd.

— Matthews Southern Comfort, 'Woodstock', at No. 1 for three weeks.

— Lindisfarne, *Nicely Out of Tune*, Charisma. Enjoying greater commercial success than any other folk-rock group of the day, Lindisfarne was formed in Newcastle upon Tyne, and combined

Alan Hull's irresistibly wistful pop with a kind of boozy folk rev-
elry forever associated with the song 'Fog on the Tyne'.

— Shelagh McDonald, *The Shelagh McDonald Album*, B&C. Debut
album.

NOVEMBER Curved Air, *Air Conditioning*, Warner Bros. Debut
album, fronted by Sonja Kristina.

— Nick Drake, *Bryter Later*, Island.

— John and Beverley Martyn, *The Road to Ruin*, Island.

— Emerson, Lake and Palmer, *Emerson, Lake and Palmer*, Island.
The prog behemoth's debut album.

DECEMBER Vashti Bunyan, *Just Another Diamond Day*, Philips.
Having been groomed by Andrew Oldham along similar lines to
Marianne Faithfull, Vashti turned her back on a pop career after a
couple of years. Her uncontrived, fragile folk debut was produced
by Joe Boyd with the assistance of arranger Robert Kirby, fresh
from working with Nick Drake.

— *** Stefan Grossman, *The Ragtime Cowboy Jew*, Transatlantic.
Sandy and Trevor Lucas sing on 'A Pretty Little Tune'; the album
features the other Fotheringay musicians throughout much of the
recording. Sandy and Trevor sing uncredited on Grossman's next
album, *Those Pleasant Days*.

1971

MARCH Carole King, *Tapestry*, Ode.

— Steeleye Span, *Please to See the King*, B&C. Having twice turned
down the opportunity to join Fairport, Martin Carthy finally
teamed up with Ashley Hutchings for the first of two albums by
this particular Steeleye line-up; *Ten Man Mop* followed later the
same year, after which Hutchings left to form the Albion Country
Band and Carthy resumed his solo career. Carthy married Norma
Waterson in 1972 and the following year became the fourth
member of the Watersons; the group had returned after a four-
year break.

— The Incredible String Band, *Be Glad for the Song Has No Ending*,

Island. Switching from Elektra to Island, the now expanded group remained on the label till 1974's *Hard Rope and Silken Twine*, before breaking up early the following year.

APRIL Anne Briggs, *Anne Briggs*, Topic. Her long-awaited debut album includes 'Go Your Way' and 'Blackwaterside'.

MAY A. L. Lloyd, Trevor Lucas and Martyn Wyndham-Read, *The Great Australian Legend – A Panorama of Bush Balladry and Song*, Topic.

JUNE Fairport Convention, *Angel Delight*, Island. Only Simon Nicol remained from the founding line-up; this was the group's sole Top Ten album.

— Bronco, *Ace of Sunlight*, Island. Intense, introverted, soulful rock; Trevor Lucas sings on 'Time Slips Away' and was an in-house assistant engineer on the album. Bronco's singer Jess Roden was retained by Island for three further albums; he sang with Sandy on 'Losing Game', one of a handful of discarded tracks recorded for *Rendezvous*.

— *** Ian Matthews, *If You Saw thro' My Eyes*, Vertigo. Sandy sings with Matthews on the title track and is featured on piano/backing vocals on 'Hearts' and 'Never Ending'.

— *** Marc Ellington, *Rains/Reins of Change*, B&C. Ellington's second album features guest spots by Sandy, Pat Donaldson, Dave Pegg, Richard Thompson, Ian Matthews and Trevor Lucas. Sandy sings backing vocals on 'I'm Leaving (America)' and 'Alligator Man'.

AUGUST Joni Mitchell, *Blue*, Reprise.

SEPTEMBER **Sandy Denny, *The North Star Grassman and the Ravens*, Island.**

OCTOBER Shirley Collins and the Albion Country Band, *No Roses*, Pegasus. Aside from launching the first of the various Albion line-ups overseen by Ashley Hutchings in the 1970s – the Albion Band and Albion Dance Band would follow – *No Roses* is one of the few trad-based folk-rock albums to rival *Liege & Lief*. In fact, Simon Nicol, Richard Thompson, Dave Mattacks and Hutchings are all involved. Collins and Hutchings had met and married that

year, and it was Collins's first venture into folk rock. 'Murder of
Maria Marten' is a tour de force.

— Cat Stevens, *Teaser and the Firecat*, Island. The singles
'Moonshadow', 'Morning Has Broken' and 'Peace Train' thrust
Stevens to international success, further consolidated by *Catch
Bull at Four* a year later, a No. 1 album in America.

*** NOVEMBER Led Zeppelin, *IV*, Atlantic. Sandy famously sings
with Robert Plant on 'The Battle of Evermore'.

— John Martyn, *Bless the Weather*, Island.

— Fairport Convention, *Babbacombe Lee*, Island. With Simon
Nicol now gone, the Fairport baton was firmly grasped by Dave
Swarbrick and relative newcomer Dave Pegg, who steered the
group through the rest of the decade.

— Lesley Duncan, *Sing Children Sing*, CBS. Debut album.

— Claire Hamill, *One House Left Standing*, Island. Debut album.

DECEMBER Bob Dylan, *More Bob Dylan Greatest Hits*, CBS.
Includes the previously unreleased 'Down in the Flood' and
'Tomorrow Is a Long Time', covered by Sandy on *North Star
Grassman* and *Sandy*.

1972

FEBRUARY Strawbs, *Grave New World*, A&M. The lines between
folk rock and prog were now obliterated and this was the group's
first major hit album.

— Nick Drake, *Pink Moon*, Island.

MARCH Neil Young, *Harvest*, Reprise. The commercial peak of
Young's singer-songwriter career.

— Little Feat, *Sailin' Shoes*, Warner Bros. Includes 'Easy to Slip',
recorded for *Rendezvous* but discarded.

*** APRIL The Bunch, *Rock On*, Island. Produced by Trevor Lucas;
Sandy sings lead on five songs: 'That'll Be the Day', 'Love's Made
a Fool of You', 'Learning the Game', 'When Will I Be Loved'
and 'Willie and the Hand Jive'. All the Fotheringay musicians
and various former Fairport members sing and play on this, the

first example of Fotheringport Confusion, as some wags dubbed
Fairport in 1974.

— Vinegar Joe, *Vinegar Joe*, Island. Debut album, fronted by Elkie
Brooks and Robert Palmer; Island showed unprecedented faith in
Palmer for almost twenty years.

MAY Wizz Jones, *Right Now*, CBS. Once described by Jansch as the
most underrated guitarist ever, Jones never made that one defining album; having made his recording debut in 1965, this comes
closest, produced by John Renbourn.

JUNE Ashley Hutchings and Friends, *Morris On*, Island.
Hutchings's more erudite and purposeful variation on the *Rock
On* format, performing English morris dance tunes and songs,
aided by Richard Thompson, Dave Mattacks, John Kirkpatrick
and Barry Dransfield.

— *** Richard Thompson, *Henry the Human Fly*, Island. His first
post-Fairport album perplexed both fans and critics in its perceived idiosyncratic approach and sold disappointingly. Sandy
plays piano and sings backing vocals on 'Painted Ladies', and provides backing vocals with Linda Peters on 'The Angels Took My
Racehorse Away', 'Cold Feet' and 'Twisted'.

JULY Jimmy Cliff, *The Harder They Come* soundtrack, Island. The
film and soundtrack introduced Jamaican music to a wider audience; a bridge from one era to the next.

— Roxy Music, *Roxy Music*, Island. Ushered in a new era for Island
Records; Roxy presented an inspired futuristic brand of art-school
rock with glam trappings and the ability to forge catchy hit singles.

— *** Sandy Denny, Christopher Logue, *Pass of Arms*, Island
7-inch. Sandy sings 'Man of Iron' and 'Here in Silence' as part of
the soundtrack to Peter Elford's short film.

SEPTEMBER **Sandy Denny, *Sandy*, Island.**

— Pentangle, *Solomon's Seal*, Reprise. The group's final album.

— Lal and Mike Waterson, *Bright Phoebus*, Trailer. A magical
album drawing together the Watersons, Tim Hart, Maddy Prior,
Ashley Hutchings and Richard Thompson; another high-water
mark for British folk rock.

*** NOVEMBER Fairport Convention, *The History of Fairport Convention*, Island. Double LP story-so-far including a contribution from the latest line-up featuring Trevor Lucas and Jerry Donahue; the gatefold sleeve sported a Pete Frame family tree and annotations by John Wood.

*** DECEMBER Lou Reizner's Production of *Tommy*, performed by the London Symphony Orchestra and Chamber Choir with Guest Soloists, Ode/Century. The studio version was launched by an all-star performance at the Rainbow, London, on 9 December. Both featured Sandy Denny as 'The Nurse'.

— *** Manfred Mann, *Swedish Fly Girls*, original soundtrack, Juno. Released in 1972 but most likely recorded in 1970; even producer Manfred Mann can't remember any details. Sandy sings on 'Water Mother', 'What Will I Do with Tomorrow', 'Are the Judges Insane?' and 'I Need You'.

1973

FEBRUARY John Martyn, *Solid Air*, Island. It's an impossibly close personal call between this and *Bless the Weather* as Martyn's finest work.

— Strawbs, *Bursting at the Seams*, A&M. This was the most mainstream Strawbs line-up, on an album which includes the hits 'Lay Down' and the timely but frivolous 'Part of the Union', the latter courtesy of John Ford and Richard Hudson, soon to depart and form Hudson Ford.

MARCH Roxy Music, *For Your Pleasure*, Island. Roxy's commercial success escalated; *Stranded* followed before Christmas that year and was a No. 1 album, but not before Bryan Ferry had already released his own spin-off solo project.

— *** Fairport Convention, *Rosie*, Island. Sandy sings on the title track. Produced by Trevor Lucas, who had joined the group in September 1972.

APRIL Bob Marley and the Wailers, *Catch a Fire*, Island. Marley, Peter Tosh and Bunny Livingston's label debut, which reaffirmed

462

Chris Blackwell's roots in Jamaican music and jazz. Marley's eventual global success propelled Island's growth internationally and effectively diminished its commitment to underground rock and folk over the next few years.

MAY **Sandy and the Strawbs, *All Our Own Work*, Hallmark**. Released at last, following the Strawbs' commercial success in the UK, then at its peak.

— Mike Oldfield, *Tubular Bells*, Virgin. Oldfield's debut and the first release by Richard Branson's Virgin label, which was licensed to Island. Branson used Sandy Denny's Island contract as a blueprint; he simply scrubbed her name off and wrote 'Mike Oldfield' instead.

OCTOBER Fairport Convention, *Nine*, Island. More or less half trad and half Trevor Lucas-penned songs, this is one of Fairport's most overlooked albums, overshadowed by speculation that Sandy might soon return to the fold; the group is pictured outside their local pub, the Brasenose Arms in Cropredy. October was also the scheduled release date for Sandy's *Like an Old Fashioned Waltz*, but the album went unreleased for nine months.

— Bryan Ferry, *These Foolish Things*, Island. Ferry's covers project was the first of many Roxy Music spin-offs by every member of the group.

— Bob Marley and the Wailers, *Burnin'*, Island. Includes 'Get Up Stand Up' and 'I Shot the Sheriff'; the album which effectively won over the initially resistant rock audience.

NOVEMBER Elton John, *Goodbye Yellow Brick Road*, DJM. Includes 'Candle in the Wind', which Sandy belatedly covered for *Rendezvous*.

DECEMBER Anne Briggs, *The Time Has Come*, CBS. Recording for a major label and, for a while, managed by Jo Lustig, the more hands-on experience left Briggs feeling ill at ease and she retired from music soon after.

— *** Maggi (Magnús Kjartansson), *Clockworking Cosmic Spirits*, MM, Iceland only. Recorded at Sound Techniques; this was a solo project by Kjartansson, who was a member of Icelandic prog

group Trúbrot. It features backing vocals by Sandy and Linda
Thompson, who wisely says she has no recollection of it. Sandy
and Linda can be heard wailing away – often none too tunefully
– on an album that's more in the Gilbert O'Sullivan vein than
anything resembling acid-folk, as it's usually described. Sandy is
very recognisably heard singing solo at the start of the slushy 'My
Sweet Little Ladyfriend'.

1974

FEBRUARY Bob Dylan, *Planet Waves*, Asylum. David Geffen chose
Island to release Dylan's first album after his break with CBS.
The live album *Before the Flood* followed in July. Six months later,
Dylan returned to CBS with the bittersweet *Blood on the Tracks*.

MARCH Steeleye Span, *Now We Are Six*, Chrysalis. Produced by
Jethro Tull's Ian Anderson and sacrificing tradition for a more
progressive Tull-like edge.

— Bryn Haworth, *Let the Days Go By*, Island. Haworth's a superb
slide guitarist and mandolinist whose music has its roots in
R & B, blues and gospel. This and 1975's *Sunny Side of the
Street* sound as if they were recorded in deepest America, not
Island Studios, London, with the usual in-house team including
Fairport's Mattacks, Pegg and Swarbrick, as well as future Fairport
drummer Bruce Rowland, then in the Greaseband.

— Brian Eno, *Here Come the Warm Jets*, Island. Having been
ejected by Roxy Music, Eno would continue to steer the Island
group in a forward-looking direction with his solo work and his
first ambient recordings for EG.

APRIL Richard and Linda Thompson, *I Want to See the Bright Lights
Tonight*, Island. The duo's delightfully doomy debut, delayed since
completion in May 1973. On 'Down Where the Drunkards Roll'
Trevor Lucas's deep bass voice harmony resonates under Linda's
on the chorus of one of the album's most affecting songs.

MAY Kevin Ayers, *Confessions of Dr Dream and Other Stories*, Island.
Label debut from the eloquently outlandish maverick whom

A & R head Muff Winwood hoped to remodel as a post-hippie matinée idol.

— Sparks, *Kimono My House*, Island. Another Muff Winwood signing; the cult LA duo's futuristic, arty camp-pop was lapped up by British audiences with a fondness for the kind of irony, eccentricity and humour that was lost on America.

JUNE **Sandy Denny, *Like an Old Fashioned Waltz*, Island**. Finally released, having been originally scheduled for October 1973.

— Kevin Ayers, John Cale, Brian Eno and Nico, *June 1, 1974*, Island. Ayers, Eno and former Velvet Underground members Nico and Cale performed a concert at the Rainbow on 1 June which was recorded and released just four weeks later, on 28 June.

— Bad Company, *Bad Company*, Island. Instant Top Three debut by the group featuring Paul Rodgers and Simon Kirke from Free and Mott the Hoople's Mick Ralphs.

JULY **Fairport Convention, *Live Convention*, Island**.

SEPTEMBER Robert Palmer, *Sneakin' Sally through the Alley*, Island. Solo debut album recorded in New Orleans with the Meters and Little Feat's Lowell George.

— Bert Jansch, *LA Turnaround*, Charisma. Jansch's albums in the 1970s were as original and distinctive as his more revered '60s work. Sensitively produced by Mike Nesmith and enhanced by Red Rhodes's pedal steel playing, it was the antithesis of the following year's over-produced *Santa Barbara Honeymoon*, recorded in LA, on which Jansch finally got round to recording 'Blues Run the Game'.

OCTOBER John Cale, *Fear*, Island. Label debut album.

NOVEMBER Nico, *The End*, Island. Label debut album.

1975

*** JANUARY Brian Maxine, *Ribbons of Stainless Steel*, EMI. Competent contemporary country covers by the British wrestling champion, recorded in August 1974. The ads claimed: 'not only does he have a golden belt but a golden voice'. Sandy and Linda

Thompson sing backing vocals, and the Fairport musicians provide backing.

MARCH Richard and Linda Thompson, *Hokey Pokey*, Island.

JUNE The Chieftains, *5*, Island. The group's label debut and first
with a major outlet. The Chieftains were now managed by Jo
Lustig and had only recently turned professional. Something of
an about-face for Island, but the Chieftains soon found themselves feted by the likes of Mick Jagger, Eric Clapton and Stanley
Kubrick, and played on Mike Oldfield's *Ommadawn* later that
year. At the same time Lustig briefly and less capably added
Fairport to his managerial client list.

JULY **Fairport Convention, *Rising for the Moon*, Island.**

OCTOBER Steeleye Span, *All Around My Hat*, Chrysalis. Produced
by Mike Batt, the title track was a Top Five single. Chrysalis, to
whom they signed in 1971, stuck with the band until they for-
mally disbanded in 1978, only to get back together again three
times during the 1980s and at regular intervals ever since.

*** NOVEMBER Charlie Drake, 'You Never Know', Charisma.
Charlie 'Hello my darlings' Drake recorded this early in the summer; it was co-written and produced by Peter Gabriel, his first
project after leaving Genesis. Sandy sings backing vocals and
performs a spoken interlude as 'the groupie'; Phil Collins, Robert
Fripp, Keith Tippett and Percy Jones are the unlikely musicians.
Robert Fripp described it as one of the strangest sessions of the
entire era.

— Kate and Anna McGarrigle, *Kate and Anna McGarrigle*, Warner
Bros. Debut album, produced by Joe Boyd and an object lesson in
how to record pure folk voices and terrific, simple songs.

— Richard and Linda Thompson, *Pour Down like Silver*, Island.
Includes 'I Wish I Was a Fool for You'; Sandy recorded it on
Rendezvous. It was the last album before the couple's eighteen-
month break from music.

— Joni Mitchell, *The Hissing of Summer Lawns*, Reprise. Mitchell
cuts loose lyrically and musically, her vocals as supple as the
album's jazzy backdrop. It was too far out for some; the usually

drooling *Rolling Stone* critics named it the worst album of the
year.

DECEMBER Burning Spear, *Marcus Garvey*, Island. Aside from
Marley, the Island roster's other big hitters by the mid-1970s
included Burning Spear, Lee Perry and Toots and the Maytals.

— Bob Marley and the Wailers, *Live*, Island. Recorded in July at
London's Lyceum, the two shows were the subject of popular
and media frenzy and effectively transformed Marley into a rock
legend.

1976

JANUARY Toots and the Maytals, *Reggae Got Soul*, Island. Produced
by Joe Boyd and Chris Blackwell.

MARCH Maddy Prior and June Tabor, *Silly Sisters*, Chrysalis. Tabor
was relatively unknown at the time. Her exquisite debut for
Topic, *Airs and Graces*, mostly traditional in scope, followed in
September and featured guitar and fiddle by Nic Jones.

MAY Fairport, *Gottle o' Gear*, Island. This was the group's final rag-
bag album for the label, the only one to drop 'Convention' from
the name above the title.

— *** Richard Thompson, *(Guitar, Vocal)* 1967–76, Island.
Includes three then unreleased Sandy Denny performances, notably the *Liege & Lief* outtake 'The Ballad of Easy Rider'.

JULY Aswad, *Aswad*, Island. Debut album from the British reggae
band formed in London's Ladbroke Grove area in 1975. Island
also signed Steel Pulse in 1978.

OCTOBER Joan Armatrading, *Joan Armatrading*, A&M. Her Glyn
Johns-produced breakthrough album, which includes her best-
known song, 'Love and Affection'.

— *** Fairport Convention, *Heyday*, BBC Sessions 1968/9, compiled by Ashley Hutchings, originally a privately distributed cassette; released by Hannibal in September 1987.

NOVEMBER Dave Swarbrick, *Dave Swarbrick*, Transatlantic. A
return to the label he first recorded for with Ian Campbell.

DECEMBER Eddie and the Hot Rods, *Teenage Depression*, Island. Island's first step into new-wave territory.

1977

JANUARY Fairport Convention, *Live at the LA Troubadour*, Island. The *Full House* band captured in full flow, recorded back in 1970.

FEBRUARY Fleetwood Mac, *Rumours*, Warner Bros.

— The Albion Dance Band, *The Prospect Before Us*, Harvest.

— Fairport Convention, *The Bonny Bunch of Roses*, Vertigo. Simon Nicol was now back full-time and this is a return to form on the improbable prog/heavy metal specialist label.

— Ultravox, *Ultravox*, Island. Debut album co-produced by Eno.

APRIL The Clash, *The Clash*, CBS. Debut album.

MAY **Sandy Denny, *Rendezvous*, Island**. The album had originally been scheduled for release in September 1976 under the title *Gold Dust*.

— Sex Pistols, 'God Save the Queen', Virgin.

— The Jam, *In the City*, Polydor. Debut album.

— Bob Marley and the Wailers, *Exodus*, Island. Marley's first UK Top Ten album; in 1999, *Time* declared it 'the most important album of the twentieth century'.

JULY Steve Winwood, *Steve Winwood*, Island. Solo debut album two years after Traffic finally called it a day.

— Al Stewart, *Year of the Cat*, RCA. Having moved to California, Stewart achieved a million-selling Top Five album in the US. *Time Passages* in 1978 fared equally well; both were smooth, FM-friendly recordings by Alan Parsons.

SEPTEMBER Grace Jones, *Portfolio*, Island. Debut album. Two years later, Jones was at the forefront of Island's new hi-tech direction with her hypnotic, post-funk, post-disco albums *Warm Leatherette* and *Nightclubbing*.

OCTOBER Joan Armatrading, *Show Some Emotion*, A&M. A Top Five album in the UK; her success was soon mirrored in America. As late as 1985 she was still enjoying Top Ten albums in the UK.

Armatrading remained on A&M until 1993, twenty years after her debut.

NOVEMBER Sex Pistols, *Never Mind the Bollocks*, Virgin. Released just days after Sandy's final tour began, it went straight to No. 1, displacing Cliff Richard's *Forty Golden Greats*. (Sandy's final show, at the Royalty Theatre on 27 November, was recorded for a potential live album but scrapped due to technical issues; it was eventually released by Universal/Island in 1998 as *Gold Dust: Live at the Royalty*.)

— John Martyn, *One World*, Island. The last folkie left standing at Island. *Grace and Danger*, his swansong, appeared in October 1980, having been delayed by Chris Blackwell for a year. Martyn would briefly return to Island in 1984.

1978

FEBRUARY Gerry Rafferty, *City to City*, United Artists. Ten years after he signed to Transatlantic with the Humblebums, 'Baker Street' turned Rafferty into an overnight, if reluctant, star. Jerry Donahue plays on both the single and the album.

— Kate Bush, *The Kick Inside*, EMI. Includes the hit 'Wuthering Heights', which reached No. 1 and remained in the charts in the weeks before Sandy Denny's death on 21 April.

MARCH The Albion Band, *Rise Up Like the Sun*, Harvest. A brief hiatus for Hutchings's various ventures followed until the National Theatre commissioned the *Lark Rise to Candleford* project in 1980.

— Buddy Holly, *Twenty Golden Greats*, EMI. Heavily TV-advertised collection that topped the charts for three weeks going into April.

— Elvis Costello and the Attractions, *This Year's Model*, Radar. While Kate Bush would become the most successful British female singer-songwriter in years to come with an artistic but carefully managed, image-aware approach, Costello emerged from the new wave to breathe further new life into a genre that no longer looked to folk clubs as its source. By now, the bubble had burst and the once thriving network of folk clubs was seriously diminishing.

MAY Fairport Convention, *Tippler's Tales*, Vertigo. Their last album for any major label. The group took great satisfaction in the fact that Vertigo paid them handsomely not to record for the label again. The live valedictory *Farewell, Farewell* was recorded a year later, utilising the Island Mobile studios, and self-released through Woodworm in September 1979.

AUGUST **Sandy Denny, *The Original Sandy Denny*, B&C** (see *It's Sandy Denny*, 1970). After Sandy's death in April, Marcel Rodd dusted down the Saga recordings again. B&C also re-released Jackson C. Frank's album under the title *Jackson Again*.

SEPTEMBER Julie Covington, *Julie Covington*, Virgin. Produced by Joe Boyd and featuring some additional vocals by Trevor Lucas, the album includes the unreleased Sandy Denny song 'By the Time It Gets Dark'.

NOVEMBER Richard and Linda Thompson, *First Light*, Chrysalis. The couple's first album in three years; Trevor Lucas sings on 'Died for Love'.

Index

Browne, Tom, 96
'Bruton Town' *see* Denny, Sandy;
  Fotheringay
Buckley, Lord, 42
Buckley, Tim, xii; 'Morning Glory', xiii,
  127, 130
Buffalo, 47
Buffalo Springfield, 219
Bull, Sandy, 36
Bunch, the: *Rock On*, 273–5; *see also*
  Lucas, Trevor
Bundrick, John 'Rabbit', 366, 368
Bunyan, Vashti, 227, 425–6
Burning Spear, 386
Burns, Hughie, 313
Burns, Tito, 98
Bush, Kate, 300, 420
'Bushes and Briars' *see* Denny, Sandy
Bushwackers, the, 414
'By the Time It Gets Dark' *see* Denny,
  Sandy
Byfield, 324–5, 401
Byrds, the, xi, 55, 95, 187, 219, 268;
  'Ballad of Easy Rider', 198
Byrne, Ossie, 170

Cage, John, 123
Cale, John, 386
Cambridge Folk Festival, 167
Cameron, Isla, 41, 69, 163, 166
Campbell, Alex: background and
  overview, 79–82; character, 83; and
  London folk scene, 36; on folk life-
  style, 67; style, 71; and budget record
  labels, 75, 81; advert, 76; influence,
  79–80; relationship with SD, 82–3;
  and drink, 82; sets up Richmond
  Folk Club, 83–4; later life, 83–4;
  Richard Thompson on, 85; and the
  folk club circle, 85–6; opinion of
  SD's talents, 87; SD records home
  tape with, 96; album recorded in
  Denmark, 96; *My Kind of Folk* TV
  show, 105–6
  ALBUMS AND SONGS: *Alex Campbell
  and His Friends*, 33, 73, 74–7, 82, 93,

424; 'Been on the Road So Long',
  77–8, 82
Campbell-Lyons, Patrick, 272
'Candle in the Wind' *see* Denny, Sandy;
  John, Elton
Cantrell, Fred, 277, 285, 342, 358–9
Capaldi, Jim, 386
'Carnival' *see* Denny, Sandy
Carr, James, 'Losing Game', 363
Carter, Sydney, 77, 78–9, 109
Carthy, Martin: and London folk
  scene, 32, 36, 40; influence, 45;
  and Felix, 62; radio performances,
  70; on Glennon, 72; on getting a
  record deal, 77; on Campbell's relationship with MacColl, 80; plays on
  Swarbrick album, 85; on sixties folk
  club world, 86–7; and Swarbrick,
  149; on SD and Fairport, 150–1;
  on Lucas, 153; Copenhagen show,
  164–5; attitude to traditional music,
  195; considered as replacement for
  SD in Fairport, 216; favourite SD
  vocal, 224; guest appearance at
  Fotheringay's last concert, 245; at
  Lincoln, 268; and SD's ambitiousness, 289; and Steeleye Span, 300;
  plays on *Gottle o' Gear*, 362–3; on
  Lucas's departure to Australia, 405;
  see also Steeleye Span
  ALBUMS AND SONGS: *Prince Heathen*,
  149; 'A Sailor's Life', 143; 'Sovay', 59
'Casey Jones' *see* Lucas, Trevor
Cattouse, Nadia, 165
Chaffinches Farm, 232–3
Charisma Records, 314
Chesterman, Ron, 91; *see also* Strawbs,
  the
Child, Francis, 60
Clapton, Eric, 58, 61–2, 330
Clare, Philippa: background, 33;
  on SD's parents, 17–18; on SD
  as performer, 33; on SD's weight
  changes, 39; on SD's relationship
  with Frank, 53; on SD's relationship
  with Campbell, 83; on proliferation

previous abortions and miscarriages, 370–1; last studio recording, 377; marital relations worsen, 378–9; carries on with drink and drugs through pregnancy, 379–80; Georgia born, 380–1; struggles with motherhood, 381–2, 383; dropped by Island, 385–7; last tour, 387–91; final decline, 391–401; money problems, 397–8; falling downstairs episodes, 400–2; final public performance, 401; Lucas takes Georgia to Australia, 402–6; death, xvi, 403–12, 418; funeral, 408–9; probate register, 413; estate and archive, xvii–xviii, 414; obituaries, 417, 419–20; author's assessment, 420–7; other gigs, xii–xiv, xv, xvi GENERAL: ambitiousness, 86–7; appearance, 9, 12, 20, 22, 38–9, 117; attitude to authority, 10, 21; attitude to pop, 116–17; clothing style, 285–6; clumsiness, 393; drama queen side, 8; emotional neediness, 186; extravagance, 232, 398; favourite books, 264; favourite music, 255; fear of flying, 182–3, 348; improvisation skills, 194–5; influences, 43, 47, 57–61, 79; need for reassurance, 287; performance nerves, 34, 38, 310, 345; personality contradictions, 256–7; relationship with brother, 8–9; relationship with Lucas, xviii–xix, 360–2, 372, 392–3, 396; relationship with parents, 15–18; rock musician friends, 256; sensitivity, 247; sexual relationships, 256; signature, 228; song introductions, 69; songwriting, 247, 256, 260–1, 355; surviving footage, 268; Swarbrick's song about, 338–9; volatility, 116 ALBUMS: Alex Campbell and His Friends, 73, 74–7, 82, 93, 424; All Our Own Work (Sandy Denny and the Strawbs), 89, 91, 93–4, 95–101, 103, 314; The Attic Track Tapes, 159; The BBC Sessions 1971–1973, 424; A

Boxful of Treasures, 423, 424; Fairport Live Convention (A Moveable Feast), 322–4, 323; Fotheringay, xv, 223–31, 225, 235, 426; Fotheringay 2, 236–8, 239; Gold Dust (live Royalty recording), 390, 424; Heyday, xiv, 141–2, 144, 145; Liege & Lief, xiv–xv, 141, 177, 190–1, 193–200, 204, 206, 207–9, 217, 426; Like an Old Fashioned Waltz, xiv, 305–9, 312, 313–14, 316–17, 320, 321–2; The North Star Grassman and the Ravens, xv, 45, 243, 248, 249, 258–72, 263, 279, 426–7; The Notes and the Words: A Collection of Demos and Rarities, 424; Rendezvous, xvi, 363–70, 369, 373–7, 378, 385, 424–5; Rising for the Moon, xvi, 267, 305, 320, 328, 330–45, 353; Rock On, 273–5, 279; Sandy, xv, 277, 278, 281–9, 284, 290–1, 301, 427; Sandy and Johnny, 73, 74–9, 78, 93, 424; Sandy Denny box set, xvii, 320, 424, 425; Sandy Denny at the BBC box set, 269, 424; Sandy Denny Solo, 310; Unhalfbricking, xv, 137, 142, 145, 146–51, 178, 183, 184, 187–9, 206, 208; What We Did on Our Holidays, xiii, xv, xvi, 99, 134, 138–41, 148; Who Knows Where the Time Goes?, 423 SONGS: 'After Halloween', 281, 338; 'All Along the Watchtower', 338; 'All I Need Is You', 100; 'All Our Days', 357, 363–4, 374–5; 'Always on My Mind', 101; 'And You Need Me', 95–6, 100–1; 'The Angels Took My Racehorse Away', 275; 'At the End of the Day', 304, 305; 'Autopsy', 120, 146–7, 148, 189, 208; 'Ballad of Easy Rider', 198; 'The Ballad of Ned Kelly', 227–8, 230; 'Balulalow', 105; 'Banks of the Nile', 208, 224–6, 230, 234, 385; 'The Battle of Evermore', 249–53, 419; 'Been on the Road So Long', 77–8, 82; 'Bird on a Wire', 209; 'Blackwaterside', 45, 69, 261,

Lamble and Jeannie Franklyn, 177,
179–83; US tour, 182–3; post-
accident regrouping, 183–5, 186–7;
Farley Chamberlayne rehearsals,
189–91, 193–5; Mattacks and
Swarbrick join, 189–90; *Top of the
Pops* performance, 191–2; SD and
Hutchings leave, 200–9; picks up
the pieces after SD's and Hutchings's
departures, 216–17; Marquee gig,
221; sends Fotheringay good-luck
telegram, 223; post-SD gigs, 229; Led
Zeppelin's relationship with, 249–50;
guest appearances by SD and Richard
Thompson, 273; Lucas and Donahue
join and Mattacks returns, 164, 236,
289–90; guest appearance by SD,
291; 1973 tours, 301–2, 305; issue of
SD rejoining, 305, 309; 1974 tours,
314; SD rejoins, 317–24; poor financial affairs, 329; Mattacks replaced
by Rowland, 335–7; SD's second
tenure, 330–50; increasing problems,
345–50; Donahue, SD and Lucas
leave, 351–3; Lucas reunites with,
414; shadow cast on ex-members,
426; other gigs, xii–xv, xvi
ALBUMS: *The Attic Track Tapes*, 159;
Fairport Convention, 122, 126, 131;
Fairport Live Convention (*A Moveable
Feast*), 322–4, 323; *From Past
Archives*, 267; *Full House*, xiv, 198,
206, 216, 217; *Gottle o' Gear*, 362–3;
Heyday, xiv, 141–2, 144, 145; *History
of Fairport Convention*, 290; *Liege &
Lief*, xiv–xv, 141, 177, 190–1, 193–
200, 204, 206, 207–9, 217, 426; *Nine*,
312–13, 331; *Rising for the Moon*, xvi,
267, 305, 320, 328, 330–45, 353;
Rosie, 289–90, 301; *Unhalfbricking*,
xv, 137, 142, 145, 146–51, 178, 183,
184, 187–9, 206, 208; *What We Did
on Our Holidays*, xiii, xv, xvi, 99, 134,
138–41, 148
SONGS: 'After Halloween', 338; 'All
Along the Watchtower', 338; 'At

the End of the Day', 305; 'Autopsy',
120, 146–7, 148, 189, 208; 'Ballad
of Easy Rider', 198; 'Bird on a Wire',
209; 'Brilliancy Medley', 345; 'Come
All Ye', 196, 197, 198; 'Country Pie',
273; 'Crazy Man Michael', 196, 197,
199–200, 206; 'Dawn', 334; 'The
Deserter', 197, 198, 206, 208; 'Down
in the Flood', 196, 291, 322–4;
'Eastern Rain', xi, xiii; 'Farewell,
Farewell', 196, 197, 198–9, 205;
'Fotheringay', xi, xii, xvi, 51, 139,
140; 'Friends', 305; 'Genesis Hall',
148; 'Hexhamshire Lass', 345; 'Hey
Joe', 250; 'I Don't Know Where I
Stand', 131; 'If I Had a Ribbon Bow',
126; 'I'll Keep It with Mine', xiii,
140; 'Iron Lion', 337; 'It'll Take a
Long Time', 345; 'Just a Little Talk
with Jesus', 196–7; 'The King and
Queen of England', 338; 'Knights
of the Road', 236, 290; 'Lark in the
Morning' medley, 197–8; 'Listen,
Listen', 345; 'Matty Groves', 197–8,
419–20; 'Meet on the Ledge', 139,
208; 'Million Dollar Bash', 145; 'Mr
Lacey', 345; 'Morning Dew', 250;
'Morning Glory', xiii, 127, 130;
'Mystery Train', 250; 'Night Time
Girl', 337; 'No End', 305; 'No More
Sad Refrains', 345; 'Nothing More',
203–4; 'Nottamun Town', 140, 141;
'One More Chance', 333–4; 'One
Sure Thing', 122; 'Open the Door,
Homer', 196; 'Pick Me Up', 377;
'The Plainsman', 290; 'The Pond and
the Stream', 203–4; 'The Quiet Joys
of Brotherhood', 198, 345; 'Reno,
Nevada', xiii, 127, 133; 'Restless',
334; 'Reynardine', 197; 'Rising for
the Moon', 330, 333, 334; 'Rosie',
345; 'A Sailor's Life', 143–4, 146,
148–9, 150, 208, 419–20; 'The
Sea', 203–4; 'She Moves through
the Fair', 134, 140, 141; 'Si tu dois
partir' ('If You Gotta Go, Go Now'),

sketched by SD, 49; at 1968 Festival
of Contemporary Song, xii, xiii, 54;
and Kingston Barge, 20; and Soho
folk clubs, 27; East London home,
29; and Les Cousins, 36, 40; and
Young Tradition, 46–7; relationship
with SD, 48–54, 56; at Le Duce, 56;
influence on SD's songs, 63, 66; SD
covers, 64; later life, 54–5; SD's song
about ('Next Time Around'), 265
ALBUMS AND SONGS: 'Blues Run the
Game', 48, 50, 64; *Jackson C. Frank*,
47, 50; 'Milk and Honey', 50, 64, 77;
'You Never Wanted Me', 50, 77
Franklin, Aretha, 255
Franklyn, Jeannie, 179, 182
Fraser, Don, 282
Free, xiv, 138, 256, 297–8
Free at Last, 168
Frey, Glenn, 398; *see also* Eagles, the
'Friends' *see* Denny, Sandy; Fairport
Convention
From Past Archives see Fairport
Convention
Frost, Geoff, 125
Full House see Fairport Convention
'Full Moon' *see* Denny, Sandy
Fury, Billy, xi, 260

Gabriel, Peter, 253
Gallagher, Benny, 374
Garfunkel, Art, 48, 50; *see also* Simon
and Garfunkel
Gaughan, Dick, 80
Genesis, 314
'Genesis Hall' *see* Denny, Sandy;
Fairport Convention; Thompson,
Richard
George, Lowell, 398–9
'Gerrard Street' *see* Denny, Sandy
Getz, Stan, 97
Gibbons, Steve, 220
Gilbert, Jerry, 103, 234–5, 309, 422
Gilmore, Thea: 'Don't Stop Singing',
361; 'London', 361; 'Long Time
Gone', 399

Glaser, Gina: background, 57; on SD's
parents, 18; takes SD to Singers Club,
27; on SD nursing, 30; befriends SD,
57–62; on SD and the Strawbs, 101–
2; on SD's appearance, 117; on SD
and Fairport, 133; on SD's relation-
ship with Lucas, 172; on SD's attitude
to traditional music, 194–5
Glasgow, 105–6
Glennon, Sandy, 71–2, 73, 141
Glynn, Prudence, 286
'Go Your Way My Love' *see* Briggs,
Annie; Denny, Sandy
Goanna, 414
Gold Dust see Denny, Sandy
'Gold Dust' *see* Denny, Sandy
Goldfrapp, Alison, 420
Good, Jack, 260
Graham, Davy, 35, 36, 40, 76, 80,
81; *Folk Roots, New Routes*, 45;
'Nottamun Town', 140
Graham, Gordon (Doon), 39, 232
Grant, Cy, 165
Grant, Peter, 250
Grease Band, 336
Great Australian Legend, The see Lloyd,
A. L.
Green, Peter, xiv
'Green Grow the Laurels' *see* Denny,
Sandy
Greer, Germaine, 158
Gretch, Rick, 258
Grossman, Stefan, 46, 174, 213, 231,
253; *The Ragtime Cowboy Jew*, 231;
Those Pleasant Days, 231
Grosvenor, Luther, *Under Open Skies*,
272
Guard, Dave, 167; *see also* Kingston
Trio
Gudmand, Ken, 97
Guest, Roy: background, 163; becomes
manager for Lucas, 162–3; and
Howff, 163, 287; SD tries to put
together group for, 171–2; becomes
manager for Fotheringay, 219; and
Fotheringay's break-up, 239, 240;

van crash, 177, 179; looks for new
repertoire, 183; decides to carry
on with Fairport post-accident,
184, 185; on Farley Chamberlayne
rehearsals, 190–1, 193, 194–5; *Top
of the Pops* performance, 191–2; on
SD's singing, 195; and *Liege & Lief*,
196; co-writes 'Come All Ye', 196,
197, 198; attitude to traditional
folk music, 202; leaves Fairport,
202–6; and Steeleye Span, 113,
205, 300; favourite SD vocal, 224;
on Fotheringay, 230; guest appearance at Fotheringay's last concert,
245; on SD's songs, 245; on SD's
personality contradictions, 257; and
SD's last tour, 390; sings 'Nadine'
on *Rock On*, 274; *see also* Fairport
Convention; Steeleye Span

'I Don't Believe You' *see* Denny, Sandy;
Dylan, Bob; Fotheringay
'I Don't Know Where I Stand' *see*
Denny, Sandy; Fairport Convention
I Want to See the Bright Lights Tonight see
Thompson, Richard
'I Wish I Was a Fool for You' *see* 'For
Shame of Doing Wrong'
Ian and Sylvia, 163
Ian Campbell Folk Group, 111, 149,
163, 216
'If I Had a Ribbon Bow' *see* Fairport
Convention
'If You Gotta Go, Go Now' ('Si tu dois
partir') *see* Denny, Sandy; Dylan,
Bob; Fairport Convention
'I'll Keep It with Mine' *see* Dylan, Bob;
Fairport Convention
'I'm a Dreamer' *see* Denny, Sandy
Incredible String Band, xii, 36, 79, 109–
10, 163, 169, 244; *The 5000 Spirits
or the Layers of the Onion*, 110; *The
Hangman's Beautiful Daughter*, 110
Ink Spots: 'Whispering Grass', xvi, 7,
306
International Pop Festival (1968), 127

'Iron Lion' *see* Denny, Sandy; Fairport
Convention; Lucas, Trevor
Irvin, Jim, 106, 231, 367, 400, 403, 410
Irving Music, 100
Irwin, Colin, 344, 379–80, 419, 420
Island Records: deal with Witchseason,
138–9; launched in USA, 218; and
Fotheringay, 228; tries to persuade
SD to record a solo album, 234, 235;
Witchseason's dependence on, 237;
buys Witchseason, 238–9, 243–4;
and Cat Stevens, 241; neglects
Witchseason artists, 243–4; SD
signs as solo artist, 245; funds *Rock
On*, 274; and *Sandy*, 277, 284–5,
291; use of Toussaint, 283; promotes
Fairport, 290; and Hamill, 297,
298; relationship with managers,
303; and *Like an Old Fashioned
Waltz*, 306, 312, 313, 314; changed
nature of label, 314–17; reaction to
SD rejoining Fairport, 321; clears
Fairport's debts, 330; and *Rising for
the Moon*, 331, 333, 342–3; asks for
new albums from SD and Fairport,
362; relationship with SD, 317–18,
377–8; and *Rendezvous*, 368–70, 373,
376–7; and Haworth, 377; drops SD
and Richard and Linda Thompson,
385–7; growth in ambition, 385–6;
and SD's last tour, 388; releases post-
humous *Who Knows Where the Time
Goes?*, 423
Isle of Wight Festival (1968), 133
'It Ain't Me Babe' *see* Denny, Sandy;
Dylan, Bob
'It Suits Me Well' *see* Denny, Sandy
'It'll Take a Long Time' *see* Denny,
Sandy; Fairport Convention
Ives, Burl, 14, 94

Jackson C. Frank see Frank, Jackson C.
James, Clive, 158
Jansch, Bert: Soho gigs, 27, 32, 34–5,
36, 37, 40; and Singers Club, 41; on
Annie Briggs, 43–4; shares flat with

plays with SD and the Strawbs, 96;
sings back-up for Fairport, 137; first
marriage, 161; comes to England,
161–6; helps form Eclection, 166–71;
relationship with Chris Collins,
171–2; relationship with SD starts,
172–5; sketched by SD, 173; drives
back from Birmingham with SD,
179, 180, 181–2; SD misses while in
USA, 183; moves in with SD, 174,
185–6; partly the reason for SD's
decision to leave Fairport, 201; forms
Fotheringay, 211, 213, 214, 218, 219,
220; Chipstead Street home, 213–14;
falsely rumoured to have been considered as replacement for SD in
Fairport, 216; life with Fotheringay,
222, 227–8, 230, 236; signature, 228;
relationship with Boyd, 231; sings on
Grossman albums, 231; love of luxury, 232; and Fotheringay's break-up,
238, 240, 244; tries record production, 244–5, 272–3; plays on *The
North Star Grassman*, 259, 272; features on *The Great Australian Legend*,
273; produces *Rock On*, 273–5; hits
on Clare, 274; produces *Sandy*, 277,
282, 284; and SD's clothes, 285; joins
Fairport, 236, 289–90; SD's worries
about his fidelity, 290, 303–4; and
SD's recording of 'No End', 291–2;
considers reforming Fotheringay,
301–2; Fairport 1973 tours, 301–2,
305; produces *Like an Old Fashioned
Waltz*, 305; rocky patch in relationship with SD, 308, 309; marries
SD, 294, 311–12; and SD rejoining
Fairport, 319; in Fairport, 320; moves
with SD to Byfield, 324–5; on SD's
stage performance, 327; and *Rising for
the Moon*, 330–1, 337, 343; drinking
and drug-taking, 346, 347–8; on
SD and alcohol, 347; tensions with
SD and Swarbrick, 349, 350; leaves
Fairport, 352, 353; country life, 357,
359; reaction to SD's flirtation with

Scientology, 359, 360; SD songs
about their relationship, 360; troubled marriage, 360–2; produces and
sings on *Rendezvous*, 363, 364, 365,
366, 367, 368, 373–4, 375–6; and
SD's pregnancy, 371, 372; on SD and
everyday life, 372; marital relations
worsen, 378–7; names Georgia, 380;
as father, 381; plays on SD's last tour,
388, 389; relationship with SD's
parents, 18, 391–2; and SD's neglect
of Georgia, 394; money problems,
397–8; and SD's falling downstairs
episodes, 401; takes Georgia to
Australia, 402–6; flies back after SD's
accident, 408; at SD's funeral, 408,
409; at SD's inquest, 410; blamed
for SD's death, 409, 411; SD's parents' bitterness, 411–14; later life
and death, xvii, 156, 414–15, 423;
estate and archive, xvii–xviii; *see
also* Eclection; Fairport Convention;
Fotheringay
ALBUMS: *Australian Folk Festival*,
159; *Eclection*, 169–70; *The Folk
Attic Presents*, 159; *Fotheringay*, xv,
223–31, 225, 235, 426; *Fotheringay 2*,
236–8, 239; *Overlander*, 153, 165–6;
Rosie, 290; *See That My Grave Is Kept
Clean*, 159
SONGS: 'The Ballad of Ned Kelly',
227–8, 230; 'Banks of the Nile/
Condamine', 166, 226; 'Bluey
Brink', 159; 'Bold Jack Donahue',
166; 'Both Sides Now', 170; 'Casey
Jones', 159; 'Dem Bones Gwine to
Rise Again', 159; 'Don't Be Cruel',
274; 'Down Where the Drunkards
Roll', 320; 'The Flash Stockman',
159; 'Iron Lion', 337; 'John Henry',
159; 'Knights of the Road', 236,
290; 'Learning the Game', 274;
'Love's Made a Fool of You', 274;
'Nadine', 274; 'Nevertheless',
169; 'Old Time Religion', 159;
'Peace in the End', 227, 230; 'The

'Soho' *see* Denny, Sandy; Jansch, Bert
'Solo' *see* Denny, Sandy; Fairport
    Convention
Solomon, Phil, 99
'Some Sweet Day' *see* Fairport
    Convention
Sonet Records, 96
Songs of Ireland see Strawbs, the
Sounds of the Seventies (radio series),
    269
Southampton, 143
'Sovay' *see* Carthy, Martin
Sparkes, Steve, 129, 192
Sparks, 315, 386
Spooky Tooth, 138, 331
Springfield, Dusty, 94, 170, 233, 298,
    420, 421–2
Springfields, the, 94
Stamp, Chris, 126
Starr, Ringo, 253; *see also* Beatles, the
'Stay Awhile with Me' *see* Denny,
    Sandy; Strawbs, the
Steel Pulse, 386
Steeleye Span, 113, 186, 268, 299–300,
    333, 348
Steppenwolf, 47
Steve Miller Band, 330
Stevens, Cat, 234, 241, 256, 271
Stevens, Meic, 80
Stewart, Al: at Festival of
    Contemporary Song, xii; on SD
    and Winnie, 20; and Les Cousins,
    36; East London home, 48; plays on
    Frank album, 50; meets SD, 51–2;
    plays with SD and Fairport, 54; on
    SD's relationship with Frank, 56; on
    SD's voice, 62–3; on SD's songwrit-
    ing, 65; signs to record label, 112; on
    SD's volatility, 116; on Dyble, 127;
    on SD and Fairport, 145; manager,
    163; on SD's Howff performance,
    310; 'Love Chronicles', xii
Stewart, Rod, 256, 270
'Still Waters Run Deep' *see* Denny,
    Sandy
Storyville record label, 96

Strange Fruit record label, 424
'Stranger to Himself' *see* Denny, Sandy;
    Fairport Convention; Swarbrick,
    Dave
Strawbs, the: overview, 91, 92–3;
    SD performs with, 71; Folk Song
    Cellar recording, 90; SD's time with,
    89–104; World Service session, 91–2;
    origins of name, 92; BBC sessions,
    92–3; style, 94–5; own publishing
    company, 100; later career, 103–5
    ALBUMS: *All Our Own Work* (*Sandy
    Denny and the Strawbs*), 89, 91,
    93–4, 95–101, 103, 314; *From the
    Witchwood*, 105; *Grave New World*,
    105; *Of a Time*, 104–5; *Songs of
    Ireland*, 93; *Strawbs*, 104–5
    SONGS: 'All I Need Is You', 100;
    'Always on My Mind', 101; 'And You
    Need Me', 95–6, 100–1; 'Nothing
    Else Will Do', 100, 101; 'Oh How
    She Changed', 104; 'On My Way',
    100; 'Sail Away to Sea', 100; 'Stay
    Awhile with Me', 95–6, 100–1;
    'Sweetling', 101; 'Tell Me What You
    See in Me', 101; 'Two Weeks Last
    Summer', 101; 'Who Knows Where
    the Time Goes?', 97, 98, 99–100,
    111, 148; 'Wild Strawberries', 101
'Strollin' Down the Highway' *see*
    Jansch, Bert
Strummer, Joe, 376
Sue and Sunny, 365
'Suzanne' *see* Cohen, Leonard; Fairport
    Convention
Swarbrick, Dave: background, 111, 149;
    and SD, 34; at Les Cousins, 40; fea-
    tured on Felix album, 62; and Lucas,
    163, 164–5; plays with Fairport, 144,
    148–50; Copenhagen show, 164–5;
    on *Far from the Madding Crowd*
    soundtrack, 166; joins Fairport, 190;
    at Farley Chamberlayne, 191, 193–4;
    Top of the Pops performance, 192;
    knowledge of traditional folk music,
    195; and *Liege & Lief*, 196, 197; on

267–8; sings on *Rock On*, 274–5; and *Henry the Human Fly*, 275; on husband's and SD's disappointment with record sales, 288–9; forms duo with Richard, 289; on SD's stage fright, 310; and *I Want to See the Bright Lights Tonight*, 315–16; SD sings with at Queen Elizabeth Hall, 342; on SD's drinking and drug-taking, 347–8; on SD's flirtation with Scientology, 359; and *Pour Down like Silver*, 363; on SD being pregnant, 379; dropped by Island, 385; on SD's last tour, 390; becomes Muslim, 393–4; and SD's decline, 393–4, 396, 397; on Lucas's departure to Australia, 404–5; on SD's death, 409–10; missing SD, 383; 'Died for Love', 414

Thompson, Richard: at 1968 Festival of Contemporary Song, xiii–xiv; plays with SD, xv; on SD's parents, 15; on SD's like for female sidekicks, 20–1; on inevitability of SD becoming folk singer, 24; and Les Cousins, 37; on SD's relationship with Frank, 53; on SD's singing, 79; on SD's relationship with Campbell, 82; on folk club circle, 85; on SD with the Strawbs, 102; and early days of Fairport, 123, 127; and SD joining Fairport, 117, 130, 134, 137–8, 140, 142; and *What We Did on Our Holidays*, 139; flat-shares with Matthews, 144; and *Unhalfbricking*, 145, 146, 148; on SD's songs, 146–7, 147–8; Swarbrick on, 150, 151, 190; on Eclection, 171; and Fairport van crash, 177, 179, 182; US tour, 183; decides to carry on with Fairport post-accident, 184; on the Band, 187; on Farley Chamberlayne rehearsals, 191; *Top of the Pops* performance, 192; and *Liege & Lief*, 196, 200, 208–9; on SD leaving Fairport, 201; decides to stay with the band pro tem, 203; on SD's Chipstead Street home,

213–14; becomes Fairport lead singer, 216; recommends Lee as guitarist for Fotheringay, 219; as subject of SD song, 226; on Briggs, 226–7; on Fotheringay's break-up, 243; Boyd's relationship with, 243–4; on SD's sensitivity, 247; and Led Zeppelin, 250; SD does session work for, 253; SD's fear of his disapproval, 254; on SD's career choices, 255; on SD's taste in music, 255; SD's crush on, 256; and Whiteman, 258; leaves Fairport, 258; co-produces and performs on *The North Star Grassman*, 258–9, 260, 261; on SD's songwriting, 261, 266; backs SD at Lincoln, 268–9; tours with Matthews, 271; backs SD on tour, 271–2; and Timi Donald, 272; guest appearances with Fairport, 273; on *Sandy*, 277; backs SD during US residencies and 1972 tour, 279–80; moves on to form duo with Linda, 289; backs McDonald, 296; on *Like an Old Fashioned Waltz*, 308; on changes at Island, 315–16; on SD working with Johns, 331–2; on *Rising for the Moon*, 340–1; SD sings with at Queen Elizabeth Hall, 342; and *Rendezvous*, 374; dropped by Island, 385; and SD's last tour, 390; becomes Muslim, 393–4; on SD's decline, 394, 396; at SD's funeral, 409; foreword to unpublished SD biography, 423–4; Fairport's shadow, 426; signs with Cooking Vinyl, xvii; *see also* Fairport Convention
ALBUMS AND SONGS: 'The Angels Took My Racehorse Away', 275; 'Beeswing', 227; 'Cold Feet', 275; 'Crazy Man Michael', 196, 197, 199–200, 206, 209; 'Died for Love', 414; 'Down Where the Drunkards Roll', 320; 'Farewell, Farewell', 196, 198–9, 205; 'For Shame of Doing Wrong', 363; 'Genesis Hall', 148, 419; *Henry the Human Fly*, 275,